# GCSE Edexcel
# Physics

GCSE Edexcel Physics can cause some con-fusion, but we've squeezed all the important facts, theory and practical skills you'll need into this brilliant all-in-one CGP book!

We've also included plenty of exam-style practice in every topic *and* a full set of practice papers. And we've included fully-worked answers, so it's easy to mark your work.

You'll also find links to our fantastic online content, with video solutions for practice questions, as well as Retrieval Quizzes to help you nail down all the facts you need to learn.

# Complete
# Revision & Practice

Everything you need to pass the exams!

Published by CGP.

From original material by Richard Parsons.

Editors: Duncan Lindsay, Jake McGuffie, Charlotte Sheridan, George Wright.

Contributors: Paddy Gannon, Gemma Hallam, Barbara Mascetti.

With thanks to Jade Sim for the copyright research.

ISBN: 978 1 78294 882 7

Data used to construct stopping distance diagram on page 39 from the Highway Code.
© Crown Copyright re-produced under the terms of the Click-Use licence.

Traffic sign on page 44 © Crown Copyright. Contains public sector information licensed under the Open Government Licence v3.0.

Printed by Elanders Ltd, Newcastle upon Tyne.
Clipart from Corel®
Illustrations by: Sandy Gardner Artist, email sandy@sandygardner.co.uk

# Contents

Throughout this book you'll see grade stamps like these:

Grade 4-6    Grade 6-7    Grade 7-9

These grade stamps help to show how difficult the questions are.
Remember — to get a top grade you need to be able to answer **all** the questions, not just the hardest ones.

In the real exams, some questions test how well you can structure an answer (as well as your scientific knowledge). In this book, we've marked these questions with an asterisk (*).

## Section 4 — Radioactivity

## Section 5 — Astronomy

## Section 6 — Forces and Energy

## Section 7 — Electricity and Circuits

## Section 8 — Electric and Magnetic Fields

## Section 9 — Matter

## Practical Skills

## Practice Exams

---

You'll see **QR codes** throughout the book that you can scan with your smartphone.

A QR code next to a tip box question takes you to a **video** that talks you through solving the question. You can access **all** the videos by scanning this code here.

A QR code on a 'Revision Summary' page takes you to a **Retrieval Quiz** for that topic. You can access **all** the quizzes by scanning this code here.

You can also find the **full set of videos** at cgpbooks.co.uk/GCSEPhys-Edex/Videos and the **full set of quizzes** at cgpbooks.co.uk/GCSEPhys-Edex/Quiz

For useful information about **What to Expect in the Exams** and other exam tips head to cgpbooks.co.uk/GCSEPhys-Edex/Exams

# The Scientific Method

*This section **isn't** about how to 'do' science — but it does show you the way **most scientists** work.*

## Scientists Come Up With **Hypotheses** — Then **Test** Them

1) Scientists try to <u>explain</u> things. They start by <u>observing</u> something they don't understand.

2) They then come up with a <u>hypothesis</u> — a possible <u>explanation</u> for what they've observed.

3) The next step is to <u>test</u> whether the hypothesis might be <u>right or not</u>. This involves making a <u>prediction</u> based on the hypothesis and testing it by <u>gathering evidence</u> (i.e. <u>data</u>) from <u>investigations</u>. If <u>evidence</u> from <u>experiments</u> backs up a prediction, you're a step closer to figuring out if the hypothesis is true.

About 100 years ago, scientists hypothesised that atoms looked like this.

## **Several Scientists** Will **Test** a Hypothesis

1) Normally, scientists <u>share</u> their <u>findings</u> in <u>peer-reviewed journals</u>, or at <u>conferences</u>.

2) <u>Peer-review</u> is where <u>other scientists</u> check results and scientific explanations to make sure they're 'scientific' (e.g. that experiments have been done in a sensible way) <u>before</u> they're published. It helps to <u>detect false claims</u>, but it doesn't mean that findings are <u>correct</u> — just that they're not wrong in any <u>obvious</u> way.

3) Once other scientists have found out about a hypothesis, they'll start basing their <u>own predictions</u> on it and carry out their <u>own experiments</u>. They'll also try to <u>reproduce</u> the original experiments to <u>check the results</u> — and if all the experiments in the world <u>back up</u> the <u>hypothesis</u>, then scientists start to think the hypothesis is <u>true</u>.

4) However, if a scientist does an experiment that <u>doesn't fit</u> with the hypothesis (and other scientists can reproduce the results) then the hypothesis may need to be <u>modified</u> or <u>scrapped</u> altogether.

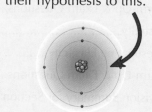

After more evidence was gathered, scientists changed their hypothesis to this.

## If **All** the **Evidence** Supports a Hypothesis, It's **Accepted** — For Now

1) <u>Accepted hypotheses</u> are often referred to as <u>theories</u>. Our <u>currently accepted</u> theories are the ones that have survived this 'trial by evidence' — they've been <u>tested many times</u> over the years and <u>survived</u>.

2) However, theories <u>never</u> become totally indisputable <u>fact</u>. If <u>new evidence</u> comes along that <u>can't be explained</u> using the existing theory, then the hypothesising and testing is likely to <u>start all over again</u>.

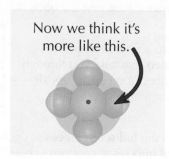

Now we think it's more like this.

---

## Scientific models are constantly being refined...

The <u>scientific method</u> has been <u>developed</u> over time. Aristotle (a Greek philosopher) was the first person to realise that theories need to be based on <u>observations</u>. Muslim scholars then introduced the ideas of creating a <u>hypothesis</u>, <u>testing</u> it, and <u>repeating</u> work to check results.

# Models and Communication

*Once scientists have made a **new discovery**, they **don't** just keep it to themselves. Oh no. Time to learn about how scientific discoveries are **communicated**, and the **models** that are used to represent theories.*

## Theories Can Involve **Different Types** of **Models**

1) A <u>representational model</u> is a <u>simplified description</u> or <u>picture</u> of what's going on in real life. Like all models, it can be used to <u>explain observations</u> and <u>make predictions</u>. E.g. the <u>Bohr model</u> of an atom is a simplified way of showing the arrangement of electrons in an atom (see p.89-91). It can be used to explain electron excitations in atoms.

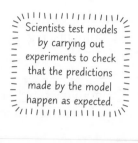
*Scientists test models by carrying out experiments to check that the predictions made by the model happen as expected.*

2) <u>Computational models</u> use computers to make <u>simulations</u> of complex real-life processes, such as climate change. They're used when there are a <u>lot</u> of different <u>variables</u> (factors that change) to consider, and because you can easily <u>change their design</u> to take into account <u>new data</u>.

3) All models have <u>limitations</u> on what they can <u>explain</u> or <u>predict</u>. E.g. <u>the Big Bang model</u> (a model used to describe the beginning of the Universe) can be used to explain why everything in the Universe is moving away from us. One of its limitations is that it <u>doesn't explain</u> the moments before the Big Bang.

## Scientific Discoveries are **Communicated** to the **General Public**

Some scientific discoveries show that people should <u>change their habits</u>, or they might provide ideas that could be <u>developed</u> into new <u>technology</u>. So scientists need to <u>tell the world</u> about their discoveries.

<u>Radioactive materials</u> are used widely in <u>medicine</u> for <u>imaging</u> and <u>treatment</u> (see p.103-104). Information about these materials needs to be communicated to <u>doctors</u> so they can <u>make use</u> of them, and to <u>patients</u>, so they can make <u>informed decisions</u> about their <u>treatment</u>.

## Scientific **Evidence** can be **Presented** in a **Biased Way**

1) Scientific discoveries that are reported in the <u>media</u> (e.g. newspapers or television) <u>aren't</u> peer-reviewed.
2) This means that, even though news stories are often <u>based</u> on data that has been peer-reviewed, the data might be <u>presented</u> in a way that is <u>over-simplified</u> or <u>inaccurate</u>, making it open to <u>misinterpretation</u>.
3) People who want to make a point can sometimes <u>present data</u> in a <u>biased way</u> (sometimes <u>without knowing</u> they're doing it). For example, a scientist might overemphasise a relationship in the data, or a newspaper article might describe details of data <u>supporting</u> an idea without giving any evidence <u>against</u> it.

## Companies can present biased data to help sell products...

Sometimes a company may only want you to see half of the story so they present the data in a <u>biased way</u>. For example, a pharmaceutical company may want to encourage you to buy their drugs by telling you about all the <u>positives</u>, but not report the results of any <u>unfavourable studies</u>.

# Issues Created by Science

*Science has helped us **make progress** in loads of areas, from advances in medicine to space travel. But science still has its **issues**. And it **can't answer everything**, as you're about to find out.*

## Scientific Developments are Great, but they can Raise Issues

Scientific <u>knowledge is increased</u> by doing experiments. And this knowledge leads to <u>scientific developments</u>, e.g. new technologies or new advice. These developments can create <u>issues</u> though. For example:

<u>Economic issues:</u> Society <u>can't</u> always <u>afford</u> to do things scientists recommend (e.g. investing in alternative energy sources) without <u>cutting back elsewhere</u>.

<u>Social issues:</u> Decisions based on scientific evidence affect <u>people</u> — e.g. should fossil fuels be taxed more highly? Would the effect on people's lifestyles be <u>acceptable</u>?

<u>Personal issues:</u> Some decisions will affect <u>individuals</u>. For example, someone might support <u>alternative energy</u>, but object if a <u>wind farm</u> was built next to their house.

<u>Environmental issues:</u> <u>Human activity</u> often affects the <u>natural environment</u>. For example, building a <u>dam</u> to produce electricity will change the <u>local habitat</u> so some species might be displaced. But it will also reduce our need for <u>fossil fuels</u>, so will help to reduce <u>climate change</u>.

## Science Can't Answer Every Question — Especially Ethical Ones

1) We don't <u>understand everything</u>. We're always finding out <u>more</u>, but we'll never know <u>all</u> the answers.

2) In order to answer scientific questions, scientists need <u>data</u> to provide <u>evidence</u> for their hypotheses.

3) Some questions can't be answered <u>yet</u> because the data <u>can't</u> currently be <u>collected</u>, or because there's <u>not enough</u> data to <u>support</u> a theory.

4) <u>Eventually</u>, as we get <u>more evidence</u>, we'll answer some of the questions that <u>currently</u> can't be answered, e.g. what the impact of global warming on sea levels will be. But there will always be the "<u>Should we be doing this at all?</u>"-type questions that experiments <u>can't</u> help us to answer...

Think about <u>new drugs which can be taken to boost your 'brain power'</u>.

- Some people think they're <u>good</u> as they could improve concentration or memory. New drugs could let people think in ways beyond the powers of normal brains.

- Other people say they're <u>bad</u> — they could give some people an <u>unfair advantage</u> in exams. And people might be <u>pressured</u> into taking them so that they could work more <u>effectively</u>, and for <u>longer hours</u>.

## There are often issues with new scientific developments...

The trouble is, there's often <u>no clear right answer</u> where these issues are concerned. Different people have <u>different views</u>, depending on their priorities. These issues are full of <u>grey areas</u>.

# Risk

*Scientific discoveries* are often great, but they can prove **risky**. With dangers all around, you've got to be aware of hazards — this includes **how likely** they are to **cause harm** and **how serious** the effects may be.

## Nothing is Completely Risk-Free

1) A hazard is something that could potentially cause harm.

2) All hazards have a risk attached to them — this is the chance that the hazard will cause harm.

3) The risks of some things seem pretty obvious, or we've known about them for a while, like the risk of causing acid rain by polluting the atmosphere, or of having a car accident when you're travelling in a car.

4) New technology arising from scientific advances can bring new risks, e.g. scientists are unsure whether nanoparticles that are being used in cosmetics and suncream might be harming the cells in our bodies. These risks need to be considered alongside the benefits of the technology, e.g. improved sun protection.

5) You can estimate the size of a risk based on how many times something happens in a big sample (e.g. 100 000 people) over a given period (e.g. a year). For example, you could assess the risk of a driver crashing by recording how many people in a group of 100 000 drivers crashed their cars over a year.

6) To make decisions about activities that involve hazards, we need to take into account the chance of the hazard causing harm, and how serious the consequences would be if it did. If an activity involves a hazard that's very likely to cause harm, with serious consequences if it does, it's considered high-risk.

## People Make Their Own Decisions About Risk

1) Not all risks have the same consequences, e.g. if you chop veg with a sharp knife you risk cutting your finger, but if you go scuba-diving you risk death. You're much more likely to cut your finger during half an hour of chopping than to die during half an hour of scuba-diving. But most people are happier to accept a higher probability of an accident if the consequences are short-lived and fairly minor.

2) People tend to be more willing to accept a risk if they choose to do something (e.g. go scuba diving), compared to having the risk imposed on them (e.g. having a nuclear power station built next door).

3) People's perception of risk (how risky they think something is) isn't always accurate. They tend to view familiar activities as low-risk and unfamiliar activities as high-risk — even if that's not the case. For example, cycling on roads is often high-risk, but many people are happy to do it because it's a familiar activity. Air travel is actually pretty safe, but a lot of people perceive it as high-risk.

4) People may over-estimate the risk of things with long-term or invisible effects, e.g. ionising radiation.

---

## The pros and cons of new technology must be weighed up...

The world's a dangerous place and it's impossible to rule out the chance of an accident altogether. But if you can recognise hazards and take steps to reduce the risks, you're more likely to stay safe.

# Designing Investigations

*Dig out your lab coat and dust off your badly-scratched safety goggles... it's **investigation time**.*

## Evidence Can **Support** or **Disprove** a **Hypothesis**

1) Scientists <u>observe</u> things and come up with <u>hypotheses</u> to explain them (see p.2). You need to be able to do the same.  For example:

> <u>Observation</u>:  People with big feet have spots.  <u>Hypothesis</u>:  Having big feet causes spots.

2) To <u>determine</u> whether or not a hypothesis is <u>right</u>, you need to do an <u>investigation</u> to gather evidence.  To do this, you need to use your hypothesis to make a <u>prediction</u> — something you think <u>will happen</u> that you can test. E.g. people who have bigger feet will have more spots.

Investigations include experiments and studies.

3) Investigations are used to see if there are <u>patterns</u> or <u>relationships</u> between <u>two variables</u>, e.g. to see if there's a pattern or relationship between the variables 'number of spots' and 'size of feet'.

## Evidence Needs to be **Repeatable, Reproducible** and **Valid**

1) <u>Repeatable</u> means that if the <u>same person</u> does an experiment again using the <u>same methods</u> and equipment, they'll get <u>similar results</u>.

2) <u>Reproducible</u> means that if <u>someone else</u> does the experiment, or a <u>different</u> method or piece of equipment is used, the results will still be <u>similar</u>.

3) If data is <u>repeatable</u> and <u>reproducible</u>, it's <u>reliable</u> and scientists are more likely to <u>have confidence</u> in it.

4) <u>Valid results</u> are both repeatable and reproducible AND they <u>answer the original question</u>. They come from experiments that were designed to be a <u>FAIR TEST</u>...

## Make an Investigation a **Fair Test** By **Controlling the Variables**

1) In a lab experiment you usually <u>change one variable</u> and <u>measure</u> how it affects <u>another variable</u>.

2) To make it a fair test, <u>everything else</u> that could affect the results should <u>stay the same</u> — otherwise you can't tell if the thing you're changing is causing the results or not.

3) The variable you <u>CHANGE</u> is called the <u>INDEPENDENT</u> variable.

4) The variable you <u>MEASURE</u> when you change the independent variable is the <u>DEPENDENT</u> variable.

5) The variables that you <u>KEEP THE SAME</u> are called <u>CONTROL</u> variables.

> You could find how <u>current</u> through a circuit component affects the <u>potential difference</u> <u>(p.d.)</u> across the component by measuring the <u>potential difference</u> at different currents. The <u>independent variable</u> is the <u>current</u>.  The <u>dependent variable</u> is the <u>potential difference</u>. <u>Control variables</u> include the <u>temperature</u> of the component, the <u>p.d.</u> of the power supply, etc.

6) Because you can't always control all the variables, you often need to use a <u>control experiment</u>.  This is an experiment that's kept under the <u>same conditions</u> as the rest of the investigation, but <u>doesn't</u> have anything <u>done</u> to it.  This is so that you can see what happens when you don't change anything at all.

# Designing Investigations

## The **Bigger** the **Sample Size** the **Better**

1) Data based on <u>small samples</u> isn't as good as data based on large samples.
   A sample should <u>represent</u> the <u>whole population</u> (i.e. it should share as many
   of the characteristics in the population as possible) — a small sample can't do
   that as well. It's also harder to spot <u>anomalies</u> if your sample size is too small.

2) The <u>bigger</u> the sample size the <u>better</u>, but scientists have to be <u>realistic</u> when
   choosing how big. For example, if you were studying the effects of <u>living</u> near a
   <u>nuclear power plant</u>, it'd be great to study <u>everyone</u> who lived near a nuclear power
   plant (a huge sample), but it'd take ages and cost a bomb. It's more realistic to
   study a thousand people, with a range of ages and races and across both genders.

## Your **Equipment** has to be **Right for the Job**

1) The measuring equipment you use has to be <u>sensitive enough</u> to measure the changes you're looking for.
   For example, if you need to measure changes of 1 cm³ you need to use a <u>measuring cylinder</u>
   that can measure in <u>1 cm³</u> steps — it'd be no good trying with one that only measures 10 cm³ steps.

2) The <u>smallest change</u> a measuring instrument can <u>detect</u> is called its <u>resolution</u>. E.g. some mass balances
   have a resolution of 1 g, some have a resolution of 0.1 g, and some are even more sensitive.

3) Also, equipment needs to be <u>calibrated</u> by measuring a known value. If there's a <u>difference</u> between
   the <u>measured</u> and <u>known value</u>, you can use this to <u>correct</u> the inaccuracy of the equipment.

## Data Should be **Repeatable**, **Reproducible**, **Accurate** and **Precise**

1) To <u>check repeatability</u> you need to <u>repeat</u> the readings and check that the results are similar.
   You need to repeat each reading at least <u>three times</u>.

2) To make sure your results are <u>reproducible</u> you can cross check them by taking
   a <u>second set of readings</u> with <u>another instrument</u> (or a <u>different observer</u>).

3) Your data also needs to be <u>accurate</u>. Really accurate
   results are those that are <u>really close</u> to the <u>true answer</u>.
   The accuracy of your results usually depends on your
   <u>method</u> — you need to make sure you're measuring the
   right thing and that you don't <u>miss anything</u> that should
   be included in the measurements. E.g. estimating the
   <u>volume</u> of an irregularly shaped solid by <u>measuring the</u>
   <u>sides</u> isn't very accurate because this will not take into
   account any gaps in the object. It's <u>more accurate</u> to
   measure the volume using a <u>eureka can</u> (see p.172).

| Repeat | Data set 1 | Data set 2 |
|--------|-----------|-----------|
| 1 | 12 | 11 |
| 2 | 14 | 17 |
| 3 | 13 | 14 |
| Mean | <u>13</u> | <u>14</u> |

Data set 1 is more precise
than data set 2.

4) Your data also needs to be <u>precise</u>. Precise results are
   ones where the data is <u>all really close</u> to the <u>mean</u>
   (average) of your repeated results (i.e. not spread out).

# Designing Investigations

## You Need to Look out for **Errors** and **Anomalous Results**

1) The results of your experiment will always <u>vary a bit</u> because of <u>random errors</u> — unpredictable differences caused by things like <u>human errors</u> in <u>measuring</u>. The errors when you make a reading from a ruler are random. You have to estimate or round the distance when it's between two marks — so sometimes your figure will be a bit above the real one, and sometimes it will be a bit below.

2) You can <u>reduce</u> the effect of random errors by taking <u>repeat readings</u> and finding the <u>mean</u>. This will make your results <u>more precise</u>.

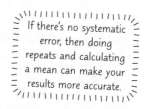
*If there's no systematic error, then doing repeats and calculating a mean can make your results more accurate.*

3) If a measurement is wrong by the <u>same amount every time</u>, it's called a <u>systematic error</u>. For example, if you measured from the very end of your ruler instead of from the 0 cm mark every time, all your measurements would be a bit small. Repeating the experiment in the exact same way and calculating a mean <u>won't</u> correct a systematic error.

4) Just to make things more complicated, if a systematic error is caused by using <u>equipment</u> that <u>isn't zeroed properly</u>, it's called a <u>zero error</u>. For example, if a mass balance always reads 1 gram before you put anything on it, all your measurements will be 1 gram too heavy.

5) You can <u>compensate</u> for some systematic errors if you know about them, e.g. if a mass balance always reads 1 gram before you put anything on it, you can subtract 1 gram from all your results.

6) Sometimes you get a result that <u>doesn't fit in</u> with the rest at all. This is called an <u>anomalous result</u>. You should investigate it and try to <u>work out what happened</u>. If you can work out what happened (e.g. you measured something wrong) you can <u>ignore</u> it when processing your results.

## Investigations Can be **Hazardous**

1) <u>Hazards</u> from science experiments might include:

- <u>Lasers</u>, e.g. if a laser is directed into the eye, this can cause blindness.
- <u>Gamma radiation</u>, e.g. gamma-emitting radioactive sources can cause cancer.
- <u>Fire</u>, e.g. an unattended Bunsen burner is a fire hazard.
- <u>Electricity</u>, e.g. faulty electrical equipment could give you a shock.

*You can find out about potential hazards by looking in textbooks, doing some internet research, or asking your teacher.*

2) Part of planning an investigation is making sure that it's <u>safe</u>.

3) You should always make sure that you <u>identify</u> all the hazards that you might encounter. Then you should think of ways of <u>reducing the risks</u> from the hazards you've identified. For example:

- If you're working with <u>springs</u>, always wear safety goggles. This will reduce the risk of the spring hitting your eye if the spring snaps.
- If you're using a <u>Bunsen burner</u>, stand it on a heat proof mat to reduce the risk of starting a fire.

---

## Designing an investigation is an involved process...

<u>Collecting data</u> is what investigations are all about. Designing a good investigation is really important to make sure that any data collected is <u>accurate</u>, <u>precise</u>, <u>repeatable</u> and <u>reproducible</u>.

# Processing Data

*Processing your data means doing some **calculations** with it to make it **more useful**.*

## Data Needs to be Organised

1) Tables are really useful for <u>organising data</u>.
2) When you draw a table <u>use a ruler</u> and make sure <u>each column</u> has a <u>heading</u> (including the <u>units</u>).

## There are Different Ways to Process Your Data

1) When you've done repeats of an experiment you should always calculate the <u>mean</u> (average). To do this <u>add together</u> all the data values and <u>divide</u> by the total number of values in the sample.

2) You can also find the <u>mode</u> of your results — this is the <u>value</u> that <u>occurs</u> the <u>most</u> in your set of results.

3) The <u>median</u> can be found by writing your results in numerical <u>order</u> — the median is the <u>middle number</u>.

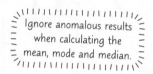
Ignore anomalous results when calculating the mean, mode and median.

**EXAMPLE**

**The results of an experiment show the extension of two springs when a force is applied to both of them. Calculate the mean, mode and median of the extension for both springs.**

| Spring | Repeat (cm) | | | | | Mean (cm) | Mode (cm) | Median (cm) |
|--------|---|---|---|---|---|-----------|-----------|-------------|
| | 1 | 2 | 3 | 4 | 5 | | | |
| A | 18 | 26 | 22 | 26 | 28 | (18 + 26 + 22 + 26 + 28) ÷ 5 = 24 | 26 | 26 |
| B | 11 | 14 | 20 | 15 | 20 | (11 + 14 + 20 + 15 + 20) ÷ 5 = 16 | 20 | 15 |

## Round to the Lowest Number of Significant Figures

The <u>first significant figure</u> of a number is the first digit that's <u>not zero</u>. The second and third significant figures come <u>straight after</u> (even if they're zeros). You should be aware of significant figures in calculations.

1) In <u>any</u> calculation, you should round the answer to the <u>lowest number of significant figures</u> (s.f.) given.
2) Remember to write down <u>how many</u> significant figures you've rounded to after your answer.
3) If your calculation has multiple steps, <u>only</u> round the <u>final</u> answer, or it won't be as accurate.

**EXAMPLE**

**The mass of a solid is 0.24 g and its volume is 0.715 cm³. Calculate the density of the solid.**

Density = 0.24 g ÷ 0.715 cm³ = 0.33566... = 0.34 g/cm³ (2 s.f.)

2 s.f.     3 s.f.        Final answer should be rounded to 2 s.f.

**EXAM TIP**

## Don't forget your calculator...

In the exam you could be given some <u>data</u> and be expected to <u>process it</u> in some way. Make sure you keep an eye on <u>significant figures</u> in your answers and <u>always write down your working</u>.

# Presenting Data

*Once you've processed your data, e.g. by calculating the mean, you can present your results in a nice **chart** or **graph**. This will help you to **spot any patterns** in your data.*

## Bar Charts Can be Used to Show Different Types of Data

Bar charts can be used to display:

1) <u>Categoric</u> data (comes in distinct categories, e.g. states of matter, types of nuclear radiation).

2) <u>Discrete</u> data (the data can be counted in chunks, where there's no in-between value, e.g. number of protons is discrete because you can't have half a proton).

3) <u>Continuous</u> data (numerical data that can have any value in a range, e.g. length or temperature).

There are some <u>golden rules</u> you need to follow for <u>drawing</u> bar charts:

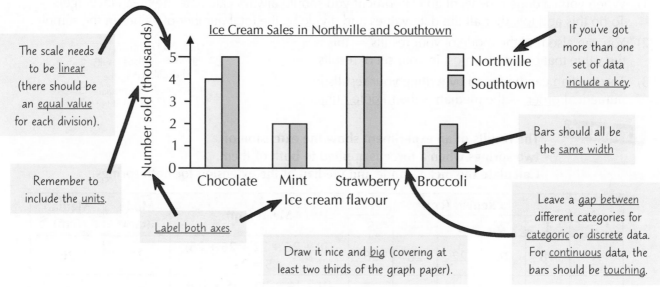

The scale needs to be <u>linear</u> (there should be an <u>equal value</u> for each division).

Remember to include the <u>units</u>.

Label both axes.

If you've got more than one set of data <u>include a key</u>.

Bars should all be the <u>same width</u>

Leave a <u>gap between</u> different categories for <u>categoric</u> or <u>discrete</u> data. For <u>continuous</u> data, the bars should be <u>touching</u>.

Draw it nice and <u>big</u> (covering at least two thirds of the graph paper).

## Graphs can be Used to Plot Continuous Data

1) If both variables are <u>continuous</u> you should use a <u>graph</u> to display the data.

2) Here are the <u>rules</u> for plotting points on a graph:

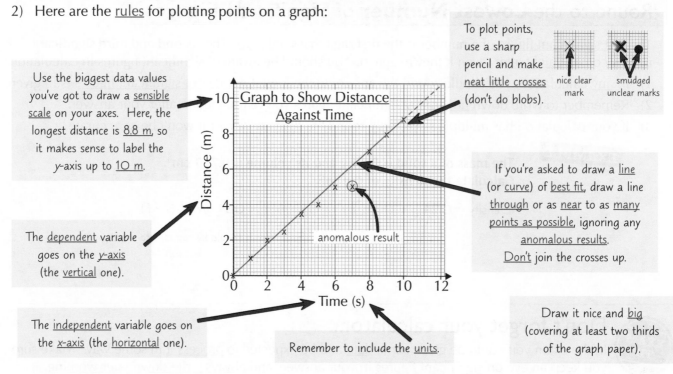

Use the biggest data values you've got to draw a <u>sensible scale</u> on your axes. Here, the longest distance is <u>8.8 m</u>, so it makes sense to label the *y*-axis up to <u>10 m</u>.

The <u>dependent</u> variable goes on the <u>*y*-axis</u> (the <u>vertical</u> one).

The <u>independent</u> variable goes on the <u>*x*-axis</u> (the <u>horizontal</u> one).

To plot points, use a sharp pencil and make <u>neat little crosses</u> (don't do blobs).

nice clear mark    smudged unclear marks

If you're asked to draw a <u>line</u> (or <u>curve</u>) of <u>best fit</u>, draw a line <u>through</u> or as <u>near</u> to as <u>many points as possible</u>, ignoring any <u>anomalous results</u>. <u>Don't</u> join the crosses up.

Remember to include the <u>units</u>.

Draw it nice and <u>big</u> (covering at least two thirds of the graph paper).

# More on Graphs

*Graphs aren't just fun to plot, they're also really useful for showing **trends** in your data.*

## Graphs Can Give You a Lot of Information About Your Data

1) The gradient (slope) of a graph tells you how quickly the dependent variable changes if you change the independent variable.

$$\text{gradient} = \frac{\text{change in } y}{\text{change in } x}$$

*You can use this method to calculate other rates from a graph, not just the rate of change of distance (which is speed). Just remember that a rate is how much something changes over time, so x needs to be the time.*

This graph shows the distance travelled by a vehicle against time. The graph is linear (it's a straight line graph), so you can simply calculate the gradient of the line to find out the speed of the vehicle.

1) To calculate the gradient, pick two points on the line that are easy to read and a good distance apart.

2) Draw a line down from one of the points and a line across from the other to make a triangle. The line drawn down the side of the triangle is the change in y and the line across the bottom is the change in x.

Change in y = 6.8 – 2.0 = 4.8 m    Change in x = 5.2 – 1.6 = 3.6 s

Rate = gradient = $\frac{\text{change in } y}{\text{change in } x}$ = $\frac{4.8\,\text{m}}{3.6\,\text{s}}$ = 1.3 m/s

*The units of the gradient are (units of y)/(units of x).*

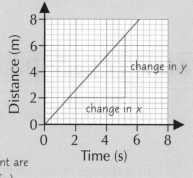

2) To find the gradient of a curve at a certain point, draw a tangent to the curve at that point and then find the gradient of the tangent. See page 22 for details on how to do this.

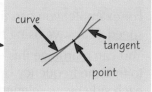

3) The intercept of a graph is where the line of best fit crosses one of the axes. The x-intercept is where the line of best fit crosses the x-axis and the y-intercept is where it crosses the y-axis.

## Graphs Show the Relationship Between Two Variables

1) You can get three types of correlation (relationship) between variables:

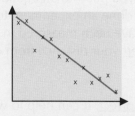

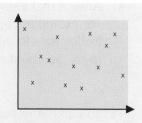

POSITIVE correlation: as one variable increases the other increases.

INVERSE (negative) correlation: as one variable increases the other decreases.

NO correlation: no relationship between the two variables.

2) Just because there's correlation, it doesn't mean the change in one variable is causing the change in the other — there might be other factors involved (see page 15).

# Units

*Graphs and maths skills are all very well, but the numbers don't mean much if you don't get the **units** right.*

## S.I. Units Are Used All Round the World

1) It wouldn't be all that useful if I defined volume in terms of <u>bath tubs</u>, you defined it in terms of <u>egg-cups</u> and my pal Fred defined it in terms of <u>balloons</u> — we'd never be able to compare our data.

2) To stop this happening, scientists have come up with a set of <u>standard units</u>, called S.I. units, that all scientists use to measure their data. Here are some S.I. units you'll see in physics:

| Quantity | S.I. Base Unit |
|---|---|
| mass | kilogram, kg |
| length | metre, m |
| time | second, s |
| temperature | kelvin, K |

## Always Check The Values Used in **Equations** Have the **Right Units**

1) Formulas and equations show <u>relationships</u> between <u>variables</u>.

2) To <u>rearrange</u> an equation, make sure that whatever you do to <u>one side</u> of the equation you also do to the <u>other side</u>.

- For example, you can find the <u>speed</u> of a wave using the equation: ⟶ wave speed = frequency × wavelength
- You can <u>rearrange</u> this equation to find the <u>frequency</u> by <u>dividing</u> <u>each side</u> by wavelength to give: ⟶ frequency = wave speed ÷ wavelength

3) To use a formula, you need to know the values of <u>all but one</u> of the variables. <u>Substitute</u> the values you do know into the formula, and do the calculation to work out the final variable.

4) Always make sure the values you put into an equation or formula have the <u>right units</u>. For example, you might have done an experiment to find the speed of a trolley. The distance the trolley travels will probably have been measured in cm, but the equation to find speed uses distance in m. So you'll have to <u>convert</u> your distance from cm to m before you put it into the equation.

5) To make sure your units are <u>correct</u>, it can help to write down the <u>units</u> on each line of your <u>calculation</u>.

## S.I. units help scientists to compare data...

You can only really <u>compare</u> things if they're in the <u>same units</u>. For example, if you measured the speed of one car in m/s, and one in km/h, it would be hard to know which car was going faster.

# Converting Units

*You can **convert units** using **scaling prefixes**. This can save you from having to write a lot of 0's...*

## Scaling Prefixes Can Be Used for Large and Small Quantities

1) Quantities come in a huge <u>range</u> of sizes. For example, the volume of a swimming pool might be around 2 000 000 000 cm³, while the volume of a cup is around 250 cm³.

2) To make the size of numbers more <u>manageable</u>, larger or smaller units are used. These are the <u>S.I. base units</u> (e.g. metres) with a <u>prefix</u> in front:

| Prefix | tera (T) | giga (G) | mega (M) | kilo (k) | deci (d) | centi (c) | milli (m) | micro (μ) | nano (n) |
|---|---|---|---|---|---|---|---|---|---|
| Multiple of Unit | $10^{12}$ | $10^{9}$ | 1 000 000 $(10^{6})$ | 1000 | 0.1 | 0.01 | 0.001 | 0.000001 $(10^{-6})$ | $10^{-9}$ |

3) These <u>prefixes</u> tell you <u>how much bigger</u> or <u>smaller</u> a unit is than the base unit. So one <u>kilometre</u> is <u>one thousand</u> metres.

4) To <u>swap</u> from one unit to another, all you need to know is what number you have to divide or multiply by to get from the original unit to the new unit — this is called the <u>conversion factor</u>.

> The conversion factor is the number of times the smaller unit goes into the larger unit.

- To go from a <u>bigger unit</u> (like m) to a <u>smaller unit</u> (like cm), you <u>multiply</u> by the conversion factor.
- To go from a <u>smaller unit</u> (like g) to a <u>bigger unit</u> (like kg), you <u>divide</u> by the conversion factor.

5) Here are some conversions that'll be useful for GCSE physics:

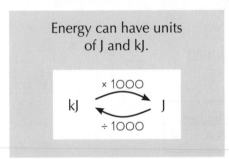

Energy can have units of J and kJ.

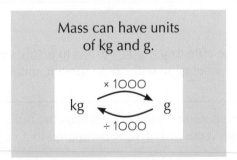

Mass can have units of kg and g.

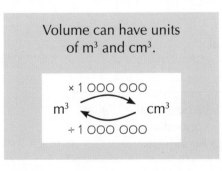

Volume can have units of m³ and cm³.

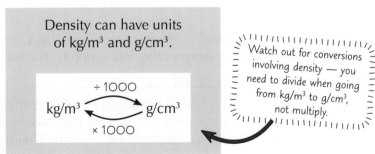

Density can have units of kg/m³ and g/cm³.

> Watch out for conversions involving density — you need to divide when going from kg/m³ to g/cm³, not multiply.

6) Numbers can also be written in <u>standard form</u>, e.g. $1 \times 10^{2}$ m = 100 m. Make sure you know how to work with standard form on <u>your calculator</u>.

## To convert from bigger units to smaller units...

...multiply by the conversion prefix. And to convert from <u>smaller units</u> to <u>bigger units</u>, <u>divide</u> by the <u>conversion factor</u>. Don't go getting this rule muddled up and the wrong way round...

# Drawing Conclusions

*Once you've designed your experiment, carried it out, processed and presented your data, it's finally time to sit down and work out exactly what your data tells you. Time for some fun with **conclusions**...*

## You Can **Only Conclude** What the Data Shows and **No More**

1) Drawing conclusions might seem pretty straightforward — you just <u>look at your data</u> and <u>say what pattern or relationship you see</u> between the dependent and independent variables.

The table on the right shows the potential difference across a light bulb for three <u>different</u> currents through the bulb:

| Current (A) | Potential difference (V) |
|:---:|:---:|
| 6 | 4 |
| 9 | 10 |
| 12 | 13 |

<u>CONCLUSION</u>: A <u>higher current</u> through the bulb gives a higher <u>potential difference</u> across the bulb.

2) But you've got to be really careful that your conclusion <u>matches the data</u> you've got and <u>doesn't go any further</u>.

> You <u>can't</u> conclude that the potential difference across <u>any circuit component</u> will be higher for a larger current — the results might be completely different.

3) You also need to be able to <u>use your results</u> to <u>justify your conclusion</u> (i.e. back up your conclusion with some specific data).

> The potential difference across the bulb was <u>9 V higher</u> with a current of 12 A compared to a current of 6 A.

4) When writing a conclusion you need to <u>refer back</u> to the original hypothesis and say whether the data <u>supports it</u> or not:

> The hypothesis for this experiment might have been that a higher current through the bulb would <u>increase</u> the potential difference across the bulb. If so, the data <u>supports</u> the hypothesis.

## You should be able to justify your conclusion with your data...

You should always be able to explain how your data <u>supports</u> your <u>conclusion</u>. It's easy to go too far with conclusions and start making <u>bold claims</u> that your data simply can't back up. When you're drawing conclusions, it's also important that you refer back to your <u>initial hypothesis</u>, the one you made right back at the start of the investigation, to see whether your data supports it or not.

# Correlation and Cause

*Don't get carried away when you're **drawing conclusions** — **correlation** doesn't always mean **cause**. There could be a few reasons why two variables appear to be linked, as you're about to find out.*

## Correlation DOES NOT Mean Cause

If two things are correlated (i.e. there's a relationship between them) it <u>doesn't</u> necessarily mean a change in one variable is <u>causing</u> the change in the other — this is <u>REALLY IMPORTANT</u> — <u>DON'T FORGET IT</u>.

## There are **Three** Possible **Reasons** for a **Correlation**

1) <u>CHANCE</u>: It might seem strange, but two things can show a correlation purely due to <u>chance</u>.

> For example, one study might find a correlation between people's hair colour and how good they are at frisbee. But other scientists <u>don't</u> get a correlation when they investigate it — the results of the first study are just a <u>fluke</u>.

2) <u>LINKED BY A 3RD VARIABLE</u>: A lot of the time it may <u>look</u> as if a change in one variable is causing a change in the other, but it <u>isn't</u> — a <u>third variable links</u> the two things.

> For example, there's a correlation between <u>water temperature</u> and <u>shark attacks</u>. This isn't because warmer water makes sharks crazy. Instead, they're linked by a third variable — the <u>number of people swimming</u> (more people swim when the water's hotter, and with more people in the water you get more shark attacks).

3) <u>CAUSE</u>: Sometimes a change in one variable does <u>cause</u> a change in the other. You can only conclude that a correlation is due to cause when you've <u>controlled all the variables</u> that could, just could, be affecting the result.

> For example, there's a correlation between <u>smoking</u> and <u>lung cancer</u>. This is because chemicals in tobacco smoke cause lung cancer. This conclusion was only made once <u>other variables</u> (such as age and exposure to other things that cause cancer) had been <u>controlled</u> and shown <u>not</u> to affect people's risk of getting lung cancer.

---

## Two variables could appear to be linked by chance...

<u>Correlation</u> doesn't necessarily mean <u>cause</u> — two variables might appear to be linked but it could just be down to <u>chance</u>, or they could be linked by a <u>third variable</u>. When you draw conclusions, make sure you're not jumping to conclusions about cause, and check that you properly <u>consider</u> all the reasons why two variables might appear to be linked.

# Uncertainty

*Uncertainty is how sure you can really be about your data. There's a little bit of **maths** to do, and also a formula to learn. But don't worry too much — it's no more than a simple bit of subtraction and division.*

## **Uncertainty** is the Amount of **Error** Your Measurements Might Have

1) When you <u>repeat</u> a measurement, you often get a <u>slightly different</u> figure each time you do it due to <u>random error</u>. This means that <u>each result</u> has some <u>uncertainty</u> to it.

2) The measurements you make will also have some uncertainty in them due to <u>limits</u> in the <u>resolution</u> of the equipment you use (see page 7).

3) This all means that the <u>mean</u> of a set of results will also have some uncertainty to it. You can calculate the uncertainty of a <u>mean result</u> using the equation:

$$\text{uncertainty} = \frac{\text{range}}{2}$$

 The range is the largest value minus the smallest value.

4) The <u>larger</u> the range, the <u>less precise</u> your results are and the <u>more uncertainty</u> there will be in your results. Uncertainties are shown using the '±' symbol.

**EXAMPLE**

**The table below shows the results of an experiment to determine the speed of the trolley as it rolls down a ramp. Calculate the uncertainty of the mean.**

| Repeat | 1 | 2 | 3 | 4 |
|---|---|---|---|---|
| Speed (m/s) | 2.01 | 1.98 | 2.00 | 2.01 |

1) First work out the range:

Range = 2.01 − 1.98 = 0.030 m/s

2) Then find the mean:

Mean = (2.01 + 1.98 + 2.00 + 2.01) ÷ 4

= 8.00 ÷ 4 = 2.00

3) Use the range to find the uncertainty:

Uncertainty = range ÷ 2 = 0.030 ÷ 2 = 0.015 m/s

So the uncertainty of the mean = 2.00 ± 0.015 m/s

5) Measuring a <u>greater amount</u> of something helps to <u>reduce uncertainty</u>. For example, in an experiment investigating speed, measuring the distance travelled over a <u>longer period</u> compared to a shorter period will <u>reduce</u> the <u>uncertainty</u> in your results.

## The smaller the uncertainty, the more precise your results...

Remember that equation for <u>uncertainty</u>. You never know when you might need it — you could be expected to use it in the exams. You need to make sure all the <u>data</u> is in the <u>same units</u> though. For example, if you had some measurements in metres, and some in centimetres, you'd need to convert them all into either metres or centimetres before you set about calculating uncertainty.

# Evaluations

*Hurrah! The end of another investigation. Well, now you have to work out all the things you did **wrong**. That's what **evaluations** are all about I'm afraid. Best get cracking with this page...*

## Evaluations — Describe **How** Experiments Could be **Improved**

An evaluation is a <u>critical analysis</u> of the whole investigation.

1) You should comment on the <u>method</u> — was it <u>valid</u>?
   Did you control all the other variables to make it a <u>fair test</u>?

2) Comment on the <u>quality</u> of the <u>results</u> — was there <u>enough evidence</u> to reach a
   valid <u>conclusion</u>? Were the results <u>repeatable</u>, <u>reproducible</u>, <u>accurate</u> and <u>precise</u>?

3) Were there any <u>anomalous</u> results? If there were <u>none</u> then <u>say so</u>.
   If there were any, try to <u>explain</u> them — were they caused by <u>errors</u> in measurement?
   Were there any other <u>variables</u> that could have <u>affected</u> the results?
   You should comment on the level of <u>uncertainty</u> in your results too.

4) All this analysis will allow you to say how <u>confident</u> you are that your conclusion is <u>right</u>.

5) Then you can suggest any <u>changes</u> to the <u>method</u> that would <u>improve</u> the quality of the results,
   so that you could have <u>more confidence</u> in your conclusion. For example, you might suggest
   <u>changing</u> the way you controlled a variable, or <u>increasing</u> the number of <u>measurements</u> you took.
   Taking more measurements at <u>narrower intervals</u> could give you a <u>more accurate result</u>.
   For example:

> <u>Springs</u> have an <u>elastic limit</u> (a maximum extension before they stop springing back to
> their original size). Say you use several <u>identical</u> springs to do an experiment to find
> the elastic limit of the springs. If you apply forces of 1 N, 2 N, 3 N, 4 N and 5 N,
> and from the results see that the elastic limit is somewhere <u>between 4 N and 5 N</u>,
> you could then <u>repeat</u> the experiment with one of the other springs, taking <u>more
> measurements between 4 N and 5 N</u> to get a <u>more accurate</u> value for the elastic limit.

6) You could also make more <u>predictions</u> based
   on your conclusion, then <u>further experiments</u>
   could be carried out to test them.

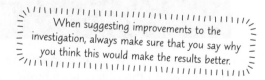
When suggesting improvements to the investigation, always make sure that you say why you think this would make the results better.

## Always look for ways to improve your investigations...

So there you have it — <u>Working Scientifically</u>. Make sure you know this stuff like the back of your hand.
It's not just in the lab, when you're carrying out your groundbreaking <u>investigations</u>, that you'll need to
know how to work scientifically. You can be asked about it in the <u>exams</u> as well. So swot up...

# Scalars and Vectors

*There are a lot of very similar **variables** on this page, but they're **different** in some **very important** ways, so prepare to pay extra close attention. It's down to whether they're a **vector** or a **scalar** quantity.*

## Vectors Have Magnitude and Direction

1) Vector quantities have a <u>magnitude</u> (size) and a <u>direction</u>.

2) Lots of <u>physical quantities</u> are vector quantities:

<u>Vector quantities</u>: force, velocity, displacement, weight, acceleration, momentum, etc.

3) Some physical quantities <u>only</u> have magnitude and <u>no direction</u>. These are called <u>scalar quantities</u>:

<u>Scalar quantities</u>: speed, distance, mass, energy, temperature, time, etc.

<u>Velocity</u> is a <u>vector</u>, but <u>speed</u> is a <u>scalar</u> quantity.
Both bikes are travelling at the same <u>speed</u>, $v$.
They have <u>different velocities</u> because
they are travelling in different <u>directions</u>.

## Distance is Scalar, Displacement is a Vector

1) <u>Distance</u> is just <u>how far</u> an object has moved. It's a <u>scalar</u> quantity so it doesn't involve <u>direction</u>.

2) Displacement is a <u>vector</u> quantity. It measures the distance and direction in a <u>straight line</u> from an object's <u>starting point</u> to its <u>finishing point</u> — e.g. the plane flew 5 metres <u>north</u>. The direction could be <u>relative to a point</u>, e.g. <u>towards the school</u>, or a <u>bearing</u> (a <u>three-digit angle from north</u>, e.g. <u>035°</u>).

3) If you walk 5 m <u>north</u>, then 5 m <u>south</u>, your <u>displacement</u> is <u>0 m</u> but the <u>distance</u> travelled is <u>10 m</u>.

## Speed and Velocity are Both How Fast You're Going

1) <u>Speed and velocity</u> both measure <u>how fast</u> you're going, but <u>speed</u> is a <u>scalar</u> and <u>velocity</u> is a <u>vector</u>:

<u>Speed</u> is just <u>how fast</u> you're going (e.g. 30 mph or 20 m/s)
with no regard to the direction.
<u>Velocity</u> is speed in a given <u>direction</u>, e.g. 30 mph north or 20 m/s, 060°.

2) This means you can have objects travelling at a <u>constant speed</u> with a <u>changing velocity</u>. This happens when the object is <u>changing direction</u> whilst staying at the <u>same speed</u>.

## When it comes to vectors the sign is important...

If you're working on a question which involves <u>vectors</u> that point in <u>opposite directions</u>, pick one direction to have a <u>positive</u> sign and the other <u>negative</u>. For example, if you decide to make all velocities pointing to the left positive, be sure that you give those pointing to the right a negative sign.

# Speed

*Speed tells you the **distance** an object travels in a **given time**. You're typically going to deal with speeds in metres per second — so you need to be able to **estimate** some everyday speeds in these units.*

## You Need to Know Some **Typical** Everyday **Speeds**

1) For an object travelling at a <u>constant</u> speed, <u>distance</u>, (average) <u>speed</u> and <u>time</u> are related by the formula:

> **distance travelled (m) = (average) speed (m/s) × time (s)**

2) Objects <u>rarely</u> travel at a <u>constant speed</u>. E.g. when you <u>walk</u>, <u>run</u> or travel in a <u>car</u>, your speed is <u>always changing</u>. Make sure you have an idea of the <u>typical speeds</u> for different transport methods:

> <u>Walking</u> — <u>1.4 m/s</u> (5 km/h)
> <u>Running</u> — <u>3 m/s</u> (11 km/h)
> <u>Cycling</u> — <u>5.5 m/s</u> (20 km/h)

> <u>Cars</u> in a <u>built-up area</u> — <u>13 m/s</u> (47 km/h)
> <u>Cars</u> on a <u>motorway</u> — <u>31 m/s</u> (112 km/h)
> <u>Aeroplanes</u> — <u>250 m/s</u> (900 km/h)
> <u>Trains</u> — up to <u>55 m/s</u> (200 km/h)
> <u>Ferries</u> — 15 m/s (54 km/h)

> <u>Wind</u> speed — <u>5 – 20 m/s</u>
> Speed of <u>sound</u> in <u>air</u> — <u>340 m/s</u>

## You can use **Different Equipment** to Measure **Distance** and **Time**

To <u>calculate</u> speed you'll need measurements of <u>distance</u> and <u>time</u>. For distances less than 1 m and times greater than 5 s, you'll probably use a <u>stopwatch</u> and a <u>metre ruler</u>, but there are <u>many different ways</u> to take distance and time measurements:

1) Light gates (p.192) are often the best option for <u>short</u> time intervals. They get rid of the <u>human error</u> caused by <u>reaction times</u> (p.36).

2) For finding something like a person's <u>walking speed</u>, the distances and times you'll look at are quite <u>large</u>. You can use a <u>rolling tape measure</u> (one of those clicky wheel things) and <u>markers</u> to measure and mark out distances.

3) If you're feeling a bit high-tech, you could also record a <u>video</u> of the moving object and look at how <u>far</u> it travels each <u>frame</u>. If you know how many <u>frames per second</u> the camera records, you can find the <u>distance</u> travelled by the object in a given number of frames and the <u>time</u> that it takes to do so.

---

## Speed is distance over time — learn it and remember it...

This all seems basic, but it's <u>vital</u> you understand it if you want to get through the <u>rest</u> of this topic.

Q1 A sprinter runs 200 m in 25 s. Calculate his average speed. [2 marks]

Q1 Video Solution

# Acceleration

*Acceleration is the **rate of change** of velocity. You need to be able estimate some day to day accelerations. This might take you a while at first, but over time you should get **faster**.*

## Acceleration is How **Quickly** You're **Speeding Up**

1) Acceleration is definitely <u>not</u> the same as <u>velocity</u> or <u>speed</u>.

2) Acceleration is the <u>change in velocity</u> in a certain amount of <u>time</u>.

3) You can find the <u>average acceleration</u> of an object using:

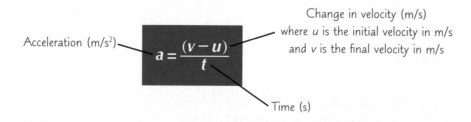

Acceleration (m/s²) ⟶ 
$$a = \frac{(v - u)}{t}$$
Change in velocity (m/s)
where *u* is the initial velocity in m/s
and *v* is the final velocity in m/s

Time (s)

4) <u>Initial velocity</u> is just the <u>starting velocity</u> of the object.

5) <u>Negative</u> acceleration is <u>deceleration</u> (if something <u>slows down</u>, the change in velocity is <u>negative</u>).

## You Need to be Able to **Estimate Accelerations**

You might have to <u>estimate</u> the <u>acceleration</u> (or <u>deceleration</u>) of an object:

**EXAMPLE**

**A car is travelling at 15 m/s, when it collides with a tree and comes to a stop. Estimate the deceleration of the car.**

1) <u>Estimate</u> how long it would take the car to <u>stop</u>.   The car comes to a stop in ~1 s.

2) Put these numbers into the <u>acceleration equation</u>.   $a = (v - u) \div t$

3) As the car has slowed down,
the <u>change in velocity</u> and so the acceleration   $= (0 - 15) \div 1$
is <u>negative</u> — the car is <u>decelerating</u>.   $= -15$ m/s²

> The ~ symbol just means it's an approximate value (or answer).

So the deceleration is about 15 m/s²

From the deceleration, you can estimate the <u>forces</u> involved too — more about that on page 38.

## Acceleration doesn't always have to mean getting faster or slower...

<u>Acceleration</u> measures how quickly <u>velocity changes</u>. Speeding up or slowing down is one way in which velocity can change — but not the only way. Velocity can also <u>change in direction</u>. So, although it might seem weird, a car driving round a roundabout at constant speed is actually experiencing acceleration.

# Acceleration

*For cases of **constant acceleration**, which includes pretty much anything that's falling, there's a really useful **equation** you can use to calculate all sorts of **variables** of **motion**.*

## Uniform Acceleration Means a Constant Acceleration

1) Constant acceleration is sometimes called uniform acceleration.

2) Acceleration due to gravity (g) is uniform for objects in free fall. It's roughly equal to 10 m/s² near the Earth's surface and has the same value as gravitational field strength (p.30).

3) You can use this equation for uniform acceleration:

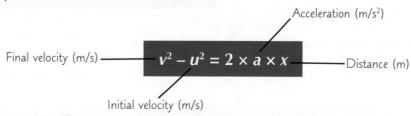

Final velocity (m/s) — $v^2 - u^2 = 2 \times a \times x$ — Distance (m)

Acceleration (m/s²)

Initial velocity (m/s)

**EXAMPLE**

**A van travelling at 23 m/s starts decelerating uniformly at 2.0 m/s² as it heads towards a built-up area 112 m away.**

**What will its speed be when it reaches the built-up area?**

1) First, rearrange the equation so $v^2$ is on one side.     $v^2 = u^2 + (2 \times a \times x)$

2) Now put the numbers in — remember a is negative because it's a deceleration.

$v^2 = 23^2 + (2 \times -2.0 \times 112)$
   $= 81$

3) Finally, square root the whole thing.     $v = \sqrt{81} = 9$ m/s

**EXAMPLE**

**A ball is launched from the ground, directly upwards, at an initial speed of 14 m/s.**

**What is the maximum height the ball will reach?  (You may ignore air resistance.)**

1) This time you'll need to rearrange the equation so x is on one side.

$x = (v^2 - u^2) \div (2 \times a)$

2) Again, put the numbers in — this is a little trickier. Remember a is negative as the ball is decelerating. Also the final velocity, at the instant the ball peaks, will be 0 m/s.

$x = (0^2 - 14^2) \div (2 \times (-10))$
$x = (-196) \div (-20)$
$x = 9.8$ m

## Acceleration due to gravity is 10 m/s² in an ideal world...

You might think 'acceleration due to gravity can't have the same value, g, for all objects — I know a bowling ball falls faster than a feather'. This is because air resistance has a much bigger effect on the feather's motion. If gravity were the only force acting, they really would accelerate at the same rate.

Q1 Video Solution

Q1     A ball is dropped from a height, h, above the ground.
        The speed of the ball just before it hits the ground is 5 m/s.
        Calculate the height the ball is dropped from. (acceleration due to gravity ≈ 10 m/s²) [2 marks]

# Distance/Time Graphs

*It's time for some exciting **graphs**. **Distance/time graphs** contain a lot of **information**, but they can look a bit complicated. Read on to get to grips with the **rules** of the graphs, and all will become clear.*

## Distance/Time Graphs Tell You **How Far** Something has **Travelled**

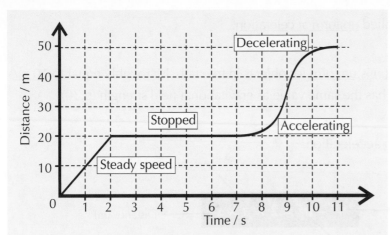

The different parts of a distance/time graph describe the <u>motion</u> of an object:

- The <u>gradient</u> (slope) at <u>any</u> point gives the <u>speed</u> of the object.
- <u>Flat</u> sections are where it's <u>stopped</u>.
- A <u>steeper</u> graph means it's going <u>faster</u>.
- <u>Curves</u> represent <u>acceleration</u>.
- A <u>curve getting steeper</u> means it's <u>speeding up</u> (increasing gradient).
- A <u>levelling off</u> curve means it's <u>slowing down</u> (decreasing gradient).

## The **Speed** of an Object can be Found From a **Distance/Time Graph**

You can find the <u>speed</u> at any time on a distance/time graph:

1) If the graph is a <u>straight line</u>, the speed at any point along that line is equal to the <u>gradient</u> of the line.

> For example, in the graph above, the speed at any time between 0 s and 2 s is:
>
> $$\text{Speed} = \text{gradient} = \frac{\text{change in the vertical}}{\text{change in the horizontal}} = \frac{20}{2} = \underline{10 \text{ m/s}}.$$

2) If the graph is <u>curved</u>, to find the speed at a certain time you need to draw a <u>tangent</u> to the curve at that point, and then find the <u>gradient</u> of the <u>tangent</u>.

⎰ A tangent is a line that is parallel
⎱ to the curve at that point.

3) You can also calculate the <u>average speed</u> of an object when it has <u>non-uniform motion</u> (i.e. it's <u>accelerating</u>) by dividing the <u>total distance travelled</u> by the <u>time it takes</u> to travel that distance.

**EXAMPLE**

**The graph shows the distance/time graph for a cyclist on his bike.**
**Calculate:**
**a) the speed of the bike 25 s into the journey.**
**b) the average speed of the cyclist from 0 to 30 s.**

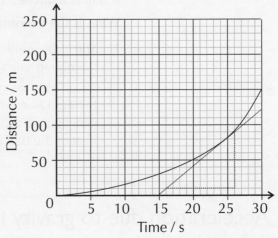

1) Draw the <u>tangent</u> to the curve at 25 s (red line).
2) Then calculate the <u>gradient</u> of the tangent (blue lines).

$$\text{gradient} = \frac{\text{change in the vertical}}{\text{change in the horizontal}} = \frac{80}{10} = 8 \text{ m/s}$$

So, the *speed of the bike 25 s into the journey is 8 m/s*.

3) Use the <u>formula</u> from page 19 to find the <u>average speed</u> of the bike.

average speed = distance ÷ time = 150 ÷ 30 = 5 m/s

## Draw a few distance/time graphs to get a feel for them.

Q1 Sketch the distance-time graph for an object that accelerates, then travels at a steady speed, and then comes to a stop.

[3 marks]

Q1 Video Solution

# Velocity/Time Graphs

*Even more graphs — **velocity/time graphs** this time. These look a lot like the **distance/time graphs** on page 22, so make sure you check the labels on the axes really carefully. You don't want to mix them up.*

## Velocity/Time Graphs can have a Positive or Negative Gradient

How an object's velocity changes over time can be plotted on a velocity/time (or *v/t*) graph.

1) Gradient = acceleration,
   since acceleration = change in velocity ÷ time.

2) Flat sections represent a steady speed.

3) The steeper the graph, the greater the acceleration or deceleration.

4) Uphill sections (/) are acceleration.

5) Downhill sections (\) are deceleration.

6) A curve means changing acceleration.

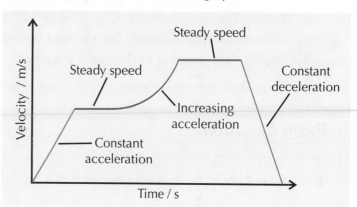

*If the graph is curved, you can use a tangent to the curve (p.22) at a point to find the acceleration at that point.*

## The Distance Travelled is the Area Under the Graph

1) The area under any section of the graph (or all of it) is equal to the distance travelled in that time interval.

2) For bits of the graph where the acceleration's constant, you can split the area into rectangles and triangles to work it out.

3) You can also find the area under the graph by counting the squares under the line and multiplying the number by the value of one square.

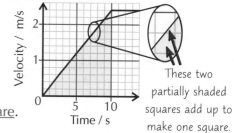

These two partially shaded squares add up to make one square.

### EXAMPLE

**The velocity/time graph of a car's journey is plotted.**

a) **Calculate the acceleration of the car over the first 10 s.**

b) **How far does the car travel in the first 15 s of the journey?**

a) This is just the gradient of the line:   $a = (v - u) \div t$
   $= (20 - 0) \div 10 = 2 \text{ m/s}^2$

b) Split the area into a triangle and a rectangle, then add together their areas — remember the area of a triangle is ½ × base × height.

   Area = (½ × 10 × 20) + (5 × 20)
        = 200 m

OR  b) Find the value of one square, count the total number of squares under the line, and then multiply these two values together.

   1 square = 2 m/s × 1 s = 2 m
   Area = 100 squares
        = 100 × 2 = 200 m

## They look similar to distance/time graphs, but don't be fooled...

Make sure you are familiar with the differences between distance/time and velocity/time graphs.

Q1 Video Solution

Q1   A stationary car starts accelerating increasingly for 10 s until it reaches a speed of 20 m/s.
     It travels at this speed for 20 s until the driver sees a hazard and brakes.
     He decelerates uniformly, coming to a stop 4 s after braking.
     Draw the velocity-time graph for this journey.                                         [3 marks]

# Warm-Up & Exam Questions

Slow down, it's not time to move on to the next topic just yet. First it's time to check that all the stuff you've just read is still running around your brain. Dive into these questions.

## Warm-Up Questions

1) What is the difference between speed and velocity?
2) Suggest the typical speeds of:   a) a person running,   b) an aeroplane,   c) sound in air.
3) How is velocity calculated from a distance-time graph?
4) Describe the shape of the line on a velocity-time graph for an object travelling at a steady speed.

## Exam Questions

1   **Figure 1** shows the velocity-time graph of a cyclist.

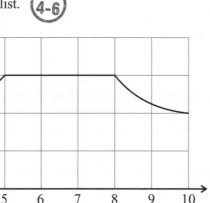

**Figure 1**

(a)   Describe the motion of the cyclist between 5 and 10 seconds.

*[2 marks]*

(b)   Calculate how far the cyclist travelled between 2 and 5 seconds.

*[2 marks]*

(c)   Calculate the acceleration of the cyclist between 2 and 5 seconds.

*[2 marks]*

(d)   Calculate the average deceleration of the cyclist between 8 and 10 seconds.

*[3 marks]*

2   A car travelling down the motorway has to perform an emergency stop.   (Grade 6-7)

(a)   Estimate the original speed of the car in metres per second.

*[1 mark]*

(b)   After pressing the brake pedal, the car decelerates uniformly for 5 seconds until reaching a complete stop.

(i)   Calculate the deceleration the car experiences.

*[2 marks]*

(ii)   Calculate the distance travelled by the car in this time.
Use the correct equation from the Physics Equation Sheet on page 268.

*[3 marks]*

# Newton's First and Second Laws

*Way back in the 1660s, some clever chap named **Isaac Newton** worked out some **Laws of Motion**...*

## A **Force** is Needed to **Change Motion**

This may seem simple, but it's important. Newton's First Law says that a resultant force (p.127) is needed to make something start moving, speed up or slow down:

> If the resultant force on a stationary object is zero, the object will remain stationary. If the resultant force on a moving object is zero, it'll just carry on moving at the same velocity (same speed and direction).

stationary bus

So, when a train or car or bus or anything else is moving at a constant velocity, the resistive and driving forces on it must all be balanced. The velocity will only change if there's a non-zero resultant force acting on the object.

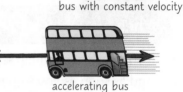
bus with constant velocity

1)  A non-zero resultant force will always produce acceleration (or deceleration) in the direction of the force.

2)  This "acceleration" can take five different forms: starting, stopping, speeding up, slowing down and changing direction.

accelerating bus

## Newton's First Law Helps to Describe **Circular Motion**

1)  Velocity is both the speed and direction of an object (p.18).

2)  If an object is travelling in a circular orbit (at a constant speed) it is constantly changing direction, so it is constantly changing velocity. This means it's accelerating.

3)  From Newton's First Law, this means there must be a resultant force (p.127) acting on it.

4)  This force acts towards the centre of the circle.

5)  This force that keeps something moving in a circle is called a centripetal force.

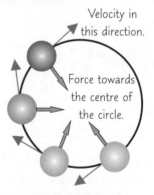
Velocity in this direction.
Force towards the centre of the circle.

## Acceleration is **Proportional** to the **Resultant Force**

1)  The larger the resultant force acting on an object, the more the object accelerates — the force and the acceleration are directly proportional. You can write this as $F \propto a$.

2)  Acceleration is also inversely proportional to the mass of the object — so an object with a larger mass will accelerate less than one with a smaller mass (for a fixed resultant force).

3)  There's an incredibly useful formula that describes Newton's Second Law:

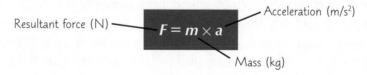
Resultant force (N) — $F = m \times a$ — Acceleration (m/s²)
Mass (kg)

## If there's no net force, then there's no acceleration...

So an object moving at a steady speed doesn't need a net force to keep moving.

Q1    Find the force needed for an 80 kg man on a 10 kg bike to accelerate at 0.25 m/s². [2 marks]

Q1 Video Solution

# Inertia and Newton's Third Law

*Newton's Third Law* and *inertia* sound pretty straightforward, but things can quickly get confusing...

## Inertia is the Tendency for **Motion** to **Remain Unchanged**

1) Until acted on by a resultant force, objects at rest stay at rest and objects moving at a constant velocity will stay moving at that velocity (Newton's First Law).

2) This tendency to keep moving with the same velocity is called inertia.

3) An object's inertial mass measures how difficult it is to change the velocity of an object.

4) Inertial mass can be found using Newton's Second Law of $F = m \times a$ (p.25). Rearranging this gives $m = F \div a$, so inertial mass is just the ratio of force over acceleration.

## Newton's Third Law — **Interaction Pairs** are **Equal** and **Opposite**

Newton's Third Law says:

> When two objects interact, the forces they exert on each other are equal and opposite.

1) If you push something, say a shopping trolley, the trolley will push back against you, just as hard.

2) And as soon as you stop pushing, so does the trolley. Kinda clever really.

3) So far so good. The slightly tricky thing to get your head round is this — if the forces are always equal, how does anything ever go anywhere? The important thing to remember is that the two forces are acting on different objects.

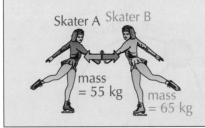

Skater A  Skater B

mass = 55 kg
mass = 65 kg

When skater A pushes on skater B, she feels an equal and opposite force from skater B's hand (the 'normal contact' force). Both skaters feel the same sized force, in opposite directions, and so accelerate away from each other.

Skater A will be accelerated more than skater B, though, because she has a smaller mass — remember $a = F \div m$.

An example of Newton's Third Law in an equilibrium situation is a man pushing against a wall. As the man pushes the wall, there is a normal contact force acting back on him. These two forces are the same size. As the man applies a force and pushes the wall, the wall 'pushes back' on him with an equal force.

Push

Normal contact force

It can be easy to get confused with Newton's Third Law when an object is in equilibrium. E.g. a book resting on a table is in equilibrium. The weight of the book is equal to the normal contact force. The weight of the book pulls it down, and the normal contact force from the table pushes it up. This is NOT Newton's Third Law. These forces are different types and they're both acting on the book.

The pairs of forces due to Newton's Third Law in this case are:

1) The weight of book is pulled down by gravity from Earth ($W_B$) and the book also pulls back up on the Earth ($W_E$).

2) The normal contact force from the table pushing up on the book ($N_B$) and the normal contact force from the book pushing down on the table ($N_T$).

$N_B$

$N_T \quad W_B$

$W_E$

## Know your interaction pairs, especially for objects in equilibrium.

Q1  A car moves at a constant velocity along a road, so that it is in equilibrium. Give an example of a pair of forces that demonstrate Newton's Third Law in this situation.  [1 mark]

Q1 Video Solution

# Warm-Up & Exam Questions

Now you've gotten yourself on the right side of the law(s of motion), it's time to put your knowledge on trial. Have a go at cross-examining these questions.

## Warm-Up Questions

1) What is the resultant force on an object moving at a constant velocity?
2) Write down the formula that links mass, force and acceleration.
3) True or false? An object travelling at a constant speed around a circular path is not accelerating.
4) Boulders A and B are accelerated from 0 m/s to 5 m/s in 10 s. Boulder A required a force of 70 N, and Boulder B required a force of 95 N. Which boulder has the greater inertial mass?
5) True or false? Two interacting objects exert equal and opposite forces on each other.

## Exam Questions

1 A student has a cricket bat with a mass of 1.2 kg.
She uses it to hit a ball with a mass of 160 g forwards with a force of 500 N.

(a) State the force that the ball exerts on the bat. Explain your answer.

*[2 marks]*

(b) State and explain whether the acceleration of the ball is greater or smaller than the acceleration of the bat.

*[2 marks]*

2 A camper van has a mass of 2500 kg. It is driven along a straight, level road
at a constant speed of 90.0 kilometres per hour, as shown in **Figure 1**.

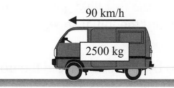

**Figure 1**

(a) A headwind begins to blow, so that the resultant force acting on the van is 200 N in the opposite direction to the van's motion. This causes the van to slow down. Calculate the van's deceleration.

*[3 marks]*

The van begins travelling at a constant speed before colliding with a stationary 4.50 kg traffic cone. The traffic cone accelerates in the direction of the van's motion with an acceleration of 28.0 m/s².

(b) Calculate the force applied to the traffic cone by the van.

*[2 marks]*

(c) Calculate the deceleration of the van, due to the force of the cone, during the collision.

*[3 marks]*

# Investigating Motion

*Here comes a **Core Practical**. This one's all about testing **Newton's Second Law**. It uses some nifty bits of kit that you may not have seen before, so make sure you follow the instructions closely.*

## You can **Investigate** the Motion of a **Trolley** on a **Ramp**

It's time for an experiment that tests Newton's 2nd Law, $F = m \times a$ (p.25).

1) Measure the <u>mass</u> of the <u>trolley</u>, the <u>unit masses</u> and the <u>hanging hook</u>.
Measure the <u>length</u> of the piece of <u>card</u> which will <u>interrupt</u> the light gate beams.
Then set up your <u>apparatus</u> as shown in the diagram below, but <u>don't</u> attach the string to the trolley.

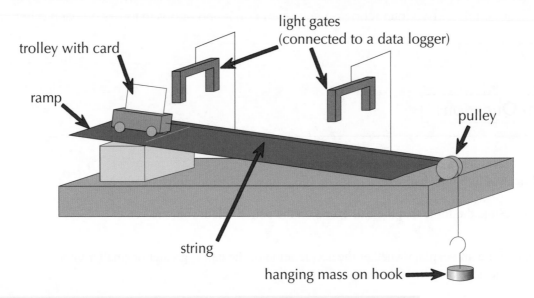

2) <u>Adjust</u> the <u>height</u> of the ramp until the trolley <u>just</u> starts to move.
This means that the <u>force due to gravity</u> acting on the <u>hanging mass</u> will
be the <u>main</u> cause of the trolley <u>accelerating</u> as it travels down the ramp.

3) Mark a <u>line</u> on the ramp just before the first <u>light gate</u>, so the trolley travels the <u>same distance</u>
every time. The light gate will record the <u>initial speed</u> of the trolley as it <u>begins to move</u>.

4) <u>Attach the trolley</u> to the hanging mass by the string. Hold the trolley <u>still</u>
at the start line, and then <u>let go</u> of it so that it starts to roll down the slope.

5) The <u>weight</u> of the <u>hook</u> and any <u>masses</u> attached to it will provide the <u>accelerating force</u>,
equal to the <u>mass of the hook</u> (*m*) × <u>acceleration due to gravity</u> (*g*).
The <u>weight</u> of the hook and masses accelerates <u>both</u> the trolley and the masses, so you
are investigating the acceleration of the <u>system</u> (the trolley <u>and</u> the masses together).

6) Each <u>light gate</u> will record the <u>time</u> when the trolley passes through it and the <u>speed</u>
of the trolley at that time. The <u>acceleration</u> of the trolley can then be found using
<u>acceleration = change in speed ÷ time</u>, with the following values:

- the <u>initial speed</u> of the trolley as it passes through the <u>first light gate</u> (it'll be <u>roughly</u> 0 m/s),
- the <u>final speed</u> of the trolley, as it passes through the <u>second light gate</u>,
- the <u>time</u> it takes the trolley to travel <u>between</u> the two light gates.

7) <u>Repeat</u> the experiment at least <u>three times</u> and calculate an <u>average acceleration</u> from the results.

# Investigating Motion

 PRACTICAL

*Now you've set up the **equipment**, and you're used to how it works, it's time to start **adjusting** your **variables**. Take care with the **method** here — there are some important points you don't want to miss.*

## Varying Mass and Force

1) To investigate how the <u>mass</u> of the system affects its <u>acceleration</u>, <u>add masses</u> one at a time to the <u>trolley</u>.

2) <u>Don't add masses to the hook</u>, as this will change the force acting on the system.

3) Each time you add a mass to the trolley, take a <u>measurement</u> of the system's <u>average acceleration</u> by using the <u>method</u> described in points 2-7 on the <u>previous page</u>.

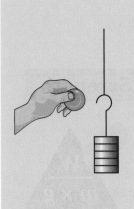

1) To investigate how the <u>force</u> acting on the system affects its <u>acceleration</u>, you need to keep the <u>total mass</u> of the <u>system</u> the <u>same</u>, but <u>change</u> the mass on the <u>hook</u>.

2) To do this, start with <u>all</u> the masses loaded onto the <u>trolley</u>, and <u>transfer</u> the masses to the hook one at a time, to increase the <u>accelerating force</u> (the weight of the hanging masses).

3) The mass of the system stays the same as you're only <u>transferring</u> the masses from <u>one part</u> of the system (the trolley) to another (the hook).

4) Each time you transfer a mass from the trolley to the hook, take a <u>measurement</u> of the system's <u>average acceleration</u> using the <u>method</u> described in points 2-7 on the <u>previous page</u>.

## Newton's Second Law Can Explain the Results

1) <u>Newton's Second Law</u> can be written as $F = m \times a$. Here, $F$ = <u>weight</u> of the <u>hanging masses</u>, $m$ = mass of the <u>whole system</u> and $a$ = <u>acceleration</u> of the <u>system</u>.

2) By <u>adding</u> masses to the <u>trolley</u>, the mass of the <u>whole system</u> increases, but the <u>force</u> applied to the system stays the <u>same</u>. This should lead to a decrease in the <u>acceleration of the trolley</u>, so $a$ is inversely proportional to $m$ ($a = F \div m$).

3) By <u>transferring masses</u> to the hook, you are <u>increasing the accelerating force</u> without changing the <u>mass</u> of the whole system. <u>Increasing</u> the force should lead to an <u>increase</u> in the acceleration of the trolley, so $a$ is proportional to $F$.

## This experiment has a lot of steps, so don't speed through it...

Make sure the <u>string</u> is the <u>right length</u> and there's <u>enough space</u> for the hanging masses to <u>fall</u>. There needs to be enough space so that the masses <u>don't</u> hit the floor <u>before</u> the trolley has <u>passed through the light gate fully</u> — if they hit the floor, the force won't be applied the whole way through the trolley's journey, so you won't get an accurate measurement for the <u>speed</u>.

# Weight

*Now for something a bit more **attractive** — the force of **gravity**. Enjoy...*

## Weight and Mass are Not the Same

1) <u>Mass</u> is just the <u>amount of 'stuff'</u> in an object. For any given object this will have the same value <u>anywhere</u> in the universe.

2) Mass is a <u>scalar</u> quantity. It's measured in <u>kilograms</u> with a <u>mass</u> balance (an old-fashioned pair of balancing scales).

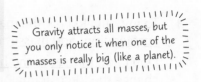
Gravity attracts all masses, but you only notice it when one of the masses is really big (like a planet).

3) <u>Weight</u> is the <u>force</u> acting on an object due to <u>gravity</u> (the <u>pull</u> of the <u>gravitational force</u> on the object). Close to Earth, this <u>force</u> is caused by the <u>gravitational field</u> around the Earth.

4) Weight is a <u>force</u> measured in <u>newtons</u>. You can think of the force as acting from a <u>single point</u> on the object, called its <u>centre of mass</u> (a point at which you assume the <u>whole</u> mass is concentrated).

5) Weight is measured using a calibrated <u>spring</u> balance (or <u>newton meter</u>).

## Weight Depends on Mass and Gravitational Field Strength

1) You can calculate the <u>weight</u> of an object if you know its <u>mass</u> ($m$) and the <u>strength</u> of the <u>gravitational field</u> that it is in ($g$):

> **weight (N) = mass (kg) × gravitational field strength (N/kg)**

$$\frac{W}{m \times g}$$

2) Gravitational field <u>strength</u> varies with <u>location</u>. It's <u>stronger</u> the <u>closer</u> you are to the mass causing the field (and <u>more massive</u> objects create <u>stronger</u> fields).

3) This means that the weight of an object <u>changes</u> with its location.

### EXAMPLE

**What is the weight, in newtons, of a 2.0 kg object on Earth (g = 10 N/kg)?**

1) Calculate the weight on <u>Earth</u> using the equation for <u>weight</u> given above.

$W = m \times g = 2.0 \times 10 = 20$ N

**The object has a weight of 16 N on a different planet.**
**What is the gravitational field strength of this other planet?**

1) <u>Rearrange</u> the weight equation for $g$.

2) <u>Substitute</u> the values in.

$g = W \div m$
$= 16 \div 2.0 = 8.0$ N/kg

Remember — the mass of the object is the same on every planet, it's the weight of the object that changes.

## You might be experiencing déjà vu...

On p.21 you saw that '$g$' was introduced as '<u>acceleration due to gravity</u>' (m/s²), and now it's being used for '<u>gravitational field strength</u>' (N/kg). These two quantities <u>have been given the same symbol</u> because acceleration due to a gravitational field will always be <u>equal</u> to the strength of that field.

Q1 Video
Solution

Q1 Calculate the weight in newtons of a 25 kg mass:
  a) on Earth (g ≈ 10 N/kg)      b) on the Moon (g ≈ 1.6 N/kg)      [4 marks]

# Warm-Up & Exam Questions

That's all you need to know about gravitational field strength... I bet that's a weight off your mind.
Try out these questions and see how much really sunk in.

## Warm-Up Questions

1) When carrying out the trolley-and-ramp practical (p.28), what is the purpose of adjusting the ramp so that the trolley is just about to move?
2) Give the definitions of mass and weight.
3) What are the units of weight?

## Exam Questions

**1** On Earth, the gravitational field strength is 10 N/kg.
Calculate the weight of an 80 kg person on Earth.

*[2 marks]*

**PRACTICAL**

**2** A student investigates how the mass of a system
affects its acceleration.
**Figure 1** is a graph of her results.

(a) Name the independent variable in this experiment.

*[1 mark]*

(b) Name the dependent variable in this experiment.

*[1 mark]*

(c) Describe the relationship between mass and acceleration.

*[1 mark]*

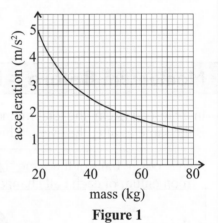

**Figure 1**

**3** The weight of a space probe on the surface of Mars
is 0.4 times its weight on the surface of Earth.

(a) The gravitational field strength on Earth is 10 N/kg.
Determine the gravitational field strength of Mars.

*[2 marks]*

(b) The weight of the probe on Mars is 3600 N. Calculate the mass of the probe.

*[3 marks]*

**PRACTICAL**

**4\*** A student is investigating how acceleration varies with force.
He has a 1 kg trolley, attached by a pulley to a 0.5 kg hanging hook.
He also has eight 100 g masses. When the trolley is released, it rolls down a ramp,
and passes through two sets of light gates which each measure its velocity.

Describe an experiment that the student can perform using this equipment
to investigate the relationship between force and acceleration.

*[6 marks]*

# Momentum

*A **large rugby player** running very **fast** has much **more momentum** than a **skinny** bloke out for a Sunday afternoon **stroll**. Momentum's something that **all moving objects have**, so you better get your head around it.*

## Momentum = Mass × Velocity

Momentum is mainly about how much 'oomph' an object has. It's a property that all moving objects have.

1) The greater the mass of an object, or the greater its velocity, the more momentum the object has.
2) Momentum is a vector quantity — it has size and direction.
3) You can work out the momentum of an object using:

$$p = m \times v$$

$$\text{momentum (kg m/s)} = \text{mass (kg)} \times \text{velocity (m/s)}$$

**EXAMPLE**

A 50 kg cheetah is running at 60 m/s. Calculate its momentum.

$p = m \times v = 50 \times 60 = 3000$ kg m/s

**EXAMPLE**

A boy has a mass of 30 kg and a momentum of 75 kg m/s. Calculate his velocity.

$v = p \div m = 75 \div 30 = 2.5$ m/s

## Momentum Before = Momentum After

In a closed system, the total momentum before an event (e.g. a collision) is the same as after the event. This is called conservation of momentum.

*A closed system is just a fancy way of saying that no external forces act.*

In snooker, balls of the same size and mass collide with each other. Each collision is an event where the momentum of each ball changes, but the overall momentum stays the same (momentum is conserved).

Before:  $m$  →$v$→  $m$

After:  $m$  →  $m$  →

The red ball is stationary, so it has zero momentum. The white ball is moving with a velocity $v$, so has momentum of $p = m \times v$.

The white ball hits the red ball, causing it to move. The red ball now has momentum. The white ball continues moving, but at a much smaller velocity (and so a much smaller momentum).

The combined momentum of the red and white ball is equal to the original momentum of the white ball, $m \times v$.

A moving car hits into the back of a parked car. The crash causes the two cars to lock together, and they continue moving in the direction that the original moving car was travelling, but at a lower velocity.

Before: The momentum was equal to mass of moving car × its velocity.
After: The mass of the moving object has increased, but its momentum is equal to the momentum before the collision. So an increase in mass causes a decrease in velocity.

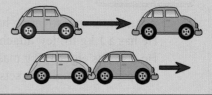

If the momentum before an event is zero, then the momentum after will also be zero. E.g. in an explosion, the momentum before is zero. After the explosion, the pieces fly off in different directions, so that the total momentum cancels out to zero.

# Momentum

*You can use the **equation** for **momentum**, along with the **conservation of momentum principle**, to **calculate** changes in **mass** and **velocity** in interactions. It's all about 'momentum before = momentum after'.*

## Calculations using Conservation of Momentum

You've already seen that momentum is conserved in a closed system (see last page).
You can use this to help you calculate things like the velocity or mass of objects in an event (e.g. a collision).

**EXAMPLE**

**Misha fires a paintball gun. A 3.0 g paintball is fired at a velocity of 90 m/s. Calculate the velocity at which the paintball gun recoils if it has a mass of 1.5 kg. Momentum is conserved.**

*The word recoil means to move backwards.*

1) Calculate the momentum of the pellet.

$$p = 0.003 \times 90 = 0.27 \text{ kg m/s}$$

2) The momentum before the gun is fired is zero.
This is equal to the total momentum after the collision.

Momentum before = momentum after

$$0 = 0.27 + (1.5 \times v)$$

3) The momentum of the gun is $1.5 \times v$.

4) Rearrange the equation to find the velocity of the gun. The minus sign shows the gun is travelling in the opposite direction to the bullet.

$$v = -(0.27 \div 1.5)$$
$$= -0.18 \text{ m/s}$$

**EXAMPLE**

**Two skaters, Skater A and Skater B, approach each other, collide and move off together as shown in the image on the right. At what velocity do they move after the collision?**

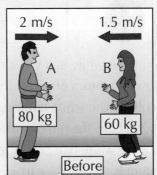
2 m/s     1.5 m/s     velocity = ?
A    B
80 kg    60 kg    (80 + 60) kg
Before     After

1) Choose which direction is positive.
I'll say "positive" means "to the right".

2) Total momentum before collision
= momentum of A + momentum of B.

Momentum before = $(80 \times 2) + (60 \times (-1.5))$
= 70 kg m/s

3) Total momentum after collision
= momentum of A and B together.

Momentum after = $140 \times v$

4) Set momentum before equal to momentum after, and rearrange for the answer.

$140 \times v = 70$, so $v = 70 \div 140$
$v = 0.5$ m/s to the right

## Momentum questions may need you to analyse a scenario...

Make sure you read any momentum questions carefully. You need to identify what the objects and momentum were before the interaction, and what they are after the interaction. The question may not be a scenario you're familiar with, so you'll need to work out what's going on.

Q1 Video Solution

Q1   A 10 kg object is travelling at 6 m/s. It hits a stationary 20 kg object and the two objects join together and keep moving in the same direction. Calculate the velocity of the combined object, assuming that momentum is conserved.    [3 marks]

# Momentum

*When a **resultant force** acts on an object, it causes the object to **change momentum**.*

## Forces Cause Changes in Momentum

1) When a resultant <u>force</u> acts on an object for a certain amount of time, it causes a <u>change in momentum</u>. <u>Newton's 2nd Law</u> can explain this:

   • A <u>resultant force</u> on an object causes it to <u>accelerate</u>: force = mass × acceleration (see p.25).

   • <u>Acceleration</u> is just <u>change in velocity</u> over <u>time</u>, so: $\text{force} = \dfrac{\text{mass} \times \text{change in velocity}}{\text{time}}$.
   This means a force applied to an object over any time interval will change the object's <u>velocity</u>.

   • <u>Mass × change in velocity</u> is equal to <u>change in momentum</u>, so you end up with the equation:

2) The <u>faster</u> a given change in momentum happens, the <u>bigger the force</u> causing the change must be (i.e. if $t$ gets <u>smaller</u> in the equation above, $F$ gets <u>bigger</u>).

3) So if someone's momentum changes <u>very quickly</u>, like in a <u>car crash</u>, the <u>forces</u> on the body will be very <u>large</u>, and more likely to cause <u>injury</u>. There's more about this on p.38.

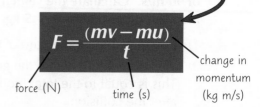

$$F = \frac{(mv - mu)}{t}$$

force (N)   time (s)   change in momentum (kg m/s)

## Conservation of Momentum Shows Newton's Third Law

The equation above can help to show <u>Newton's Third Law</u> (<u>reaction</u> forces are <u>equal</u> and <u>opposite</u>). Take this example using <u>snooker balls</u> below:

Before | During | After

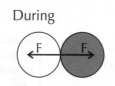

(0.15 kg) —4 m/s→ (0.15 kg)   |   (F ← | → F)   |   (0.15 kg) —1 m/s→ (0.15 kg) —3 m/s→

1) <u>Before</u> the collision, the <u>white</u> ball has a momentum of 0.15 × 4 = 0.6 kg m/s.

2) The <u>red</u> ball has a momentum of <u>zero</u>. The <u>total momentum</u> of the system is 0.6 kg m/s.

3) When the balls collide, the <u>white</u> ball exerts a <u>force</u> on the <u>red</u> ball.

4) Due to <u>Newton's 3rd Law</u>, the <u>red</u> ball also exerts an <u>equal</u> but <u>opposite</u> force on the <u>white</u> ball.

5) <u>After</u> the collision, the white ball <u>continues moving</u> at 1 m/s. The red ball <u>begins moving</u> at 3 m/s.

6) The total momentum is (0.15 × 1) + (0.15 × 3) = 0.6 kg m/s. Momentum is <u>conserved</u>.

7) The collision lasted 0.1 s. Given this information, you can <u>calculate</u> the size of the <u>force</u> that caused this <u>change of velocity</u> (and so <u>change of momentum</u>) for each ball:

### Red Ball

$$F = \frac{(mv - mu)}{t}$$
$$= \frac{(0.15 \times 3) - (0.15 \times 0)}{0.1}$$
$$= \frac{0.45}{0.1} = 4.5 \text{ N}$$

### White Ball

$$F = \frac{(mv - mu)}{t}$$
$$= \frac{(0.15 \times 1) - (0.15 \times 4)}{0.1}$$
$$= \frac{-0.45}{0.1} = -4.5 \text{ N}$$

8) The <u>force exerted on the white ball</u> (by the red ball) is <u>equal and opposite</u> to the force exerted <u>on the red ball</u> (by the white ball). This shows <u>Newton's Third Law</u>.

---

## The larger the force, the larger the change in momentum...

<u>Momentum</u> is a <u>fundamental</u> bit of physics — learn it well. Then have a go at this question.

Q1    Calculate the force a tennis racket needs to apply to a 58 g tennis ball to accelerate it from rest to 34 m/s in 11.6 ms.            [3 marks]

Q1 Video Solution

# Warm-Up & Exam Questions

Don't lose momentum now. Throw yourself into these questions and you'll be done before you know it.

## Warm-Up Questions

1) What are the units of momentum?
2) What is meant by the conservation of momentum?
3) What is the total momentum before and after an explosion?
4) How does increasing the time over which an object changes momentum change the force on it?

## Exam Questions

1   A 60 kg gymnast lands on a crash mat. When they hit the crash mat, they are moving at
    5.0 m/s and come to a stop in a period of 1.2 seconds (after which their momentum is zero).

   (a)  State the equation linking momentum, mass and velocity.

   *[1 mark]*

   (b)  Calculate the momentum of the gymnast immediately before they hit the crash mat.

   *[2 marks]*

   (c)  Calculate the size of the average force acting on the gymnast as they land on the crash mat.
        Use the correct equation from the Physics Equation Sheet on page 268.

   *[2 marks]*

2   In a demolition derby, cars drive around an arena and crash into each other.

   (a)  One car has a mass of 650 kg and a velocity of 15.0 m/s.
        Calculate the momentum of the car.

   *[2 marks]*

   (b)  The car collides head-on with another car with a mass of 750 kg. The two cars stick together.
        Calculate the combined velocity of the two cars immediately after the collision if the other car had
        a velocity of −10.0 m/s before the collision. Give your answer to 3 significant figures.

   *[4 marks]*

3   A fast-moving neutron collides with a uranium-235 atom and bounces off.
    **Figure 1** shows the particles before and after the collision.
    The masses given in **Figure 1** are relative masses.

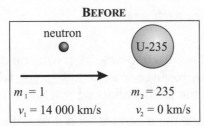
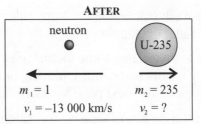

BEFORE

neutron   U-235

$m_1 = 1$        $m_2 = 235$
$v_1 = 14\,000$ km/s    $v_2 = 0$ km/s

AFTER

neutron   U-235

$m_1 = 1$        $m_2 = 235$
$v_1 = -13\,000$ km/s    $v_2 = ?$

**Figure 1**

Calculate the velocity of the U-235 atom after the collision. Give your answer to 3 significant figures.

   *[4 marks]*

# Reaction Times

*Believe it or not, **reaction times** measure how quickly you react. They're also super easy to **test** for yourself. Read on for a simple **experiment** you can do in the lab.*

## You can **Measure** Reaction Times with the **Ruler Drop Test**

Everyone's <u>reaction time</u> is different and many different factors can affect it.

You can do <u>simple experiments</u> to investigate your reaction time, but as reaction times are <u>so short</u>, you haven't got a chance of measuring one with a <u>stopwatch</u>. One way of measuring reaction times is to use a <u>computer-based test</u> (e.g. <u>clicking a mouse</u> when the screen changes colour). Another is the <u>ruler drop test</u>.

Here's how to carry it out:

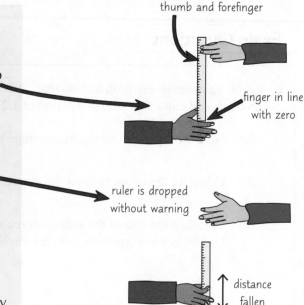

ruler hanging between thumb and forefinger

finger in line with zero

ruler is dropped without warning

distance fallen

ruler caught between thumb and finger

1) Sit with your arm resting on the edge of a table (this should stop you moving your arm up or down during the test). Get someone else to hold a ruler so it <u>hangs between</u> your thumb and forefinger, lined up with <u>zero</u>. You may need a <u>third person</u> to be at <u>eye level with the ruler</u> to check it's lined up.

2) Without giving any warning, the person holding the ruler should <u>drop it</u>. Close your thumb and finger to try to <u>catch the ruler as quickly as possible</u>.

3) The measurement on the ruler at the point where it is caught is <u>how far</u> the ruler dropped in the time it takes you to react.

4) The <u>longer</u> the <u>distance</u>, the <u>longer</u> the <u>reaction time</u>.

5) You can calculate <u>how long</u> the ruler falls for (the <u>reaction</u> time) because <u>acceleration due to gravity is constant</u> (roughly 10 m/s²).

E.g. say you catch the ruler at 20 cm. From p.21 you know: $\underline{v^2 - u^2 = 2 \times a \times x}$.
$u = 0$, $a = 10$ m/s² and $x = 0.2$ m, so: $v = \sqrt{2 \times 10 \times 0.2 + 0} = \underline{2 \text{ m/s}}$
$v$ is equal to the <u>change in velocity</u> of the ruler.
From page 20 you also know: $\underline{a = (v - u) \div t}$ so $\underline{t = (v - u) \div a = 2 \div 10 = 0.2 \text{ s}}$
This gives your <u>reaction time</u>.

6) It's <u>pretty hard</u> to do this experiment <u>accurately</u>, so you should do a lot of <u>repeats</u> and calculate a <u>mean reaction time</u>. The results will be better if the ruler falls <u>straight down</u> — you could add a <u>blob of modelling clay</u> to the bottom to stop it from waving about.

7) Make sure it's a <u>fair test</u> — use the <u>same ruler</u> for each repeat, and have the <u>same person</u> dropping it.

8) You could try to investigate some factors affecting reaction time, e.g. you could introduce <u>distractions</u> by having some <u>music</u> playing or by having someone <u>talk to you</u> while the test takes place (see the next page for more on the factors affecting reaction time).

9) Remember to still do lots of <u>repeats</u> and calculate the <u>mean</u> reaction time with distractions, which you can <u>compare</u> to the mean reaction time <u>without</u> distractions.

For an experiment like this, a typical reaction time is around <u>0.2-0.6 s</u>.
A person's reaction time in a <u>real</u> situation (e.g. when driving) will be <u>longer</u> than that, though.
Typically, an <u>alert</u> driver will have a reaction time of about <u>1 s</u>.

# Stopping Distances

*Knowing what affects **stopping distances** is especially useful for everyday life, as well as the exam.*

## Stopping Distance = Thinking Distance + Braking Distance

In an emergency, a driver may perform an emergency stop. This is where the maximum force is applied by the brakes in order to stop the car in the shortest possible distance. The longer it takes a car to stop after seeing a hazard, the higher the risk of crashing.

The distance it takes to stop a car (stopping distance) is found by:

**Stopping Distance = Thinking Distance + Braking Distance**

Thinking distance is the distance the car travels in the driver's reaction time (the time between noticing the hazard and applying the brakes).

Braking distance is the distance taken to stop once the brakes have been applied.

## Many Factors Affect Your Total Stopping Distance

Thinking distance is affected by:

- Your speed — the faster you're going the further you'll travel during the time you take to react.
- Your reaction time — the longer your reaction time (see next page), the longer your thinking distance. This can be affected by tiredness, drugs or alcohol. Distractions can affect your ability to react.

Braking distance is affected by:

- Your speed — for a given braking force, the faster a vehicle travels, the longer it takes to stop (p.39).
- How much friction is between your tyres and the road — you're more likely to skid if the road is dirty, if it's icy or wet or if the tyres are bald (tyres must have a minimum tread depth of 1.6 mm).
- How good your brakes are — if brakes are worn or faulty, they won't be able to apply as much force as well-maintained brakes, which could be dangerous when you need to brake hard.
- The mass of the car — a car full of people and luggage won't stop as quickly as an empty car.

In the exam, you may need to spot the factors affecting thinking and braking distance in different situations.

> E.g. if a parent is driving her children to school early in the morning on an autumn day, her thinking distance could be affected by tiredness, or by her children distracting her. Her braking distance could be affected by ice, or by leaves on the road reducing the friction/grip.

## Stopping distance = thinking distance + braking distance...

The exam might ask you to give factors, other than speed, which affect thinking or braking distances, so make sure you know all the factors that affect each of these and what their effects are.

# Stopping Safely

*Plotting a graph is always handy when there's a lot of info to take in. These **velocity/time graphs** illustrate really clearly how high speeds affect both **thinking and braking distances**.*

## Thinking and Braking Distance can be Seen on *v/t* Graphs

The graph below shows the velocity of a vehicle as the driver performs an emergency stop.

See p.23 for more on v/t graphs.

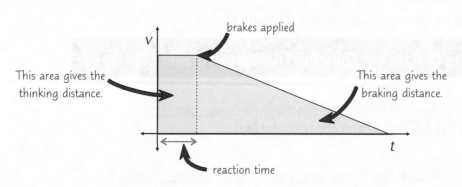

But if the driver is going faster, and he's a bit tired....

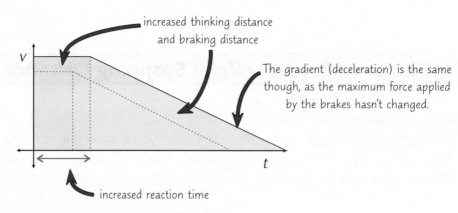

## Large Decelerations can be **Dangerous**

1) Large decelerations of objects and people (e.g. in car crashes) can cause serious injuries. This is because a large deceleration requires a large force — $F = m \times a$.

2) The force can be lowered by slowing the object down over a longer time, i.e. decreasing its deceleration.

3) Safety features in vehicles are designed to increase collision times, which reduces the force, and so reduces the risk of injury. For example, seat belts stretch slightly and air bags slow you down gradually. Crumple zones are areas at the front and back of a vehicle which crumple up easily in a collision, increasing the time taken to stop.

**EXAMPLE**

**Estimate the resultant force acting on a car stopping quickly from 15 m/s.**

1) Estimate the deceleration of the car — you did that for this example on page 20.

2) Estimate the mass of the car.

3) Put these numbers into Newton's 2nd Law.

The car comes to a stop in ~1 s.
$a = (v - u) \div t = (0 - 15) \div 1 = -15$ m/s$^2$

Mass of a car is ~1000 kg.

$F = m \times a$
$= 1000 \times -15 = -15\ 000$ N

*The force here is negative as it acts in the opposite direction to the motion of the car.*

4) The brakes of a vehicle do work on its wheels (see p.123). This transfers energy from the vehicle's kinetic energy store to the thermal energy store of the brakes. Very large decelerations may cause the brakes to overheat (so they don't work as well). They could also cause the vehicle to skid.

# Stopping Safely

*So now you know what affects a car's **stopping distance**, let's have a look at the **facts and figures**.*

## Drivers Need to Leave Enough **Space** to **Stop**

1) These <u>typical stopping distances</u> are from the <u>Highway Code</u>.

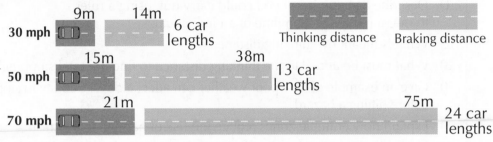

2) To <u>avoid an accident</u>, drivers must leave <u>enough space</u> in front so they could stop <u>safely</u> — <u>at least</u> equal to the <u>stopping distance</u> for their speed.

30 mph — 9m — 14m — 6 car lengths

50 mph — 15m — 38m — 13 car lengths

70 mph — 21m — 75m — 24 car lengths

Thinking distance | Braking distance

3) <u>Speed limits</u> are really important because <u>speed</u> affects stopping distances so much. (Remember, weather and road conditions can affect them too.)

4) As <u>speed increases</u>, <u>thinking distance increases</u> at the <u>same rate</u>. This is because the driver's <u>reaction time</u> stays fairly <u>constant</u>, but the higher the speed, the further you go in that time ($d = s \times t$, p.19).

5) However, <u>braking distance</u> and <u>speed</u> have a <u>squared</u> relationship — if speed <u>doubles</u>, braking distance increases by a <u>factor of 4</u> ($2^2$), and if speed <u>trebles</u>, braking distance increases by a <u>factor of 9</u> ($3^2$).

You saw on the previous page that the <u>brakes</u> of a car <u>do work</u> on the car's wheels, which <u>transfers energy</u> from the car's <u>kinetic energy store</u> to the <u>thermal energy store</u> of the <u>brakes</u>. To stop a car, the brakes must transfer <u>all</u> of this energy, so:

*There's more on these equations on pages 42 and 123.*

**Energy in the car's kinetic energy store = Work done by the brakes**

$$\tfrac{1}{2} \times m \times v^2 \qquad = \qquad F \times d$$

mass of the car    speed of car      braking force    braking distance

*This means doubling the mass doubles the braking distance.*

## You can **Estimate** the **Distances** Involved in **Stopping**

**EXAMPLE**

**A car travelling at 25 m/s makes an emergency stop to avoid a hazard. The braking force applied to the car is 5000 N. Estimate the total distance taken to stop.**

1) Estimate the driver's <u>reaction time</u>.

2) Calculate the <u>thinking distance</u>.

3) To work out the <u>braking distance</u>, rearrange the equation above for *d*, and <u>estimate</u> the <u>mass</u> of the car.

4) Add the thinking distance and braking distance to give the <u>stopping distance</u>.

Reaction time is ~1 s.

$d = s \times t = 25 \times 1 = 25$ m

$d = (\tfrac{1}{2} \times m \times v^2) \div F$

Mass of a car is ~1000 kg

$d = (\tfrac{1}{2} \times 1000 \times 25^2) \div 5000$

$= 62.5$ m

$25 + 62.5 = 87.5$ m    Distance is ~90 m

*Make sure you can estimate the mass of objects. A car's mass is ~1000 kg. A single decker bus is ~10 000 kg and a loaded lorry is ~30 000 kg.*

## Learn the mass of typical vehicles — it's massively important.

Q1    A driver performs an emergency stop.
His thinking distance and braking distance are both 6 m.
Estimate his total stopping distance if he had been travelling three times as quickly.    [4 marks]

Q1 Video Solution

# Warm-Up & Exam Questions

Time to apply the brakes for a second and put your brain through an MOT. Try out these questions. If you can handle these, your exam should be clear of hazards.

## Warm-Up Questions

1) Describe an experiment you could carry out, using a ruler, to measure the reaction time of an individual.

2) What is meant by 'thinking distance'?

3) What must be added to the thinking distance to find the total stopping distance of a car?

4) Give an example of how poor weather can affect a driver's ability to stop a car before hitting a hazard.

5) Explain how crumple zones reduce the risk of harm in a car crash.

6) How will a vehicle's braking distance change if the speed of the vehicle is tripled?

## Exam Question

1    **Figure 1** shows how thinking distance and stopping distance vary with speed for a car travelling on a clear day on a dry road.

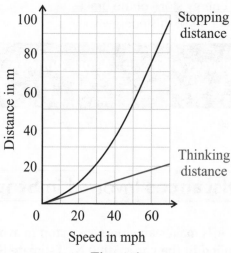

**Figure 1**

(a) Use **Figure 1** to determine the braking distance for a car travelling at 40 mph.

*[3 marks]*

(b) Using **Figure 1**, determine whether the thinking distance or braking distance is greater at 50 miles per hour.

*[1 mark]*

(c) Using **Figure 1**, determine whether stopping distance is directly proportional to speed. Explain your answer.

*[1 mark]*

(d) Describe how the shape of each of the graphs on **Figure 1** would change if the data was taken for the same driver travelling on an icy road.

*[2 marks]*

# Revision Summary for Section 1

That wraps up <u>Section 1</u> — time to put yourself to the test and find out <u>how much you really know</u>.
- Try these questions and <u>tick off each one</u> when you <u>get it right</u>.
- When you're <u>completely happy</u> with a sub-topic, tick it off.

For even more practice, try the Retrieval Quiz for Section 1 — just scan this QR code!

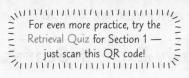 

Section 1 Quiz

## Motion (p.18-23) ☑

1) What is the difference between a scalar and a vector quantity? Give two examples of each. ☑
2) Give the equation relating distance travelled, speed and time. ☑
3) Estimate typical speeds for...
   a) ... walking...
   b) ... cycling...
   c) ... a car in a built-up area. ☑
4) Suggest appropriate equipment for measuring a person's walking speed. ☑
5) Define acceleration in terms of velocity and time. ☑
6) What is the value of acceleration due to gravity near the Earth's surface? ☑
7) What does the gradient represent on
   a) ... a distance/time graph?
   b) ... a velocity/time graph? ☑
8) How would you find the distance travelled by an object from its velocity/time graph? ☑

## Newton's Laws, Forces and Momentum (p.25-34) ☑

9) State Newton's First and Second Laws of Motion. ☑
10) Explain why there must be a force acting to produce circular motion. What is the name of the force? ☑
11) What is inertial mass? ☑
12) What is Newton's Third Law of Motion? Give an example of it in action. ☑
13) What piece of equipment is appropriate for measuring the speed of a trolley rolling down a ramp? ☑
14) What is the formula for calculating the weight of an object? ☑
15) State the formula used to calculate an object's momentum. ☑
16) True or false? For an object's momentum to change more quickly, a greater force on the object is needed. ☑

## Car Safety (p.36-39) ☑

17) What is meant by a person's reaction time? ☑
18) State two factors that can affect the thinking distance for a stopping car. ☑
19) State four things that can affect the braking distance of a vehicle. ☑
20) Explain why cars have safety features to reduce the decelerations experienced by passengers. ☑
21) What is the typical braking distance for a car travelling at 70 mph? ☑
22) What is the relationship between braking distance and speed? ☑
23) Which energy store is energy transferred to when a car's brakes do work on its wheels? ☑

# Energy Stores

*Energy is **never used up**. Instead it's just **transferred** between different **energy stores** and different objects...*

## Energy Exists in Stores

Energy can be transferred between and held in different <u>energy stores</u>. There are eight you need to know:

<u>Thermal</u> — any object — the <u>hotter</u> it is, the <u>more</u> energy it has in this <u>store</u>.

<u>Kinetic</u> — anything <u>moving</u> has energy in this store (see below).

<u>Gravitational potential</u> — anything in a <u>gravitational field</u> (i.e. anything that can <u>fall</u>) (see below).

<u>Elastic potential</u> — anything <u>stretched</u>, like springs, rubber bands, etc. (p.186).

<u>Chemical</u> — anything that can release energy by a <u>chemical reaction</u>, e.g. food, fuels.

<u>Magnetic</u> — e.g. two <u>magnets</u> that attract and repel each other.

<u>Electrostatic</u> — e.g. two <u>charges</u> that attract and repel each other.

<u>Nuclear</u> — <u>atomic nuclei</u> release energy from this store in <u>nuclear reactions</u>.

## Movement Means Energy in an Object's Kinetic Energy Store

1) Anything that is <u>moving</u> has energy in its <u>kinetic energy store</u>. Energy is transferred <u>to</u> this store when an object <u>speeds up</u> and is transferred <u>away</u> from this store when an object <u>slows down</u>.

2) The energy in the <u>kinetic energy store</u> depends on the object's <u>mass</u> and <u>speed</u>. The <u>greater its mass</u> and the <u>faster</u> it's going, the <u>more energy</u> there will be in its kinetic energy store.

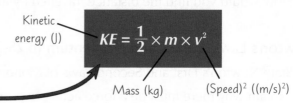
Kinetic energy (J) $\qquad KE = \frac{1}{2} \times m \times v^2$ $\qquad$ Mass (kg) $\qquad$ (Speed)² ((m/s)²)

3) There's a <u>slightly tricky</u> formula for it, so you have to concentrate <u>a little bit harder</u> for this one.

**EXAMPLE**

**A car of mass 2500 kg is travelling at 20 m/s. Calculate the energy in its kinetic energy store.**

$KE = \frac{1}{2} \times m \times v^2 = \frac{1}{2} \times 2500 \times 20^2 = 500\ 000$ J

## Raised Objects Store Energy in Gravitational Potential Energy Stores

1) <u>Lifting</u> an object in a <u>gravitational field</u> causes a <u>transfer of energy</u> to the <u>gravitational potential energy</u> (g.p.e.) store of the raised object. The <u>higher</u> the object is lifted, the <u>more</u> energy is transferred to this store.

2) The amount of energy in a gravitational potential energy store depends on the object's <u>mass</u>, its <u>height</u> and the <u>strength</u> of the gravitational field the object is in.

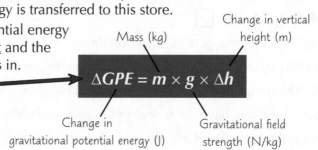
Mass (kg) $\qquad$ Change in vertical height (m) $\qquad \Delta GPE = m \times g \times \Delta h \qquad$ Change in gravitational potential energy (J) $\qquad$ Gravitational field strength (N/kg)

3) You can use this equation to find the <u>change in energy</u> in an object's gravitational potential energy store for a <u>change in vertical height</u>, $\Delta h$.

## No speed means no kinetic energy...

Remember, the <u>faster</u> an object is travelling, the <u>more</u> energy it has in its kinetic energy store — just don't forget that <u>squared sign</u> when you're doing kinetic energy calculations.

Q1 Video Solution

Q1 A 2 kg object is dropped from a height of 10 m. Calculate the speed of the object after it has fallen 5 m, assuming there is no air resistance. $g = 10$ N/kg. [5 marks]

# Energy Stores and Transfers

*Now you know about the different energy stores, it's time to find out how energy is **transferred** between them.*

## Energy is **Never Created** or **Destroyed**

This is a <u>really important</u> principle in physics, it is called <u>conservation of energy</u>:

<u>Energy</u> can be <u>stored</u>, <u>transferred</u> between <u>stores</u>, and <u>dissipated</u>, but it can never be <u>created or destroyed</u>.

See page 46 for more on dissipation.

## The **Total Energy** of a **Closed System** Doesn't Change

1) A <u>closed system</u> is just a system (a collection of objects) that can be treated <u>completely on its own</u>.  The <u>total energy</u> of a closed system has <u>no net change</u>.

2) If you get a question where the energy of a system <u>increases</u> or <u>decreases</u>, then it's <u>not closed</u>.

3) But you can <u>make it into a closed system</u> by <u>increasing the number of things</u> you treat as part of it.

> For example, a <u>pan of water</u> heating on a hob <u>isn't</u> a closed system, but the <u>pan</u>, the <u>gas</u> and the <u>oxygen</u> that burn to heat it, and <u>their surroundings</u> (e.g. if they're in a perfectly insulated room) are a <u>closed system</u>.

## You Need to Identify **Different Types** of **Energy Transfer**

1) When a system <u>changes</u>, <u>energy is transferred</u>.  Energy is <u>transferred</u> in <u>four different ways</u>:

- <u>Mechanically</u> — a <u>force</u> acting on an object (and doing <u>work</u>, p.123), e.g. pushing, stretching, squashing.
- <u>Electrically</u> — a <u>charge</u> doing <u>work</u> (p.135), e.g. charges moving round a circuit.
- <u>By heating</u> — energy transferred from a <u>hotter</u> object to a <u>colder</u> object, e.g. heating a pan on a hob.
- <u>By radiation</u> — energy transferred by <u>waves</u>, e.g. energy from the Sun reaching Earth by light.

2) You need to be able to describe how <u>energy</u> gets <u>transferred</u> from <u>store to store</u>.  Here's one <u>example</u> (there's more on the next page):

> <u>A ball rolling up a slope</u>
> The ball <u>does work</u> against the gravitational force, so energy is transferred <u>mechanically</u> from the <u>kinetic energy store</u> of the ball to its <u>gravitational potential energy store</u>.
>
> Before: the ball has energy in it's kinetic energy store.
>
> After: energy has been transferred to the ball's gravitational potential energy store.

**EXAM TIP**

## No matter what store it's in, it's all energy...

In the exam, make sure you refer to <u>energy</u> in terms of the <u>store</u> it's in.  For example, if you're describing energy in a <u>hot object</u>, say it 'has energy in its thermal energy store'.

# Energy Stores and Transfers

*You can keep track of complicated **energy transfers** much more easily if you draw a **diagram**.*

## More Examples of **Energy Transfers**

Here come a few more <u>examples</u> of everyday <u>energy transfers</u> that you need to get to grips with...

<u>A bat hitting a ball</u>

The bat has energy in its <u>kinetic energy store</u>. Some of this is transferred <u>mechanically</u> to the ball's <u>kinetic energy store</u>. Some energy is also transferred <u>mechanically</u> to the <u>thermal energy stores</u> of the bat and the ball (and to the <u>surroundings</u> by <u>heating</u>). The <u>rest</u> is carried away by <u>sound</u>.

<u>A rock dropped from a cliff</u>

Assuming there's <u>no air resistance</u>, <u>gravity</u> does work on the rock, so the rock constantly <u>accelerates</u> towards the ground. Energy is transferred <u>mechanically</u> from the rock's <u>gravitational potential</u> energy store to its <u>kinetic</u> energy store.

<u>A car slowing down (without braking)</u>

Energy in the <u>kinetic energy store</u> of the car is transferred <u>mechanically</u> (due to <u>friction</u> between the tyres and road), and then by <u>heating</u>, to the <u>thermal energy stores</u> of the car and road.

<u>A kettle boiling water</u>

Energy is transferred <u>electrically</u> from the mains to the heating element of the kettle, and then by <u>heating</u> to the <u>thermal energy store</u> of the water.

## You can **Draw Diagrams** to Show Energy Transfers

Diagrams can make it <u>easier</u> to see <u>what's going on</u> when energy is transferred. The diagram below shows the energy transferred when a ball is thrown upwards, taking air resistance into account. The <u>boxes</u> represent <u>stores</u> and the <u>arrows</u> show <u>transfers</u>:

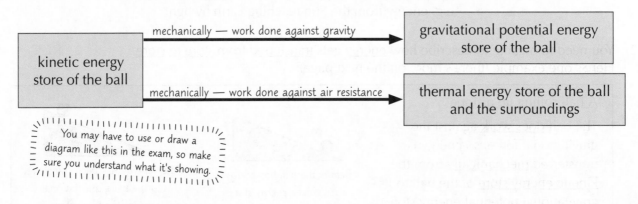

*You may have to use or draw a diagram like this in the exam, so make sure you understand what it's showing.*

# Energy is transferred between the different stores of objects...

Energy stores pop up <u>everywhere</u> in physics. You need to be able to describe <u>how energy is transferred</u>, and <u>which stores</u> it gets transferred between, for <u>any scenario</u>. So, it's time to make sure you know all the <u>energy stores</u> and <u>transfer methods</u> like the back of your hand.

Q1    Describe the energy transfers that occur when the wind causes a windmill to spin.    [3 marks]

Q1 Video Solution

# Warm-Up & Exam Questions

These questions give you chance to use your knowledge about energy stores and energy transfers.

## Warm-Up Questions

1) State the equation that links energy in an object's kinetic energy store with mass and speed.
2) Which has more energy in its kinetic energy store: a person walking at 3 miles per hour, or a lorry travelling at 60 miles per hour?
3) Give two methods of energy transfer.
4) Describe the main energy transfer that takes place when the sun warms a glass of water.

## Exam Questions

**1**   A motor lifts a load of mass 20 kg.
The load gains 140 J of energy in its gravitational potential energy store.

(a)   State the equation that links change in gravitational potential energy, mass, gravitational field strength and change in vertical height.

Use this equation to calculate the height through which the motor lifts the load.
Assume the gravitational field strength = 10 N/kg.

*[4 marks]*

(b)   The motor releases the load and the load falls.
Ignoring air resistance, describe the changes in the way energy is stored that take place as the load falls.

*[2 marks]*

(c)   Describe how your answer to (b) would differ if air resistance was not ignored.

*[1 mark]*

**2**   A sling-shot is used to catapult a 60 g rock directly upwards.
**Figure 1** shows how the rock's height changes over time.

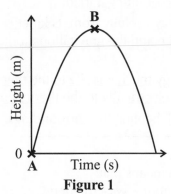

**Figure 1**

(a)   From launch (**A**) to the peak of the rock's flight (**B**), describe how energy is transferred.

*[3 marks]*

(b)   Initially, the speed of the rock is 18 m/s.
Calculate the amount of energy in the rock's kinetic energy store at this time.

*[2 marks]*

(c)   Use your answer to (b) to calculate the height of the rock at **B**.

*[3 marks]*

# Unwanted Energy Transfers

*So energy is **transferred** between different **stores**. But not all of the energy is transferred to **useful** stores.*

## Most **Energy Transfers** Involve Some **Losses**, Often by **Heating**

1) You've already met the <u>principle of conservation of energy</u> on page 43, but another <u>important principle</u> you need to know is:

> Energy is <u>only useful</u> when it is <u>transferred</u> from one store to a <u>useful store</u>.

2) <u>Useful devices</u> can <u>transfer energy</u> from <u>one store</u> to a <u>useful store</u>.

3) However, some of the <u>input energy</u> is always <u>dissipated or wasted</u>, often to <u>thermal energy stores</u> of the surroundings.

> Dissipated is a fancy way of saying the energy is spread out and so is 'lost'.

4) Whenever work is done <u>mechanically</u> (see p.43), <u>frictional forces</u> have to be overcome, including things like <u>moving parts rubbing</u> together, and <u>air resistance</u>. The energy needed to overcome these frictional forces is transferred to the <u>thermal energy stores</u> of whatever's doing the work and the <u>surroundings</u>.

5) This energy usually <u>isn't useful</u>, and is <u>quickly dissipated</u>.

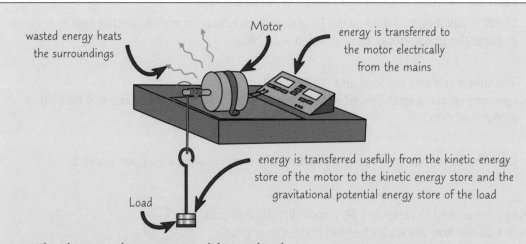

wasted energy heats the surroundings

Motor

energy is transferred to the motor electrically from the mains

Load

energy is transferred usefully from the kinetic energy store of the motor to the kinetic energy store and the gravitational potential energy store of the load

- The diagram shows a <u>motor</u> lifting a load.
- The motor transfers energy usefully from its <u>kinetic energy store</u> to the <u>kinetic</u> energy store and the <u>gravitational potential</u> energy store of the <u>load</u>.
- But it also transfers energy <u>mechanically</u> to the <u>thermal energy stores</u> of its moving parts, and <u>electrically</u> to the <u>thermal energy stores</u> of its <u>circuits</u>.
- This energy is <u>dissipated</u>, heating the surroundings.

6) The conservation of energy principle means that:
   <u>total energy input = useful energy output + wasted energy</u>.

7) The <u>less energy</u> that's <u>wasted</u>, the <u>more efficient</u> the device is said to be. The amount of energy that's wasted can often be <u>reduced</u> — see page 48.

## Before you know what's waste, you've got to know what's useful...

If you're trying to work out <u>how</u> a device is <u>wasting energy</u>, the first thing you should do is figure out which store is <u>useful</u>. For example, for a <u>phone charger</u>, only energy transferred to the <u>chemical energy store</u> of the phone's battery is <u>useful</u>. Then you know energy that ends up <u>anywhere else</u> is <u>wasted</u>.

# Efficiency

*Devices have **energy transferred** to them, but only transfer **some** of that energy to **useful energy stores**.*
*Wouldn't it be great if we could tell **how much** the device **usefully transfers**? That's where **efficiency** comes in.*

## You can **Calculate** the **Efficiency** of an **Energy Transfer**

The efficiency of any device is defined as:

$$\text{efficiency} = \frac{\text{useful energy transferred by the device (J)}}{\text{total energy supplied to the device (J)}}$$

*This will give the efficiency as a decimal. To give it as a percentage, you need to multiply the answer by 100.*

**EXAMPLE**

**A toaster transfers 216 000 J of energy electrically from the mains.**
**84 000 J of energy is transferred to the bread's thermal energy store.**
**Calculate the efficiency of the toaster.**

*This could also be written as 39% (to 2 s.f.).*

$$\text{efficiency} = \frac{\text{useful energy transferred by the device}}{\text{total energy supplied to the device}} = \frac{84\,000}{216\,000} = 0.388... = 0.39 \text{ (to 2 s.f.)}$$

All devices have an efficiency, but because some energy is <u>always wasted</u>,
the efficiency <u>can never be</u> equal to or higher than <u>1 (or 100%)</u>.

## You can Use **Diagrams** to Show **Efficiency**

<u>No device</u> is 100% efficient, but some are <u>more efficient</u> than others. You can use diagrams
like the one below to show the different <u>energy transfers</u> made by a device, and so how <u>efficient</u> it is:

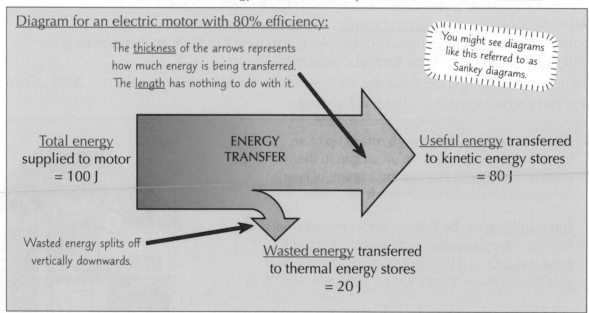

Diagram for an electric motor with 80% efficiency:

The <u>thickness</u> of the arrows represents how much energy is being transferred. The <u>length</u> has nothing to do with it.

*You might see diagrams like this referred to as Sankey diagrams.*

Total energy supplied to motor = 100 J

ENERGY TRANSFER

Useful energy transferred to kinetic energy stores = 80 J

Wasted energy splits off vertically downwards.

Wasted energy transferred to thermal energy stores = 20 J

You can <u>reduce</u> the amount of energy that's <u>wasted</u> in various ways — including by <u>lubrication</u> and by
<u>thermal insulation</u>. <u>Decreasing</u> the amount of <u>wasted energy</u> means that a <u>higher proportion</u> of the <u>supplied</u>
energy is transferred to <u>useful</u> stores, so the <u>efficiency</u> of the process is <u>increased</u>.

## There's no such thing as perfect efficiency...

One really important thing to take from here — devices that <u>transfer energy</u> from
one store to other stores will <u>always</u> transfer some energy to stores that aren't <u>useful</u>.

Q1 Video Solution

Q1    An electrical device wastes 420 J of energy when it has an input energy of 500 J.
      Calculate the efficiency of the device as a percentage.                    [3 marks]

# Reducing Unwanted Energy Transfers

*There are a few ways you can **reduce** the amount of energy scampering off to a **completely useless** store — **lubrication** and **thermal insulation** are the ones you need to know about. Read on to find out more...*

## Lubrication Reduces Energy Transferred by Friction

1) Whenever something moves, there's usually at least one frictional force acting against it.
2) This transfers energy mechanically (work is done against friction) to the thermal energy store of the objects involved, which is then dissipated by heating to the surroundings.
3) For example, pushing a box along the ground causes energy to be transferred mechanically to the thermal energy stores of the box and the ground. This energy is then radiated away to the thermal energy store of the surroundings.

For objects that are touching each other, lubricants can be used to reduce the friction between the objects' surfaces when they move.

Lubricants are usually liquids (like oil), so they can flow easily between objects and coat them.

## Insulation Reduces the Rate of Energy Transfer by Heating

1) When one side of an object is heated, the particles in the hotter part vibrate more and collide with each other. This transfers energy from their kinetic energy stores to other particles, which then vibrate faster.
2) This process is called conduction. It transfers energy through the object.
3) All materials have a thermal conductivity — it describes how well a material transfers energy by conduction. For example, metals have a high thermal conductivity and gases (like air) have a low thermal conductivity.
4) To reduce a building's rate of cooling, walls should be thick and have low thermal conductivity.
5) You can also use thermal insulation in buildings:

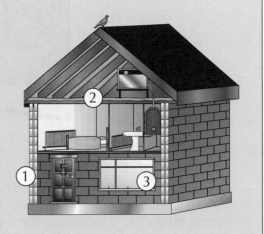

1) Some houses have cavity walls, made up of an inner and an outer wall with an air gap in the middle. The air gap reduces the amount of energy transferred by conduction through the walls.

2) Loft insulation can be laid out across the loft floor and ceiling. Fibreglass wool is often used which is a good insulator as it has pockets of trapped air. Loft insulation reduces energy loss by conduction.

3) Double-glazed windows work in the same way as cavity walls — they have an air gap between two sheets of glass to prevent energy transfer by conduction through the windows.

## Having a well-insulated house can reduce your heating bills...

When people talk of energy loss, it's not that the energy has disappeared. It still exists (see conservation of energy on page 43), just not in the store we want. For example, in a car, you want the energy to transfer to the kinetic energy store of the wheels, and not to the thermal energy stores of the moving components.

# Warm-Up & Exam Questions

Don't let your energy dissipate. These questions will let you see how efficient your revision has been.

## Warm-Up Questions

1) Which energy store does wasted energy typically end up in?
2) Why is the efficiency of an appliance always less than 100%?
3) Give one way you could reduce the frictional forces in the hinge of an automatic door.
4) For a given material, how does its thermal conductivity affect the rate of energy transfer through it?
5) How does the thickness of a building's walls affect the building's rate of cooling?

## Exam Questions

1   Torch A transfers 1200 J of energy per minute.
    480 J of this is transferred away usefully as light, 690 J is transferred
    to useless thermal energy stores and 30 J is transferred away as sound.

   (a)   Write down the equation linking efficiency, useful energy transferred by the device
         and total energy supplied to the device.

                                                                                    *[1 mark]*

   (b)   Calculate the efficiency of torch A.

                                                                                    *[2 marks]*

   Torch B transfers 10 J of energy away usefully as light each second.

   (c)   Torch B has an efficiency of 0.55.  Calculate the total energy supplied to torch B each second.

                                                                                    *[3 marks]*

   (d)   Each torch is powered by an identical battery.  A student claims that the battery in torch B will
         go 'flat' quicker than in torch A because it transfers more energy away as light each minute.
         Explain whether or not you agree with the student.

                                                                                    *[1 mark]*

2   A student investigates which type of window is the best at reducing unwanted energy transfers.
    The student places different samples of windows on a hot plate and measures
    how long it takes for the top surface of the window sample to reach 30 °C.

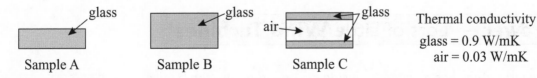

**Figure 1**

**Figure 1** shows the cross-sections of each window sample.  Rank them from best to worst for reducing
unwanted energy transfers from a house and explain your choices.

                                                                                    *[4 marks]*

# Energy Resources

*There are lots of **energy resources** available on Earth. They are either **renewable** or **non-renewable** resources.*

## Non-Renewable Energy Resources Will Run Out One Day

Non-renewable energy resources are fossil fuels and nuclear fuel (e.g. uranium and plutonium). Fossil fuels are natural resources that form underground over millions of years. They are typically burnt to provide energy. The three main fossil fuels are:

1) Coal
2) Oil
3) (Natural) Gas

- These will all 'run out' one day.
- They all do damage to the environment.
- But they are reliable.

## Renewable Energy Resources Will Never Run Out

Renewable energy resources include:

1) The Sun (Solar)
2) Wind
3) Hydro-electricity
4) Bio-fuel
5) Tides

- These will never run out — the energy can be 'renewed' as it is used.
- Most of them do damage the environment, but in less nasty ways than non-renewables.
- The trouble is they don't provide much energy and some of them are unreliable because they depend on the weather.

## Solar Cells — Expensive but No Environmental Damage

1) Solar cells are made from materials that use energy transferred by light to create an electric current.
2) Solar power is often used in remote places where there's not much choice (e.g. the Australian outback) and to power electric road signs and satellites.
3) There's no pollution. (Although they do require quite a lot of energy to make.)
4) Initial costs are high, but there are basically no running costs.
5) They're mainly used to generate electricity on a relatively small scale.
6) Solar power is best in sunny countries, but it can be used in cloudy countries like Britain.
7) You can't make solar power at night or increase production when there's extra demand.

## Wind Power — Lots of Little Wind Turbines

1) Each wind turbine has a generator inside it — wind rotates the blades, which turn the generator and produce electricity. So there's no pollution.
2) Initial costs are quite high, but running costs are minimal.
3) But lots of them are needed to produce as much power as, for example, a coal power plant. This means they can spoil the view. They can also be noisy, which can be annoying for people living nearby.
4) They only work when it's windy, so you can't always supply electricity, or respond to high demand.

# More Renewable Energy Resources

*Bio-fuels*, *hydro-electricity* and ***tidal barrages*** — *three more energy resources to get your head around.*

## Bio-fuels are Made from **Plants** and **Waste**

1) Bio-fuels are renewable energy resources created from either plant products or animal dung. They can be solid, liquid or gas and can be burnt to produce electricity or run cars.

2) They are supposedly carbon neutral, although there is some debate about this as it's only really true if you keep growing plants (or raising animals) at the rate that you're burning things.

3) Bio-fuels are fairly reliable, as crops take a relatively short time to grow and different crops can be grown all year round. However, they cannot respond to immediate energy demands. To combat this, bio-fuels are continuously produced and stored for when they are needed.

4) The cost to refine bio-fuels is very high. Also, some worry that growing crops specifically for bio-fuels will mean there isn't enough space or water for crops that are grown for food.

5) In some regions, large areas of forest have been cleared to make room to grow bio-fuels, resulting in lots of species losing their natural habitats. The decay or burning of this cleared vegetation also increases methane and $CO_2$ emissions.

## Hydro-electricity — Building **Dams** and **Flooding Valleys**

1) Producing hydro-electricity usually involves flooding a valley by building a big dam. Rainwater is caught and allowed out through turbines. There is no pollution (as such).

2) There is a big impact on the environment due to the flooding of the valley and possible loss of habitat for some species.

3) A big advantage is it can immediately respond to increased electricity demand — more water can be let out through the turbines to generate more electricity.

4) Initial costs are often high but there are minimal running costs and it's generally a reliable energy source.

## Tidal Barrages — Using the Sun and Moon's **Gravity**

1) Tidal barrages are big dams built across river estuaries with turbines in them.

2) As the tide comes in it fills up the estuary. The water is then let out through turbines at a controlled speed to generate electricity.

3) There is no pollution but they affect boat access, can spoil the view and they alter the habitat for wildlife, e.g. wading birds.

4) Tides are pretty reliable (they're caused by the Sun and Moon's gravity and always happen twice a day). But the height of the tides is variable and barrages don't work when the water level is the same either side.

5) Initial costs are moderately high, but there are no fuel costs and minimal running costs.

# Non-Renewable Resources

*Renewable resources may sound like **great news** for the **environment**. But when it comes down to it, they **don't** currently meet all our needs so we still need those nasty, polluting **non-renewables**.*

## Non-Renewables are Reliable and Cost Effective...

1) Fossil fuels and nuclear energy are reliable. There's enough fossil and nuclear fuels to meet current demand, and they are extracted from the Earth at a fast enough rate that power plants always have fuel in stock. This means that the power plants can respond quickly to changes in demand.

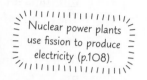

Nuclear power plants use fission to produce electricity (p.108).

2) While the set-up costs of power plants can be quite high compared to some other energy resources, the running costs aren't that expensive. Combined with fairly low fuel extraction costs, using fossil fuels is a cost effective way to produce energy (which is why it's so popular).

## ...But Create Other Problems

1) Coal, oil and gas release carbon dioxide ($CO_2$) into the atmosphere when they're burned. All this $CO_2$ adds to the greenhouse effect, and contributes to global warming.

2) Burning coal and oil also releases sulfur dioxide, which causes acid rain — which can be harmful to trees and soils and can have far-reaching effects in ecosystems.

3) Acid rain can be reduced by taking the sulfur out before the fuel is burned, or cleaning up the emissions.

4) Views can be spoilt by fossil fuel power plants, and coal mining makes a mess of the landscape, especially "open-cast mining".

5) Oil spillages cause serious environmental problems, affecting mammals and birds that live in and around the sea. We try to avoid them, but they'll always happen.

6) Nuclear power is clean, since it does not directly release $CO_2$, but the nuclear waste is very dangerous and difficult to dispose of.

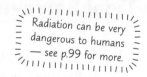

Radiation can be very dangerous to humans — see p.99 for more.

7) Nuclear fuel (e.g. uranium or plutonium) is relatively cheap but the overall cost of nuclear power is high due to the cost of the power plant and final decommissioning.

8) Nuclear power always carries the risk of a major catastrophe like the Fukushima disaster in Japan.

# Trends in Energy Resource Use

*Over time, the types of **energy resources** we use **change**. There are lots of reasons for this — breakthroughs in **technology**, understanding more about how they affect the **environment** or changes in **cost** are just a few.*

## Currently We Depend on Fossil Fuels

1) Over the 20th century, the electricity use of the UK <u>hugely increased</u> as the <u>population grew</u> and people began to use electricity for <u>more and more</u> things.

2) Since the beginning of the 21st century, electricity use in the UK has been <u>decreasing</u> (slowly), as we make appliances more <u>efficient</u> (p.47) and become <u>more careful</u> with energy use in our homes.

3) Some of our electricity is produced using <u>fossil fuels</u> and from <u>nuclear power</u>.

4) Generating electricity isn't the only reason we burn fossil fuels — <u>oil</u> (diesel and petrol) is used to <u>fuel cars</u>, and <u>gas</u> is used to <u>heat</u> homes and cook food.

5) However, renewable energy resources can be used for these purposes as well. <u>Bio-fuels</u> can be used to <u>exclusively</u> power <u>vehicles</u>, and <u>solar water heaters</u> can be used to <u>heat buildings</u>.

## The Aim is to Increase Renewable Energy Use

1) Burning fossil fuels has a lot of <u>negative effects</u> on the <u>environment</u> (p.52). This has led to many people wanting to use more renewable energy resources that have <u>less</u> of an effect on the <u>environment</u>.

2) <u>Pressure from other countries</u> and the <u>public</u> has meant that governments have begun to introduce <u>targets</u> for using renewable resources. This in turn puts pressure on <u>energy providers</u> to build new power plants that use renewable resources to make sure they do not lose <u>business</u> and <u>money</u>.

3) <u>Car companies</u> have also been affected by this change in attitude towards the environment as the demand for <u>electric cars</u> is gradually increasing.

## The Use of Renewables is Usually Limited by Reliability and Money

1) <u>Building</u> new renewable power plants costs <u>money</u>, so some smaller energy providers are <u>reluctant</u> to do this — especially when fossil fuels are such a <u>cost effective</u> way of <u>meeting demand</u>.

2) Even if <u>new power plants</u> are built, there are a lot of <u>arguments</u> over where they should be. E.g. many people don't want to live next to a <u>wind farm</u>, which can lead to <u>protests</u>.

3) Energy resources like wind power are not as <u>reliable</u> as traditional fossil fuels, whilst others cannot increase their power output <u>on demand</u>. This would mean either having to use a <u>combination</u> of <u>different</u> power plants (which would be <u>expensive</u>) or <u>researching</u> ways to <u>improve</u> reliability.

4) <u>Research</u> into improving the <u>reliability</u> and <u>cost</u> of renewable resources takes <u>time and money</u>. This means that, even with funding, it might be <u>years</u> before improvements are made. In the meantime, dependable, <u>non-renewable</u> power stations have to be used.

5) Making <u>personal changes</u> can be <u>expensive</u> or <u>impractical</u>. Things like <u>solar panels</u> for your home are still quite pricey and <u>electric cars</u> need to be <u>charged</u> which is harder in rural areas. The cost of these things is <u>slowly going down</u> and <u>infrastructure</u> is improving, but they are still not an option for many people.

*Infrastructure is just the basic systems or services needed across the country for something to work, e.g. charging points for cars.*

## Going green is on-trend this season...

So with some people wanting to <u>help the environment</u>, others not wanting to be <u>inconvenienced</u>, and greener alternatives being <u>expensive to set up</u>, the energy resources we use are <u>changing</u>. Just <u>not</u> particularly <u>quickly</u>.

# Warm-Up & Exam Questions

This is the last set of warm-up and exam questions on Section 2. They're not too horrendous, I promise.

## Warm-Up Questions

1) Name three non-renewable energy resources.
2) Give one advantage and one disadvantage associated with solar power.
3) Give two ways in which using coal as an energy resource causes environmental problems.
4) Suggest two reasons why we can't just stop using fossil fuels immediately.

## Exam Questions

1 The government of a country needs to generate more electricity to support a growing population. They want to use renewable energy resources in order to achieve this.

(a) The government has considered using wind, tides and hydro-electric power to generate electricity. Suggest **two** other renewable energy resources they could use.

*[2 marks]*

(b) In hydro-electric power stations, such as the one shown in **Figure 1**, water is held back behind a dam before being allowed to flow out through turbines.

Give **one** environmental impact the government might be concerned about if they chose hydro-electric power to generate electricity.

*[1 mark]*

**Figure 1**

(c) The government choose to generate electricity using tidal barrages. Give **one** environmental advantage of generating electricity using tidal barrages.

*[1 mark]*

2 A family want to install solar panels on their roof. They have 8 m² of space on their roof for the solar panels. They use 32 500 000 J of energy per day. A 1 m² solar panel has an output of 200 J each second in good sunlight.

(a) Calculate the minimum number of 1 m² solar panels required to cover the family's daily energy use, assuming there are 5 hours of good sunlight in a day.

*[4 marks]*

(b) Determine, using your answer from (a), whether the family can install enough solar panels to provide all of the energy they use, assuming there are 5 hours of good sunlight every day.

*[1 mark]*

(c) In reality, the number of hours of good sunlight in a day varies based on the weather and time of year. Discuss the reliability of energy from solar panels compared to from a local coal-fired power station.

*[3 marks]*

# Revision Summary for Section 2

Well, that's that for <u>Section 2</u> — this is when you find out <u>how much of it went in</u>.
- Try these questions and <u>tick off each one</u> when you <u>get it right</u>.
- When you're <u>completely happy</u> with a sub-topic, tick it off.

For even more practice, try the Retrieval Quiz for Section 2 — just scan this QR code!

Section 2 Quiz

## Energy Stores and Transfers (p.42-44) ☑

1) Write down four energy stores.

2) What kind of energy store is energy transferred to when you compress a spring?

3) If energy is transferred to an object's kinetic energy store, what happens to its speed?

4) Give the equation for finding the change in an object's gravitational potential energy.

5) True or false? Energy can be destroyed.

6) What is a closed system?

7) Give the name of the transfer in which energy moves from a hotter object to a cooler object.

8) Describe the energy transfers that occur when an electric kettle boils water.

## Reducing Unwanted Energy Transfers and Improving Efficiency (p.46-48) ☑

9) Explain what is meant by the term 'dissipate'.

10) True or false? It is possible to manufacture appliances with an efficiency greater than 1.

11) How can you reduce unwanted energy transfers in a machine with moving components?

12) True or false? A high thermal conductivity means there is a high rate of energy transfer.

13) True or false? Thicker walls make a house cool down quicker.

14) Give three ways to prevent unwanted energy transfers in a home.

## Energy Resources and Trends in their Use (p.50-53) ☐

15) Name four renewable energy resources.

16) What is the difference between renewable and non-renewable energy resources?

17) Give one advantage and one disadvantage associated with generating electricity using wind power.

18) Give one potential environmental impact of bio-fuels.

19) Give one environmental benefit of using nuclear power.

20) Explain why the UK plans to use more renewable energy resources in the future.

# Wave Basics

*Waves **transfer energy** from one place to another **without** transferring any **matter** (stuff).*

## Energy and Information are Transferred by Waves

1) <u>Waves</u> transfer <u>energy</u> and <u>information</u> in the <u>direction</u> they are <u>travelling</u>.

2) When waves travel through a medium, the <u>particles</u> of the medium <u>vibrate</u> and <u>transfer energy and information</u> between each other.

3) But overall, the particles stay in the <u>same place</u> — <u>only energy and information</u> are transferred.

> For example, if you drop a twig into a calm pool of water, <u>ripples</u> form on the water's surface. The ripples <u>don't</u> carry the <u>water</u> (or the twig) away with them though.
>
> Similarly, if you strum a <u>guitar string</u> and create <u>sound waves</u>, the sound waves don't carry the <u>air</u> away from the guitar and create a <u>vacuum</u>.

## Waves have Amplitude, Wavelength and Frequency

1) The <u>amplitude</u> of a wave is the <u>displacement</u> from the <u>rest position</u> to a <u>crest</u> or <u>trough</u>.

2) The <u>wavelength</u> is the length of a <u>full cycle</u> of the wave, e.g. from <u>crest to crest</u> (see below) or from <u>compression</u> to <u>compression</u> (see the next page).

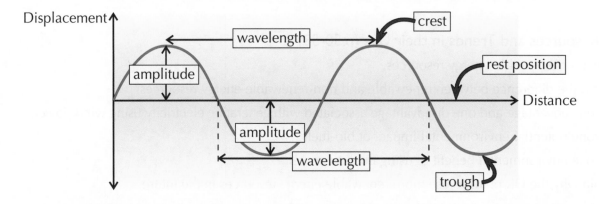

3) <u>Frequency</u> is the <u>number of complete cycles</u> of the wave passing a certain point <u>per second</u>. Frequency is measured in <u>hertz</u> (<u>Hz</u>). 1 Hz is <u>1 wave per second</u>.

4) The <u>period</u> of a wave is the <u>number of seconds</u> it takes for a <u>full cycle</u> of the wave to pass a point. Period = 1 ÷ frequency.

## Waves only transfer energy and information...

It's <u>really</u> important that you understand this stuff <u>really</u> well, or the rest of this topic will simply be a blur. Make sure you can sketch the <u>wave diagram</u> above and can <u>label</u> all the features from memory.

# Transverse and Longitudinal Waves

*All waves are either **transverse** or **longitudinal**. Read on to find out more...*

## Transverse Waves Have Sideways Vibrations

1) In <u>transverse waves</u>, the vibrations are <u>perpendicular</u> (at 90°) to the <u>direction</u> the wave travels.

2) A spring wiggled <u>up and down</u> gives a <u>transverse wave</u>:

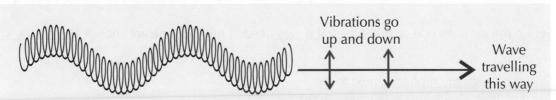

Vibrations go up and down

Wave travelling this way

3) <u>Most waves</u> are transverse, including:
   - <u>All electromagnetic waves</u>, e.g. light (p.77).
   - <u>S-waves</u> (a type of seismic wave, p.69).
   - <u>Ripples</u> and waves in <u>water</u> (see p.58).

## Longitudinal Waves Have Parallel Vibrations

1) In <u>longitudinal waves</u>, the vibrations are <u>parallel</u> to the <u>direction</u> the wave travels.

2) Longitudinal waves <u>squash up</u> and <u>stretch out</u> the arrangement of particles in the medium they pass through, making <u>compressions</u> (<u>high pressure</u>, lots of particles) and <u>rarefactions</u> (<u>low pressure</u>, fewer particles).

3) If you <u>push</u> the end of a <u>spring</u>, you get a <u>longitudinal wave</u>:

One wavelength       rarefactions

Vibrations in same direction as wave is travelling

A wavelength is still one complete cycle, e.g. from the middle of one compression to the middle of another.

compressions

4) Other examples of longitudinal waves are:
   - <u>Sound waves</u> (p.66)
   - <u>P-waves</u> (a type of seismic wave p.69).

## Wave Speed = Frequency × Wavelength

1) <u>Wave speed</u> is no different to any other speed — it tells you how <u>quickly</u> a <u>wave</u> moves through space.

2) There are <u>two</u> ways to calculate <u>wave speed</u>:

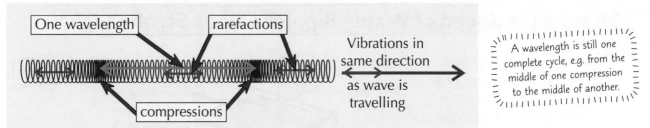

Wave speed (m/s) — $v = \dfrac{x}{t}$ — Distance (m) / Time (s)

Wave speed (m/s) — $v = f \times \lambda$ — Wavelength (m) / Frequency (Hz)

3) $v = f \times \lambda$ is sometimes referred to as '<u>the wave equation</u>'.

4) Remember, <u>velocity</u> is <u>speed</u> in a given <u>direction</u> (p.18). So, if you know the <u>direction</u> of a wave, you can use these equations to work out <u>wave velocity</u>.

## Learn both of those wave speed equations...

Whether a wave is <u>transverse</u> or <u>longitudinal</u>, you can find its speed using the wave equation.

Q1    A wave has a speed of 0.15 m/s and a wavelength of 7.5 cm. Calculate its frequency. [3 marks]

Q1 Video Solution

# Investigating Waves

*The **speeds**, **frequencies** and **wavelengths** of waves can vary by huge amounts. So you have to use **suitable** **equipment** to measure waves in different materials, to make sure you get **accurate** and **precise** results.*

## Use an **Oscilloscope** to Measure the **Speed** of **Sound**

By attaching a signal generator to a speaker you can generate sounds with a specific frequency. You can use two microphones and an oscilloscope to find the wavelength of the sound waves generated.

1) Set up the oscilloscope so the detected waves at each microphone are shown as separate waves.

2) Start with both microphones next to the speaker, then slowly move one away until the two waves are aligned on the display, but have moved exactly one wavelength apart.

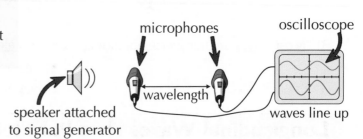

microphones      oscilloscope

wavelength

speaker attached to signal generator

waves line up

3) Measure the distance between the microphones to find one wavelength (λ).

4) You can then use the formula $v = f \times \lambda$ (see previous page) to find the speed (v) of the sound waves passing through the air — the frequency (f) is whatever you set the signal generator to in the first place.

*The speed of sound in air is around 340 m/s, so check your results roughly agree with this.*

## Measure the **Speed** of **Water Ripples** Using a **Strobe Light**

**PRACTICAL**

1) Using a signal generator attached to the dipper of a ripple tank you can create water waves at a set frequency.

2) Dim the lights and turn on the strobe light — you'll see a wave pattern made by the shadows of the wave crests on the screen below the tank.

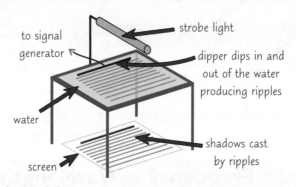

to signal generator

strobe light

dipper dips in and out of the water producing ripples

water

screen

shadows cast by ripples

3) Alter the frequency of the strobe light until the wave pattern on the screen appears to 'freeze' and stop moving. This happens when the frequency of the waves and the strobe light are equal — the waves appear not to move because they are being lit at the same point in their cycle each time.

4) The distance between each shadow line is equal to one wavelength. Measure the distance between lines that are 10 wavelengths apart, then find the average wavelength.

*If you don't know the frequency of the strobe light, you can find the frequency by using a regular light, so you can see the waves moving. Count how many waves pass a mark on the screen in a given time, then divide this by the time in seconds to find the frequency.*

5) Use $v = f \times \lambda$ to calculate the speed of the waves.

- Depending on the exact set-up of your apparatus, the waves seen on the screen may be magnified. In this case you'll need to work out the scale factor before you can find the wavelength.

- An easy way to do this it to stick a piece of tape of a known length, e.g. 10 cm, to the bottom of the ripple tank. Then measure the length of its shadow. If the shadow is longer than the tape, then what you're seeing on the screen is magnified.

- The length of the tape's shadow divided by the actual length of the tape will give the scale factor.

# Investigating Waves

*There's one more **wave experiment** coming up. This time, it's to do with **waves in a solid**.*

## Use **Peak Frequency** to find the **Speed** of **Waves in Solids**

1) You can find the speed of waves in a solid by measuring the frequency of the sound waves produced when you hit the object, e.g. a rod, with a hammer.

2) Hitting the rod causes waves to be produced along the rod.

3) These waves make the rod vibrate and produce sound waves in the air around the rod (this is how a percussion triangle works).

4) These sound waves have the same frequencies as the waves in the rod.

5) Here is a method for measuring the speed of waves in a metal rod:

- Measure and record the length of a metal rod, e.g. a brass rod.

- Set up the apparatus shown in the diagram below, making sure to secure the rod at its centre.

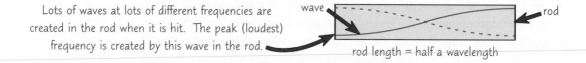

clamps

microphone

elastic bands

hammer

to computer

rod

- Tap the rod with the hammer. Write down the peak frequency displayed by the computer.

Lots of waves at lots of different frequencies are created in the rod when it is hit. The peak (loudest) frequency is created by this wave in the rod.

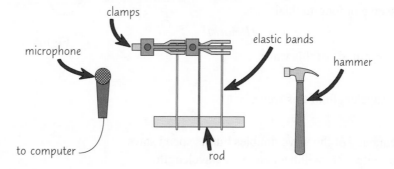

wave

rod

rod length = half a wavelength

- Repeat this three times to get an average peak frequency.

- Calculate the speed of the wave using $v = f \times \lambda$, where $\lambda$ is equal to twice the length of the rod.

6) The peak frequency wave always has $\lambda$ = rod length × 2, whatever the rod is made from. So this set-up is suitable for finding the wave speed in a rod of any type of solid material.

---

## Learn the methods for all these practicals...

These experiments might seem quite different, but the aim in all of them is to try and find values for $f$ and $\lambda$. All the experiments then use the wave equation, $v = f \times \lambda$, to calculate wave speed.

# Warm-Up & Exam Questions

Now to check what's actually stuck in your mind over the last four pages...

## Warm-Up Questions

1) A twig is dropped on a pool of water and creates water ripples.
   Explain why the twig stays where it is, rather than being carried away by the ripples.

2) What are the units of frequency?

3) Give one example of a longitudinal wave.

4) State the equation that relates wave speed, frequency and wavelength.

## Exam Questions

**1**    **Figure 1** shows a graph of a water ripple.

*Grade 4-6*

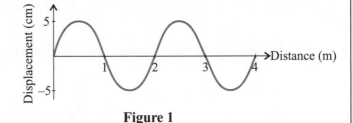

**Figure 1**

   (a)   State whether water ripples are transverse or longitudinal.

   *[1 mark]*

   (b)   Give the amplitude of this wave.

   *[1 mark]*

   (c)   Find the wavelength of this wave.

   *[1 mark]*

   (d)   If the frequency of the wave doubles but its speed stays the same, state what will happen to its wavelength.

   *[1 mark]*

**PRACTICAL**

**2**    **Figure 2** shows how an oscilloscope can be used to display sound waves by connecting microphones to it. Trace 1 shows the sound waves detected by microphone 1 and trace 2 shows the sound waves detected by microphone 2.

*Grade 6-7*

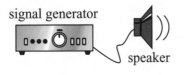 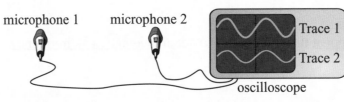

signal generator          microphone 1     microphone 2

speaker                                                        oscilloscope

Trace 1

Trace 2

**Figure 2**

A student begins with both microphones at equal distances from the speaker and the signal generator set at a fixed frequency. He gradually moves microphone 2 away from the speaker, which causes trace 2 to move. He stops moving microphone 2 when both traces line up again as shown in **Figure 2**. He then measures the distance between the microphones.

   (a)   Explain how his measurement could be used to work out the speed of sound in air.

   *[2 marks]*

   (b)   With the frequency set to 50 Hz, the distance between the microphones was measured as 6.8 m.
         Calculate the speed of sound in air.

   *[2 marks]*

# Wave Behaviour at Boundaries

*How a wave behaves when it reaches a **boundary** depends on the **properties** of the **materials** either side of the boundary. It also depends on the **wavelength** of the wave.*

## Waves are **Absorbed, Transmitted** and **Reflected** at **Boundaries**

When a <u>wave</u> meets a <u>boundary</u> between two materials (a <u>material interface</u>), <u>three</u> things can happen:

1) The wave is <u>absorbed</u> by the second material — the wave <u>transfers energy</u> to the material's energy stores. Often, the energy is transferred to a <u>thermal</u> energy store, which leads to <u>heating</u> (this is how a <u>microwave</u> works, see page 79).

2) The wave is <u>transmitted</u> through the second material — the wave <u>carries on travelling</u> through the new material. This often leads to <u>refraction</u> (see below). Refraction can be used in <u>communications</u> (p.80) as well as in the lenses of <u>glasses</u> and <u>cameras</u> (p.73).

3) The wave is <u>reflected</u> — this is where the incoming ray is neither <u>absorbed</u> nor <u>transmitted</u>, but instead is 'sent back' away from the second material (see p.64). This is how <u>echoes</u> are created.

What actually happens depends on the <u>wavelength</u> of the wave and the <u>properties</u> of the <u>materials</u> involved.

## Refraction — Waves **Changing Direction** at a **Boundary**

1) Waves travel at <u>different speeds</u> in materials with <u>different densities</u>. So when a wave crosses a <u>boundary</u> between materials it <u>changes speed</u>.

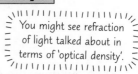

You might see refraction of light talked about in terms of 'optical density'.

2) If a wave hits a boundary at an <u>angle</u>, the change of <u>speed</u> causes a <u>change in direction</u> — <u>refraction</u>.

3) If the wave is travelling <u>along the normal</u> (see next page) it will <u>change speed</u>, but it's <u>not refracted</u>.

4) The <u>greater</u> the <u>change</u> in speed, the <u>more</u> a wave <u>bends</u> (changes direction).

5) The wave bends <u>towards the normal</u> if it <u>slows down</u>, and <u>away</u> from the normal if it <u>speeds up</u>.

6) <u>Electromagnetic</u> (EM) waves (see p.77) like light usually travel more <u>slowly</u> in <u>denser</u> materials.

7) How <u>much</u> an <u>EM wave</u> refracts can be affected by its <u>wavelength</u>. <u>Shorter</u> wavelengths <u>bend more</u>. This can lead to the <u>wavelengths spreading out</u> (<u>dispersion</u>), e.g. <u>white</u> light becoming a <u>spectrum</u>.

8) The <u>frequency</u> of a wave <u>stays the same</u> when it crosses a boundary. As <u>$v = f \times \lambda$</u>, this means that the <u>change in speed</u> is caused by a <u>change in wavelength</u> — the wavelength <u>decreases</u> if the wave <u>slows down</u>, and <u>increases</u> if it <u>speeds up</u>.

9) You can show <u>refraction</u> using <u>wavefront diagrams</u>. When one part of the wavefront <u>crosses</u> a boundary into a <u>denser</u> material, that part travels <u>slower</u> than the rest of the wavefront, so the wave <u>bends</u>.

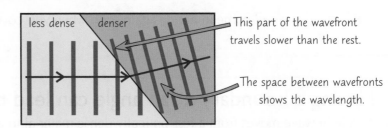

less dense    denser

This part of the wavefront travels slower than the rest.

The space between wavefronts shows the wavelength.

# Refraction and Ray Diagrams

*Refraction — what you really need is a clear diagram to show what's going on. Cue **ray diagrams**.*

## You can **Construct** a **Ray Diagram** to show **Refraction**

A <u>ray</u> is a <u>line</u> showing the <u>path</u> a wave travels in. Rays are always drawn as <u>straight lines</u>.
Ray diagrams can be drawn to show how a light ray <u>refracts</u> at the <u>boundary</u> between two materials:

1) First, start by drawing the <u>boundary</u> between your two materials and the <u>normal</u>. The <u>normal</u> is an <u>imaginary line</u> that's <u>perpendicular</u> (at right angles) to the <u>surface</u> at the <u>point of incidence</u> (the point where the wave <u>hits</u> the boundary). The normal is usually shown as a <u>dotted line</u>.

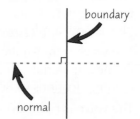

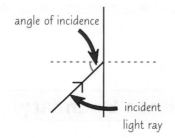

2) Draw an <u>incident ray</u> that <u>meets</u> the <u>normal</u> at the <u>boundary</u>. The angle <u>between</u> the <u>ray</u> and the <u>normal</u> is the <u>angle of incidence</u>. (If you're <u>given</u> this angle, make sure to draw it <u>carefully</u> using a <u>protractor</u>.)

3) Now draw the <u>refracted ray</u> on the other side of the boundary. The <u>angle</u> between this ray and the <u>normal</u> is the <u>angle of refraction</u>. If the second material is <u>optically denser</u> than the first, the refracted ray <u>bends towards</u> the normal. The angle of <u>refraction</u> is <u>smaller</u> than the <u>angle of incidence</u>.

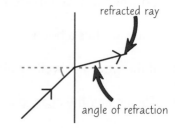

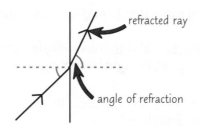

4) If the second material is less <u>dense</u> than the first, the refracted ray <u>bends away</u> from the normal. The angle of <u>refraction</u> is <u>larger</u> than the <u>angle of incidence</u>.

<u>Ray diagrams</u> will come in handy again soon when you cover <u>reflection</u> (p.64) and <u>lenses</u> (p.75).

---

## Hitting a boundary at an angle can lead to refraction...

As a light wave moves from a <u>less optically dense</u> material to a <u>more optically dense</u> material, it will <u>slow down</u>. If it crosses a boundary like this at an <u>angle</u>, its path will bend <u>towards the normal</u>.

Q1 Draw a ray diagram for light entering a less optically dense medium, 40° to the normal.

[3 marks]

**Q1 Video Solution**

# Investigating Refraction

*It's time to whip out your ray box and get some **refraction** going on. This is just one practical that covers how **electromagnetic waves** (p.77) behave — there are a couple more over on page 86.*

## You Need to Do This **Experiment** in a **Dim Room**

1) This experiment uses a <u>ray of light</u>, so it's best to do it in a <u>dim room</u> so you can <u>clearly</u> see the ray.
2) The ray of light must be thin, so you can easily see the <u>middle</u> of the ray when <u>tracing</u> it and <u>measuring angles</u> from it.
3) To do this, you can use a <u>ray box</u> — an enclosed box that contains a <u>light bulb</u>. A <u>thin slit</u> is cut into one of the sides — allowing a <u>thin ray of light</u> out of the box that you can use for your experiment.

## You Can Use a **Glass Block** to Investigate **Refraction**

Light is refracted at the <u>boundary</u> between <u>air</u> and <u>glass</u>. You can investigate this by looking at how much light is <u>refracted</u> when it passes through a glass block.

1) Place a <u>rectangular glass block</u> on a piece of <u>paper</u> and <u>trace around it</u>. Use a <u>ray box</u> to shine a ray of light at the <u>middle</u> of one side of the block.

2) <u>Trace</u> the <u>incident ray</u> and the <u>emergent ray</u> on the other side of the block. Remove the block and, with a <u>straight line</u>, <u>join up</u> the <u>incident ray</u> and the emergent ray to show the path of the <u>refracted ray</u> through the block.

3) Draw the <u>normal</u> at the <u>point</u> where the light ray <u>entered</u> the block. Use a protractor to measure the <u>angle</u> between the <u>incident</u> ray and the <u>normal</u> (the <u>angle of incidence</u>, *I*) and the angle between the <u>refracted</u> ray and the <u>normal</u> (the <u>angle of refraction</u>, *R*).

4) Do the <u>same</u> for the point where the ray <u>emerges</u> from the block.

5) You should end up with a <u>diagram</u> that looks like <u>this</u>. ➡

6) <u>Repeat</u> this three times, keeping the angle of incidence as the ray <u>enters</u> the block <u>the same</u>. Calculate an <u>average</u> for each of the angles.

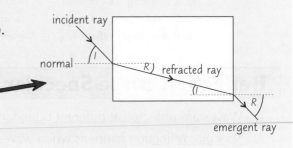

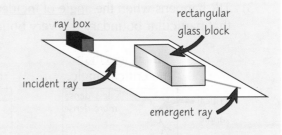

Here's what you should find:

- You should see that the ray of light <u>bends towards</u> the normal as it <u>enters</u> the block (so the <u>angle of refraction</u> is <u>less than</u> the <u>angle of incidence</u>). This is because <u>air</u> has a <u>lower optical density</u> than <u>glass</u>, so the light ray will always <u>slow down</u> when it enters the block.

- You should then see the ray of light bends <u>away from the normal</u> as it <u>leaves</u> the block. This is because the light ray <u>speeds up</u> as it leaves the block and travels through the air.

- It's important to remember that <u>all electromagnetic waves</u> can be refracted — this experiment uses <u>visible light</u> so that you can actually <u>see</u> the ray being <u>refracted</u> as it travels through the block.

## Ray boxes produce a thin beam of light...

A thin, bright beam of light will be much <u>easier</u> to trace than a thicker, dimmer one. Not only will you be able to see the light <u>more clearly</u>, but your measurements will be <u>more accurate</u> too.

# Reflection

*You can also use **ray diagrams** to see what's happening when a wave is **reflected**.*

## You Can Draw a Simple **Ray Diagram** for **Reflection**

The <u>law of reflection</u> is true for <u>all</u> reflected waves:

Angle of incidence = Angle of reflection

Where <u>the angle of reflection</u> is the angle between the <u>reflected ray</u> and the normal.

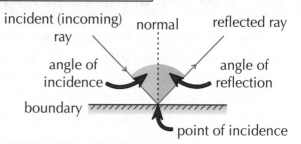

## Total Internal Reflection Depends on the Critical Angle

1) A wave crossing a boundary can experience <u>total internal reflection</u> (TIR). This means it is <u>reflected back</u> into the material.

2) This can only happen when the wave travels <u>through a dense material</u> like glass or water <u>towards a less dense</u> substance like air.

3) TIR happens when the <u>angle of incidence</u>, *i*, is <u>larger</u> than the <u>critical angle</u> for that particular boundary — every boundary has its <u>own</u>, <u>different</u> critical angle.

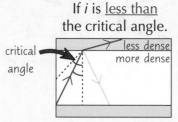

If *i* is <u>less than</u> the critical angle.

Most of the light is refracted into the outer layer, but some of it is internally reflected.

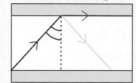

If *i* is <u>equal to</u> the critical angle.

The ray would go along the surface (with quite a bit of internal reflection as well).

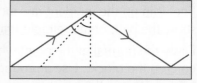

If *i* is <u>larger than</u> the critical angle.

No light comes out. It's all internally reflected, i.e. total internal reflection.

## Reflection can be Specular or Diffuse

1) Waves are reflected at <u>different boundaries</u> in <u>different ways</u>.

2) <u>Specular reflection</u> happens when waves are reflected in a <u>single direction</u> by a <u>smooth</u> surface.

3) This means you get a <u>clear reflection</u>, e.g. when <u>light</u> is reflected by a <u>mirror</u>.

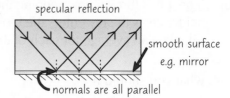

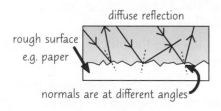

4) <u>Diffuse reflection</u> occurs when waves are reflected by a <u>rough surface</u> (e.g. paper) and the waves are <u>reflected</u> in <u>all directions</u>.

5) This happens because the <u>normal</u> is <u>different</u> for each incident ray, so each ray has a different <u>angle of incidence</u>. The rule <u>angle of incidence = angle of reflection</u> still applies.

6) When light is reflected by <u>something rough</u>, the surface looks <u>matte</u>, and you <u>don't</u> get a clear reflection.

## The law of reflection — it's simple, but don't overlook it...

Remember, the angle of incidence is <u>always equal to</u> the angle of reflection of a wave.

Q1    A light ray is incident on a mirror at an angle of 30°. Draw a ray diagram to show its reflection.

[3 marks]

Q1 Video Solution

# Warm-Up & Exam Questions

There you go — a little reflection, a lot of refraction. Here are a few questions to check it all went in.

## Warm-Up Questions

1) List the three things that can happen when a wave meets a boundary.
2) True or false? The shorter the wavelength of an electromagnetic wave, the less the wave is refracted at a boundary.
3) A wave's speed increases as it crosses the boundary between two materials. Assuming the wave hits the boundary at an angle to the normal, will the wave bend towards or away from the normal as it refracts?
4) Name a piece of equipment that can be used to produce a thin beam of light for use in refraction experiments.
5) State the law of reflection.
6) True or false? An incoming wave will be totally internally reflected at a boundary if its angle of incidence is less than the boundary's critical angle.

## Exam Questions

1 **Figure 1** shows a student looking at a pencil from behind a screen using a mirror. **Grade 4-6**

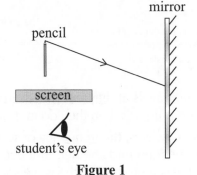

**Figure 1**

(a) State the type of reflection that occurs in **Figure 1** as light is reflected from the pencil tip to the student's eye.

*[1 mark]*

(b) Complete the ray diagram in **Figure 1** to show how the light reflected by the tip of the pencil travels to the student's eye. Mark the angle of incidence and the angle of reflection.

*[3 marks]*

**PRACTICAL**

2 **Figure 2** shows a ray of red light entering a glass prism. Red light travels slower in glass than in air. **Grade 7-9**

(a) Complete the diagram to show the ray passing through the prism and emerging from the other side. Label the angles of incidence, *I*, and refraction, *R*, for both boundaries.

*[3 marks]*

(b) Describe an experiment that could be carried out to measure *I* and *R* at both boundaries.

*[4 marks]*

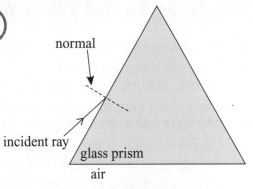

**Figure 2**

# Sound

*Time to learn all about the **properties** of **sound waves** and how they cause us to **hear** things. Don't panic though — you won't be quizzed on each individual part of the **ear**, just make sure you have a general idea.*

## Sound Travels as a Wave

1) <u>Sound waves</u> are caused by <u>vibrating objects</u>.

2) The vibrations are passed through the surrounding medium as a series of <u>compressions</u> and <u>rarefactions</u>. Sound waves are a type of <u>longitudinal wave</u> (see page 57).

3) When a sound wave travels <u>through a solid</u> it does so by causing <u>particles</u> in the solid to <u>vibrate</u>.

4) However, not all <u>frequencies</u> of sound can be transferred through an object. An object's <u>size</u>, <u>shape</u> and <u>structure</u> determines which frequencies it can transmit.

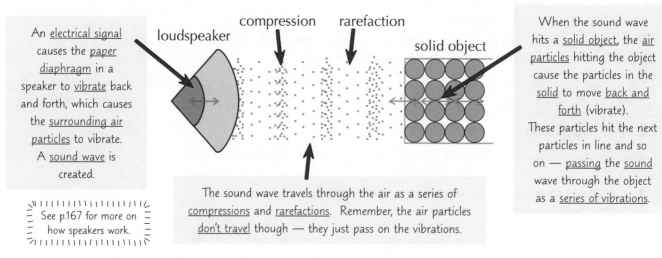

An <u>electrical signal</u> causes the <u>paper diaphragm</u> in a speaker to <u>vibrate</u> back and forth, which causes the <u>surrounding air particles</u> to vibrate. A <u>sound wave</u> is created.

loudspeaker   compression   rarefaction   solid object

When the sound wave hits a <u>solid object</u>, the <u>air particles</u> hitting the object cause the particles in the <u>solid</u> to move <u>back and forth</u> (vibrate). These particles hit the next particles in line and so on — <u>passing</u> the <u>sound</u> wave through the object as a <u>series of vibrations</u>.

See p.167 for more on how speakers work.

The sound wave travels through the air as a series of <u>compressions</u> and <u>rarefactions</u>. Remember, the air particles <u>don't travel</u> though — they just pass on the vibrations.

5) Sound travels at <u>different speeds</u> in <u>different media</u> — sound waves generally travel <u>faster</u> in <u>liquids</u> than they do in <u>gases</u>, and faster in <u>solids</u> than they do in <u>liquids</u>.

6) Like all waves, the <u>frequency</u> of sound <u>doesn't change</u> when it passes from one medium into another. But because $v = f \times \lambda$ the <u>wavelength</u> does — it gets <u>longer</u> when the wave <u>speeds up</u>, and <u>shorter</u> when it <u>slows down</u>.

7) So sound waves can <u>refract</u> as they enter <u>different media</u>. (However, since sound waves are always spreading out so much, the change in direction is <u>hard to spot</u> under normal circumstances.)

8) <u>Sound waves</u> will be <u>reflected</u> by <u>hard, flat surfaces</u>. <u>Echoes</u> are just reflected sound waves.

9) Sound can't travel in <u>space</u> because it's mostly a <u>vacuum</u> (there are no particles to move or vibrate).

## You Hear Sound When Your Eardrum Vibrates

1) Sound waves that reach your <u>eardrum</u> cause it to <u>vibrate</u>.

2) These <u>vibrations</u> are passed on to <u>tiny bones</u> in your ear called <u>ossicles</u>, through the <u>semicircular canals</u> and to the <u>cochlea</u>.

3) The <u>cochlea</u> turns these vibrations into <u>electrical signals</u> which get sent to your <u>brain</u>.

4) The brain <u>interprets</u> the signals as sounds of different <u>pitches</u> and <u>volumes</u>, depending on their <u>frequency</u> and <u>intensity</u>. A <u>higher frequency</u> sound wave has a <u>higher pitch</u>.

5) <u>Human hearing</u> is limited by the <u>size</u> and <u>shape</u> of our <u>eardrum</u>, and the <u>structure</u> of all the parts within the ear that <u>vibrate</u> to transmit the sound wave.

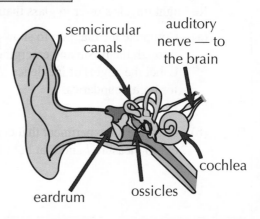

semicircular canals   auditory nerve — to the brain

cochlea

ossicles

eardrum

# Infrasound and Ultrasound

*Can you hear **that**? If not, '**that**' could be **ultrasound**, or even **infrasound**.*

## Infrasound is Sound with **Frequencies Lower** than **20 Hz**

1) Infrasound waves are sound waves so low in frequency that we can't hear them — they're under 20 Hz.

2) Some animals communicate using infrasound — for example elephants and whales. By detecting infrasound, scientists are able to track these animals for conservation purposes.

3) Natural events like erupting volcanoes, avalanches and earthquakes also produce infrasound in the local area. Scientists can monitor infrasound to try to predict events, e.g. if a volcano will shortly erupt.

4) Earthquakes also produce waves that travel through the different layers of the Earth. Some of these waves have frequencies less than 20 Hz — i.e. they're infrasound waves. We can use these waves to explore the structure of the Earth (see p.69).

## Ultrasound is Sound with **Frequencies Higher** than **20 000 Hz**

1) Electrical devices can be made which produce electrical oscillations of any frequency.

2) These can easily be converted into mechanical vibrations to produce sound waves beyond the range of human hearing (i.e. frequencies above 20 000 Hz).

3) This is called ultrasound and it pops up all over the place.

## Ultrasound Waves Get **Partially Reflected** at **Boundaries**

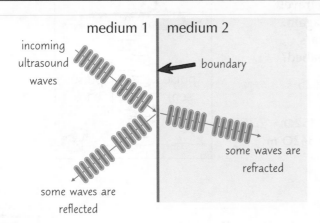

medium 1  medium 2

incoming ultrasound waves

boundary

some waves are refracted

some waves are reflected

1) When a wave passes from one medium into another, some of the wave is reflected off the boundary between the two media, and some is transmitted (and refracted). This is partial reflection.

2) What this means is that you can point a pulse (short burst) of ultrasound at an object, and wherever there are boundaries between one substance and another, some of the ultrasound gets reflected back.

3) The time it takes for the reflections to reach a detector can be used to measure how far away the boundary is.

## Infrasound is too low to hear, ultrasound is too high...

Sandwiched between infrasound and ultrasound, spanning from 20 Hz to 20 000 Hz, is the range of frequencies that most people are able to hear. These sound waves are often referred to as 'audible'.

# Exploring Structures with Waves

*Pulses of **ultrasound** are super useful — they can be used to **scan** things that are ordinarily hidden from view.*

## Ultrasound is Useful in Lots of Different Ways

1) <u>Ultrasound</u> can be used in <u>medical imaging</u>, e.g. the prenatal scanning of a foetus.

2) <u>Ultrasound waves</u> can pass through the body, but whenever they reach a boundary between <u>two different media</u> (like fluid in the womb and the skin of the foetus) some of the wave is <u>reflected back</u> and <u>detected</u>.

3) The exact <u>timing and distribution</u> of these <u>echoes</u> are processed by a computer to produce a <u>video image</u> of the foetus.

4) So far as we know, ultrasound imaging is <u>completely safe</u>.

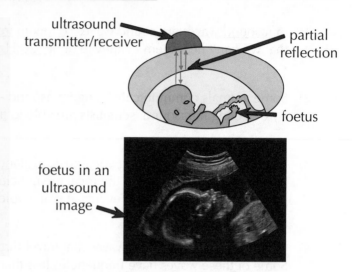

ultrasound transmitter/receiver

partial reflection

foetus

foetus in an ultrasound image

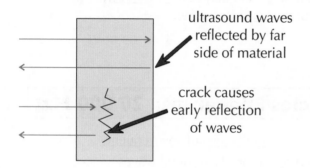

ultrasound waves reflected by far side of material

crack causes early reflection of waves

5) Ultrasound can also be used in <u>industrial imaging</u>, e.g. to find <u>flaws</u> in objects such as <u>pipes</u>, or <u>materials</u> such as wood or metal.

6) Ultrasound waves entering a material will usually be <u>reflected</u> by the <u>far side</u> of the material.

7) If there is a flaw such as a <u>crack</u> inside the material, the wave will be <u>reflected sooner</u>.

8) Ultrasound is also used in <u>echo sounding</u>, which is a type of <u>sonar</u> used by boats and submarines to find out the <u>distance to the seabed</u> or to <u>locate</u> objects in <u>deep water</u>.

### EXAMPLE

**A pulse of ultrasound takes 4.5 seconds to travel from a submarine to the seabed and back again. If the speed of sound in seawater is 1520 m/s, how far away is the submarine from the seabed?**

1) The 4.5 s is for there <u>and</u> back, so <u>halve</u> the time.

$4.5 \div 2 = 2.25$ s

2) Use the <u>wave speed</u> <u>formula</u> from p.57.

$x = v \times t = 1520 \times 2.25$
$= 3420$ m

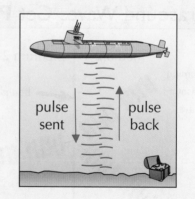

pulse sent

pulse back

## Make sure you can use $x = v \times t$ to work out distances...

You should be familiar with the equation linking <u>distance</u>, <u>wave speed</u> and <u>time</u> from page 57. Remember, if you're given the time taken for an <u>ultrasound pulse</u> to travel from an emitter to a boundary and back, you must <u>divide your answer by two</u> to find just the distance to the boundary.

Q1   Calculate how long it takes for an ultrasound pulse to return to a submarine, if the speed of sound in seawater is 1520 m/s and the submarine is 2500 m above the seabed.   [3 marks]

Q1 Video Solution

# Exploring Structures with Waves

*All seismic waves are **not** the same. There are **surface waves** which travel along the Earth's surface. There are also **body waves** which travel through the Earth — it's these you need to know about.*

## Earthquakes and Explosions Cause Seismic Waves

1) When there's an earthquake somewhere, it produces seismic waves at a range of frequencies which travel out through the Earth. We detect these waves all over the surface of the planet using seismometers.

2) Seismologists work out the time it takes for the shock waves to reach each seismometer. They also note which parts of the Earth don't receive the waves at all.

3) When seismic waves reach a boundary between different layers of material (which all have different properties, like density), some waves will be absorbed and some will be refracted. (They may also be reflected).

4) Most of the time, if the waves are refracted they change speed gradually, resulting in a curved path. But when the properties change suddenly, the wave speed changes abruptly, and the path has a kink.

## Seismic Waves Provide Evidence for the Earth's Structure

By observing how seismic waves are absorbed and refracted, scientists have been able to work out where the properties of the Earth change dramatically.

Our current understanding of the internal structure of the Earth and the size of the Earth's core is based on these observations.

There are two different types of seismic waves you need to learn — P waves and S waves (see below).

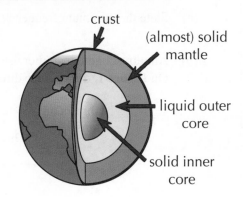

crust
(almost) solid mantle
liquid outer core
solid inner core

## P-waves can Travel through the Earth's Core...

1) P-waves are longitudinal.

2) They travel through solids and liquids.

3) They travel faster than S-waves.

## ...S-waves can't

1) S-waves are transverse.

2) They can only travel through solids.

3) They're slower than P-waves.

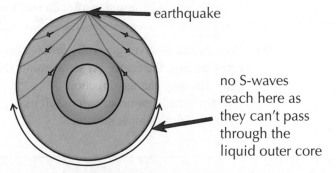

earthquake

no P-waves reach here

P-waves pass through core and are detected here

earthquake

no S-waves reach here as they can't pass through the liquid outer core

*Section 3 — Waves and the Electromagnetic Spectrum*

# Warm-Up & Exam Questions

Here are some questions for you, to check if your understanding of the last few pages is sound.

## Warm-Up Questions

1) What sort of wave is a sound wave — transverse or longitudinal?
2) Which property of a sound wave stays constant as it passes from one medium to another — its wave speed, frequency or wavelength?
3) Why can humans only hear sound with a limited range of frequencies?
4) What name is given to sound waves with a frequency below 20 Hz?
5) State one use of ultrasound.
6) Which type of seismic wave is longitudinal?

## Exam Questions

1   Ultrasound waves have frequencies above the normal range of human hearing.

    (a)   State the minimum frequency of an ultrasound wave.

*[1 mark]*

    (b)   An ultrasound transmitter uses mechanical vibrations to produce ultrasound waves.
On **Figure 1**, draw on the direction of the mechanical vibrations.

*[1 mark]*

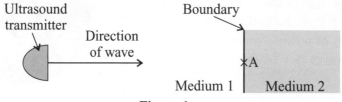

**Figure 1**

    (c)   State what will happen to the ultrasound wave when it reaches point A.

*[1 mark]*

2   Ultrasound is used to scan a crack inside a steel girder. The ultrasound scanner is placed against the steel girder and an ultrasound pulse is emitted. The pulse of ultrasound takes 35 μs  to travel to the crack and back to the ultrasound scanner, where it is detected. The speed of ultrasound in steel is 5800 m/s. Calculate the distance of the crack from the ultrasound scanner.

*[3 marks]*

3   **Figure 2** shows the internal structure of the Earth.

    (a)   Explain which part(s) of the Earth, A, B or C, S-waves would be found in after an earthquake.

*[3 marks]*

    (b)   Both P- and S-waves generally follow curved paths through the Earth. At some points their paths abruptly change direction. Explain what these observations tell us about the Earth's inner structure.

*[3 marks]*

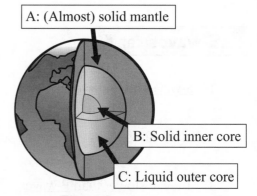

**Figure 2**

A: (Almost) solid mantle

B: Solid inner core

C: Liquid outer core

# Visible Light and Colour

*The **colour** something appears to be is all about what **wavelengths** of light we're **seeing** when we look at it.*

## Visible Light is Made Up of a Range of Colours

1) Our eyes can only detect a <u>small part</u> of the <u>electromagnetic spectrum</u> —
the <u>visible light</u> spectrum (see p.77 for more on the electromagnetic spectrum).

2) The visible light spectrum is a <u>range</u> of wavelengths that we perceive as <u>different colours</u>.
<u>Each colour</u> has its own narrow <u>range</u> of <u>wavelengths</u> ranging from <u>violets</u> up to <u>reds</u>.

long wavelength        short wavelength

low frequency        high frequency

3) <u>White light</u> is a mixture of <u>all</u> the different <u>colours</u> of light.

## Colour and Transparency Depend on Absorbed Wavelengths

1) Different objects <u>absorb</u>, <u>transmit</u> and <u>reflect</u> different <u>wavelengths</u> of light in different ways (p.61).

2) <u>Opaque</u> objects are objects that <u>do not transmit light</u>. When visible light
waves hit them, they <u>absorb</u> some wavelengths of light and <u>reflect</u> others.

3) The <u>colour</u> of an opaque object depends on <u>which wavelengths</u> of light
are <u>reflected</u>. E.g. a red apple appears to be red because the wavelengths
corresponding to the <u>red part</u> of the <u>visible spectrum</u> are reflected.

<u>White</u> light <u>hits</u> the apple, and <u>red</u> light
is <u>reflected</u> — all other colours are
absorbed. The apple looks red.

4) Colours can also <u>mix together</u> to make other colours. The only colours you <u>can't</u>
make by mixing are the <u>primary</u> colours: pure <u>red</u>, <u>green</u> and <u>blue</u>. So a banana may look
<u>yellow</u> because it's <u>reflecting yellow light</u> OR because it's reflecting <u>both red and green light</u>.

5) <u>White</u> objects <u>reflect all</u> of the wavelengths of visible light <u>equally</u>.

6) <u>Black</u> objects <u>absorb all</u> wavelengths of visible light.
Your eyes see black as the <u>lack of</u> any visible light (i.e. the lack of any <u>colour</u>).

7) <u>Transparent</u> (see-through) and <u>translucent</u> (partially see-through) objects <u>transmit light</u>,
i.e. not all light that hits the surface of the object is absorbed or reflected —
some (or most for transparent objects) can <u>pass through</u>.

8) Some wavelengths of light may be <u>absorbed</u> or <u>reflected</u> by translucent and (to a lesser extent)
transparent objects. These objects will appear to be the colour of light that corresponds to the
wavelengths most <u>strongly transmitted</u> by the object.

## We see the colour of light that objects reflect into our eyes...

The only thing that makes red stuff red is the fact that it <u>reflects</u> (or <u>transmits</u>) the 'red' wavelengths of light
and <u>absorbs</u> the rest. So what colour is it in the dark when there's no light to reflect? The mind boggles.

# Colour Filters

*Colour filters are **transparent objects** that absorb most wavelengths of light and just let some through. E.g. red cellophane — everything viewed through it appears to be either a shade of red or black. Here's why...*

## Colour Filters Only Let Through Particular Wavelengths

1) Colour filters are used to <u>filter out</u> different <u>wavelengths</u> of light, so that only certain colours (wavelengths) are <u>transmitted</u> — the rest are <u>absorbed</u>.

2) A <u>primary colour filter</u> only <u>transmits</u> that <u>colour</u>, e.g. if <u>white light</u> is shone at a <u>blue</u> colour filter, <u>only</u> blue light will be let through. The rest of the light will be <u>absorbed</u>.

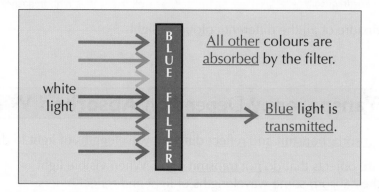

<u>All other</u> colours are <u>absorbed</u> by the filter.

white light

<u>Blue</u> light is <u>transmitted</u>.

3) If you look at a <u>blue object</u> through a blue <u>colour filter</u>, it would still look <u>blue</u>. Blue light is <u>reflected</u> from the object's surface and is <u>transmitted</u> by the filter.

4) However, if the object was e.g. <u>red</u> (or any colour <u>not made from blue light</u>), the object would appear <u>black</u> when viewed through a blue filter. <u>All</u> of the light <u>reflected</u> by the object will be <u>absorbed</u> by the filter.

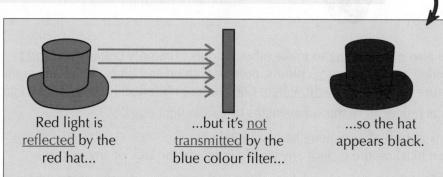

Red light is <u>reflected</u> by the red hat...

...but it's <u>not</u> <u>transmitted</u> by the blue colour filter...

...so the hat appears black.

5) <u>Filters</u> that <u>aren't</u> for <u>primary</u> colours let through <u>both</u> the <u>wavelengths</u> of light corresponding to that <u>colour</u> and the wavelengths of the <u>primary</u> colours that can be added together to make that colour. E.g. <u>cyan</u> can be made from <u>blue</u> and <u>green</u> light mixed together. So a <u>cyan</u> colour filter will let through the <u>wavelengths</u> of light that correspond to <u>cyan</u>, <u>blue</u> and <u>green</u>.

## Colour filters only let their own colour of light through...

Hopefully you now know enough about <u>absorption</u> and <u>reflection</u> that you're feeling pretty confident about how colour filters work. Once you absorb the <u>basic facts</u>, the stuff on this page and on the previous page is pretty easy — red objects reflect red light and red filters let red light through. Simple.

# Lenses

*This bit is about **how light acts** when it hits a **lens**.  Be ready for lots of diagrams on the next few pages.*

## Lenses Refract Light to Form an Image

Lenses form images by <u>refracting</u> light (p.61) and changing its direction.  There are <u>two main types</u> of lens — <u>converging</u> and <u>diverging</u>.  They have different shapes and have <u>opposite effects</u> on light rays.

1)  A <u>converging</u> lens <u>bulges outwards</u> in the middle.  It causes parallel rays of <u>light</u> to be <u>brought together</u> (<u>converge</u>) at the <u>principal focus</u>.  They're sometimes called <u>convex</u> lenses.

2)  A <u>diverging</u> (or concave) lens <u>caves inwards</u>.  It causes parallel rays of <u>light</u> to <u>spread out</u> (<u>diverge</u>).

3)  The <u>axis</u> of a lens is a line passing through the <u>middle</u> of the lens and the <u>centre</u> of its <u>curved surfaces</u> (see the diagrams below).

4)  The <u>principal focus</u> of a <u>converging lens</u> is where rays hitting the lens parallel to the axis all <u>meet</u>.

5)  The <u>principal focus</u> of a <u>diverging lens</u> is the point where rays hitting the lens parallel to the axis <u>appear</u> to all <u>come from</u> — you can trace them back until they all appear to <u>meet up</u> at a point behind the lens.

6)  There is a principal focus on <u>each side</u> of the lens.  The <u>distance</u> from the <u>centre of the lens</u> to the <u>principal focus</u> (F) is called the <u>focal length</u>.

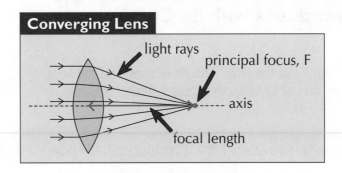

Converging Lens
light rays
principal focus, F
axis
focal length

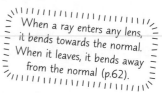

When a ray enters any lens, it bends towards the normal. When it leaves, it bends away from the normal (p.62).

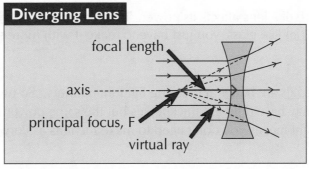

Diverging Lens
focal length
axis
principal focus, F
virtual ray

## All lenses have a principal focus...

In fact <u>every</u> lens has <u>two principal focuses</u> — one on either side of it.  Which one you're interested in depends on which <u>side</u> light is coming from and whether the lens is converging or diverging.

# Images and Lens Power

*Lenses can refract light to form **two** types of image — a **real** or a **virtual** image.*
*How much lenses refract light depends on the **power** of the lens.*

## Lenses can Produce **Real** and **Virtual** Images

Images are formed at points where all the light rays from a certain point on an object appear to come together.
There are two types of images that can be formed by lenses:

A real image is formed when the light rays actually come together to form the image. The image can be captured on a screen, because the light rays actually meet at the place where the image seems to be. E.g. the image formed on the eye's retina.

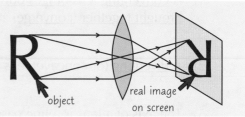

object
real image on screen

A virtual image is when the light rays from the object appear to be coming from a completely different place to where they're actually coming from.

The light rays don't actually come together at the point where the image seems to be, so it cannot be captured on a screen.
E.g. magnifying glasses create virtual images.

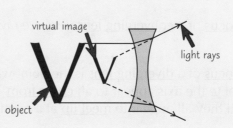

virtual image
light rays
object

To describe an image, say if it's bigger or smaller than the object, if it's upright or inverted and if it's real or virtual.

## The **Power** of a Lens **Increases** with its **Curvature**

1) Focal length is related to the power of the lens. The more powerful the lens, the more strongly it converges rays of light, so the shorter the focal length.

2) For a converging lens, the power is positive. For a diverging lens, the power is negative.

3) The curvature of a lens affects its power. To make a more powerful lens from a certain material like glass, you just have to make it with more strongly curved surfaces.

4) Some materials are better at focusing light than others. So two lenses made from different materials may have different thicknesses but the same power (using a material that's better at focusing light means you don't need to make the lens as curved to get the same focal length).

## Make sure you know what's real and what's virtual...

A virtual image will always be formed on the same side of the lens as the object. A real image will form on the opposite side of the lens to the object and, unlike a virtual image, it can be captured on a screen.

# Lenses and Ray Diagrams

*You need to be able to draw **ray diagrams** for **converging** and **diverging lenses**.*

## Draw a **Ray Diagram** for an **Image** Through a **Diverging Lens**

1) Pick a point on the <u>top</u> of the object. Draw a ray going from the object to the lens <u>parallel</u> to the axis of the lens.

2) Draw another ray from the <u>top</u> of the object going right through the <u>middle</u> of the lens.

3) The incident ray that's <u>parallel</u> to the axis is <u>refracted</u> so it appears to have come from the <u>principal focus</u> (F). Draw a <u>ray</u> from the principal focus. Make it <u>dotted</u> before it reaches the lens (as it's virtual here).

4) The ray passing through the <u>middle</u> of the lens <u>doesn't bend</u>.

5) Mark where this ray meets the <u>virtual ray</u>. That's the <u>top</u> of the image.

6) <u>Repeat</u> the process for a point on the <u>bottom</u> of the object. When the bottom of the object is on the <u>axis</u>, the bottom of the image is <u>also</u> on the axis.

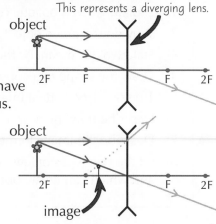

> A <u>diverging</u> lens always produces a <u>virtual image</u>. The image is <u>the right way up</u>, <u>smaller</u> than the object and on the <u>same side of the lens as the object</u> — <u>no matter where the object is</u>.

*If you get a lens that looks like this in your exam, you don't need to show how the light refracts inside it.*

## Draw a **Ray Diagram** for an **Image** Through a **Converging Lens**

1) Pick a point on the <u>top</u> of the object. Draw a ray going from the object to the lens <u>parallel</u> to the axis of the lens.

2) Draw another ray from the <u>top</u> of the object going right through the <u>middle</u> of the lens.

3) The incident ray that's <u>parallel</u> to the axis is <u>refracted</u> through the <u>principal focus</u> (F). Draw a <u>refracted ray</u> passing through F.

4) The ray passing through the <u>middle</u> of the lens doesn't bend.

5) Mark where the rays <u>meet</u>. That's the <u>top of the image</u>.

6) Repeat the process for a point on the bottom of the object. When the bottom of the object is on the <u>axis</u>, the bottom of the image is <u>also</u> on the axis.

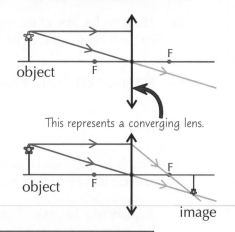

*This represents a converging lens.*

## **Distance** from the Lens Affects the **Size** and **Position** of the **Image**

1) An object <u>at 2F</u> (two focal lengths) from the lens produces a <u>real</u>, <u>inverted</u> (upside down) image the <u>same size</u> as the object, and <u>at 2F</u> on the other side of the lens.

2) <u>Between F and 2F</u> it'll make a <u>real</u>, <u>inverted</u> image <u>bigger</u> than the object, and <u>beyond 2F</u>.

3) An object <u>nearer than F</u> will make a <u>virtual</u> image that is <u>upright</u>, <u>bigger</u> than the object and on the <u>same side</u> of the lens.

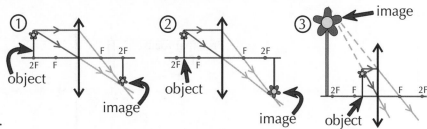

## Get lots of practice at drawing ray diagrams for lenses...

That's everything you need to know about <u>lenses</u>. Time to try out a <u>practice question</u>.

Q1   Draw a ray diagram for an object at a distance of 2F in front of a converging lens.   [3 marks]

Q1 Video Solution

# Warm-Up & Exam Questions

That's all you need to know about visible light and lenses. Have a go at focusing on these questions.

## Warm-Up Questions

1) Explain why an opaque red object appears red.
2) Why does a green object viewed through a red filter appear black?
3) State what is meant by the focal length of a lens.
4) Draw the shape of a converging lens.
5) True or false? Virtual images may be captured on a screen.
6) Describe how the power of a lens is related to its focal length.
7) Describe the image formed when an object is placed at a distance of 2F from a converging lens.
8) Of the two types of lens, which always creates a virtual image and which can create both real and virtual images?

## Exam Questions

1   **Figure 1** shows a ray diagram for a lens refracting parallel rays of light.  Grade 4-6

   (a)   Name the type of lens that is shown in **Figure 1**.

   *[1 mark]*

   (b)   Mark the location of the lens's principal focus on the left-hand side of the lens.

   *[2 marks]*

   (c)   Find the focal length of this lens.

   *[1 mark]*

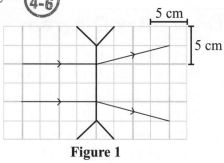

**Figure 1**

2   A student is trying to start a campfire by focusing sunlight through his spectacle lens onto the firewood.  The lens is a diverging lens.  Grade 6-7

   (a)   Explain why he cannot focus the sunlight onto the wood using this lens.

   *[2 marks]*

   (b)   The student finds a slug and uses a magnifying glass to look at it. Complete **Figure 2** to show where the image of the slug is formed.

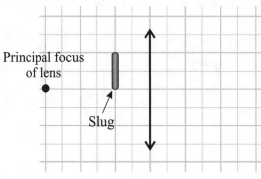

Principal focus of lens

Slug

**Figure 2**

   *[3 marks]*

# Electromagnetic Waves

*There are lots of different types of **electromagnetic wave**. Well, **seven** to be exact...*

## There's a **Continuous Spectrum** of **EM Waves**

1) Electromagnetic (EM) waves are transverse waves (p.57).

2) They all travel at the same speed through a vacuum (space). But they travel at different speeds in different materials (which can lead to refraction and dispersion, p.61).

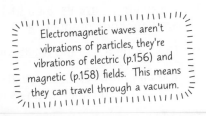

Electromagnetic waves aren't vibrations of particles, they're vibrations of electric (p.156) and magnetic (p.158) fields. This means they can travel through a vacuum.

3) EM waves vary in wavelength from around $10^{-15}$ m to more than $10^4$ m.

4) We group them based on their wavelength and frequency — there are seven basic types, but the different groups merge to form a continuous spectrum.

| RADIO WAVES | MICRO WAVES | INFRA RED | VISIBLE LIGHT | ULTRA VIOLET | X-RAYS | GAMMA RAYS |
|---|---|---|---|---|---|---|
| $1\text{ m} - 10^4\text{ m}$ | $10^{-2}\text{ m}$ | $10^{-5}\text{ m}$ | $10^{-7}\text{ m}$ | $10^{-8}\text{ m}$ | $10^{-10}\text{ m}$ | $10^{-15}\text{ m}$ |

Wavelength

INCREASING FREQUENCY AND DECREASING WAVELENGTH

5) EM waves are generated by a variety of changes in atoms and their nuclei, giving a large range of frequencies. E.g. changes in the nucleus of an atom create gamma rays (p.94) and visible light is often produced by changes in an electron's energy level (p.91). This also explains why atoms can absorb a range of frequencies — each one causes a different change.

6) Our eyes can only detect a small part of this spectrum — visible light. Different colours of light have different wavelengths — from longest to shortest: red, orange, yellow, green, blue, indigo, violet.

7) All EM waves transfer energy from a source to an absorber. For example, when you warm yourself by an electric heater, infrared waves transfer energy from the thermal energy store of the heater (the source) to your thermal energy store (the absorber).

8) The higher the frequency of the EM wave, the more energy it transfers (and so the more dangerous it may be to humans — see p.82).

EM waves are sometimes called EM radiation.

---

REVISION TIP

## You need to remember all seven types of EM waves...

You need to know the order of the EM waves too. A mnemonic can make this a whole lot easier. My favourite's 'Raging Martians Invaded Venus Using X-ray Guns'. You can make up your own.

# Uses of EM Waves

*This page is all about how **radio waves** are **generated** and what they can be **used for**.*

## Radio Waves are Made by Oscillating Charges

1) EM waves are made up of oscillating electric and magnetic fields.

2) Alternating currents (a.c.) (p.148) are made up of oscillating charges. As the charges oscillate, they produce oscillating electric and magnetic fields, i.e. electromagnetic waves.

3) The frequency of the waves produced will be equal to the frequency of the alternating current.

4) You can produce radio waves using an alternating current in an electrical circuit. The object in which charges (electrons) oscillate to create the radio waves is called a transmitter.

5) When transmitted radio waves reach a receiver, the radio waves are absorbed.

6) The energy transferred by the waves is transferred to the electrons in the material of the receiver.

7) This energy causes the electrons to oscillate and, if the receiver is part of a complete electrical circuit, it generates an alternating current.

8) This current has the same frequency as the radio waves that generated it.

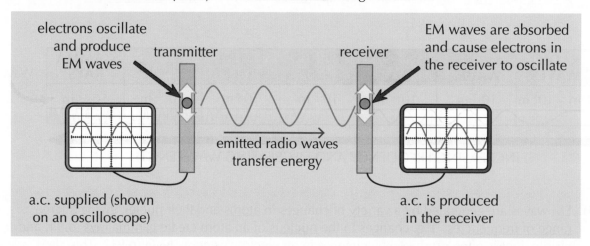

## Radio Waves are Used for Communication and Broadcasting

1) Long-wave radio signals (wavelengths of 1 – 10 km) can be received halfway round the world from where they started, because long wavelengths bend around the curved surface of the Earth. This makes it possible for radio signals to be received even if the receiver isn't in the line of sight of the transmitter.

2) Short-wave radio signals (wavelengths of about 10 m – 100 m) can, like long-wave, be received at long distances from the transmitter. That's because they are reflected by the Earth's atmosphere.

3) Bluetooth® uses short-wave radio waves to send data over short distances between devices without wires (e.g. wireless headsets so you can use your phone while driving a car).

4) The radio waves used for TV and FM radio transmissions have very short wavelengths. To get reception, you must be in direct sight of the transmitter — the signal doesn't bend or travel far through buildings.

# Uses of EM Waves

*Believe it or not, **microwaves** are used in **microwave ovens**. For more uses of microwaves, read on.*

## Microwaves and Radio Waves are Used by Satellites

1) Communication to and from satellites (including satellite TV signals and satellite phones) uses EM waves which can pass easily through the Earth's watery atmosphere.

2) These waves are usually microwaves, but can sometimes be relatively high frequency radio waves.

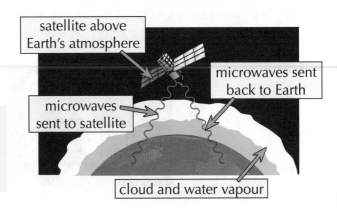

satellite above Earth's atmosphere

microwaves sent back to Earth

microwaves sent to satellite

cloud and water vapour

3) For satellite TV, the signal from a transmitter is transmitted into space and picked up by the satellite receiver dish orbiting thousands of kilometres above the Earth.

4) The satellite transmits the signal back to Earth in a different direction, where it's received by a satellite dish on the ground.

## Microwave Ovens Also Use Microwaves

1) In microwave ovens, the microwaves are absorbed by water molecules in food.

2) The microwaves penetrate up to a few centimetres into the food before being absorbed and transferring the energy they are carrying to the water molecules in the food, causing the water to heat up.

3) The water molecules then transfer this energy to the rest of the molecules in the food by heating — which quickly cooks the food.

## Some microwaves pass through water, others are absorbed by water...

The wavelength of an EM wave affects whether it is absorbed, transmitted or reflected by a substance (p.61). The microwaves used in a microwave oven are absorbed by water (and sometimes fat). So if you put something that contains no water or fat in a microwave it won't absorb any microwaves and won't get hot.

# Uses of EM Waves

*Infrared radiation is another ridiculously useful EM wave. You can use it to **cook** your dinner, **catch criminals** in the dark, and change the **TV channel** without getting up from your favourite chair.*

## Infrared Radiation Can be Used to **Monitor Temperature**...

1) Infrared (IR) radiation is given out by all hot objects —
the hotter the object, the more IR radiation it gives out.

2) Infrared cameras can be used to detect infrared radiation and monitor temperature.

3) The camera detects the IR radiation and turns it into an electrical signal,
which is displayed on a screen as a picture. This is called thermal imaging.

Different colours represent different amounts of IR radiation being detected. Here, the redder the colour, the more infrared radiation is being detected.

4) Thermal imaging is used by police to see suspects that are trying to escape or hide in the dark.

5) Infrared sensors can be used in security systems.
If a change in infrared radiation is detected, an alarm sounds or a security light turns on.

## ...Or **Increase** it

1) Absorbing IR radiation causes objects to get hotter. Food can be cooked using IR radiation —
the temperature of the food increases when it absorbs IR radiation, e.g. from a toaster's heating element.

2) Electric heaters heat a room in the same way. Electric heaters contain a long piece
of wire that heats up when a current flows through it. This wire then emits lots of
infrared radiation (and a little visible light — the wire glows). The emitted IR radiation
is absorbed by objects and the air in the room — energy is transferred by the IR waves
to the thermal energy stores of the objects, causing their temperature to increase.

## Infrared Can Also Transfer Information

Infrared radiation can also be used to transfer information.

1) For example, it can be used to send files between mobile phones or laptops.
The distances must be fairly small and the receiver must be in the line of sight of the emitter.

2) This is also how TV remote controls work. In fact, some mobile phones now have built in
software which means that you can use your phone as a TV remote.

3) Optical fibres are thin glass or plastic fibres that can carry data (e.g. from telephones or
computers) over long distances as pulses of infrared radiation. They usually use a single
wavelength to prevent dispersion (p.61), which can otherwise cause some information to be lost.

4) They use total internal reflection (p.64) to send lots of data over long distances.

# Uses of EM Waves

*And we're still not finished with **uses** of EM **waves** — there's just no end to their talents...*

## Photography Uses **Visible Light**

1) <u>Visible light</u> is the light that we can <u>see</u>. We use it for <u>illuminating</u> things so that we can see them.
2) <u>Photographic film</u> reacts to light to form an image. This is how traditional <u>cameras</u> create <u>photographs</u>.
3) <u>Digital cameras</u> contain <u>image sensors</u>, which detect <u>visible light</u> and generate an electrical signal. This signal is then <u>converted</u> into an image that can be stored digitally or <u>printed</u>.

## Ultraviolet is Used in **Fluorescent Lamps**

1) <u>Fluorescence</u> is a property of certain chemicals, where <u>ultraviolet</u> (<u>UV</u>) radiation is <u>absorbed</u> and then <u>visible light</u> is <u>emitted</u>. That's why fluorescent colours look so <u>bright</u> — they actually <u>emit light</u>.
2) <u>Fluorescent lights</u> use UV to <u>emit</u> visible light. They're <u>energy-efficient</u> (p.47) so they're good to use when light is needed for <u>long periods</u> (like in your <u>classroom</u>).
3) <u>Security pens</u> can be used to <u>mark</u> property (e.g. laptops). Under <u>UV light</u> the ink will <u>glow</u>, but it's <u>invisible</u> otherwise, helping to <u>identify</u> stolen property.
4) <u>Bank notes</u> and <u>passports</u> use a similar technique to detect <u>forgeries</u> — genuine notes and passports have <u>special markings</u> that only show up under UV light.
5) Ultraviolet radiation is sometimes used to <u>sterilise water</u>. It <u>kills bacteria</u> in the water, making it <u>safe</u> to drink. (Gamma rays are used in a similar way, see below.)

## X-rays Let Us See **Inside** Things

1) <u>X-rays</u> can be used to view the <u>internal structure</u> of <u>objects</u> and <u>materials,</u> including our <u>bodies</u>.
2) They affect <u>photographic</u> film in the same way as <u>light</u>, meaning you can take <u>X-ray photographs</u>. But X-ray images are usually formed <u>electronically</u> these days.
3) <u>Radiographers</u> in <u>hospitals</u> take <u>X-ray images</u> to help doctors diagnose <u>broken bones</u> — X-rays are <u>transmitted by flesh</u> but are <u>absorbed</u> by <u>denser material</u> like <u>bones</u> or metal.

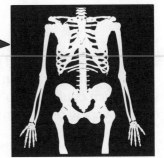

4) To produce an <u>X-ray image</u>, X-ray radiation is directed <u>through the object</u> or <u>body</u> onto a <u>detector</u>. The <u>brighter bits</u> of the image are where <u>fewer X-rays</u> get through, producing a <u>negative image</u> (the plate starts off <u>all white</u>).
5) X-rays are also used in <u>airport security scanners</u> to detect hidden objects that can't be detected with <u>metal detectors</u>.

## Gamma Rays are Used for **Sterilising Things**

1) <u>Gamma rays</u> are used to <u>sterilise</u> medical instruments — they <u>kill</u> microbes (e.g. bacteria).
2) <u>Food</u> can be <u>sterilised</u> in the same way — again by <u>killing microbes</u>. This keeps the food <u>fresh for longer</u>, without having to freeze it, cook it or preserve it some other way, and it's <u>perfectly safe</u> to eat.
3) Some <u>medical imaging</u> techniques such as <u>tracers</u> (p.102) use gamma rays to <u>detect cancer</u>.
4) Gamma radiation is used in <u>cancer treatment</u> (p.104), radiation is targeted at cancer cells to <u>kill them</u>. Doctors have to be careful to <u>minimise</u> the damage to <u>healthy cells</u> when treating cancer like this.

# Dangers of EM Waves

*Okay, so you know how **useful** electromagnetic radiation can be — well, it can also be pretty **dangerous**.*

## EM Radiation Can be Harmful to People

1) As you saw on p.61, when EM waves meet a boundary they can be absorbed, transmitted, refracted or reflected.

2) What happens depends on the materials at the boundary and the wavelength of the EM wave. E.g. some materials absorb some wavelengths of light but reflect others. This is what causes things to be a certain colour (p.71).

3) Differences in how EM waves are transmitted, reflected and absorbed have implications for human health.

> In general, the higher the frequency of the EM wave, the more energy it transfers and so the more potentially dangerous it is for humans.

## Different EM Waves Have Different Effects on the Body

1) Radio waves are transmitted through the body without being absorbed.

2) Some wavelengths of microwaves can be absorbed, causing heating of cells, which may be dangerous.

3) Infrared (IR) and visible light are mostly reflected or absorbed by the skin, causing some heating too. IR can cause burns if the skin gets too hot.

4) Ultraviolet (UV) is also absorbed by the skin. But it has a higher frequency, so it is potentially more dangerous. It's a type of ionising radiation (p.94) and when absorbed it can cause damage to cells on the surface of your skin, which could lead to skin cancer. It can also damage your eyes and cause a variety of eye conditions or even blindness.

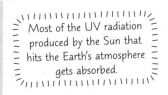
Most of the UV radiation produced by the Sun that hits the Earth's atmosphere gets absorbed.

5) X-rays and gamma rays are also ionising, so they can cause mutations and damage cells too (which can lead to cancer). But they have even higher frequencies, so transfer even more energy, causing even more damage. They can also pass through the skin and be absorbed by deeper tissues.

---

## The risks and benefits must be weighed up...

Ionising radiation can be dangerous, but the risk can be worth taking. X-ray machines used to be installed in shoe shops for use in shoe fittings. They were removed when people realised X-rays were harmful and the risks far outweighed the benefits of using X-rays rather than tape measures...

# Warm-Up & Exam Questions

EM radiation — so many uses, so many risks. Test your memory by answering these questions.

## Warm-Up Questions

1) Are EM waves transverse or longitudinal?
2) True or false? The speed at which an EM wave travels in a vacuum depends on its wavelength.
3) Which type of EM wave has the highest frequency?
4) True or false? Changes in atoms can generate EM waves.
5) State one possible use of radio waves.
6) Explain how microwave ovens heat food.
7) What type of radiation is used in optical fibres?
8) Give one use of gamma radiation.
9) True or false? The higher the frequency of EM radiation, the more potentially dangerous it is for humans.

## Exam Questions

**1** **Figure 1** shows an image of the bones in a patient's foot.

   (a) Name a type of EM radiation that could have been used to produce this photograph.

       *[1 mark]*

   (b) State **one** risk to the patient from being exposed to this type of radiation.

       *[1 mark]*

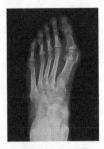
**Figure 1**

**2** An alternating current is passed through a transmitter in order to produce radio waves with a wavelength of 8 km. The radio waves reach a receiver which is connected to a complete electrical circuit.

   (a) Describe the effect of the incoming wave on the receiver and its circuit.

       *[3 marks]*

The receiver is located in a built-up area. A resident is concerned that being exposed to radio waves may cause health problems.

   (b) Explain whether the resident is right to be concerned.

       *[1 mark]*

**3** A patient is suffering with a skin condition called psoriasis. She is offered UVB phototherapy to treat the condition, where she will be exposed to ultraviolet radiation three times a week.

Describe the possible dangers involved with this treatment and any precautions that may be taken to minimise the risk of the patient being harmed by this treatment.

       *[4 marks]*

# EM Radiation and Temperature

*The **hotter** an object is, the **more EM radiation** it emits. And no matter how hot an object is, it will always be **absorbing** radiation from its surroundings as well as **emitting** it.*

## Every Object Absorbs and Emits EM Radiation

1) <u>All objects</u> are <u>continually emitting</u> (radiating) and <u>absorbing</u> EM radiation over a <u>range of wavelengths</u>.

2) The <u>distribution</u> and <u>intensity</u> of these wavelengths <u>only</u> depends on the object's <u>temperature</u>. <u>Intensity</u> is the <u>power per unit area</u> (power is <u>energy transferred per second</u>, p.124).

3) As the <u>temperature</u> of an object <u>increases</u>, the <u>intensity</u> of <u>every emitted wavelength</u> increases.

4) However, the intensity <u>increases more rapidly</u> for <u>shorter wavelengths</u> than longer wavelengths. This causes the <u>peak wavelength</u> (the wavelength with the <u>highest intensity</u>) to <u>decrease</u>.

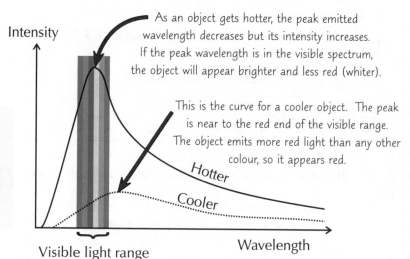

As an object gets hotter, the peak emitted wavelength decreases but its intensity increases. If the peak wavelength is in the visible spectrum, the object will appear brighter and less red (whiter).

This is the curve for a cooler object. The peak is near to the red end of the visible range. The object emits more red light than any other colour, so it appears red.

## Temperature is Constant When Emission Equals Absorption

The <u>rate</u> at which an object <u>absorbs</u> and <u>radiates</u> EM radiation also <u>affects its temperature</u>:

1) If the average power <u>emitted</u> by an object is <u>greater than</u> the average power it <u>absorbs</u>, the object's <u>temperature will fall</u>.

2) If the average power <u>emitted</u> by an object is <u>less than</u> the average power it <u>absorbs</u>, the object's <u>temperature will rise</u>.

3) For an object's temperature to stay <u>constant</u>, the average power it <u>emits</u> must be <u>equal</u> to the average power it <u>absorbs</u>.

The hot chocolate (and the mug) is warmer than the air around it, so the average power it emits is greater than the average power it absorbs. Its temperature will fall.

---

## Peak wavelength decreases as temperature goes up...

The graph above is the key to understanding this rather tricky stuff. Make sure you can <u>sketch</u> it and <u>label</u> it from memory — then practise <u>explaining</u> it to yourself until it's firmly lodged in your brain.

Q1    The peak wavelength of light from the Sun is about 500 nm. The peak wavelength of light from a second star is at about 850 nm. Which star is cooler? Explain your answer. [2 marks]

# Earth and Radiation

*It's lucky for us that the **Sun** is close by (well, about 150 million km away) and transfers energy to us by **EM radiation**. It's also lucky for us that a lot of this energy is **reflected** or **emitted** back into space.*

## Radiation Affects the **Earth's Temperature**

The overall temperature of the Earth depends on the amount of EM radiation it reflects, absorbs and emits.

1) During the day, lots of radiation (including light) is transferred to the Earth from the Sun.

2) Some of this is reflected, but most of it is absorbed. The radiation is reflected and absorbed by the Earth's atmosphere, clouds and surface. This causes an increase in local temperature.

3) At night, radiation is emitted by the atmosphere, clouds and the Earth's surface. This causes a decrease in the local temperature.

4) Overall, the temperature of the Earth stays fairly constant. You can show the flow of radiation for the Earth on a handy diagram.

Some radiation is reflected by the atmosphere, clouds and the Earth's surface.

Some radiation is emitted by the atmosphere.

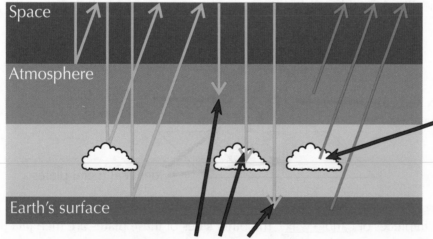

Some of the radiation emitted by the surface is reflected or absorbed (and later emitted) by the clouds.

Some radiation is absorbed by the atmosphere, clouds and the Earth's surface.

5) Changes to the atmosphere can cause a change to the Earth's overall temperature. If the atmosphere starts to absorb more radiation without emitting the same amount, the overall temperature will rise until absorption and emission are equal again.

## Absorbed radiation means a rise in temperature...

Greenhouse gases, such as carbon dioxide, are good absorbers of radiation. That's why adding more of them to the atmosphere causes the Earth's atmosphere to warm up as more radiation is absorbed by the atmosphere and less is emitted back into space. This is the mechanism behind global warming.

# Investigating Emission and Absorption

*On this page you'll find a couple of straightforward **experiments** that you can use to **investigate** how an object's **surface** affects the rate at which it will **emit or absorb** EM radiation.*

## Black Surfaces are Better Emitters than White Ones

PRACTICAL

You can <u>investigate</u> how well <u>different surfaces</u> emit radiation with this simple <u>experiment</u>:

1) Wrap four <u>identical test tubes</u> with material, e.g. paper. The material covering each test tube should be the <u>same</u>, but each one should have a <u>different surface</u> or be a different <u>colour</u>, e.g. <u>black</u> and <u>white</u> paper, <u>glossy</u> and <u>matte</u> paper.

2) <u>Boil</u> water in a kettle and <u>fill</u> each test tube with the <u>same volume</u> of water.

3) Use a <u>thermometer</u> to measure the <u>temperature</u> of the <u>water</u> in the test tubes <u>every minute</u>. <u>Seal</u> the test tubes with <u>bungs</u> between measurements.

The <u>temperature</u> of the <u>water</u> will <u>decrease quicker</u> for the test tubes surrounded by surfaces that are <u>better emitters</u> of radiation. You should find that <u>matte</u> (or <u>dull</u>) surfaces are <u>better</u> emitters than <u>shiny</u> ones and that <u>black</u> surfaces emit radiation <u>better</u> than <u>white</u> ones.

## You Can Investigate Absorption by Melting Wax

PRACTICAL

The amount of infrared radiation <u>absorbed</u> by different materials also depends on their <u>surface</u>. You can do an experiment to show this, using a <u>Bunsen burner</u> and some <u>candle wax</u>.

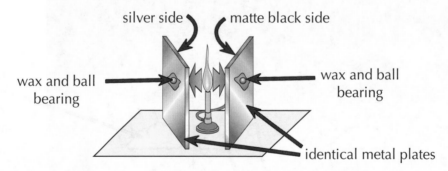

silver side    matte black side

wax and ball bearing    wax and ball bearing

identical metal plates

1) Set up the equipment as shown above. Two <u>ball bearings</u> are each stuck to <u>one side</u> of a <u>metal plate</u> with solid pieces of <u>candle wax</u>. The other sides of these plates are then faced towards the <u>flame</u>. The plates are placed the <u>same distance</u> away from the flame.

2) The sides of the plates that are facing towards the flame each have a different <u>surface colour</u> — one is <u>matt black</u> and the other is <u>silver</u>.

3) The ball bearing on the black plate will <u>fall first</u> as the black surface <u>absorbs more</u> infrared radiation — <u>transferring</u> more energy to the <u>thermal energy store</u> of the wax. This means the wax on the <u>black</u> plate melts <u>before</u> the wax on the <u>silver</u> plate.

---

**PRACTICAL TIP**

## Make sure you work safely during these practicals...

It might sound obvious, but you need to be <u>really careful</u> when handling the <u>hot objects</u> in these practicals. Make sure you use <u>protective gloves</u> when handling hot objects, be careful pouring the <u>boiling water</u> into test tubes and <u>turn off</u> the Bunsen burner when you're not using it.

# Warm-Up & Exam Questions

Now it's time to test how much of this information you've actually absorbed by answering a few questions.

## Warm-Up Questions

1) True or false? As an object's temperature increases, the peak wavelength of the radiation it emits will become shorter.

2) If an object's temperature is constant, what can be said about the average power emitted and absorbed by that object?

3) True or false? Radiation from the Sun can be absorbed by the Earth's atmosphere.

4) Which is a better emitter of radiation, a matte black surface or a shiny white surface?

5) Describe how you could test which of two surfaces absorbs more radiation, using a ball bearing stuck to the other side of each surface with some wax.

## Exam Question

**PRACTICAL**

1    A student is investigating the radiation emitted by different surfaces. They use a cube that is filled with hot water and whose four vertical sides are coated with different surface types (as shown in **Figure 1**). The student records how long it takes the temperature on each thermometer to increase by 5 °C.

(a)  Suggest **one** thing the student should do to make the experiment a fair test.

*[1 mark]*

(b)  In which of the following orders (fastest to slowest) would you expect the thermometers to increase by 5 °C?

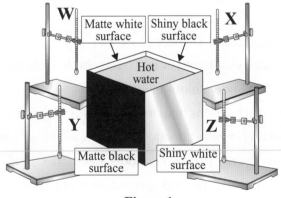

**Figure 1**

  ☐  **A**    W, X, Y, Z

  ☐  **B**    Y, W, X, Z

  ☐  **C**    Z, Y, X, W

  ☐  **D**    X, W, Z, Y

*[1 mark]*

(c)  The water used in the experiment was initially at boiling point, 100 °C.
The experiment is repeated using water at 60 °C.
Predict how this would affect the results. Explain your prediction.

*[2 marks]*

(d)  Each thermometer used measures the temperature to the nearest °C.
Another student suggests that using digital thermometers connected to data loggers to measure the temperatures would improve the investigation.
The digital thermometers measure temperature in °C to two decimal places.
Give **two** reasons why this student is correct.

*[2 marks]*

# Revision Summary for Section 3

Wave goodbye to <u>Section 3</u> — you've finally reached the end. Time to see how much you've learnt.

- Try these questions and <u>tick off each one</u> when you <u>get it right</u>.
- When you're <u>completely happy</u> with a sub-topic, tick it off.

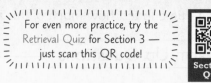

For even more practice, try the Retrieval Quiz for Section 3 — just scan this QR code!

Section 3
Quiz

## Wave Properties (p.56-59) ☑

1) What is the amplitude, wavelength, frequency and period of a wave? ☑
2) Describe the difference between transverse and longitudinal waves and give an example of each. ☑
3) State the equation that relates wave speed, distance and time. ☑
4) Describe an experiment you could do to measure the speed of ripples in water. ☑

## Refraction and Reflection (p.61-64) ☑

5) Explain, in terms of wave speed, what is meant by refraction. ☑
6) Draw a ray diagram for a light ray entering a more optically dense material at an angle to the normal. ☑
7) State why experiments investigating the refraction of light should be conducted in a dim room. ☑
8) What conditions are needed for total internal reflection to occur? ☑
9) Define specular and diffuse reflection. ☑

## Sound and Exploring Structures with Waves (p.66-69) ☑

10) What affects an object's ability to transmit given frequencies of sound? ☑
11) Explain how ultrasound is used in echo sounding. ☑
12) Describe how S-waves and P-waves can be used to explore the structure of the Earth's core. ☑

## Visible Light and Lenses (p.71-75) ☑

13) Explain what happens to white light that hits an opaque white object. ☑
14) Describe how colour filters work. ☑
15) Explain the terms 'real image' and 'virtual image'. ☑
16) Explain how the curvature of a lens affects its power. ☑
17) Draw the ray diagram symbols for a converging lens and a diverging lens. ☑
18) True or false? Diverging lenses always produce real images. ☑

## Uses and Dangers of Electromagnetic Waves (p.77-86) ☑

19) True or false? All electromagnetic waves are transverse. ☑
20) True or false? The human eye can detect all types of EM wave. ☑
21) What kind of current is used to generate radio waves in an antenna? ☑
22) What type of radiation is used in thermal imaging cameras? ☑
23) Give a non-medical use of X-rays. ☑
24) Give one potential danger of X-rays and gamma rays. ☑
25) Describe the average power absorption and radiation for an object that is cooling down. ☑
26) Explain how absorption, reflection and emission of radiation affects the Earth's temperature. ☑

# Developing the Model of the Atom

*We used to think **atoms** were tiny solid spheres (like ball bearings), but they're **much more complex** than that.*

## The Theory of **Atomic Structure** Has **Changed** Over Time

1) In 1897 <u>J. J. Thomson</u> discovered that <u>electrons</u> could be <u>removed</u> from atoms, so atoms must be made up of smaller bits. He suggested the '<u>plum-pudding' model</u> — that atoms were <u>spheres of positive charge</u> with tiny negative electrons <u>stuck in them</u> like fruit in a plum pudding.

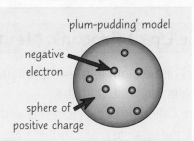
'plum-pudding' model
negative electron
sphere of positive charge

2) That "plum pudding" theory didn't last very long though. In 1909, <u>Rutherford</u> and <u>Marsden</u> tried firing a beam of <u>alpha particles</u> (see p.94) at <u>thin gold foil</u>. From the plum-pudding model, they expected the particles to <u>pass straight through</u> the gold sheet, or only be <u>slightly deflected</u>.

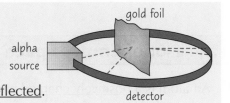
gold foil
alpha source
detector

3) But although most of the particles did go <u>straight through</u> the sheet, some were deflected more than they had expected, and a few were <u>deflected back</u> the way they had come — something the plum-pudding model <u>couldn't explain</u>.

4) Rutherford realised this meant that <u>most of the mass</u> of the atom was concentrated at the <u>centre</u> in a <u>tiny nucleus</u>.

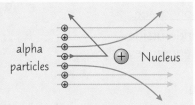
alpha particles
⊕ Nucleus

5) He also realised that most of an atom is just <u>empty space</u>, and that the nucleus must have a <u>positive charge</u>, since it repelled the positive alpha particles.

6) This led to the creation of the <u>nuclear model</u> of the atom (see next page).

7) <u>Niels Bohr</u> tweaked Rutherford's idea a few years later by proposing a model where the electrons were in <u>fixed orbits</u> at <u>set distances</u> from the nucleus. These fixed orbits were called <u>energy levels</u> (p.91).

8) He suggested that electrons can <u>only</u> exist in these fixed orbits (or <u>shells</u>), and not anywhere in between.

9) This is known as the <u>Bohr model</u> and is <u>pretty close</u> to our currently accepted model of the atom.

WORKING SCIENTIFICALLY

## Rutherford's experiment helped adapt the model of the atom...

Rutherford and his lab of scientists made a <u>hypothesis</u>, did an <u>investigation</u> and then <u>analysed</u> the data they got from it. By doing this, they showed that the plum pudding model of the atom must be wrong, so it was <u>changed</u>. This is a great example of the <u>scientific method</u> (see page 2) in action.

# Current Model of the Atom

*Due to lots of scientists doing lots of **experiments**, we now have a better idea of what the atom's really like. We now know about the particles in atoms — **protons**, **neutrons** and **electrons**.*

## The **Current Model** of the Atom

### **Atoms** are Made Up **of Protons, Neutrons** and **Electrons**...

1) The <u>current model</u> of the atom tells us that all atoms are made out of <u>three different particles</u>.
2) These particles are called <u>protons</u>, <u>electrons</u> and <u>neutrons</u>.
3) You need to know the <u>relative mass</u> and <u>relative charge</u> of each of these particles.

| Particle | Relative Mass | Relative Charge |
|----------|---------------|-----------------|
| Proton | 1 | +1 |
| Neutron | 1 | 0 |
| Electron | 0.0005 | −1 |

### ... and a lot of **Empty Space**

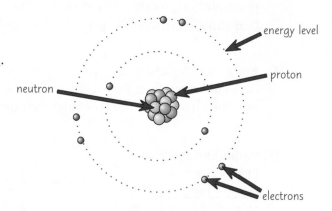

energy level

proton

neutron

electrons

1) An atom is a <u>positively charged nucleus</u> surrounded by <u>negatively charged electrons</u>.
2) Virtually all the <u>mass</u> of the atom is in the <u>nucleus</u>. The nucleus is <u>tiny</u> — about <u>10 000</u> times <u>smaller</u> than the whole atom. It contains <u>protons</u> (which are <u>positively charged</u>) and <u>neutrons</u> (which are <u>neutral</u>). The rest of the atom is mostly <u>empty space</u>.
3) The <u>negative electrons</u> whizz round outside the nucleus in <u>fixed orbits</u> called <u>energy levels</u> or <u>shells</u>. They give the atom its <u>overall size</u> of around $1 \times 10^{-10}$ m.
4) Atoms are <u>neutral</u>, so <u>the number of protons = the number of electrons</u>. This is because <u>protons</u> and <u>electrons</u> have an <u>equal</u> but <u>opposite</u> charge.
5) If an atom <u>loses an electron</u> it becomes a <u>positive ion</u>. If it <u>gains</u> an electron it becomes a <u>negative ion</u> (p.91).
6) Atoms can <u>join together</u> to form <u>molecules</u> — e.g. molecules of <u>oxygen</u> gas are made up of two oxygen atoms bonded together. <u>Small molecules</u> like this have a typical size of $1 \times 10^{-10}$ m — the <u>same sort of scale</u> as an atom.

## Lots of Atomic Quantities use **Standard Form**

The quantities to do with atoms are <u>really tiny</u>, so they're written in <u>standard form</u>:

A is a number between 1 and 10.

$A \times 10^n$

*n* is the number of places the decimal point would move if you wrote the number out in decimal form.

If *n* is positive you know you're dealing with a large number. If *n* is negative you're dealing with a small number.

**MATHS TIP**

## You'll find standard form all over the place...

Physics covers everything from tiny particles to giant stars. That means dealing with some <u>really big numbers</u> and some <u>really small numbers</u>. So, unless you want to spend all day writing zeros you've got to get used to <u>standard form</u>. $1 \times 10^{-10}$ m is a lot easier than writing 0.0000000001 m.

# Electron Energy Levels

*There's some **quirky** stuff on this page — and the best part is that you can tell everyone you've been doing a little **quantum physics** today. Honestly. And if you study physics to a higher level, things get even **quirkier**.*

## Electrons can be Excited to Higher Energy Levels

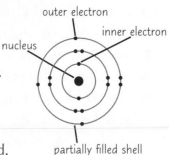

1) <u>Electrons</u> in an atom sit in <u>different energy levels</u> or shells.
2) Each <u>energy level</u> is a different distance from the <u>nucleus</u>.
3) An inner electron can <u>move up</u> to a higher energy level if it <u>absorbs electromagnetic (EM) radiation</u> with the right amount of <u>energy</u>.
4) When it does move up, it moves to an <u>empty</u> or <u>partially filled shell</u> and is said to be '<u>excited</u>'.
5) The electron will then quickly <u>fall back</u> to its <u>original energy level</u>, and in doing so will <u>emit</u> (lose) the <u>same amount</u> of <u>energy</u> it <u>absorbed</u>.
6) The energy is <u>carried away</u> by <u>EM radiation</u>.

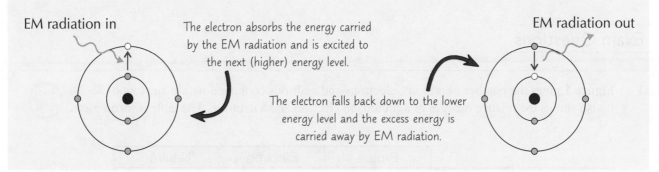

EM radiation in

The electron absorbs the energy carried by the EM radiation and is excited to the next (higher) energy level.

EM radiation out

The electron falls back down to the lower energy level and the excess energy is carried away by EM radiation.

7) The part of the <u>EM spectrum</u> the radiation <u>emitted from the atom</u> is from depends on its <u>energy</u>. This depends on <u>the energy levels</u> the electron moves between. A <u>higher energy</u> means a <u>higher frequency</u> of EM radiation — p.77.

- As you move <u>further out</u> from the nucleus, the energy levels get <u>closer together</u> (so the <u>difference in energy</u> between two levels <u>next to</u> each other gets <u>smaller</u>).
- This means that an <u>excited</u> electron <u>falling</u> from the <u>third</u> energy level to the <u>second</u> would release <u>less energy</u> than an excited electron falling from the <u>second</u> energy level to the <u>first</u>. So the <u>frequency</u> of the generated radiation <u>decreases</u> as you get <u>further</u> from the <u>nucleus</u>.

8) Often, <u>visible light</u> is released when electrons move between energy levels.
9) Changes <u>within the nucleus itself</u> lead to the production of high energy, high frequency <u>gamma rays</u> (p.94).

## An Atom is Ionised if it Loses an Electron

1) If an <u>outer electron</u> absorbs radiation with <u>enough energy</u>, it can move <u>so far</u> that it <u>leaves the atom</u>.

2) It is now a <u>free electron</u> and the atom is said to have been <u>ionised</u>.

3) The atom is now a <u>positive ion</u>. It's <u>positive</u> because there are now <u>more protons</u> than <u>electrons</u>.

4) An atom can lose <u>more than one electron</u>. The <u>more</u> electrons it loses, the <u>greater</u> its positive charge.

# Warm-Up & Exam Questions

Atoms may be tiny, but you could bag some big marks in your exams if you know them inside out.
Here are some questions to check just how great your understanding of atoms really is...

## Warm-Up Questions

1) Describe Thompson's 'plum pudding' model of the atom.
2) What are the relative masses of protons, neutrons and electrons?
3) True or false?  Most of an atom's volume is made up of empty space.
4) In the current model of the atom, where are the protons located?
5) What is the overall charge of an atom?
6) What is the typical size of an atom?
7) True or false?  An atom must gain an electron in order to become a positively charged ion.

## Exam Questions

1    **Figure 1** gives the number of protons, electrons and neutrons contained within an atom of Si-28.
     It also shows the relative charges of a proton, an electron and a neutron.  The table is incomplete.

|  | Proton | Electron | Neutron |
|---|---|---|---|
| Relative Charge | +1 | -1 |  |
| Number Present in Si-28 | 14 |  | 14 |

**Figure 1**

(a)   Complete **Figure 1**.

*[2 marks]*

(b)   Describe how electrons are arranged in the Bohr model of the atom.

*[2 marks]*

An electron in Si-28 absorbs $6.9 \times 10^{-19}$ J of energy and as a result is excited to a higher energy level.
After some time the electron returns to its original energy level by emitting electromagnetic radiation.

(c)   State how much energy is emitted by the electron as it returns to its original energy level.

*[1 mark]*

Now the electron absorbs enough energy to be completely removed from the atom.

(d)   State the relative charge of the silicon ion that is formed as a result.

*[1 mark]*

2    Rutherford investigated the structure of the atom by firing a beam of alpha particles at gold foil.
     Describe the results that Rutherford observed and the conclusions they led him to.

*[4 marks]*

# Isotopes

*Isotopes* of an element look pretty similar, but watch out — they have ***different numbers of neutrons***.

## Atoms of the **Same Element** have the **Same Number** of **Protons**

1) All atoms of each <u>element</u> have a <u>set number</u> of <u>protons</u> (so each nucleus has a given <u>positive charge</u>).

2) The <u>number</u> of protons in an atom is its <u>atomic number</u> or its <u>proton number</u>.

3) The <u>mass (nucleon) number</u> of an atom (the <u>mass</u> of the <u>nucleus</u>) is the <u>number of protons</u> + the <u>number of neutrons</u> in its nucleus.

Example: An oxygen atom has the chemical symbol $^{16}_{8}O$.

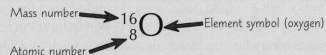

Mass number → 16 O ← Element symbol (oxygen)
8
Atomic number →

- Oxygen has an <u>atomic number</u> of 8. All oxygen atoms have <u>8 protons</u>.
- This atom of oxygen has a <u>mass number</u> of 16.
  Since it has 8 protons, it must have $16 - 8 = $ <u>8 neutrons</u>.

## Isotopes are **Different Forms** of the **Same Element**

1) <u>Isotopes</u> of an element are atoms with the <u>same</u> number of <u>protons</u> (the same <u>atomic number</u>) but a different number of <u>neutrons</u> (a different <u>mass number</u>).

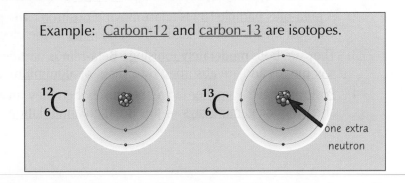

Example: <u>Carbon-12</u> and <u>carbon-13</u> are isotopes.

$^{12}_{6}C$     $^{13}_{6}C$

one extra neutron

2) <u>Isotopes</u> can be written as, e.g., <u>oxygen-18</u>. This means that the <u>mass</u> number is <u>18</u>.

3) <u>All</u> elements have different isotopes, but there are usually only one or two <u>stable</u> ones.

4) The other <u>unstable</u> isotopes tend to <u>decay</u> into <u>other elements</u> and give out <u>radiation</u> as they try to become <u>more stable</u>. This process is called <u>radioactive decay</u>.

5) Radioactive substances <u>spit out</u> one or more types of <u>ionising</u> radiation when they decay: <u>alpha</u>, <u>beta</u> or <u>gamma</u> (see next page). They can also emit <u>neutrons</u> (n).

## Isotopes — Same-same, but different...

<u>Isotopes</u> of an element have lots in common — they have the <u>same number</u> of <u>protons</u> and <u>electrons</u>. What's <u>different</u> is their <u>mass numbers</u> — this is because they have different numbers of <u>neutrons</u>.

# Ionising Radiation

*Alpha, beta and gamma radiation* — *they all come from the nucleus, but they have some **key differences**...*

## Nuclear Radiation Ionises Atoms

1) <u>Ionising radiation</u> is <u>any radiation</u> that can knock electrons from atoms.
2) <u>How likely</u> it is that each type of radiation will ionise an atom <u>varies</u>.

## Alpha Particles are **Helium Nuclei**

1) Alpha radiation is when an <u>alpha particle</u> ($\alpha$) is emitted from the nucleus. An $\alpha$-particle is <u>two neutrons</u> and <u>two protons</u> (like a <u>helium nucleus</u>).
2) They <u>don't</u> penetrate very far into materials and are <u>stopped quickly</u> — they can only travel a <u>few cm in air</u> and are <u>absorbed</u> by a thin sheet of <u>paper</u>.
3) Because of their size they are <u>strongly ionising</u>.

## Beta Particles can be **Electrons** or **Positrons**

1) A <u>beta-minus particle</u> ($\beta^-$) is simply a fast-moving <u>electron</u> released by the nucleus. Beta-minus particles have virtually <u>no mass</u> and a relative charge of –1.
2) A <u>beta-plus particle</u> ($\beta^+$) is a fast-moving <u>positron</u>. The positron is the <u>antiparticle</u> of the electron. This just means it has exactly the same <u>mass</u> as the electron, but a <u>positive (+1) charge</u>.
3) They are both <u>moderately ionising</u>. Beta-minus particles have a <u>range in air</u> of a <u>few metres</u> and are <u>absorbed</u> by a sheet of <u>aluminium</u> (around <u>5 mm</u> thick).
4) <u>Positrons</u> have a <u>smaller</u> range, because when they hit an <u>electron</u> the two <u>destroy</u> each other and produce <u>gamma rays</u> — this is called <u>annihilation</u> and it's used in PET scanning (see p.103).

## Gamma Rays are **EM Waves** with a Short Wavelength

1) After a nucleus has <u>decayed</u>, it often undergoes <u>nuclear rearrangement</u> and releases some energy. <u>Gamma rays</u> ($\gamma$) are waves of <u>EM radiation</u> (p.77) released by the nucleus that carry away this energy.
2) They <u>penetrate far into materials</u> without being stopped and will travel a <u>long distance</u> through <u>air</u>.
3) This means they are <u>weakly</u> ionising because they tend to <u>pass through</u> rather than collide with atoms. Eventually they <u>hit something</u> and do <u>damage</u>.
4) They can be <u>absorbed</u> by thick sheets of <u>lead</u> or metres of <u>concrete</u>.

## Alpha particles are more ionising than beta particles...

... and <u>beta particles</u> are <u>more ionising</u> than <u>gamma rays</u>. Make sure you've got that clearly memorised, as well as what makes up each type of <u>radiation</u>, as this isn't the last you'll see of this stuff. No siree.

# Nuclear Equations

*Nuclear equations* show *radioactive decay* and once you get the hang of them they're *dead easy*. Get going.

## Mass and Atomic Numbers Have to Balance

1) Nuclear equations are a way of showing radioactive decay by using element symbols (p.93).
2) They're written in the form: atom before decay → atom after decay + radiation emitted.
3) There is one golden rule to remember: the total mass and atomic numbers must be equal on both sides.

## Alpha Decay Decreases the Charge and Mass of the Nucleus

When a nucleus emits an alpha particle, it loses two protons and two neutrons, so:

- the mass number decreases by 4.
- the atomic number decreases by 2.

$$^{238}_{92}\text{U} \rightarrow \,^{234}_{90}\text{Th} + \,^{4}_{2}\alpha$$

mass number: $238 \rightarrow 234 + 4 \,(= 238)$
atomic number: $92 \rightarrow 90 + 2 \,(= 92)$

## Beta-minus Decay Increases the Charge of the Nucleus

In a beta-minus decay, a neutron changes into a proton and an electron, so:

- the mass number doesn't change — as it has lost a neutron but gained a proton.
- the atomic number increases by 1 — because it has one more proton.

$$^{14}_{6}\text{C} \rightarrow \,^{14}_{7}\text{N} + \,^{0}_{-1}\beta$$

mass number: $14 \rightarrow 14 + 0 \quad (= 14)$
atomic number: $6 \rightarrow 7 + (-1) \,(= 6)$

## Positron Emission Decreases the Charge of the Nucleus

In beta-plus decay, a proton changes into a neutron and a positron, so:

- the mass number doesn't change — as it has lost a proton but gained a neutron.
- the atomic number decreases by 1 — because it has one less proton.

$$^{18}_{9}\text{F} \rightarrow \,^{18}_{8}\text{O} + \,^{0}_{1}\beta$$

mass number: $18 \rightarrow 18 + 0 \quad (= 18)$
atomic number: $9 \rightarrow 8 + 1 \quad (= 9)$

## Neutron Emission Decreases the Mass of the Nucleus

When a nucleus emits a neutron:

- the mass number decreases by 1 — as it has lost a neutron.
- the atomic number stays the same.

$$^{13}_{4}\text{Be} \rightarrow \,^{12}_{4}\text{Be} + \,^{1}_{0}\text{n}$$

mass number: $13 \rightarrow 12 + 1 \quad (= 13)$
atomic number: $4 \rightarrow 4 + 0 \quad (= 4)$

## Gamma Rays Don't Change the Charge or Mass of the Nucleus

1) Gamma rays (γ) are a way of getting rid of excess energy from an atom. The nucleus goes from an excited state to a more stable state by emitting a gamma ray.
2) The mass and atomic numbers stay the same after a gamma ray has been emitted.

---

## Make sure your equations are balanced on both sides...

Nuclear equations look intimidating, but they're quite straightforward once you get the hang of them.

Q1    Write the nuclear equation for $^{219}_{86}\text{Rn}$ forming polonium (Po) by alpha decay.    [3 marks]

Q1 Video Solution

# Warm-Up & Exam Questions

Knowing different kinds of radiation and what can absorb them could bag you easy marks in an exam.
Here are a few questions so you can show off all you've learnt about ionising radiation...

## Warm-Up Questions

1) An atom of sodium has a mass number of 23 and an atomic number of 11.
   How many neutrons does it have?

2) True or false? Isotopes of an element have different atomic numbers.

3) What is meant by the term 'ionising radiation'?

4) Which type of ionising radiation has the greatest mass: alpha, beta or gamma?

5) True or false? A 5 mm sheet of aluminium will completely block gamma rays.

6) An atom undergoes a single beta-plus decay. What is the change in its atomic number?

7) An atom of Ar-40 undergoes gamma decay. What is the mass number of the resulting nucleus?

## Exam Questions

1   Alpha, beta and gamma radiation sources were used to direct radiation at thin
    sheets of paper and aluminium. A detector was used to measure where radiation
    had passed through the sheets. The results are shown in **Figure 1**.

    **Grade 4-6**

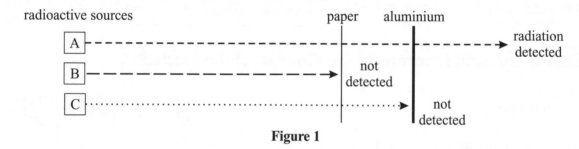

**Figure 1**

Name the type of radiation that source C emits. Explain your answer.

*[2 marks]*

2   **Figure 2** contains information
    about three atoms.

    **Grade 6-7**

| | Mass number | Atomic number |
|---|---|---|
| **Atom A** | 32 | 17 |
| **Atom B** | 33 | 17 |
| **Atom C** | 32 | 16 |

**Figure 2**

(a) Define the term 'mass number'
    in the context of atoms.

    *[1 mark]*

(b) State and explain which two atoms in **Figure 2** are isotopes of the same element.

*[2 marks]*

(c) Plutonium-219 decays by alpha emission to form an
    isotope of uranium. **Figure 3** shows an incomplete
    nuclear equation for this decay.

    $$^{239}_{94}\text{Pu} \rightarrow {}^{235}_{X}\text{U} + {}^{4}_{2}\alpha$$

    **Figure 3**

    Determine the atomic number, $X$, of the uranium atom.

*[1 mark]*

# Background Radiation and Activity

*Forget love — **radiation** is **all around**. Don't panic too much though — it's usually a pretty **small amount**.*

## Background Radiation Comes from Many Sources

Background radiation is the low-level radiation that's around us all the time. It comes from:

1) Radioactivity of naturally occurring unstable isotopes which are all around us — in the air, in some foods, in building materials and in some of the rocks under our feet.

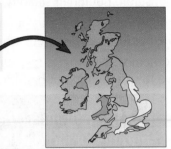

Coloured bits indicate more radiation from rocks.

2) Radiation from space, which is known as cosmic rays. These come mostly from the Sun. Luckily, the Earth's atmosphere protects us from much of this radiation.

3) Radiation due to human activity, e.g. fallout from nuclear explosions or radiation from nuclear waste. But this represents a tiny proportion of the total background radiation.

## Radioactivity is a Totally Random Process

1) Radioactive sources contain radioactive isotopes that give out radiation from the nuclei of their atoms.

2) This process is entirely random. This means that if you have 1000 unstable nuclei, you can't say when any one of them is going to decay, or which one will decay next.

3) If there are lots of nuclei though, you can predict how many will have decayed in a given time based on the half-life of the source (see next page). The rate at which a source decays is called its activity.

4) Activity is measured in becquerels, Bq. 1 Bq is 1 decay per second.

5) Activity can be measured with a Geiger-Müller tube, which clicks each time it detects radiation. The tube can be attached to a counter, which displays the number of clicks per second (the count-rate).

6) You can also detect radiation using photographic film. The more radiation the film's exposed to, the darker it becomes (just like when you expose it to light).

## Your exposure to background radiation depends on where you live...

Background radiation comes from many sources, from food and drink to cosmic rays, but mostly it comes from the ground and is given out by certain rocks, like granite. That's why some parts of the UK have higher levels of background radiation than others. Areas like Cornwall and Devon, where there's lots of granite, have higher background radiation levels than is average for the UK. But they do have lovely beaches.

# Half-Life

*How quickly **unstable nuclei** decay is measured using **activity** and **half-life** — two very important terms.*

## The **Radioactivity** of a Source **Decreases Over Time**

1) Each time a radioactive nucleus <u>decays</u>, that radioactive nucleus <u>disappears</u>.
   As the <u>unstable nuclei</u> all steadily disappear, the activity <u>as a whole</u> will <u>decrease</u>.

2) For <u>some</u> isotopes it takes <u>just a few hours</u> before nearly all the
   unstable nuclei have <u>decayed</u>, whilst others last for <u>millions of years</u>.

3) The problem with trying to <u>measure</u> this is that <u>the activity never reaches zero</u>, so
   we have to use the idea of <u>half-life</u> to measure how quickly the activity <u>drops off</u>.

> The <u>half-life</u> is the <u>average</u> time taken for the
> <u>number of radioactive nuclei</u> of an isotope to <u>halve</u>.

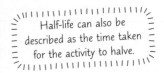
Half-life can also be described as the time taken for the activity to halve.

4) A <u>short half-life</u> means the <u>activity falls quickly</u>, because the nuclei are very <u>unstable</u> and <u>rapidly decay</u>.

5) Sources with a short half-life are <u>dangerous</u> because of the <u>high</u> amount
   of radiation they emit at the start, but they <u>quickly</u> become <u>safe</u>.

6) A <u>long half-life</u> means the activity <u>falls more slowly</u> because <u>most</u> of the nuclei don't decay
   <u>for a long time</u> — the source just sits there, releasing <u>small</u> amounts of radiation for a <u>long time</u>.

7) This can be dangerous because <u>nearby areas</u> are <u>exposed</u> to radiation for <u>(millions of)</u> <u>years</u>.

**EXAMPLE**

**The activity of a radioactive sample is measured as 640 Bq.
Two hours later it has fallen to 40 Bq. Find its half-life.**

1) Count how many half-lives it took to fall to 40 Bq.

   Initial activity:  after 1 half-life:  after 2 half-lives:  after 3 half-lives:  after 4 half-lives:
   640  $(\div 2) \rightarrow$  320  $(\div 2) \rightarrow$  160  $(\div 2) \rightarrow$  80  $(\div 2) \rightarrow$  40

2) Calculate the half-life of the sample.

   Two hours is four half-lives — so the half-life is 2 hours ÷ 4 = 30 min

## Finding the **Half-Life** of a Sample using a **Graph**

1) If you plot a graph of <u>activity</u>
   <u>against time</u> (taking into account
   <u>background radiation</u>, see
   previous page), it will <u>always</u>
   be shaped like this one.

2) The <u>half-life</u> is found from
   the graph by finding the
   <u>time interval</u> on the <u>bottom axis</u>
   corresponding to a <u>halving</u> of
   the <u>activity</u> on the <u>vertical axis</u>.

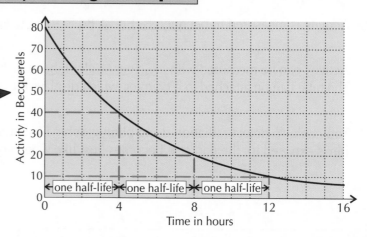

## Isotopes with short half-lives decay quickly...

<u>Half-life</u> — the average time for the number of radioactive nuclei or the activity to <u>halve</u>. Simple.

Q1  The initial activity of a sample is 40 Bq. Show that the ratio of
    its final activity to its initial activity is 1:8 after three half-lives.

[3 marks]

Q1 Video Solution

# Dangers of Radiation

*Ionising radiation can be **dangerous** stuff — it all depends on **how much** you're exposed to and for **how long**.*

## Radiation **Damages** Cells by **Ionisation**

1) Radiation can <u>enter living cells</u> and <u>ionise atoms and molecules</u> within them. This can lead to <u>tissue damage</u>.

2) <u>Lower doses</u> tend to cause <u>minor damage</u> without <u>killing</u> the cells. This can give rise to <u>mutant cells</u> which <u>divide uncontrollably</u>. This is <u>cancer</u>.

3) <u>Higher doses</u> tend to <u>kill cells completely</u>, causing <u>radiation sickness</u> (leading to vomiting, tiredness and hair loss) if a lot of cells <u>all get affected at once</u>.

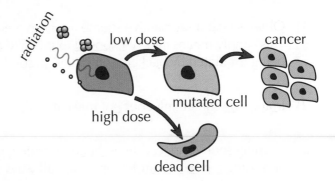

## How **Hazardous** a Radioactive **Source is** Depends on its **Half-Life**

1) The <u>lower</u> the <u>activity</u> (see p.97) of a <u>radioactive source</u>, the <u>safer</u> it is to be around.

- If two sources that produce the <u>same type</u> of radiation start off with the <u>same activity</u>, the one with the <u>longer</u> half-life will be <u>more dangerous</u>.
- This is because, after <u>any period</u> of time, the activity of the source with the <u>shorter half-life</u> will have <u>fallen more</u> than the activity of the source with the <u>longer half-life</u>.

- If the two sources have <u>different initial activities</u>, the danger associated with them changes over time.
- Even if its <u>initial activity</u> is lower (so it is <u>initially safer</u>), the source with the <u>longer half-life</u> will be <u>more dangerous</u> after a certain period of time because its <u>activity</u> falls <u>more slowly</u>.

2) When choosing a radioactive source for an application, it's important to find a <u>balance</u> between a source that has the <u>right level of activity</u> for the right amount of <u>time</u>, and that isn't <u>too dangerous</u> for too long.

3) <u>Careful planning</u> of <u>storage</u> and <u>disposal</u> of sources is needed, especially for sources with <u>long half-lives</u>.

## Ignoring the risks of radiation is a dangerous omission...

Whenever <u>ionising radiation</u> is in the picture, there is a <u>risk</u> of harm. This risk depends on <u>how much radiation</u> is emitted, the <u>activity</u> of the radiation, the <u>type</u> of radiation and the <u>safety precautions</u> put in place (see next page). So it's really important that if people are going to be exposed to ionising radiation that the level of risk is carefully assessed.

# Irradiation and Contamination

*Radioactive contamination comes about from **touching** and **handling** radioactive substances, whereas **irradiation** can result from just being near a source.*

## Exposure to Radiation is called Irradiation

1) Objects <u>near</u> a radioactive source are <u>irradiated</u> by it. This simply means they're <u>exposed</u> to it (we're <u>always</u> being irradiated by <u>background radiation</u> sources).

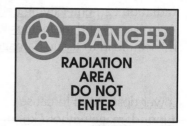

2) <u>Irradiating</u> something does <u>not</u> make it <u>radioactive</u>.

3) Keeping sources in <u>lead-lined boxes</u>, standing behind <u>barriers</u> or being in a <u>different room</u> and using <u>remote-controlled arms</u> are all ways of reducing the effects of <u>irradiation</u>.

4) <u>Medical</u> staff who work with radiation wear <u>photographic film badges</u> to <u>monitor</u> their exposure.

## Contamination is Radioactive Particles Getting onto Objects

1) If <u>unwanted radioactive atoms</u> get onto an object, the object is said to be <u>contaminated</u>. E.g. if you <u>touch</u> a radioactive source without wearing <u>gloves</u>, your hands would be <u>contaminated</u>.

2) These <u>contaminating atoms</u> might then decay, releasing <u>radiation</u> which could cause you <u>harm</u>.

3) Contamination is especially dangerous because radioactive particles could get <u>inside your body</u>.

4) Once a person is <u>contaminated</u>, they are at <u>risk of harm</u> until either the contamination is <u>removed</u> (which isn't always possible) or <u>all</u> the radioactive atoms have <u>decayed</u>.

5) <u>Gloves</u> and <u>tongs</u> should be used when handling sources, to avoid particles getting stuck to your <u>skin</u> or <u>under your nails</u>.

6) Some industrial workers wear <u>protective suits</u> to stop them <u>breathing in</u> particles.

## Risk of Irradiation and Contamination Depends on the Radiation

1) Outside the body, <u>beta</u> and <u>gamma</u> radiation are the most dangerous, because they can penetrate the body and get to the delicate <u>organs</u>. Alpha is <u>less</u> dangerous, because it <u>can't penetrate the skin</u>.

2) <u>Inside the body</u>, <u>alpha</u> sources are the most dangerous. Alpha particles are <u>strongly ionising</u>, so they do all their damage in a <u>very localised area</u>. That means <u>contamination</u>, rather than <u>irradiation</u>, is the major concern when working with alpha sources.

# Warm-Up & Exam Questions

High activity is dangerous? Time for a rest then... But only a short one — because here's
a shiny new set of questions about radiation for you to wrap your brain around.

## Warm-Up Questions

1) Give three sources of background radiation.
2) What does it mean if a radioactive source is said to have an activity of 1 becquerel?
3) Give an example of a detector that could be used to detect radiation.
4) A radioactive source has a half-life of three days.
   How long would it take for the source's activity to decrease by a factor of four?
5) What is the difference between radioactive contamination and irradiation?
6) Explain why you should wear gloves when handling radioactive materials.
7) Why is contamination by an alpha source more dangerous
   to humans than irradiation by an alpha source?

## Exam Questions

1   Two different radioactive sources are being considered for use in a medical treatment.
    Their safety needs to be assessed.

    (a)   Give **two** possible effects of being exposed to a dose of ionising radiation.

    [2 marks]

    Both sources are beta-plus emitters.
    Source A has a half-life of four hours.  Source B has a half-life of 6 days.

    (b)   Explain which of the sources presents a greater danger to staff and patients.

    [1 mark]

    (c)   Suggest **one** precaution the hospital should take when storing radioactive substances.

    [1 mark]

2   A radioactive sample has a half-life of 40 seconds.
    The initial activity of the sample is 8000 Bq.

    (a)   Calculate the activity after 2 minutes.  Give your answer in becquerels.

    [2 marks]

    (b)   Determine the number of half-lives it would take for the activity to fall to 250 Bq.

    [2 marks]

    (c)   The radioactive source is left until its activity falls to 100 Bq.
          Calculate the final activity as a percentage of the initial activity.

    [2 marks]

# Uses of Nuclear Radiation

*Despite its dangers, **radiation** can be pretty useful. We use it in our **homes**, in **medicine** and in **industry**.*

## Household **Fire Alarms** Use **Alpha Radiation**

1) A <u>weak</u> source of alpha radiation (p.94) is placed in a smoke detector, close to <u>two electrodes</u>.
2) The source causes <u>ionisation</u>, and a <u>current</u> of charged particles flows.
3) If there is a fire then smoke will <u>absorb</u> the charged particles — the current falls and the <u>alarm sounds</u>.

## **Food** and **Equipment** can be **Sterilised** Using **Gamma Rays**

1) <u>Food</u> can be <u>irradiated</u> (p.100) with a <u>high dose</u> of <u>gamma rays</u> which will <u>kill</u> all <u>microbes</u>. This means that the food doesn't go bad as quickly as it would do otherwise.

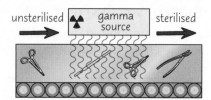

2) Similarly, <u>medical equipment</u> can be <u>sterilised</u> using gamma rays instead of being <u>boiled</u>.
3) <u>Irradiation</u> is a particularly good method of sterilisation because, unlike boiling, it doesn't involve <u>high temperatures</u>, so <u>fresh fruit</u> or <u>plastic instruments</u> can be totally <u>sterilised</u> without being <u>damaged</u>.
4) The radioactive source used for this needs to be a <u>very strong</u> emitter of <u>gamma rays</u> with a <u>reasonably long half-life</u> (at least several months) so that it doesn't need <u>replacing</u> too often.

## **Radiation** is Used in **Tracers** and **Thickness Gauges**

1) Certain radioactive isotopes can be used as <u>tracers</u>. A <u>medical</u> tracer is <u>injected</u> into a patient (or <u>swallowed</u>) and its progress around the body is followed using an <u>external detector</u>. This method can be used to <u>detect</u> and <u>diagnose medical conditions</u> (e.g. cancer).

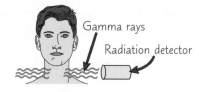

2) <u>All isotopes</u> which are taken <u>into the body</u> must be <u>beta or gamma</u> emitters (never alpha). This is because beta and gamma particles are able to <u>pass out of the body</u> and reach the detector. They're also <u>weakly ionising</u> enough to not do too much <u>damage</u>. They should only last <u>a few hours</u>, so that the radioactivity inside the patient <u>quickly</u> <u>disappears</u> (i.e. they should have a <u>short half-life</u>).
3) <u>Gamma emitting tracers</u> are also used in <u>industry</u> to detect <u>leaks</u> in <u>underground pipes</u>.
4) <u>Beta radiation</u> is used in <u>thickness control</u>. You direct radiation <u>through</u> the product being made (e.g. paper), and put a <u>detector</u> on the <u>other side</u>, connected to a control unit. When the amount of <u>detected</u> radiation <u>changes</u>, it means the paper is coming out <u>too thick</u> or <u>too thin</u>, so the control unit <u>adjusts</u> the rollers to give the correct thickness.

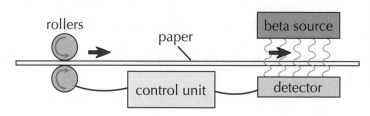

---

## Each type of radiation has its own uses...

Before you move on, make sure you can <u>describe why</u> different types of radiation have different uses.

Q1 In order to sterilise medical equipment, radiation is directed at the equipment while it is sealed in packaging. Explain whether alpha radiation would be suitable for this use. [2 marks]

# PET Scanning

*And the **uses** keep on coming — we use radiation in lots of **medical** scanners like the **PET** scanner.*

## PET Scanning Can Help **Diagnose Illnesses**

1) Positron emission tomography or PET scanning is a technique used to show tissue or organ function, and it can be used to diagnose medical conditions.

2) For example, it can identify active tumours by showing metabolic activity in tissue.

3) Cancer cells have a much higher metabolism than healthy cells because they're growing like mad. And here's how it all works:

1) Inject the patient with a substance used by the body, e.g. glucose, containing a positron-emitting radioactive isotope with a short half-life so it acts as a tracer, e.g. $^{11}$C, $^{13}$N, $^{15}$O or $^{18}$F. Over an hour or so the tracer moves through the body to the organs.

2) Positrons (see page 94) emitted by the isotope meet electrons in an organ and annihilate, emitting high-energy gamma rays in opposite directions.

3) Detectors around the body detect pairs of gamma rays — the tumour will lie along the same path as each pair. By detecting at least three pairs from the tumour, the location of the tumour can be found by triangulation.

4) The distribution of radioactivity matches up with metabolic activity. This is because more of the radioactive glucose (or whatever) injected into the patient is taken up and used by cells that are doing more work (cells with an increased metabolism, in other words).

5) The isotopes used in PET scanning have short half-lives, so it's important that they're made close to where they'll be used. Some hospitals have their own cyclotron to make the isotopes on-site.

6) Otherwise, if the isotopes had to be transported over a large distance, their activity could be too low by the time they arrived at the hospital, making them no longer as useful.

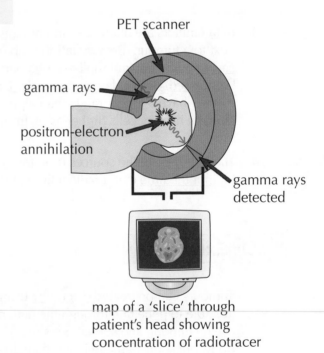

PET scanner

gamma rays

positron-electron annihilation

gamma rays detected

map of a 'slice' through patient's head showing concentration of radiotracer

## Welcome to the high-tech world of PET...

PET is definitely a really tricky topic to get your head around. One important point to remember is that the gamma rays the scanner detects are not directly emitted by the radioactive isotope. The isotope actually emits a positron which goes on to annihilate, producing the gamma rays.

# Radiotherapy

*Radiotherapy* harnesses the harmful nature of ionising **radiation** and turns it on **cancer cells**.

## Radiation can be Used to **Treat Cancer**

Targeted doses of radiation can be used to kill cancer cells. Treatment that exposes patients to radiation is known as radiotherapy. Radiotherapy treatments may be delivered either internally or externally.

## Radiation can be delivered **Internally...**

1) With internal radiation therapy, a radioactive material is placed inside the body into or near a tumour. This can be done in many ways, e.g. by injecting or implanting a small amount of radioactive substance.

2) Alpha emitters are usually injected near to the tumour. As alpha particles are strongly ionising, they do lots of damage to the nearby area (the cancerous cells), but the damage to normal tissue surrounding the tumour is limited because they have such a short range.

3) Beta emitters are often used in implants, placed inside or next to a tumour. Beta radiation is able to penetrate the casing of the implant (unlike alpha particles, which would be stopped) before damaging nearby cancerous cells. As they have a longer range than alpha particles, they can damage healthy cells further away from the cancerous cells.

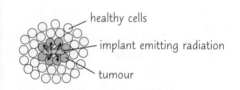

healthy cells

implant emitting radiation

tumour

4) The half-lives of the sources used for internal treatments are usually short, to limit the time that a radioactive substance is inside the patient's body.

## ...Or **Externally**

1) Tumours can be treated externally using gamma rays aimed at the tumour, as these are able to penetrate through the patient's body. The radiation is carefully focused on the tumour, and sometimes shielding is placed on other areas of the patient's body, but some damage is still done to surrounding healthy cells.

High dose of radiation directed at cancer cells only.
Ionisation causes lots of damage to the cells.

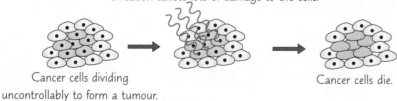

Cancer cells dividing uncontrollably to form a tumour.

Cancer cells die.

2) The sources used in external radiotherapy treatments should have long half-lives, so they don't have to be replaced often.

3) The machines used for radiotherapy are often surrounded by shielding and kept in a designated room to reduce the risk to staff and patients in the hospital.

# Warm-Up & Exam Questions

Radiation has pros and cons, and one of its downsides is that you need to know about it for your exam. So have a go at the practice exam questions below to see if you're radiating radiation knowledge.

## Warm-Up Questions

1) Which type of radiation is used in household fire alarms?
2) What radiation is used to sterilise food?
3) Give another example of radiation being used to sterilise objects.
4) Explain why alpha radiation would not be suitable for use as a medical tracer.
5) Why do isotopes used in PET scans have to be made nearby?
6) Give one method of delivering a dose of internal radiation for the treatment of cancer.
7) Why is alpha radiation not used for external radiation therapy?

## Exam Questions

1    A source of beta-minus radiation is used in controlling
     the thickness of aluminium foil during the production process.
     The source is placed on one side of the foil, whilst a detector is placed on the other.

   (a)   Suggest what would happen to the count-rate measured
         by the detector if the foil were to increase in thickness.

                                                                                  *[1 mark]*

   (b)   Explain why gamma radiation would be unsuitable for this task.

                                                                                  *[2 marks]*

   (c)   Give an application of gamma radiation.

                                                                                  *[1 mark]*

2    **Figure 1** shows the properties of three radioactive isotopes.

| Isotope | Half-life | Type of emission |
|---|---|---|
| technetium-99m | 6 hours | gamma |
| phosphorus-32 | 14 days | beta |
| cobalt-60 | 5 years | beta/gamma |

**Figure 1**

State which of these would be best to use as a medical tracer.  Explain your answer.

                                                                                  *[3 marks]*

3    Cancer cells use more glucose than healthy,
     non-cancerous cells.  **Figure 2** shows a patient
     having a PET scan who has been injected with
     glucose that contains positron-emitting isotopes.

     Describe how the PET scan uses the radioactive
     glucose as a tracer to locate tumours.

                                              *[4 marks]*
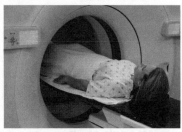

**Figure 2**

# Nuclear Fission

*It's amazing how much **energy** there is **trapped** in a tiny atom. This energy can be released by **nuclear fission**.*

## Nuclear Fission — the **Splitting Up** of Big Atomic Nuclei

Nuclear fission is a type of nuclear reaction that is used to release energy from uranium (or plutonium) atoms, e.g. in a nuclear reactor. Huge amounts of energy can be released this way by using a chain reaction...

## The **Chain Reaction**:

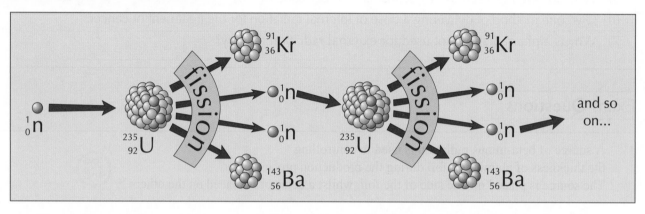

1) A slow-moving neutron is fired at a large, unstable nucleus — often uranium-235. The neutron is absorbed by the nucleus — this makes the atom more unstable and causes it to split.

2) When the U-235 atom splits it forms two new lighter elements ('daughter nuclei') and energy is released.

3) There are lots of different pairs of atoms that uranium can split into, e.g. krypton-91 and barium-143, but all these new nuclei are radioactive.

4) Each time a uranium atom splits up, it also spits out two or more neutrons, which can hit other uranium nuclei, causing them to split also, and so on and so on. This is a chain reaction.

*A neutron can be absorbed by the nucleus because it has no charge — i.e. it's not repelled by the positive charge of the nucleus.*

## Chain Reactions in Reactors Must be **Carefully Controlled**

1) The neutrons released by fission reactions in a nuclear reactor have a lot of energy.

2) These neutrons will only cause other nuclear fissions (and cause a chain reaction) if they are moving slowly enough to be captured by the uranium nuclei in the fuel rods.

3) Such slow-moving neutrons are called thermal neutrons.

4) To produce thermal neutrons, the uranium fuel rods are placed in a moderator (for example, graphite) to slow down the fast-moving neutrons.

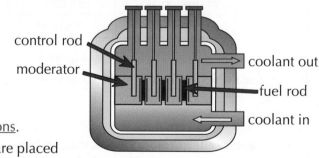

5) Control rods, often made of boron, limit the rate of fission by absorbing excess neutrons. They are placed in between the fuel rods and are raised and lowered into the reactor to control the chain reaction.

6) This creates a steady rate of nuclear fission, where each fission produces another fission.

7) If the chain reaction in a nuclear reactor is left to continue unchecked, large amounts of energy can be released in a very short time. Many new fissions will follow each fission, causing a runaway reaction which could lead to a meltdown.

# Nuclear Fusion

*If you bring **two small nuclei** very close together they will **combine** to form a single, heavier nucleus. This process releases a **lot of energy**. Sounds great, but the reality is a little more complicated. Read on...*

## Nuclear **Fusion — Joining Small Nuclei**

1) <u>Nuclear fusion</u> is the opposite of nuclear fission. In nuclear fusion, two <u>light nuclei collide</u> at high speed and <u>join</u> (fuse) to create a <u>larger</u>, heavier nucleus. For example, <u>hydrogen</u> nuclei can fuse to produce a <u>helium nucleus</u>.

2) This <u>heavier</u> nucleus does not have as much <u>mass</u> as the two <u>separate</u>, light nuclei did. Some of the mass of the lighter nuclei is converted to <u>energy</u> (<u>don't panic</u>, you don't need to know <u>how</u>) and <u>released</u>.

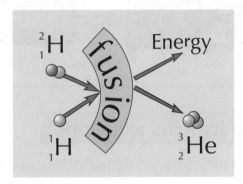

3) Nuclear fusion is the <u>energy source</u> of <u>stars</u> (p.114).

## Fusion Only Happens at **High Temperatures** and **Pressures**

1) The <u>big problem</u> is that fusion only happens at <u>really high pressures and temperatures</u> (about <u>10 000 000 °C</u>). This is because the <u>positively charged</u> nuclei have to get <u>very close</u> to fuse, so the large <u>force</u> due to <u>electrostatic repulsion</u> (p.153) has to be overcome.

2) It's <u>really hard</u> to create the <u>right conditions</u> for fusion. <u>No material</u> can withstand that kind of temperature — it would just be <u>vaporised</u>. So fusion reactors are <u>really hard</u> and <u>expensive</u> to try to build.

3) There are a few <u>experimental</u> reactors around at the moment, but none of them are generating electricity yet. It takes <u>more</u> power to get up to temperature than the reactors can produce.

## Why do we even bother?

Building a working <u>fusion</u> reactor is a real headache. It's <u>expensive</u>, <u>difficult</u> and no one's got it quite right yet. So what's the point? Well, apart from a tonne of <u>energy</u>, all a fusion reactor would produce is <u>helium</u>, which is <u>neither radioactive nor a greenhouse gas</u> — some people believe this could solve the <u>current energy crisis</u>.

# Nuclear Power

*Nuclear* power has a bit of a **scary reputation**, but going nuclear does have some **advantages**...

## Nuclear Power Stations are Really Glorified Steam Engines

1) Nuclear power stations are powered by <u>nuclear reactors</u> that create controlled chain reactions.

2) The <u>energy</u> released by <u>fission</u> is transferred to the <u>thermal</u> energy store of the <u>moderator</u>. This is then transferred to the <u>thermal</u> energy store of the <u>coolant</u>, and then to the <u>thermal energy store</u> of the <u>cold water</u> passing through the <u>boiler</u>. This causes the water to <u>boil</u> and energy to be transferred to the <u>kinetic</u> energy store of the <u>steam</u>.

3) This energy is then <u>transferred</u> to the <u>kinetic</u> energy store of a <u>turbine</u> and then to the <u>kinetic</u> energy store of a <u>generator</u>. The energy is then <u>transferred away</u> from the generator <u>electrically</u>.

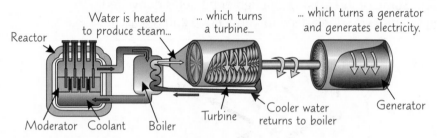

Reactor — Water is heated to produce steam... — ... which turns a turbine... — ... which turns a generator and generates electricity.

Moderator — Coolant — Boiler — Turbine — Cooler water returns to boiler — Generator

## Using Nuclear Power Has Its Pros and Cons

Nuclear power has a lot going for it, but some people are completely against it being used.

1) <u>Public perception</u> of nuclear power can be <u>very negative</u> — it's seen by many to be <u>very dangerous</u>.

2) Some people worry that nuclear waste can <u>never be disposed of safely</u>. The waste products from nuclear fission have <u>very long half-lives</u>, meaning they'll be <u>radioactive</u> for <u>hundreds</u> or <u>thousands</u> (even millions) of <u>years</u>. There is always a danger that they could <u>leak out</u> and <u>pollute</u> land, rivers and oceans.

3) <u>Nuclear power</u> also carries the risk of <u>leaks</u> directly from the power station or a <u>major catastrophe</u> like those at <u>Chernobyl</u> and <u>Fukushima</u>.

4) However, nuclear power is generally a <u>pretty safe</u> way of generating electricity — it's not as <u>risky</u> as <u>some people may think</u> it is.

5) And it's not all doom and gloom. Nuclear power is a <u>very reliable</u> energy resource and reduces the need for fossil fuels (which are already running low — see p.50).

6) <u>Fossil fuels</u> (coal, oil and gas) all release carbon dioxide ($CO_2$) when they're burnt. This adds to the <u>greenhouse effect</u> and <u>global warming</u>. Burning coal and oil also releases <u>sulfur dioxide</u> that can cause <u>acid rain</u>. Nuclear fission <u>doesn't</u> release these gases, so in this way it is a very <u>clean</u> source of energy.

7) <u>Huge</u> amounts of energy can be generated from a relatively <u>small</u> amount of <u>nuclear material</u>. Nuclear <u>fuel</u> (i.e. the uranium) is <u>cheap</u> and <u>readily available</u>.

8) However, the <u>overall cost</u> of nuclear power is <u>high</u> due to the initial cost of the <u>power plant</u> and final <u>decommissioning</u> — dismantling a nuclear plant safely takes <u>decades</u>.

# Warm-Up & Exam Questions

Nuclear power — it's not always popular, despite having some great benefits.  Sounds similar to revision.
Have a go at these questions and see how much has stuck.

## Warm-Up Questions

1) True or false?  Nuclear fission is the process of releasing energy by splitting a large nucleus.
2) What happens when a uranium-235 nucleus absorbs a slow-moving neutron?
3) What are daughter nuclei in a fission reaction?
4) What is the role of the moderator in a nuclear reactor?
5) True or false?  Nuclear fission is the energy source of stars.
6) Why are fusion reactors so difficult to build?
7) Describe the energy transfers that take place in a nuclear power station.
8) Give one advantage of nuclear power when compared to fossil fuels.

## Exam Questions

**1** Nuclear reactors often use uranium-235 as fuel.  (Grade 4-6)

 (a) Describe the steps involved in a chain reaction of uranium-235.

*[3 marks]*

 (b) In a nuclear reactor, control rods are used to control the reaction.
 State what could happen if the nuclear reaction is not controlled.

*[1 mark]*

 (c) Give **two** disadvantages of using nuclear power.

*[2 marks]*

**2** When two small nuclei fuse, energy is released.  (Grade 4-6)

 (a) Which of the following statements is true for a fusion reaction?

 ☐ **A** The combined mass of the reacting nuclei is less than the mass of the product.

 ☐ **B** The combined mass of the reacting nuclei is equal to the mass of the product.

 ☐ **C** The combined mass of the reacting nuclei is more than the mass of the product.

 ☐ **D** The reacting nuclei and the product have no mass.

*[1 mark]*

 (b) Fusion will only take place under conditions of extremely high temperature and pressure.
 Explain why these conditions are necessary.

*[2 marks]*

 (c) Explain why nuclear fusion is not currently used as a commercial energy resource.

*[1 mark]*

# Revision Summary for Section 4

That's the end of <u>Section 4</u> — hopefully it wasn't too painful. Time to see how much you've absorbed.

- Try these questions and <u>tick off each one</u> when you <u>get it right</u>.
- When you're <u>completely happy</u> with a sub-topic, tick it off.

For even more practice, try the Retrieval Quiz for Section 4 — just scan this QR code!

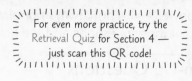

Section 4 Quiz

## The Atomic Model (p.89-91) ☑

1) Briefly describe how the model of an atom has changed over time. ☑
2) Describe the experiment that confirmed the existence of a small positively charged nucleus. ☑
3) Which has the lowest mass: a proton, an electron or a neutron? ☑
4) Draw a sketch to show our currently accepted model of the atom. ☑
5) True or false? Most of an atom's mass is contained within its nucleus. ☑
6) Describe the process of an electron moving to a higher energy level. ☑
7) What happens to an atom if it loses one or more of its outer electrons? ☑

## Isotopes and Nuclear Decay (p.93-95) ☑

8) What is the atomic number of an atom? ☑
9) Which number defines what element an atom is: the atomic number or the mass number? ☑
10) How do isotopes of the same element differ? ☑
11) Name four things that may be emitted during radioactive decay. ☑
12) For alpha, beta and gamma radiation, give: a) their ionising power, b) their range in air. ☑
13) Which type of radiation has the same structure as a helium nucleus? ☑
14) What type of nuclear decay doesn't change the mass or charge of the nucleus? ☑

## Half-life and the Dangers of Radiation (p.97-100) ☑

15) What is background radiation? ☑
16) True or false? It is possible to predict when a particular nucleus will decay. ☑
17) What is the activity of a source? What are its units? ☑
18) True or false? The half-life of a radioactive source decreases over time. ☑
19) Explain how you would find the half-life of a source, given a graph of its activity over time. ☑
20) Explain the dangers of a radioactive source with a long half-life. ☑
21) Define irradiation and contamination. ☑
22) What precautions can be put in place to reduce contamination? ☑

## Uses of Nuclear Radiation (p.102-108) ☑

23) Give one use of alpha radiation. ☑
24) Describe how radioactive isotopes are used as medical tracers. ☑
25) Describe how beta radiation is used in controlling the thickness of paper. ☑
26) What is the difference between internal radiation therapy and external radiation therapy? ☑
27) What is the difference between nuclear fission and nuclear fusion? ☑
28) Name two factors that contribute to negative perceptions of nuclear power. ☑

# The Solar System

*The **Sun** is the centre of our **Solar System**. It's **orbited** by **eight planets**, along with a bunch of other objects.*

## Our Solar System has **One** Star — The **Sun**

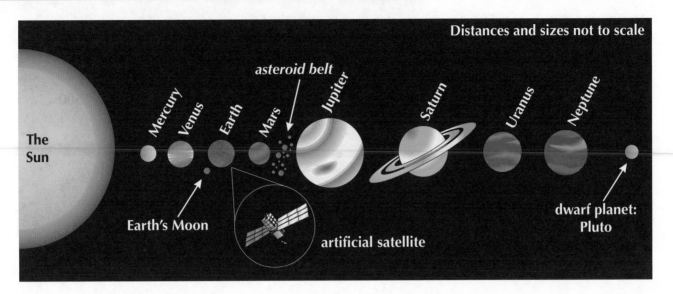

Distances and sizes not to scale

asteroid belt

Mercury Venus Earth Mars Jupiter Saturn Uranus Neptune

The Sun

Earth's Moon

artificial satellite

dwarf planet: Pluto

The <u>Solar System</u> includes things like:

1) <u>Planets</u> — these are large objects that <u>orbit a star</u>. The <u>eight</u> planets in our Solar System are, in order (from the Sun outwards): Mercury, Venus, Earth, Mars, Jupiter, Saturn, Uranus and Neptune.

2) <u>Dwarf planets</u>, like our pal Pluto. These are planet-like objects that <u>aren't big enough</u> to be planets.

3) <u>Moons</u> — these orbit <u>planets</u> with (usually) <u>almost circular</u> orbits. They're a type of <u>natural satellite</u> (i.e. they're not man-made).

> A satellite is an object that orbits a second, more massive object.

4) <u>Artificial satellites</u> (ones humans have built) that usually orbit the <u>Earth</u> in fairly <u>circular orbits</u>.

5) <u>Asteroids</u> — lumps of <u>rock</u> and <u>metals</u> that orbit the <u>Sun</u>. They're usually found in the <u>asteroid belt</u>.

6) <u>Comets</u> — lumps of <u>ice</u> and <u>dust</u> that orbit the <u>Sun</u>. Their orbits are usually <u>highly elliptical</u> (a very stretched out circle) — some travel from near to the Sun to the <u>outskirts</u> of our <u>Solar System</u>.

REVISION TIP

## The Sun is orbited by planets, comets and asteroids...

You need to <u>memorise</u> the <u>eight planets</u> in order, starting with Mercury — the closest to the Sun. One way to do this is to use a <u>mnemonic</u>, like My Very Exhausted Mother Just Slept Until Noon.

# Changing Ideas About the Solar System

*Over time*, *we've come up with different ideas about **how our Solar System looks**.*

## Geocentric Model — the Earth is the Centre of the Solar System

1) The geocentric model is a theory which suggested that the Sun,
   Moon, planets and stars all orbited the Earth in perfect circles.

2) It arose because people on Earth didn't have telescopes and saw the Sun and
   Moon travelling across the sky in the same way every day and night.

3) It was the accepted model of the Universe from the time of the ancient Greeks until the 1500s.

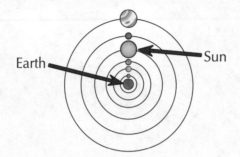

## Heliocentric Model — the Sun is the Centre of the Solar System

1) Next up was the heliocentric model, which said the Sun was at the centre of the Solar System.

2) It originally said that the Earth and all of the planets orbited the Sun in perfect circles.

3) Galileo found one of the best pieces of evidence for this theory — the moons around Jupiter.

> • Whilst looking at Jupiter with a telescope,
>   Galileo noticed some stars in a line near the planet.
> • When he looked again, he saw these 'stars' never moved away
>   from Jupiter and seemed to be carried along with the planet.
> • This showed not everything was in orbit around the Earth
>   — evidence that the geocentric model was wrong.

4) Gradually, evidence for the heliocentric model increased thanks to more technological advances.

5) The current model still says that the planets in our Solar System orbit the Sun — but that these orbits
   are actually elliptical rather than circular (we treat them as circular to make life easier though).

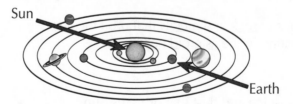

6) People also used to think that the Sun was at the centre of the Universe.
   We now know that this is not the case.

---

 ## Don't get confused between geocentric and heliocentric...

If you have a hard time remembering which model is which, you can remind yourself by thinking
of words like geography and geology, which are to do with studying and describing the Earth.

# Orbits

*The structure of the **Solar System** is determined by **orbits** — the paths that objects take as they move around each other in space. I bet you can't wait to find out more. Well, read on...*

## Gravity Provides the Force That Creates Orbits

1) The planets move around the Sun in almost circular orbits (the same goes for the Moon orbiting Earth).

2) You saw on p.25 that an object moving in a circular orbit at a constant speed is constantly accelerating (as its velocity is changing).

3) The force causing this acceleration is the centripetal force. It acts towards the centre of the circle.

4) This force would cause the object to fall towards whatever it was orbiting, but as the object is already moving, it just causes it to change direction.

5) The object keeps accelerating towards what it's orbiting but the instantaneous velocity (which is at a right angle to the acceleration) keeps it travelling in a circle.

6) The force that makes this happen is provided by the gravitational force (gravity) between the planet and the Sun (or between the planet and its satellite).

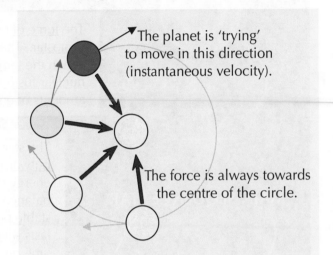

The planet is 'trying' to move in this direction (instantaneous velocity).

The force is always towards the centre of the circle.

## The Force due to Gravity Depends on Mass and Distance

1) Back on page 30 you saw that the weight (i.e. the force on an object due to gravity) of any object varies depending on the strength (g) of the gravitational field that it is in.

2) Gravitational field strength depends on the mass of the body creating the field. The larger the mass of the body, the stronger its gravitational field. (The Earth is more massive than the Moon, so an object would weigh more on Earth than it would on the Moon.)

3) Gravitational field strength also varies with distance. The closer you get to a star or planet, the stronger the gravitational force is.

4) In circular motion, the stronger the force, the larger the instantaneous velocity needed to balance it.

5) So the closer to a star or planet you get, the faster you need to go to remain in orbit.

6) For an object in a stable orbit, if the speed of the object changes, the size (radius) of its orbit must do so too.

7) Faster moving objects will move in a stable orbit with a smaller radius than slower moving ones.

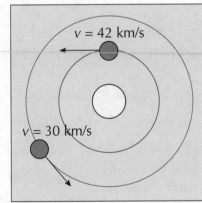

v = 42 km/s

v = 30 km/s

## Objects are kept in orbit by gravity...

The gravitational force acting on an orbiting object is always towards the body it is orbiting. It is what causes the orbiting object to change direction, which means its velocity changes and it accelerates.

Q1 Video Solution

Q1     If the distance between the Moon and the Earth was smaller, how would the orbital speed of the Moon compare to its current orbital speed? Explain your answer.     [3 marks]

# Life Cycle of Stars

*Stars go through some **dramatic transformations** during their life cycle.*

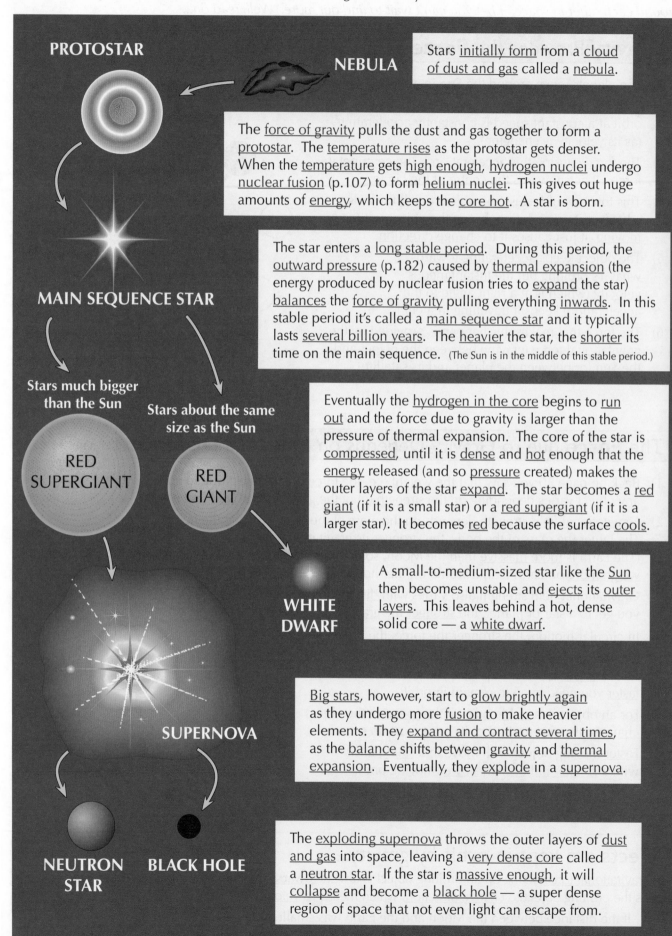

**PROTOSTAR**

**NEBULA**

Stars <u>initially form</u> from a <u>cloud of dust and gas</u> called a <u>nebula</u>.

The <u>force of gravity</u> pulls the dust and gas together to form a <u>protostar</u>. The <u>temperature rises</u> as the protostar gets denser. When the <u>temperature</u> gets <u>high enough</u>, <u>hydrogen nuclei</u> undergo <u>nuclear fusion</u> (p.107) to form <u>helium nuclei</u>. This gives out huge amounts of <u>energy</u>, which keeps the <u>core hot</u>. A star is born.

**MAIN SEQUENCE STAR**

The star enters a <u>long stable period</u>. During this period, the <u>outward pressure</u> (p.182) caused by <u>thermal expansion</u> (the energy produced by nuclear fusion tries to <u>expand</u> the star) <u>balances</u> the <u>force of gravity</u> pulling everything <u>inwards</u>. In this stable period it's called a <u>main sequence star</u> and it typically lasts <u>several billion years</u>. The <u>heavier</u> the star, the <u>shorter</u> its time on the main sequence. (The Sun is in the middle of this stable period.)

**Stars much bigger than the Sun**

**Stars about the same size as the Sun**

**RED SUPERGIANT**

**RED GIANT**

Eventually the <u>hydrogen in the core</u> begins to <u>run out</u> and the force due to gravity is larger than the pressure of thermal expansion. The core of the star is <u>compressed</u>, until it is <u>dense</u> and <u>hot</u> enough that the <u>energy</u> released (and so <u>pressure</u> created) makes the outer layers of the star <u>expand</u>. The star becomes a <u>red giant</u> (if it is a small star) or a <u>red supergiant</u> (if it is a larger star). It becomes <u>red</u> because the surface <u>cools</u>.

**WHITE DWARF**

A small-to-medium-sized star like the <u>Sun</u> then becomes unstable and <u>ejects</u> its <u>outer layers</u>. This leaves behind a hot, dense solid core — a <u>white dwarf</u>.

**SUPERNOVA**

<u>Big stars</u>, however, start to <u>glow brightly again</u> as they undergo more <u>fusion</u> to make heavier elements. They <u>expand and contract several times</u>, as the <u>balance</u> shifts between <u>gravity</u> and <u>thermal expansion</u>. Eventually, they <u>explode</u> in a <u>supernova</u>.

**NEUTRON STAR**

**BLACK HOLE**

The <u>exploding supernova</u> throws the outer layers of <u>dust and gas</u> into space, leaving a <u>very dense core</u> called a <u>neutron star</u>. If the star is <u>massive enough</u>, it will <u>collapse</u> and become a <u>black hole</u> — a super dense region of space that not even light can escape from.

# Warm-Up & Exam Questions

Astronomy has some pretty cool stuff, but that doesn't mean you can escape a few practice questions...

## Warm-Up Questions

1) Name the eight planets in our Solar System, in the order of nearest to furthest from the Sun.
2) Apart from planets, name two other types of object in the Solar System that orbit the Sun.
3) Describe the geocentric model of the Solar System.
4) What is the force responsible for keeping planets in orbit?
5) Explain why a 1 kg mass has a greater weight on the Earth's surface than the Moon's surface.
6) What is a nebula?
7) Immediately after the end of its main sequence phase, what does a star much larger than the Sun become?

## Exam Questions

1   Which of the following statements is true about the Earth's orbit around the Sun?    Grade 4-6
    You can assume that the Earth has a perfectly circular, stable orbit.

    ☐   **A**   The orbital speed of the Earth constantly changes during the course of its orbit.

    ☐   **B**   The orbital velocity of the Earth remains constant during the course of its orbit.

    ☐   **C**   Gravity provides the centripetal force that causes the Earth to move along a circular path.

    ☐   **D**   The Earth does not accelerate during the course of its orbit.

*[1 mark]*

2   Two identical satellites are orbiting Earth.    Grade 6-7
    The radius of the orbit of satellite A is 1000 km.
    The radius of the orbit of satellite B is 1500 km.

    Explain which satellite is orbiting at a greater speed.

*[3 marks]*

3   Stars go through many stages in their lives.    Grade 6-7

    (a)   Describe how a star is formed.

*[3 marks]*

    (b)   The stable period of a main sequence star can last billions of years.
          Explain why main sequence stars undergo a stable period.

*[2 marks]*

    When main sequence stars begin to run out of hydrogen in their core, they swell
    and become either a red giant or a red supergiant, depending on their size.

    (c)   Describe what happens to stars after their red giant phase.

*[2 marks]*

    (d)   Describe what happens to stars after they have expanded and
          contracted several times during their red supergiant phase.

*[2 marks]*

# Red-Shift

*Red-shift suggests that galaxies are moving away from us and that the Universe is expanding.*

## Red-Shift is Observed When a Source Moves Away from the Observer

1) If a wave source is moving away from an observer, the observed wave frequency will be slightly lower and the wavelength slightly longer than the wave originally emitted by the source.

You've probably heard this from the vrrr-oom of a racing car or the sound of an ambulance as it drives past you. The noise sounds lower-pitched when it's travelling away from you because it drops in frequency (the Doppler effect).

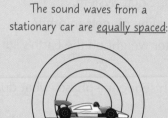

The sound waves from a stationary car are equally spaced:

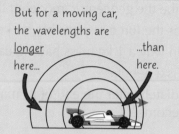

But for a moving car, the wavelengths are longer here... ...than here.

So the frequency of the sound waves is lower if the car is moving away from you.

2) For electromagnetic waves, this observed shift towards lower frequencies is known as red-shift (as waves are shifted towards the red end of the spectrum).

## Red-Shift Suggests the Universe is Expanding

1) Measurements of red-shift of distant galaxies suggest that they are all moving away from us very quickly — and it's the same result whichever direction you look in.

2) Measurements also show that most galaxies seem to be moving away from each other.

3) You can measure red-shift by comparing absorption spectra:

> 1) Different elements absorb different frequencies (or wavelengths) of light.
>
> 2) As a result, each element produces an absorption spectrum — a specific pattern of dark lines at the frequencies it absorbs in the visible part of the EM spectrum (p.77).
>
> 3) By taking a particular pattern and looking at how far each absorption line (caused by absorption in a distant galaxy) has moved compared to light produced in a lab, you can measure the change in wavelength and calculate red-shift.

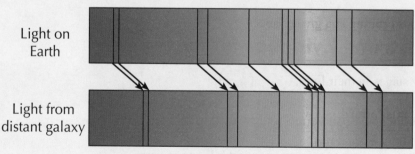

Light on Earth

Light from distant galaxy

4) More distant galaxies have greater red-shifts than nearer ones — they show a bigger observed increase in wavelength.

5) This means that more distant galaxies are moving away faster than nearer ones. This provides evidence that the whole Universe is expanding.

## Light from distant galaxies has been red-shifted...

Remember, when light has been shifted towards the red end of the spectrum, the light has an increased wavelength and decreased frequency compared to the light originally emitted by the source. And if the light has been red-shifted, that means the wave source must be moving away from the observer.

# The Origin of the Universe

*'How did it all begin?' is a tricky question. Currently, the most **widely-accepted theory** is the **Big Bang theory**.*

## Theories for the **Creation** of the Universe Have **Changed over Time**

1) As big as the Universe already is, it looks like it's getting even <u>bigger</u> (it's <u>expanding</u>).

2) This observation has led to the creation of numerous <u>models</u> that try to explain the <u>creation of the Universe</u>.

3) These are the <u>two</u> you need to know about:

## Steady State — **Matter** is **Always** Being Created

1) The '<u>Steady State</u>' theory says that the Universe <u>has always</u> existed <u>as it is now</u>, and it <u>always will</u> do. It's based on the idea that the Universe appears pretty much <u>the same everywhere</u>.

2) As the Universe <u>expands</u>, new matter is <u>constantly being created</u>.

3) This means that the <u>density</u> (p.172) of the Universe is always roughly the <u>same</u>.

4) In this theory there is <u>no beginning</u> or <u>end</u> to the Universe.

## The Big Bang — the Universe **Started** with an **Explosion**

1) Initially, <u>all</u> the matter in the Universe occupied <u>a very small space</u>.

2) This tiny space was very <u>dense</u> and so was very <u>hot</u>.

3) Then it '<u>exploded</u>' — space started expanding, and the <u>expansion</u> is still going on.

4) This theory gives a <u>finite age</u> for the Universe (around 13.8 billion years).

## CMB radiation is **Strong Evidence** for the Big Bang

1) <u>Red-shift</u> can be explained by <u>both</u> the Steady State and Big Bang theories.

2) In both models, objects are <u>moving away</u> from the observer as the Universe expands, so red-shift would be observed for either model.

3) However, scientists have also detected <u>low frequency electromagnetic radiation</u> coming from <u>all parts</u> of the Universe. This radiation is mainly in the <u>microwave</u> part of the EM spectrum, and is known as the <u>cosmic microwave background radiation</u> (CMB radiation).

4) The presence of CMB radiation shows that the Universe was once much <u>hotter</u> and <u>denser</u>. This suggests that the Universe had a <u>beginning</u>, so CMB radiation <u>only</u> supports the <u>Big Bang model</u>.

5) As there is good evidence to support it, the <u>Big Bang theory</u> is currently our <u>accepted model</u> for the start of the Universe.

## We can't say for sure if the Big Bang theory is correct...

It's just the <u>best theory</u> that we have <u>at the moment</u>. Theories about the origin of the Universe are a great example of how <u>new evidence</u> leads to theories being <u>disproved</u> or <u>adapted</u>.

# Looking into Space

*We've all seen **stars** in the **night sky** — but to the **naked eye**, they simply look like **twinkly dots**. **Telescopes** allow you to see the night sky in much **greater detail**.*

## Telescopes are Used to Observe the Universe

Telescopes use refraction (p.61) and reflection (p.64) to allow you to see distant objects clearly. There are loads of different kinds and they all work in different ways. You're most likely to have seen an optical telescope — one that detects visible light.

You need to know how to improve the quality of the image you can see using them:

1) Increase the aperture of the telescope. This is the diameter of the objective lens — the big lens at the end of the telescope where light from the distant object enters the telescope.

2) Use a higher quality objective lens.

## Space Telescopes Have a Clearer View Than Those on Earth

1) The location of the telescope can also have a large effect on image quality.

2) If you're trying to detect light coming from space, Earth's atmosphere gets in the way — it absorbs a lot of the light coming from space before it can reach us.

3) To fully observe these absorbed frequencies, you have to go above the atmosphere.

Night sky in urban area with light pollution.

4) Then there's pollution. Light pollution (light thrown up into the sky from street lamps, etc.) can make it hard to pick out dim objects.

5) And air pollution can reflect and absorb light coming from space.

6) So to get the best view possible from Earth, a telescope should be on top of a mountain (where there's less atmosphere above it), and in a dark place away from cities (e.g. on a mountain in Hawaii).

Night sky in rural area with no light pollution.

7) To avoid the problem of the atmosphere completely, you can put your telescope in space.

---

## Remember, dark and high up is good, but space is better...

Make sure you know how the image produced by a telescope can be improved. For example, using a larger aperture and a higher quality objective lens improves the image quality. The telescope's location also matters — image quality can be reduced by air pollution, light pollution and the Earth's atmosphere.

# Looking into Space

*It's not just **visible light** that we can see these days — there are **telescopes** for all different types of EM waves.*

## Different Telescopes Detect Different Types of EM Wave

To get as full a picture of the Universe as possible, you need to detect <u>different</u> kinds of <u>EM wave</u>.

1) The earliest telescopes were all <u>optical telescopes</u>. They're used to look at objects close by and in other galaxies. But many objects in the Universe <u>aren't</u> detectable using visible light — so <u>other</u> types of EM telescopes are needed to observe them.

2) From the 1930s, telescopes began to be developed for <u>all other</u> parts of the <u>EM spectrum</u>. These modern telescopes mean we can now '<u>see</u>' parts of the Universe that we couldn't see before and learn more about the Universe, e.g. its <u>structure</u>.

3) <u>X-ray telescopes</u> are a good way to 'see' violent, <u>high-temperature events</u> in space, like <u>exploding stars</u>.

4) <u>Radio telescopes</u> were responsible for the discovery of the <u>cosmic microwave background radiation</u> (p.117) — this helped scientists to learn more about the <u>origin</u> of the Universe.

A radio telescope.

## Telescopes Have Improved over Time

1) Telescopes are <u>improving</u> all the time:
   - <u>Bigger</u> telescopes give us better <u>resolution</u> (i.e. more detail) and can <u>gather more light</u>, so we can see things that were <u>too faint</u> to see before.
   - Improved <u>magnification</u> means we can now look <u>further</u> into space — more and more galaxies are being <u>discovered</u>.

2) Modern telescopes often work alongside <u>computers</u>. Computers make it easy to <u>capture</u> images so they can be analysed later. They also help to create <u>clearer</u> and <u>sharper</u> images.

3) Computers make it possible to collect and store <u>huge amounts</u> of data, 24 hours a day, without having to rely on <u>humans</u>. They also make it easier and quicker to <u>analyse</u> all this data.

## Modern telescopes observe the Universe like never before...

<u>Different bodies</u> in space <u>emit different frequencies</u> of EM radiation, so it makes sense to use different telescopes to <u>detect</u> these different frequencies. Otherwise, a lot of the Universe would be <u>invisible</u> to us.

# Warm-Up & Exam Questions

You're so close to the end of the section. Time for just a few more questions before you can take a break, have a brew and give yourself a pat on the back for making it this far.

## Warm-Up Questions

1) What is the name given to the observed increase in the wavelength of light from distant galaxies?
2) True or false? An expanding Universe means that the more distant a galaxy is from Earth, the faster it is moving away from Earth.
3) What does 'CMB' stand for in 'CMB radiation'?
4) Name the currently accepted theory for the origin of the Universe.
5) A telescope contains an objective lens. Give two ways to improve the telescope so it produces better quality images.

## Exam Questions

1 (a) Red-shift occurs when a wave source is moving away from an observer. Which one of the following statements is true for the observed waves compared to those emitted by the source? *Grade 4-6*

- A the wavelength of the observed waves stays the same, but the frequency changes
- B the wavelength of the observed waves changes, but the frequency stays the same
- C both the frequency and wavelength of the observed waves change
- D the observed waves are no different for a moving source than for a stationary source

*[1 mark]*

(b) Red-shift observations support the Steady State theory. Which one of the following statements is part of the Steady State theory?

- A the density of the Universe is constantly changing
- B matter is constantly being created in the Universe
- C the Universe has a beginning and an end
- D the Universe has always been the same size

*[1 mark]*

2 **Figure 1** shows an image of part of a nebula that has been captured using a telescope in space. *Grade 6-7*

Explain the benefits of positioning a telescope in space.

*[3 marks]*

**Figure 1**

3* Explain how observations of both red-shift and CMB radiation provide evidence that supports the Big Bang theory. *Grade 7-9*

*[6 marks]*

# Revision Summary for Section 5

Well that's the end of <u>Section 5</u> — now it's time to check if you've filled all that space in your head.

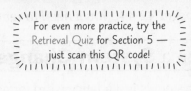
For even more practice, try the Retrieval Quiz for Section 5 — just scan this QR code!

Section 5 Quiz

- Try these questions and <u>tick off each one</u> when you <u>get it right</u>.
- When you're <u>completely happy</u> with a sub-topic, tick it off.

## The Solar System and Orbits (p.111-113) ☑

1) What is the sixth furthest planet from the Sun in our Solar System? ☑
2) What do moons orbit? ☑
3) Describe the orbits of comets. ☑
4) Describe the heliocentric model of the Solar System. ☑
5) True or false? A satellite in a stable orbit is constantly changing velocity. ☑
6) How does the gravitational field strength of a planet relate to a planet's mass? ☑
7) How does the speed of a planet (in a stable orbit) relate to its distance from the star it's orbiting? ☑

## The Life Cycle of Stars (p.114) ☑

8) What causes the outward pressure in a main sequence star that prevents it from collapsing inwards under the force of gravity? ☑
9) How does the mass of a star affect how long it is a main sequence star for? ☑
10) Describe the life cycle of a star the same size as the Sun. ☑
11) What is a supernova? ☑
12) Name the two astronomical bodies that could be left behind after a supernova. ☑

## The Origin of the Universe (p.116-117) ☑

13) Describe what is meant by red-shift. ☑
14) Describe how absorption spectra are used to determine if the light from distant galaxies has been red-shifted. ☑
15) Describe one piece of evidence that shows the Universe is expanding. ☑
16) Compare the Steady State and Big Bang theories. Which is the currently accepted theory? ☑
17) Explain how both the Steady State and Big Bang theories can account for red-shift. ☑
18) What is CMB radiation? ☑

## Looking into Space (p.118-119) ☑

19) How would using a telescope with a wider aperture affect image quality? ☑
20) How do air pollution and light pollution affect the image quality of a telescope at the Earth's surface? ☑
21) State two ways in which telescopes have improved over time. ☑

# Section 6 — Forces and Energy

## Energy Transfers

*Re-read* pages 42-44. *You'll need to remember everything on those pages for this section.*

## When a **System Changes, Energy** is **Transferred**

1) A system is just a fancy word for a single object (e.g. the air in a piston) or a group of objects (e.g. two colliding vehicles) that you're interested in. You can define your system to be anything you like.

2) When a system changes, energy is transferred. It can be transferred into or away from the system, between different objects in the system or between different types of energy stores (p.42).

3) Whenever a system changes, some energy is dissipated and stored in less useful ways (p.46).

4) The efficiency of a transfer is the proportion of the total energy supplied that ends up in useful energy stores (p.47).

5) You can use diagrams to show how efficient a transfer is, and which stores the energy is transferred to (see p.44 and 47).

6) How you define your system changes how you describe the energy transfers that take place (see below). A closed system is one that's defined so that the net change in energy is zero (p.43).

## **Energy** can be **Transferred** by **Heating...**

1) A pan of water is heated on a gas camping stove.

2) When the system is the pan of water, energy is transferred into the system by heating to the thermal energy stores of the pan and the water, which increases their temperature.

3) When the system is the camping stove and the pan, energy is transferred within the system — from the chemical energy store of the gas to the thermal energy stores of the pan and the water, increasing their temperature.

## ...by Forces **Doing Work...**

1) A box is lifted up off of the floor. The box is the system.

2) As the box is lifted, work is done (see next page) against gravity.

3) This causes energy to be transferred to the box's kinetic and gravitational potential energy (GPE) stores.

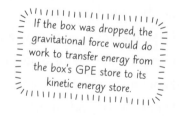

If the box was dropped, the gravitational force would do work to transfer energy from the box's GPE store to its kinetic energy store.

## ...or by **Electrical Equipment**

1) Electrical devices work by transferring energy between different energy stores.

2) For example, electric irons transfer energy electrically from the mains power supply to the thermal energy store of their metal plates.

An electric toothbrush is a system. It transfers energy electrically from the chemical energy store of its battery to the kinetic energy store of its bristles.

Some of this energy is transferred out of the system to the surroundings by sound and by heating.

A hair dryer is a system. It transfers energy into the system electrically from the mains supply to the kinetic energy store of the fan inside of it.

It also transfers energy electrically to the thermal energy store of the heating element and some energy is transferred away from the system by sound.

# Work Done

*I'm sure you're no stranger to **doing work**, but in physics it's all to do with **forces** and **energy**.*

## If A Force **Moves** An Object, **Work is Done**

> When a <u>force</u> moves an object through a <u>distance</u>, <u>work is done</u> on the object and <u>energy is transferred</u>.

1) To make something <u>move</u>, some sort of <u>force</u> needs to act on it. The thing <u>applying the force</u> needs a <u>source</u> of <u>energy</u> (like <u>fuel</u> or <u>food</u>).

2) The force does '<u>work</u>' to <u>move</u> the object and <u>energy</u> is <u>transferred mechanically</u> from one <u>store</u> to another.

3) Remember, you can calculate the amount of energy in the <u>kinetic energy</u> and <u>gravitational potential energy</u> stores using $\underline{KE = \frac{1}{2} \times m \times v^2}$ and $\underline{\Delta GPE = m \times g \times \Delta h}$ (p.42).

4) Whether energy is transferred '<u>usefully</u>' (e.g. <u>lifting a load</u>) or is '<u>wasted</u>' (p.46) you can still say that '<u>work is done</u>'.

5) You can find out <u>how much</u> work has been done using: 

6) <u>One joule of work</u> is done when a <u>force of one newton</u> causes an object to move a <u>distance of one metre</u>. You can also write this as 1 J = 1 Nm (newton metre).

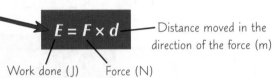

$$E = F \times d$$

Distance moved in the direction of the force (m)

Work done (J)   Force (N)

---

**EXAMPLE**

**A sled is pulled with a force of 10 N, for a distance of 4 m. Calculate the work done on the sled.**

work done = force × distance = 10 × 4 = 40 J

**The sled started at rest. After travelling 4 m, its final velocity is 4 m/s.**
**Calculate the sled's mass, assuming all the energy was transferred to the sled's kinetic energy store.**

1) <u>Rearrange</u> the kinetic energy equation for *m*.      $m = \dfrac{2 \times KE}{v^2}$

2) <u>Substitute</u> the values in.      $= \dfrac{2 \times 40}{4^2} = 5 \text{ kg}$

---

## Doing **Work** Often Causes a **Rise in Temperature**

1) A force doing work often causes a <u>rise in temperature</u> as energy is dissipated to the <u>thermal</u> energy stores of a moving object and its surroundings.

2) This means that the process is often <u>wasteful</u> and so the <u>efficiency</u> of the process is <u>reduced</u>.
Remember, efficiency $= \dfrac{\text{useful energy transferred by the device}}{\text{total energy supplied to the device}}$ (p.47).

> When you push something along a <u>rough surface</u> (like a <u>carpet</u>) you are doing work <u>against frictional</u> <u>forces</u>. Energy is being <u>transferred</u> to the <u>kinetic energy store</u> of the <u>object</u> because it starts <u>moving</u>, but some is also being transferred to <u>thermal energy stores</u> due to the friction. This causes the overall <u>temperature</u> of the object to <u>increase</u>. (Like <u>rubbing your hands together</u> to warm them up.)

3) <u>Lubrication</u> (p.48) <u>reduces friction</u> and unwanted energy transfers to <u>thermal energy stores</u>.

---

## Get comfortable with work done calculations...

Make sure you're happy using the <u>equations</u> on this page before you move on.

Q1    A constant force of 20 N pushes an object 20 cm.
       Calculate the work done on the object.                                              [2 marks]

Q1 Video
Solution

# Power

*The **more powerful** a device is, the **more energy** it will transfer in a certain amount of **time**.*

## Power is How Much Work is Done per Second

1) Power is the rate of energy transfer.

2) The unit of power is the watt (W).  1 W = 1 J/s.

3) Remember, when work is done, energy is transferred (see previous page).

4) So, another way of describing power is how much work is being done every second.

5) This is the very easy formula for power:

$$\text{power (W)} = \frac{\text{work done (J)}}{\text{time taken (s)}} \qquad \text{or} \qquad P = \frac{E}{t}$$

The larger the power of an object, the more work it does per second.  E.g. if an electric heater has a power of 600 W this means it transfers 600 J of energy every second.  A 1200 W heater would transfer twice as much energy per second and so would heat a room quicker than the 600 W heater.

### EXAMPLE

**A microwave transfers 105 kJ of energy in 2 minutes.  Find its power output.**

1) Convert the values to the correct units first (p.12-13).  105 kJ = 105 000 J and 2 mins = 120 s
2) Substitute the values into the power equation.      $P = E \div t = 105\,000 \div 120 = 875$ W

### EXAMPLE

**A 300 W motor lifts a 50 kg mass 5 m vertically upwards.  Calculate the amount of energy transferred to the gravitational potential energy store of the mass.**

Substitute values into the        $\Delta GPE = m \times g \times \Delta h$
equation for $\Delta GPE$ (p.42).          $= 50 \times 10 \times 5 = 2500$ J

**Calculate how long it takes the motor to lift the mass.**

1) Rearrange the power equation for $t$.    $t = E \div P$
2) Substitute the values in.          $= 2500 \div 300 = 8.33...$ s
                                         $= 8$ s (to 1 s.f.)

## A large power doesn't necessarily mean a large force...

A powerful device is not necessarily one which can exert a strong force (although it usually ends up that way).  A powerful device is one which transfers a lot of energy in a short space of time.

# Warm-Up & Exam Questions

Do some work by answering these questions and transfer some knowledge to your brain store.

## Warm-Up Questions

1) What is meant by the word 'system'?
2) True or false?  Energy can be transferred into a system.
3) Describe the useful energy transfer that occurs in a battery powered fan.
4) State the equation linking work done, force and distance moved in the direction of the force.
5) True or false?  Power measures how quickly energy is transferred.
6) Which unit for power is equivalent to joules per second?

## Exam Questions

**1**  A ball rolls down a ramp, as shown in **Figure 1**.

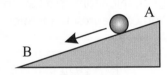

   (a)  The ball and ramp are assumed to be a closed system.
        Describe the energy transfer that takes place as the ball rolls
        from point A to point B.

        *[2 marks]*

**Figure 1**

   (b)  State the change in total energy of the ball and ramp as this energy transfer occurs.

        *[1 mark]*

**2**  The motor of an electric scooter moves the scooter 10 metres along a flat, horizontal
       course in 20 seconds.  During this time the motor does a total of 1000 J of work.

   (a)  (i)  Write down the equation that links power, work done and time taken.

        *[1 mark]*

        (ii) Calculate the power of the motor.

        *[1 mark]*

   (b)  Whilst completing the course, 480 J of energy was transferred usefully to the
        kinetic energy stores of the scooter and its rider.  Calculate the efficiency of the scooter.

        *[2 marks]*

   (c)  The scooter's motor is replaced with a more powerful, but otherwise identical, motor.
        It moves along the same 10 m course.
        Describe how its performance will differ from before.  Explain your answer.

        *[2 marks]*

**3**  A train, initially at rest, moves 700 m in a straight line along a flat track.
       The force acting on the train is 42 000 N forwards along the track.
       You can assume there are no frictional forces acting on the train.
       The train has a mass of 150 000 kg.

   (a)  Calculate the work done by the force as the train moves 700 m.  Give your answer in kJ.

        *[3 marks]*

   (b)  Assuming that all of this energy was transferred to the train's kinetic energy store,
        calculate the final speed of the train.

        *[3 marks]*

# Forces

*Force is a **vector** — it has both a **size** and a **direction** (unlike **scalar** quantities which only have a **size** — p.18). This means you can use **arrows** to represent the forces acting on an object or a system.*

## Interactions Between Objects Cause Forces

1) A <u>force</u> is a <u>push</u> or a <u>pull</u> on an object that is caused by it <u>interacting</u> with something.

2) Sometimes, objects need to be <u>touching</u> for a force to act.
E.g. the <u>normal contact force</u> that acts between <u>all</u> touching objects, or <u>friction</u> between a car's <u>tyre</u> and the <u>road</u>. These are <u>contact forces</u>.

3) Other forces can act between objects that <u>aren't touching</u> (<u>non-contact forces</u>). They're usually caused by <u>interacting fields</u>. E.g. the <u>gravitational attraction</u> between objects (like the <u>Earth</u> and the <u>Sun</u>) is caused by their <u>gravitational fields</u> interacting.

4) <u>Interacting magnetic fields</u> (p.158) cause <u>attraction</u> or <u>repulsion</u> between <u>magnetic</u> objects, and the electrostatic force causing <u>attraction</u> and <u>repulsion</u> between <u>electrical charges</u> (p.153) is due to interactions between their <u>electric fields</u> (p.156).

5) Whenever two objects <u>interact</u>, both objects feel an equal but opposite <u>force</u> (Newton's 3rd Law, p.26). This pair of forces is called an <u>interaction pair</u>. You can represent an interaction pair with a pair of <u>vectors</u> (<u>arrows</u>).

---

A <u>chair</u> exerts a force on the <u>ground</u>, whilst the ground pushes back at the chair with the <u>same</u> force (the <u>normal contact</u> force).

<u>Equal</u> but <u>opposite</u> forces are felt by <u>both</u> the chair and the ground.

This is <u>NOT</u> a free body force diagram (see below) — the forces are acting on <u>different objects</u>.

Chair pushes on ground

Ground pushes on chair

---

## Free Body Force Diagrams Show All the Forces Acting on Objects

1) A <u>free body force diagram</u> shows an <u>isolated body</u> (an object or system on its own), and <u>all</u> the <u>forces</u> acting on it.

2) It should include <u>every</u> force acting <u>on the body</u>, but <u>none</u> of the forces it <u>exerts</u> on the rest of the world.

3) The <u>sizes</u> of the arrows show the <u>relative magnitudes</u> of the forces and the <u>directions</u> show the directions of the forces.

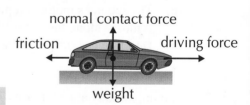

normal contact force

friction

driving force

weight

---

# Drawing free body force diagrams can be relatively tricky...

Be careful — the <u>arrows</u> you draw need to have <u>clearly different lengths</u> for different sized <u>forces</u>.

Q1    A car has a driving force of 2000 N and a weight of 1600 N.
There is a total resistive force of 1200 N acting against the driving force.
Draw the free body force diagram for the car.                    [2 marks]

Q1 Video Solution

# Resultant Forces

*The **resultant force** acting on an object is found by **adding together** or **subtracting** all the forces acting on*

## A **Resultant Force** is the **Overall Force** on a Point or Object

1) In most <u>real</u> situations there are at least <u>two forces</u> acting on an object along any direction.

2) If you have a <u>number of forces</u> acting at a single point, you can replace them with a <u>single force</u> (so long as the single force has the <u>same effect</u> as all the original forces together).

3) This single force is called the <u>resultant force</u> (or sometimes the <u>net force</u> on an object).

4) If the forces all act along the <u>same line</u> (they're all parallel), the <u>overall effect</u> is found by <u>adding</u> those going in the <u>same</u> direction and <u>subtracting</u> any going in the opposite direction.

5) Objects in <u>equilibrium</u> have a resultant force of <u>zero</u> — see the next page. Objects in equilibrium are either <u>stationary</u>, or moving at a <u>steady speed</u> (this is Newton's 1st Law — p.25).

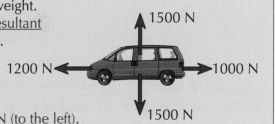

- The <u>normal contact force</u> felt by the car is <u>equal</u> to its weight. These forces act in <u>opposite directions</u>, so there is <u>no resultant force</u> in the <u>vertical</u> direction (1500 N – 1500 N = 0 N).
- The <u>frictional</u> force acting on the car is <u>smaller</u> than the <u>driving</u> force pushing it forward, so there is a <u>resultant force</u> in the <u>horizontal</u> direction.
- 1200 N – 1000 N = 200 N. The resultant force is <u>200 N (to the left)</u>.

## Use **Scale Drawings** to Find **Resultant Forces**

<u>Scale drawings</u> can help you <u>resolve</u> forces (see next page) or <u>work out</u> the <u>resultant force</u>.

1) Draw all the <u>forces</u> acting on an object, to scale, 'tip-to-tail'.

2) Then draw a <u>straight line</u> from the start of the <u>first force</u> to the <u>end</u> of the <u>last force</u> — this is the <u>resultant</u> (or <u>net</u>) force.

3) Measure the <u>length</u> of the <u>resultant force</u> on the diagram to find the <u>magnitude</u> of the force and the <u>angle</u> to find its <u>direction</u>.

*Make sure the scale you use is sensible. You want large, clear diagrams that make your calculations easier to do.*

**EXAMPLE**

**A man is on an electric bicycle that has a driving force of 4 N north. However, the wind produces a force of 3 N east. Find the net force acting on the man.**

1) Start by drawing a <u>scale drawing</u> of the forces acting.

2) Make sure you choose a <u>sensible scale</u> (e.g. 1 cm = 1 N).

3) Draw the <u>net force</u> from the tail of the first arrow to the tip of the last arrow.

4) Measure the <u>length</u> of the net force with a <u>ruler</u> and use the <u>scale</u> to find the force in N.

5) Use a <u>protractor</u> to measure the direction as a <u>bearing</u>.

*A bearing is an angle measured clockwise from north, given as a 3-digit number, e.g. 10° = 010°.*

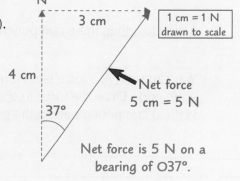

N

3 cm

1 cm = 1 N
drawn to scale

4 cm

37°

Net force
5 cm = 5 N

Net force is 5 N on a bearing of 037°.

## When it comes to scale drawings, bigger is better...

**EXAM TIP** If you're asked to draw a scale drawing in an exam, try to use up as <u>much</u> of the <u>space</u> provided as possible. This will help you to measure <u>angles</u> and <u>lengths</u> more <u>accurately</u>.

# Resolving Forces

e **added tip-to-tail** to give a single **resultant force**. Sometimes it's helpful to reverse
) a single force into components — this is known as **resolving a force**.

## Equilibrium if the **Forces** on it are **Balanced**

1) If <u>all</u> of the forces acting on an object <u>combine</u> to give
   a resultant force of <u>zero</u>, the object is in <u>equilibrium</u>.

2) On a <u>scale diagram</u>, this means that the <u>tip</u> of the <u>last</u> force you draw should end where the <u>tail</u>
   of the first <u>force</u> you drew begins.

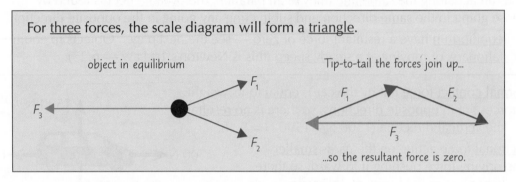

For <u>three</u> forces, the scale diagram will form a <u>triangle</u>.

object in equilibrium

$F_1$

$F_3$

$F_2$

Tip-to-tail the forces join up...

$F_1$

$F_2$

$F_3$

...so the resultant force is zero.

3) You might be <u>given</u> forces acting on an <u>object</u> and told to <u>find</u>
   a <u>missing force</u>, given that the object is in <u>equilibrium</u>.

4) To do this, draw out the forces you <u>do</u> know (to <u>scale</u> and <u>tip-to-tail</u>),
   then <u>join</u> the <u>end</u> of the <u>last force</u> to the <u>start</u> of the <u>first force</u>.
   Make sure you draw this last force in the <u>right direction</u> — it's in
   the <u>opposite</u> direction to how you'd draw a <u>resultant</u> force.

5) This line is the <u>missing force</u>, you can measure its <u>size</u> and <u>direction</u>.

## You Can **Split** a Force into **Components**

1) Not <u>all</u> forces act <u>horizontally</u> or <u>vertically</u> — some act at <u>awkward angles</u>.

2) To make these <u>easier</u> to deal with, they can be <u>split</u> into two <u>components</u>
   at <u>right angles</u> to each other (usually horizontal and vertical).

3) Acting <u>together</u>, these components have the <u>same effect</u> as the single force.

4) You can <u>resolve</u> a force (split it into components) by drawing it on a
   scale grid. Draw the force <u>to scale</u>, and then add the <u>horizontal</u> and
   <u>vertical</u> components along the <u>gridlines</u>. Then you can just <u>measure</u> them.

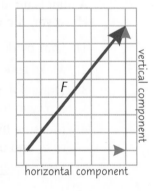

*F*

vertical component

horizontal component

## You might be given a scale to work with...

Scale drawings are really <u>useful</u>, so you need to make sure you're happy using <u>different scales</u>.

Q1  An object in equilibrium is being acted on by three forces.
    The first force is 0.50 N acting south and the second force is 0.30 N acting
    on a bearing of 045°. Find the magnitude and bearing of the third force.     [3 marks]

Q1 Video
Solution

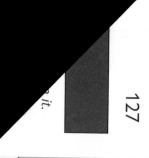

# Moments

*This page is all about how forces can make objects **rotate**.  Give it a read, it'll only take a **moment**.*

## A **Moment** is the **Turning Effect** of a Force

A <u>force</u>, or several forces, can cause an object to <u>rotate</u>.  The <u>turning effect</u> of a force is called its <u>moment</u>.
The <u>size</u> of the <u>moment</u> of the force is given by:

> ### moment of a force (Nm) = force (N) × distance (m)

*This is actually 'distance normal to the direction of the force'.*

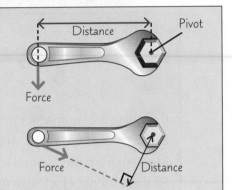

1)  The <u>force</u> on the spanner causes a <u>turning effect</u> or <u>moment</u> on the nut (which acts as a pivot).

2)  A <u>larger force</u> or a <u>longer distance</u> (i.e. a longer spanner) would mean a <u>larger</u> moment.

3)  To get the <u>maximum</u> moment (or turning effect) you need to push at <u>right angles</u> (<u>perpendicular</u>) to the spanner.

4)  Pushing at <u>any other angle</u> means a <u>smaller distance</u>, and so a <u>smaller moment</u>.  This is what the '<u>normal to the direction of the force</u>' bit means.

The <u>principle of moments</u> states that for an object in <u>equilibrium</u> (one that's <u>not turning</u>):

> ### the sum of the clockwise moments = the sum of the anticlockwise moments

**EXAMPLE**

**A 6 m long, massless plank rests horizontally on a pole 1 m from one end.
A mass, weighing 1000 N, is placed halfway along the plank.
What is the tension in a supporting cable attached vertically to the other end?**

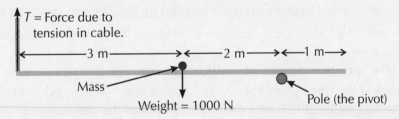

*T* = Force due to tension in cable.

├───3 m───┤├──2 m──┤├─1 m─┤

Mass
Weight = 1000 N
Pole (the pivot)

1)  For the plank to balance, the <u>total anticlockwise</u> moment should <u>equal</u> the <u>total clockwise</u> moment.  So start by calculating the total anti-clockwise moment.

Moment = force × distance
Total anticlockwise moment = 1000 × 2
= 2000 Nm

2)  Then, write an expression for the <u>total clockwise moment</u>.

Total clockwise moment = *T* × (3 + 2)
= 5 × *T*

3)  Set the moments equal to each other and <u>rearrange for *T*</u>.

2000 = 5 × *T*
*T* = 2000 ÷ 5 = 400 N

---

## Check if a moment is clockwise or anticlockwise...

Don't just dive into a question — check if the force will cause a <u>clockwise</u> or <u>anticlockwise</u> moment.

**Q1**  Your brother weighs 300 N and sits 2 m from the pivot of a seesaw.
If you weigh 600 N, what distance from the pivot, on the other side
of the seesaw, should you sit to balance it?

[3 marks]

Q1 Video Solution

# Levers and Gears

*Moments play a part in a lot of mechanical devices, from clocks to wheelbarrows. They can help you get the most out of a **small force**, and allow you to **transmit** forces across a distance.*

## Levers Make it Easier for us to Do Work

1) Levers transfer the turning effect of a force — push one end of a lever down and the rotation around the pivot causes the other end to rise.

2) Levers make it easier to do work as they increase the distance from the pivot at which a force is applied — the longer the lever, the smaller the force needed to give the same moment.

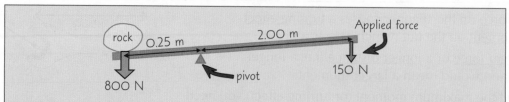

Calculate the moments from each force:

Moment from the rock's weight = $F \times d = 800 \times 0.25 = $ 200 Nm anticlockwise

Moment from the applied force = $F \times d = 150 \times 2.00 = $ 300 Nm clockwise

So there's a net clockwise moment of 100 Nm, meaning the rock will rise.

## Gears Fit Together to Transmit Turning Effects

1) Gears are circular cogs with 'teeth' around their edge. Their teeth interlock so that turning one causes another to turn, in the opposite direction.

2) They are used to transmit the rotational effect of a force from one place to another.

3) A force applied to a small gear creates a small moment. This gear applies the same force to the next gear. If this next gear is larger, this force is applied further from its pivot, so the moment is larger.

4) Interlocked gears will rotate at different speeds — the larger the gear, the slower it spins.

---

You can work out how speeds and moments will change between gears by looking at the gear ratios.

- For example, look at the three gears above. The largest gear has 16 teeth and the medium gear has 8 teeth. The ratio of teeth between the largest gear and the medium gear is 16 : 8 = 2 : 1.

- This means that for every 1 turn the largest gear does, the medium gear will do 2 turns.

- The force applied to each gear is the same, and the radius of a gear is equal to the distance of the applied force from the pivot.

- As moment = force × distance, this means that the ratio of moments of two gears is equal to the ratio of the gears' radii, and therefore equal to the ratio of teeth.

- For the gears above, the moment of the largest gear to the medium gear is also 2 : 1 — so the moment gets doubled.

---

5) Gears are often lubricated (p.48) to improve the efficiency of machines.

---

## You need to be able to explain how gears and levers work...

Gears can be tricky to keep track of. Remember that, when you have a series of connected gears, the direction of rotation changes each time the rotational effect is transferred. Try drawing arrows to show how the gears move, so you can more easily follow how the turning effect is transmitted.

# Warm-Up & Exam Questions

Time to test your ability to force new information into your mind. That's right, there's more questions.
Work through the warm-ups and when you're feeling happy with them, dive into the exam questions.

## Warm-Up Questions

1) True or false? Objects can only exert a force on one another if they are touching.
2) What does the length of an arrow on a free body diagram represent?
3) What is meant by the resultant force acting on an object?
4) If an object is equilibrium, what will you find if you draw all the forces acting on it, to scale and tip-to-tail?
5) State the principal of moments.
6) True or false? Using a longer lever means a smaller force is needed to give the same moment.
7) True or false? Two interlocking gears rotate in the same direction.

## Exam Questions

1   **Figure 1** shows two hot air balloons, labelled with the forces acting on them.

Grade 4-6

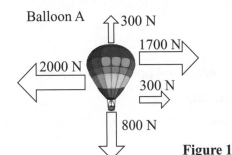 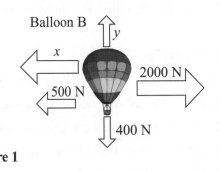

Balloon A — 300 N, 1700 N, 2000 N, 300 N, 800 N

Balloon B — y, x, 2000 N, 500 N, 400 N

**Figure 1**

(a)   Calculate the size of the resultant force acting on Balloon A and give its direction.

*[3 marks]*

(b)   The resultant force acting on Balloon B is zero. Calculate the size of forces *x* and *y*.

*[2 marks]*

2   Bolts are often secured using an Allen key, as shown in **Figure 2**. One end of the Allen key is put into the bolt and the other is turned to tighten the bolt.

Grade 6-7

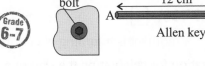

bolt — A, 12 cm, Allen key, 3 cm, B

**Figure 2**

(a)   Calculate the moment on the bolt when end A of the Allen key is put into the bolt and a force of 15 N is applied to end B.

*[3 marks]*

(b)   Calculate the moment on the bolt when end B of the Allen key is put into the bolt and a force of 15 N is applied to end A.

*[3 marks]*

(c)   State and explain which end of the Allen key (A or B) should be put into the bolt to make it easier to tighten.

*[1 mark]*

# Revision Summary for Section 6

That's <u>Section 6</u> done and dusted — now you've got a chance to see <u>how much has stuck</u>.

- Try these questions and <u>tick off each one</u> when you <u>get it right</u>.
- When you're <u>completely happy</u> with a sub-topic, tick it off.

For even more practice, try the Retrieval Quiz for Section 6 — just scan this QR code!

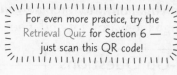 

Section 6 Quiz

## Energy, Work Done and Power (p.122-124) ☑

1) True or false? When a system changes, energy is transferred. ☑

2) Energy may be transferred electrically or by heating. Name a third way of transferring energy. ☑

3) Give the equation that links kinetic energy, mass and speed. ☑

4) Give the equation that links change in gravitational potential energy, mass, gravitational field strength and change in vertical height. ☑

5) Work done can be measured in joules or newton metres. How many joules is one newton metre equivalent to? ☑

6) True or false? A force doing work can cause a rise in temperature. ☑

7) Give the equation that links efficiency, useful energy transferred by the device and total energy supplied to the device. ☑

8) Often, energy is lost doing work against frictional forces. Suggest a way to reduce friction. ☑

9) Give the equation that links power, work done and time taken. ☑

## Forces (p.126-128) ☑

10) Explain the difference between contact and non-contact forces. ☑

11) True or false? Friction is a non-contact force. ☑

12) What force causes the repulsion of two like electrical charges? What causes this force? ☑

13) What is a free body force diagram? ☑

14) Describe how you would use a scale diagram to work out the resultant force acting on an object. ☑

15) True or false? The arrows on a scale diagram for the forces on an object in equilibrium join up to create a closed shape. ☑

16) Describe how you would resolve a force into horizontal and vertical components using a scale drawing. ☑

## Moments (p.129-130) ☑

17) True or false? A moment is a turning effect of a force. ☑

18) State the equation for calculating the size of a moment of a force. ☑

19) How would the moment of a force change if the force were applied further from the pivot? ☑

20) If a seesaw is balanced, what can you say about the moments of the forces acting on the seesaw? ☑

21) True or false? For a given force, a larger gear will turn slower than a smaller gear. ☑

# Circuit Basics

*Current, **potential difference** and **resistance** are key to understanding circuits. But first up, **circuit symbols**.*

## Circuit Symbols You Should Know

You need to be able to use these symbols to <u>interpret</u> and <u>draw circuit diagrams</u>.

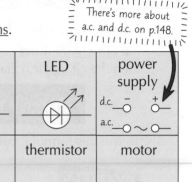
*There's more about a.c. and d.c. on p.148.*

| cell | battery | open switch | closed switch | filament lamp | fuse | LED | power supply |
|---|---|---|---|---|---|---|---|
| ⊣⊢ | ⊣⊢--⊣⊢ | —o/ o— | —o⌐o— | —⊗— | —▭— | ⊳⊢ | d.c. — + a.c. —o~o— |

| resistor | variable resistor | ammeter | voltmeter | diode | LDR | thermistor | motor |
|---|---|---|---|---|---|---|---|
| —▭— | —▱— | —(A)— | —(V)— | —⊳⊢— | —(□)— | —▱— | —(M)— |

## Current is the Flow of Electrical Charge

1) <u>Current</u> is the <u>flow</u> of electric charge (e.g. electrons, see below) around the circuit.

2) The unit of current is the <u>ampere</u>, A.

3) <u>Potential difference</u> (or voltage) is the <u>driving force</u> that <u>pushes</u> the charge round.

4) The unit of potential difference is the <u>volt</u>, V.

5) <u>Resistance</u> is anything that <u>slows the flow</u> down.

6) The unit of resistance is the <u>ohm</u>, Ω.

7) Current will <u>only flow</u> through an electrical component if there is a <u>potential difference</u> across that component, and if the circuit is <u>closed</u> (complete).

8) The current flowing <u>through a component</u> depends on the <u>potential difference</u> across it and the <u>resistance</u> of the component (p.135).

9) Generally speaking, the <u>higher the potential difference</u> across a component, the <u>higher the current</u> will be. And the <u>greater the resistance</u> of a component, the <u>smaller the current</u> that flows (for a given potential difference across the component). There's more on resistance on p.135.

*potential difference of supply provides the 'push'*

*+ve* ⊣⊢ *−ve*

*R*

*current flows*

*resistance — opposes the flow*

## Current in Metals is the Flow of Free Electrons

1) All <u>atoms</u> contain <u>positive protons</u> and <u>neutral neutrons</u> in the <u>nucleus</u>, with <u>negatively charged electrons orbiting</u> the nucleus (p.90).

2) The atoms in <u>metals</u> are bonded in such a way that metals are made up of a <u>lattice</u> (a grid) of <u>positive ions</u> (p.91) surrounded by <u>free electrons</u>.

3) These electrons are <u>free to move</u> through the whole metal. The <u>current</u> in metals is the flow of these free electrons.

*positive ion*

*free electron*

## Electrons flow the opposite way to the current...

<u>Electrons</u> in circuits actually move <u>from −ve to +ve</u>, but it's conventional to draw <u>current</u> as though it's flowing from <u>+ve to −ve</u>. It's what early physicists thought (before they discovered electrons), and it's stuck.

# Circuit Basics

*Charges **transfer energy** round a circuit — you can work out **how much** with a couple of equations...*

## Total Charge Through a Circuit Depends on Current and Time

1) <u>Current</u> is the <u>rate of flow</u> of <u>charge</u>.

2) If a <u>current</u> (*I*) flows past a point in a circuit for a length of <u>time</u> (*t*),
   then the <u>charge</u> (*Q*) that has passed this point is given by this formula:

$$\text{charge} = \text{current} \times \text{time}$$ or $$Q = I \times t$$

*More charge passes around the circuit in a given time when a greater current flows.*

3) To use this formula, you need <u>current</u> in <u>amperes</u>, A, <u>charge</u> in <u>coulombs</u>, C, and <u>time</u> in <u>seconds</u>, s.

> **EXAMPLE**
>
> **A battery charger passes 18 000 C of charge to a battery over a period of 2.5 hours.
> Calculate the current flowing between the battery charger and the battery.**
>
> 1) <u>Convert</u> the time into seconds.     $2.5 \times 60 \times 60 = 9000$ s
> 2) <u>Rearrange</u> the equation for current.     $I = Q \div t$
> 3) <u>Substitute</u> into the rearranged equation.     $= 18\ 000 \div 9000 = 2$ A

## Potential Difference is the Energy Transferred Per Unit Charge

1) The <u>potential difference</u> is the <u>energy transferred per coulomb of charge</u>
   that passes between <u>two points</u> in an electrical circuit.

2) You can calculate energy transferred (*E*), from charge moved (*Q*),
   and potential difference (*V*), using <u>this formula</u>:

$$\text{energy transferred} = \text{charge moved} \times \text{potential difference}$$ or $$E = Q \times V$$

3) To use this formula, you need <u>energy transferred</u> in <u>joules</u>, J, <u>charge moved</u>
   in <u>coulombs</u>, C, and <u>potential difference</u> in <u>volts</u>, V.

4) So, the <u>potential difference</u> (p.d.) across an electrical component is the <u>amount of energy</u>
   transferred by that electrical component (e.g. the amount of energy transferred by a motor
   to its kinetic energy store) <u>per unit charge</u> passed.  One <u>volt</u> is one <u>joule per coulomb</u>.

5) Potential difference is sometimes called <u>voltage</u>.  They're the same thing.

> **EXAMPLE**
>
> **The motor in an electric toothbrush is attached to a 3 V battery.
> 140 C of charge passes through the circuit as it is used.
> Calculate the energy transferred.**
>
> $E = Q \times V = 140 \times 3 = 420$ J

---

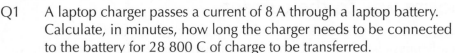

## Understanding potential difference is potentially difficult...

<u>Potential difference</u> can be harder to visualise than current or resistance.  But if you know the
<u>definition</u> for p.d. and are comfortable using the <u>equations</u>, you can't go far wrong.

Q1 Video Solution

Q1   A laptop charger passes a current of 8 A through a laptop battery.
     Calculate, in minutes, how long the charger needs to be connected
     to the battery for 28 800 C of charge to be transferred.          [4 marks]

# Potential Difference and Resistance

*Prepare yourself to meet one of the most **important equations** in electronics. It's all about **resistance**, **current** and **potential difference**... Now if that doesn't tempt you on to read this page, I don't know what will.*

## Resistance, Potential Difference and Current: $V = I \times R$

1) Potential difference ($V$), current ($I$), and resistance ($R$) are all related through this formula:

> **potential difference = current × resistance**     or     $V = I \times R$

2) To use this formula, you need potential difference in volts, V, current in amperes, A, and resistance in ohms, Ω.

3) If you rearrange this equation, you can use it to calculate the resistance of a component from measurements of potential difference and current (e.g. from the experiment on the next page).

**EXAMPLE**

**A 4.0 Ω resistor in a circuit has a potential difference of 6.0 V across it. What is the current through the resistor?**

1) Rearrange the equation for current.     $I = V \div R$

2) Substitute into the rearranged equation.     $= 6.0 \div 4.0 = 1.5$ A

## Resistance **Increases** with **Temperature** (Usually)

1) When an electrical charge flows through a component, it has to do work against resistance.

2) This causes an electrical transfer of energy (work done = energy transferred, p.123).

3) Some of this energy is transferred usefully but some of it is dissipated to the thermal energy stores of the component and the surroundings.

4) So when a current flows through a resistor, the resistor heats up.

5) This happens because the electrons collide with the ions in the lattice that make up the resistor as they flow through it.

6) This gives the ions energy, which causes them to vibrate more (and the energy in the thermal energy store of the resistor to increase — see p.174).

7) The more the ions vibrate, the harder it is for electrons to get through the resistor (because there are more collisions).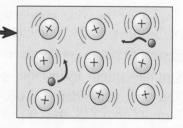

8) So for a given p.d. the current decreases as the resistor heats up.

9) If the resistor gets too hot, no current will be able to flow.

10) There is one exception to this — the resistance of a thermistor decreases with an increase in temperature (p.137).

11) Low resistance wires (p.169) can be used to reduce the energy dissipated to thermal stores as the current flows between components.

---

## The more ions vibrate, the lower the current passing through...

As a resistor heats up, current can't flow through it as easily — make sure you can explain why.

Q1     An appliance is connected to a 230 V source.
Calculate the resistance of the appliance if a current of 5.0 A is flowing through it.   [3 marks]

Q1 Video Solution

*ical — the **set-up** described on this page can be used to **investigate any component**. Handy.*

## You Can **Investigate** How **P.d.** Changes with **Current**

To investigate the <u>relationship</u> between <u>current</u> ($I$), <u>p.d.</u> ($V$) and <u>resistance</u> ($R$) for a range of components, such as a <u>filament bulb</u> or a <u>fixed resistor</u>:

1) Set up the <u>test circuit</u> as shown below.

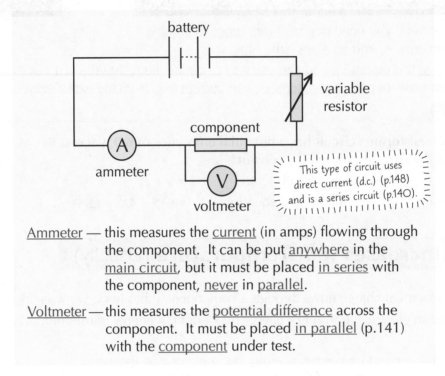

Ammeter — this measures the <u>current</u> (in amps) flowing through the component. It can be put <u>anywhere</u> in the <u>main circuit</u>, but it must be placed <u>in series</u> with the component, <u>never</u> in <u>parallel</u>.

Voltmeter — this measures the <u>potential difference</u> across the component. It must be placed <u>in parallel</u> (p.141) with the <u>component</u> under test.

2) The variable resistor is used to <u>change</u> the <u>current</u> in the circuit.

3) As $I = V \div R$ (p.135), <u>increasing</u> the resistance of the variable resistor <u>lowers</u> the current through the circuit at a fixed supply p.d.. This changes the <u>potential difference</u> across the <u>component</u>.

4) Now you need to get <u>sets</u> of <u>current</u> and <u>potential difference</u> readings:

• Set the <u>resistance</u> of the variable resistor.

• Measure the <u>current</u> through and <u>potential difference</u> across the component.

• Take measurements at a number of <u>different</u> resistances.

5) <u>Swap</u> over the wires connected to the battery to reverse the <u>direction of the current</u>. The ammeter should now display <u>negative readings</u>.

6) <u>Repeat</u> step 4 to get results for negative values of current.

7) <u>Plot</u> the <u>current</u> against the <u>potential difference</u> to get *I-V* graphs like the ones on the next page.

8) You can use this data to work out the component's <u>resistance</u> for <u>each measurement</u> of *I* and *V*, using the formula on p.135, so you can see if the resistance of the component <u>changes</u> as *I* and *V* change.

9) Make sure the circuit doesn't get <u>too hot</u> over the course of your experiment, as this will mess up your results (see previous page). If the circuit starts to warm up, <u>disconnect</u> it for a while between readings so it can cool down. And, like any experiment, you should do repeats and <u>calculate means</u>.

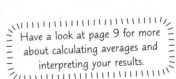
Have a look at page 9 for more about calculating averages and interpreting your results.

WORKING SCIENTIFICALLY

## In this experiment, temperature is a control variable...

The <u>temperature</u> of the component needs to be kept <u>constant</u>, otherwise the investigation would not be a <u>fair test</u>. Variables that need to be kept the same are called <u>control variables</u> (page 6).

# Circuit Devices

*With your current and your potential difference measured, you can now make some **sweet** graphs...*

## Three Important Current-Potential Difference Graphs

*I-V* graphs show how the <u>current</u> varies as you <u>change</u> the <u>potential difference</u> (p.d.).
Here are three examples, plotted from the <u>experiment</u> on the previous page:

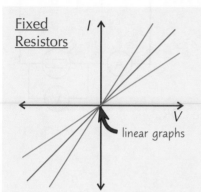

Fixed
Resistors

linear graphs

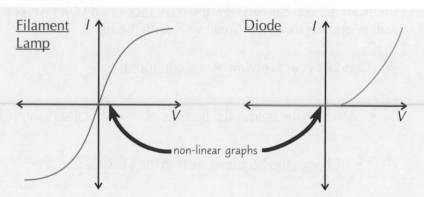

Filament
Lamp

Diode

non-linear graphs

Current is directly proportional to p.d. (if the temperature stays the same). Different resistors have different resistances, so their *I-V* graphs have different slopes.

The increasing current increases the temperature of the filament, which makes the resistance increase (p.135) so their *I-V* graphs are curved.

Current will only flow through a diode in one direction, as shown. The diode has very high resistance in the opposite direction. Current flows this way through a diode:

1) <u>Linear</u> components have an *I-V* graph that's a <u>straight line</u> (e.g. a fixed resistor). <u>Non-linear</u> components have a <u>curved</u> *I-V* graph (e.g. a filament lamp or a diode).

2) For <u>linear</u> components, if the line goes through <u>(0,0)</u>, the resistance of the component equals the <u>inverse</u> of the <u>gradient</u> of the line, or "<u>1/gradient</u>". The <u>steeper</u> the graph, the <u>lower</u> the resistance.

3) You can find the <u>resistance</u> for <u>any point</u> on any *I-V* graph by reading the <u>p.d.</u> and <u>current</u> at that point and sticking them into $V = I \times R$ (p.135).

## LDR is Short for Light Dependent Resistor

1) An LDR is a resistor that is <u>dependent</u> on the <u>intensity</u> of <u>light</u>. Simple really.

2) In <u>bright light</u>, the resistance <u>falls</u>.

3) In <u>darkness</u>, the resistance is <u>highest</u>.

4) They have lots of applications including <u>automatic</u> <u>night lights</u>, outdoor lighting and <u>burglar detectors</u>.

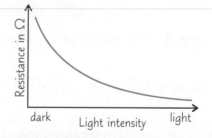

## A Thermistor's Resistance Decreases as Temperature Increases

1) A <u>thermistor</u> is a <u>temperature dependent</u> resistor.

2) For <u>negative temperature coefficient</u> thermistors:
   - Their resistance <u>drops</u> in <u>hotter</u> conditions.
   - Their resistance <u>goes up</u> in <u>cooler</u> conditions.

3) Thermistors make useful <u>temperature detectors</u>, e.g. <u>car engine</u> temperature sensors and electronic <u>thermostats</u>.

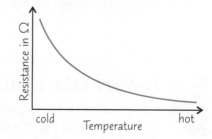

# Investigating LDRs and Thermistors

*...meter, I feel another **experiment** coming on — this time it's **thermistors** and **LDRs**.*

## You can **Investigate** How **Resistance** Changes for **LDRs**

1) You can create <u>I-V graphs</u> for <u>LDRs</u> using the method on p.136.
2) But the <u>resistance</u> of LDRs can <u>depend on</u> things <u>other than</u> current.
3) For example, you can test how the <u>resistance</u> of an LDR changes with brightness using the circuit shown on the right:

- Conduct your experiment in a <u>dim room</u>.

- Measure the <u>potential difference</u> across and <u>current</u> through the LDR.

- <u>Change the light level</u> near to the LDR.

- Measure the <u>p.d.</u> and <u>current</u> again. <u>Repeat</u> this for a <u>range</u> of light levels.

- Calculate the <u>resistance</u> for each measurement using $R = V \div I$.

4) You should find that as the light level gets <u>brighter</u>, the <u>current</u> through the LDR <u>increases</u> as the <u>resistance decreases</u>.

## You can **Investigate** How **Resistance** Changes for **Thermistors**

1) As with LDRs, you can use the method on p.136 to create <u>I-V graphs</u> for <u>thermistors</u>.
2) Also, you can test how the <u>resistance</u> of a thermistor changes with <u>temperature</u> using the circuit on the right:

- Measure the <u>p.d. across</u> and <u>current through</u> the thermistor.

- <u>Change the temperature</u> of the thermistor by heating it.

- Measure the <u>current</u> and <u>p.d.</u> for a range of <u>different temperatures</u>.

- Calculate the <u>resistance</u> for each measurement using $R = V \div I$.

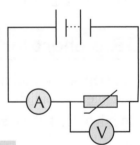

3) You should find that as the <u>temperature increases</u>, the <u>current</u> through the thermistor <u>increases</u> — showing that the <u>resistance decreases</u>.

## Always take a moment to think about safety...

When you plan any experiment always <u>assess</u> the <u>risks</u> to try and <u>reduce</u> them as much as possible. So if you're working in a dim room, check there are <u>no wires</u> trailing across the floor.

# Warm-Up & Exam Questions

Now you've had an intro to some circuit basics, check you've understood it all by trying these questions.

## Warm-Up Questions

1) Draw the symbol for an LED.
2) What are the units of resistance?
3) True or false? Current in metals is the flow of positive ions.
4) State the equation linking energy transferred, charge moved and potential difference.
5) Explain, in terms of electrons and ions, why energy is transferred to a resistor's thermal energy store when a current flows through it.
6) How should a voltmeter be connected in a circuit to measure the p.d. across a component?
7) Sketch the current-potential difference graph for a filament lamp.
8) How does a thermistor's resistance change as the temperature of its surroundings increases?

## Exam Questions

1   **Figure 1** shows a circuit diagram for a standard test circuit. When the switch is closed, the ammeter reads 0.30 A and the voltmeter reads 1.5 V.

Grade 6-7

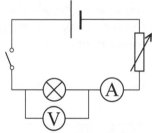

(a) (i) The switch is closed for 35 seconds. Calculate the total charge that flows through the filament lamp during this time.

[2 marks]

**Figure 1**

(ii) Calculate the energy transferred to the filament lamp during this time.

[2 marks]

(b) The variable resistor is used to increase the resistance in the test circuit. State how this will affect the current flowing through the circuit.

[1 mark]

**PRACTICAL**

2   A student carried out an experiment to measure what happened to the potential difference across a diode as the current through it was varied. **Figure 2** shows a graph of her results.

Grade 6-7

(a) State **one** variable that should be controlled in this experiment.

[1 mark]

(b) Calculate the resistance of the diode at the point marked A in **Figure 2**.

[4 marks]

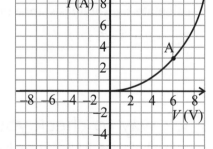

**Figure 2**

# Series Circuits

*You'll need to make sure you know the **rules** for **current** and **p.d.** in series circuits. You also need to be able to explain what happens to a circuit's **total resistance** when you connect **resistors** in **series**.*

## Series Circuits — All or Nothing

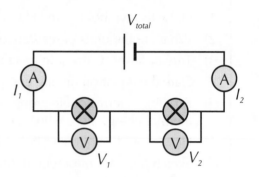

$V_{total}$

1) In series circuits, the different components are connected in a line, end to end, between the +ve and –ve of the power supply (except for voltmeters, which are always connected in parallel, but they don't count as part of the circuit).

2) If you remove or disconnect one component, the circuit is broken and they all stop working. This is generally not very handy, and in practice very few things are connected in series.

3) You can use the following rules to design series circuits to measure quantities and test components. For a series circuit:

- There's a bigger supply p.d. when more cells are in series (if they're all connected the same way). E.g. when two cells with a p.d. of 1.5 V are connected in series they supply 3 V between them.

- The current is the same everywhere. $I_1 = I_2$ etc. The size of the current depends on the total p.d. and the total resistance of the circuit ($I = V \div R$).

- The total potential difference of the supply is shared between components. The p.d. for each component depends on its resistance. The bigger a component's resistance, the bigger its share of the total potential difference.

- The total resistance of the circuit increases as you add resistors (see below).

## Adding Resistors in Series Increases Total Resistance

1) In series circuits the total resistance of two components is just the sum of their resistances.

2) This is because by adding a resistor in series, the two resistors have to share the total p.d..

3) The potential difference across each resistor is lower, so the current through each resistor is also lower. In a series circuit, the current is the same everywhere so the total current in the circuit is reduced when a resistor is added. This means the total resistance of the circuit increases.

**For the circuit diagram shown, calculate the total resistance of the circuit.**

$R_{total}$ = 2 + 3 = 5 $\Omega$

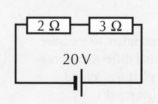

## A quick way to check your p.d. calculations...

The ratio in which p.d. is shared out between components in series is the same as the ratio of their resistances. So if a resistor has a resistance three times greater than a light bulb, the resistor will receive a share of the battery's p.d. that is three times larger than that received by the bulb.

Q1 Video Solution

Q1    A battery is connected in series with a 4 $\Omega$ resistor, a 5 $\Omega$ resistor and a 6 $\Omega$ resistor.
A current of 0.6 A flows through the circuit.
Calculate the potential difference of the battery.                    [3 marks]

# Parallel Circuits

*Parallel circuits can be a little bit trickier to wrap your head around, but they're much more **useful** than series circuits. Most electronics use a combination of series and parallel circuitry.*

## Parallel Circuits — Everything is Independent

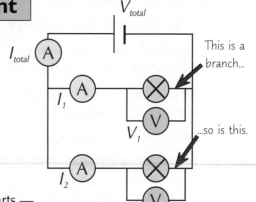

1) In parallel circuits, each component is separately connected to the +ve and –ve of the supply (except ammeters, which are always connected in series).

2) If you remove or disconnect one of them, it will hardly affect the others at all.

3) This is obviously how most things must be connected, for example in cars and in household electrics. You have to be able to switch everything on and off separately.

4) Everyday circuits often include a mixture of series and parallel parts — when looking at components on the same branch the rules for series circuits apply.

### Potential Difference in Parallel Circuits

1) In parallel circuits all components get the full source p.d., so the voltage is the same across all components: $$V_1 = V_2 = V_3 = ...$$

2) This means that identical bulbs connected in parallel will all be at the same brightness.

### Current in Parallel Circuits

1) In parallel circuits the current is shared between branches.

2) The total current flowing around the circuit is equal to the total of all the currents through the separate components: $$I_{total} = I_1 + I_2 + ...$$

3) In a parallel circuit, there are junctions where the current either splits or rejoins. The total current going into a junction has to equal the total current leaving it.

4) If two identical components are connected in parallel then the same current will flow through each component.

## Adding a Resistor in Parallel Reduces the Total Resistance

1) If you have two resistors in parallel, their total resistance is less than the resistance of the smallest of the two resistors.

2) This can be tough to get your head around, but think about it like this:

- In parallel, both resistors have the same potential difference across them as the source.
- This means the 'pushing force' making the current flow is the same as the source potential difference for each resistor that you add.
- But by adding another loop, the current has more than one direction to go in.
- This increases the total current that can flow around the circuit. Using $V = I \times R$, an increase in current means a decrease in the total resistance of the circuit.

## Learn the difference between series and parallel circuits...

In series circuits, current is the same everywhere and p.d. is split between components.
In parallel circuits, p.d. is the same across each branch and current is split between branches.

Q1 Video Solution

Q1   A circuit contains three resistors, each connected in parallel with a cell. Explain what happens to the total current and resistance in the circuit when one resistor is removed.

[4 marks]

# Investigating Circuits

...*ment to see how placing **components** in series or parallel can affect a circuit's total resistance.*

## You Can **Investigate** Adding **Resistors** in **Series**...

1) First, you'll need to find at least four <u>identical resistors</u>.

2) Then build the circuit shown on the right using <u>one</u> of the resistors. Make a note of the <u>potential difference</u> of the <u>battery</u> (V).

3) Measure the <u>current</u> through the circuit using the ammeter. Use this to <u>calculate the total resistance</u> of the circuit using $R = V \div I$.

4) Add another <u>resistor</u>, in <u>series</u> with the first.

5) Again, measure the current through the circuit and use this and the <u>potential difference</u> of the battery to <u>calculate</u> the <u>total resistance</u> of the circuit.

6) Repeat <u>steps 4 and 5</u> until you've added all of your resistors.

7) <u>Plot a graph</u> of the <u>number of resistors</u> against the <u>total resistance</u> of the circuit (see below).

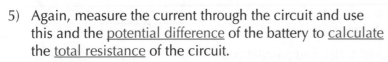

## ... or in **Parallel**

1) Using the <u>same equipment</u> as before (so the experiment is a <u>fair test</u>), build the same <u>initial circuit</u>.

2) Measure the <u>total current</u> through the circuit and <u>calculate the total resistance</u> of the circuit using $R = V \div I$ (again, V is the potential difference of the <u>battery</u>).

3) Next, add another <u>resistor</u>, in <u>parallel</u> with the first.

4) Measure the <u>total current</u> through the circuit and use this and the <u>potential difference</u> of the battery to calculate the <u>total resistance of the circuit</u>.

5) Repeat <u>steps 3 and 4</u> until you've added all of your resistors.

6) Plot a <u>graph</u> of the <u>number of resistors</u> in the circuit against the <u>total resistance</u>.

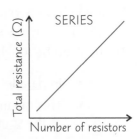

## Your Results Should **Match** the **Resistance Rules**

You should find that adding resistors in <u>series increases</u> the total <u>resistance</u> of the circuit (adding a resistor <u>decreases</u> the total <u>current</u> through the circuit).

The <u>more</u> resistors you add, the <u>larger</u> the resistance of the whole circuit.

If you measured the <u>p.d.</u> across one of the resistors, you would find the p.d. <u>decreases</u> as more resistors are added in series.

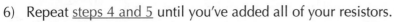

When you add resistors in <u>parallel</u>, the <u>total current</u> through the circuit <u>increases</u> — so the total resistance of the circuit has <u>decreased</u>.

The <u>more</u> resistors you add, the <u>smaller</u> the overall resistance becomes.

If you measured the <u>p.d.</u> across one of the resistors, you would find the p.d. <u>remains the same</u> regardless of how many resistors are added in parallel.

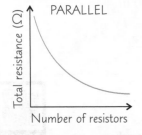

You can also do the experiments on this page with <u>filament lamps</u> instead of resistors:

- The lamps should get <u>dimmer</u> when a lamp is added in <u>series</u> (as the p.d. is being <u>shared out</u>).
- The lamps should be the <u>same brightness</u> in <u>parallel</u> (as they each have the <u>same p.d.</u>).

# Warm-Up & Exam Questions

Time to see what you can remember about parallel and series circuits.

## Warm-Up Questions

1) True or false?  Current is the same everywhere in a series circuit.

2) How is the total resistance of a series circuit calculated from the resistance of each component in the circuit?

3) Two identical resistors are connected in parallel across a 3 V cell.
   What is the potential difference across each resistor?

4) Which circuit has the higher total resistance: two resistors connected in series,
   or the same two resistors connected in parallel?

5) Describe an experiment that could be used to investigate how increasing the number of resistors connected in series affects the total resistance of a circuit.

## Exam Questions

1    **Figure 1** shows a series circuit.    (Grade 4-6)

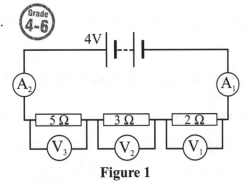

**Figure 1**

(a)    Calculate the total resistance in the circuit.

*[1 mark]*

(b)    The reading on $A_1$ is 0.4 A.
       Explain what the reading on $A_2$ is.

*[2 marks]*

(c)    $V_1$ reads 0.8 V and $V_2$ reads 1.2 V.
       Calculate the reading on $V_3$.

*[1 mark]*

2    A parallel circuit is connected as shown in **Figure 2**.    (Grade 7-9)

(a)    Find the reading on voltmeter $V_1$.

*[1 mark]*

(b)    Calculate the reading on ammeter $A_1$.

*[3 marks]*

(c)    Calculate the reading on ammeter $A_2$.

*[1 mark]*

(d)    A third resistor is added to the circuit,
       connected in series with the 3 Ω resistor.
       Explain how this would affect the reading on $A_2$.

*[3 marks]*

**Figure 2**

# Energy in Circuits

*You can think about **electrical circuits** in terms of **energy transfer** — the charge carriers take energy around the circuit. When they go through an electrical component energy is transferred to make the component work.*

## Energy Transferred Depends on Current, p.d. and Time

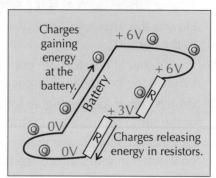

Charges gaining energy at the battery.

Charges releasing energy in resistors.

1) When an electrical charge goes through a change in potential difference, then energy is transferred (as work is done against resistance — p.135).

2) Energy is supplied to the charge at the power source to 'raise' it through a potential.

3) The charge gives up this energy when it 'falls' through any potential drop in components elsewhere in the circuit.

4) To find the energy transferred to an electrical component, you can use the equation:

$$E = I \times V \times t$$

*This equation comes from combining the two equations from p.134.*

Where $E$ is energy transferred in joules (J), $I$ is current in amps (A), $V$ is p.d. in volts (V) and $t$ is time in seconds (s).

5) The larger the current through, or p.d. across, a component, the more energy is transferred to it.

> **EXAMPLE**
>
> **A bulb is connected to a circuit. The p.d. across the bulb is 250 V and the current through the bulb is 0.4 A.**
> **Calculate how long it will take for 1 kJ of energy to be transferred to the bulb.**
>
> 1) Convert the energy from kilojoules to joules.     1 kJ = 1000 J
>
> 2) Then rearrange $E = I \times V \times t$ for $t$.    $t = \dfrac{E}{I \times V}$
>
> 3) Substitute into the rearranged equation    $t = \dfrac{1000}{0.4 \times 250} = 10$ s

## Energy is Transferred from Cells and Other Sources

1) Electrical appliances are designed to transfer energy to components in the circuit when a current flows.

| | |
|---|---|
| Kettles transfer energy electrically from the mains a.c. supply to the thermal energy store of the heating element inside the kettle.  | Energy is transferred electrically from the battery of a handheld fan to the kinetic energy store of the fan's motor.  |

2) Of course, no appliance transfers all energy completely usefully. The higher the current, the more energy is transferred to the thermal energy stores of the components (and then the surroundings).

3) This heating usually increases the resistance of the components, like you saw on page 135.

---

## $I \times V \times t$ will give the total energy transferred to a component...

The equation won't tell you how much of that energy is then transferred usefully by the component, or how much is wasted. To find that out, you need to know the component's efficiency (p.47).

Q1 Video Solution

Q1   A charger is connected to a 230 V source for an hour. A current of 4.0 A flows through it. Calculate the energy transferred by the charger. Give your answer to 2 significant figures.

[3 marks]

# Heating in Circuits and Power Ratings

*Electrical devices* are built to *transfer energy*. But nothing is perfect and some of this transferred energy ends up in *thermal* stores. This isn't always a bad thing though — devices like *toasters* and *heaters* make use of it.

## Heating a **Circuit** isn't Always Bad

1) Heating up a component generally <u>reduces</u> its <u>efficiency</u> (p.47) — less energy is transferred to <u>useful</u> energy stores because more of it is being transferred to the <u>thermal</u> energy store of the component.

2) If the temperature gets <u>too high</u>, this can cause components in the circuit to <u>melt</u> — which means the circuit will <u>stop working</u>, or not work <u>properly</u>.

3) <u>Fuses</u> use this effect to <u>protect</u> circuits — they <u>melt</u> and <u>break</u> the circuit if the current gets too high (there's more on fuses on p.149).

4) The heating effect of an electric current can have other <u>advantages</u>. For example, it's ace if you want to heat something. Toasters contain a coil of wire with a really high <u>resistance</u>. When a current passes through the coil, its temperature increases so much that it <u>glows</u> and gives off <u>infrared radiation</u>. This radiation <u>transfers energy</u> to the bread and <u>cooks</u> it.

5) <u>Filament bulbs</u> and <u>electric heaters</u> work in a similar way.

## Appliances Often Have a **Power Rating**

1) The <u>total</u> energy transferred by an appliance depends on <u>how long</u> the appliance is on for and its <u>power</u>.

2) The <u>power</u> of an appliance is the energy that it <u>transfers per second</u>. So the <u>more</u> energy it transfers in a given time, the <u>higher</u> its power. Power is measured in <u>watts</u>.

3) Appliances are often given a <u>power rating</u> — they're labelled with the <u>maximum</u> safe power that they can operate at. You can usually take this to be their <u>maximum operating power</u>.

4) The power rating tells you the <u>maximum</u> amount of <u>energy</u> transferred between stores <u>per second</u> when the appliance is in use.

> Microwaves have a range of <u>power ratings</u>. A microwave with a power rating of 500 W will take <u>longer</u> to cook food than one with a power rating of 750 W. This is because the 500 W microwave transfers <u>less</u> energy <u>per second</u> to the <u>thermal</u> energy store of the food, so it takes longer to cook.

5) This can help customers choose between models — the <u>lower</u> the power rating, the <u>less</u> electricity an appliance uses in a <u>given time</u>.

6) But, a higher power <u>doesn't</u> necessarily mean that it transfers <u>more</u> energy <u>usefully</u>. An appliance may be <u>more powerful</u> than another, <u>but less efficient</u>, meaning that it might still only transfer the <u>same amount</u> of energy (or even <u>less</u>) to useful stores (see p.46).

## A higher power rating means more electricity is used per second...

The <u>amount of electricity</u> used by an appliance depends on its <u>power rating</u> and the amount of <u>time</u> it's <u>switched on</u> for. For example, the <u>power rating</u> of an electric <u>lawn mower</u> is typically about <u>ten times higher</u> than the power rating of a <u>fridge</u> (so the lawn mower will use <u>more electricity per second</u>), but a fridge probably uses more electricity in, for example, one year as it's <u>always switched on</u>.

# Power in Circuits

*Here come three equations for **calculating** electrical **power**, just for you. An equation for every occasion.*

## You can **Calculate** the **Power** of an Appliance

1) The <u>power</u> of an appliance can be found using:

> **Power (W) = Energy transferred (J) ÷ Time (s)**   or   $P = \dfrac{E}{t}$

2) The <u>power transferred</u> by an appliance also depends on the <u>potential difference</u> (p.d.) across it, and the <u>current</u> flowing through it.

3) The <u>p.d.</u> tells you how much <u>energy each unit of charge transfers</u> (p.134), and the <u>current</u> tells you <u>how much charge</u> passes per unit time. So <u>both</u> will affect the rate that <u>energy is transferred</u> to an appliance, and the rate at which it <u>transfers energy</u> to other stores.

4) The <u>power</u> of an appliance can be found with:

> **Electrical power (W) = Current (A) × Potential difference (V)**   or   $P = I \times V$

### EXAMPLE

**A blender is connected to the mains electricity supply. In one minute, 20 700 J of energy is transferred to the blender. Calculate the power of the blender.**

$P = E ÷ t = 20\ 700 ÷ 60 = 345\ W$

**The potential difference of the mains electricity supply is 230 V. Calculate the current through the blender during this one minute period.**

1) <u>Rearrange</u> $P = I \times V$ for $I$.   $I = P ÷ V$
2) <u>Substitute</u> into the rearranged equation.   $I = 345 ÷ 230 = 1.5\ A$

## You can also Calculate **Power** Using **Current** and **Resistance**

You can also find the power of an appliance if you <u>don't know</u> the <u>potential difference</u>. To do this, stick $V = I \times R$ from page 135 into $P = I \times V$, which gives you:

> $P = I^2 \times R$

Where $P$ is the electrical power in watts (W), $I$ is current in amperes (A) and $R$ is the resistance in ohms (Ω).

### EXAMPLE

**A current of 5 A is passing through a motor, which has a resistance of 48 Ω. Calculate the power of the motor.**

$P = I^2 \times R = 5^2 \times 48 = 1200\ W$

---

## Make sure you use the right power equation...

Q1 Video Solution

If you're struggling to pick which <u>power equation</u> to use, it can be helpful to <u>list</u> the variables in the question, then decide which equation is suitable from the variables <u>you've been given</u>.

Q1    Calculate the difference in the amount of energy transferred by a 250 W TV and a 375 W TV when they are both used for two hours.    [3 marks]

# Warm-Up & Exam Questions

Put the brakes on — it's time to see what you can remember about energy and power in circuits.

1) State the equation relating energy transferred, current, potential difference and time.
2) Describe the main energy transfer that occurs in an electric toaster when it's plugged into the mains and turned on.
3) Name one appliance that makes use of the heating effect of an electric current.
4) Give the unit used to measure power.
5) Will a 60 W light bulb or a 40 W light bulb transfer more energy in a given amount of time?
6) State the equation that relates electrical power, current and resistance.

## Exam Questions

**1** **Figure 1** shows the power ratings for two kettles and the potential difference across each kettle.

|  | **Power (kW)** | **Potential Difference (V)** |
|---|---|---|
| **Kettle A** | 2.8 | 230 |
| **Kettle B** | 3.0 | 230 |

**Figure 1**

(a) State the equation linking electrical power, current and potential difference.

*[1 mark]*

(b) Calculate the current drawn from the mains supply by kettle A.

*[3 marks]*

(c) A student is deciding whether to buy kettle A or kettle B.
She wants to buy the kettle that boils water faster. Both kettles have the same efficiency.
State and explain which kettle she should choose.

*[2 marks]*

**2** A torch uses a 3.0 V power supply. A current of 0.5 A passes through a torch bulb.

(a) The torch is on for half an hour.
Calculate the amount of energy transferred from the power supply in this time.
Use the correct equation from the Physics Equation Sheet on page 268.

*[3 marks]*

(b) The torch bulb is replaced. When the new torch bulb is connected
to the 3.0 V power supply, 0.25 A of current passes through it.
State how the power of the torch will be affected by this change.

*[1 mark]*

**3** A single 1.5 V battery contains 13 000 J of energy in its chemical energy store.
One of these batteries can be used to power a clock.
A current of 0.2 mA passes through the clock when the battery is connected.

Calculate how many batteries are needed to power the clock for 10 years.
Use the correct equation from the Physics Equation Sheet on page 268.

*[3 marks]*

# Electricity in the Home

*Now you've learnt the basics of **electrical circuits**, it's time to see how **electricity** is used in **everyday life**.*

## Mains Supply is **a.c.**, Battery Supply is **d.c.**

1) There are two types of electricity supplies — <u>alternating current</u> (a.c.) and <u>direct current</u> (d.c.).

2) In <u>a.c. supplies</u> the movement of the charges is <u>constantly</u> changing direction. <u>Alternating currents</u> are produced by <u>alternating voltages</u> (the <u>positive</u> and <u>negative</u> ends of the p.d. keep <u>alternating</u>).

3) The <u>UK mains supply</u> (the electricity in your home) is an a.c. supply at around <u>230 V</u>.

4) The frequency of the a.c. mains supply is <u>50 cycles per second</u> or <u>50 Hz</u> (hertz).

5) By contrast, cells and batteries supply <u>direct current</u> (d.c.).

6) In <u>direct current</u> the movement of the charges is only in one <u>direction</u>. It's created by a <u>direct voltage</u> (a p.d. that is <u>only positive</u> or <u>negative</u>, not both).

*You can turn a.c. into d.c. by using a diode (p.137).*

## Most Cables Have **Three** Separate **Wires**

1) Most electrical appliances are connected to the mains supply by <u>three-core</u> cables. This means that they have <u>three wires</u> inside them, each with a <u>core of copper</u> and a <u>coloured plastic coating</u>.

2) The <u>colour</u> of the insulation on each cable shows its <u>purpose</u>.

3) The colours are <u>always</u> the <u>same</u> for <u>every</u> appliance. This is so that it is easy to tell the different wires <u>apart</u>.

<u>LIVE WIRE</u> — <u>brown</u>.
The live wire carries the voltage (potential difference, p.d.). It alternates between a <u>high +ve and −ve voltage</u> of about <u>230 V</u>.

<u>NEUTRAL WIRE</u> — <u>blue</u>.
The neutral wire <u>completes</u> the circuit — when the appliance is operating normally, current flows through the <u>live</u> and <u>neutral</u> wires. It is around <u>0 V</u>.

<u>EARTH WIRE</u> — <u>green</u> and <u>yellow</u>.
The earth wire is for <u>safety</u> and <u>protecting</u> the <u>wiring</u>. It carries the current away if something goes <u>wrong</u> and stops the appliance casing becoming <u>live</u>. It's <u>also</u> at 0 V.

- The <u>p.d.</u> between the <u>live wire</u> and the <u>neutral wire</u> equals the <u>supply p.d.</u> (<u>230 V</u> for the mains).
- The <u>p.d.</u> between the <u>live wire</u> and the <u>earth wire</u> is also <u>230 V</u> for a mains-connected appliance.
- There is <u>no p.d.</u> between the <u>neutral wire</u> and the <u>earth wire</u> — they're both at 0 V.

4) <u>Plug sockets</u> have <u>switches</u> which are connected in the <u>live wire</u> of the circuit. This is so the circuit can be <u>broken</u> — the appliance becomes <u>isolated</u> and the risk of an <u>electric shock</u> is reduced.

5) <u>Fuses</u> and <u>circuit breakers</u> are also attached to the <u>live wire</u> in order to <u>isolate</u> the appliance if something goes wrong (p.149).

## Mains electricity is always 230 V in the UK...

Make sure you can remember the <u>potential differences</u> between the three wires in mains wiring. Only the <u>live wire</u> has a potential difference that <u>isn't zero</u>, so there's a potential difference between the live wire and each of the other two wires (of 230 V). The potential difference between the earth and neutral wires is <u>zero</u>.

# Electrical Safety

*The **live wire** is capable of giving a dangerous **electric shock**, so safety precautions such as **fuses** are needed.*

## Touching the **Live Wire** Gives You an **Electric Shock**

1) Your <u>body</u> (just like the earth) is at <u>0 V</u>.

2) This means that if you touch the <u>live wire</u>, a <u>large potential difference</u> is produced across your body and a <u>current</u> flows through you.

3) This causes a large <u>electric shock</u> which could injure or even kill you.

4) Even if a plug socket is turned <u>off</u> (i.e. the switch is <u>open</u>) there is still a <u>danger</u> of an electric shock. A current <u>isn't flowing</u>, but there is still a p.d. in the live wire. If you made <u>contact</u> with the live wire, your body would provide a <u>link</u> between the supply and the earth, so a <u>current</u> would flow <u>through you</u>.

5) <u>Any</u> connection between <u>live</u> and <u>neutral</u> can be <u>dangerous</u>. If the link creates a <u>low resistance</u> path to earth, a huge current will flow, which could result in a fire.

## **Earthing** and **Fuses** Prevent **Electrical Overloads**

1) <u>Surges</u> (sudden increases) in <u>current</u> can occur because of <u>changes in a circuit</u> (e.g. an appliance suddenly switching off) or because of a <u>fault</u> in an electrical <u>appliance</u>.

2) Current surges can lead to the <u>circuits and wiring</u> in your appliances <u>melting</u> or causing a <u>fire</u>, and <u>faulty</u> appliances can cause deadly <u>electric shocks</u>.

3) The <u>earth wire</u> and a <u>fuse</u> are included in electrical appliances to prevent this from happening. The example below shows how they work:

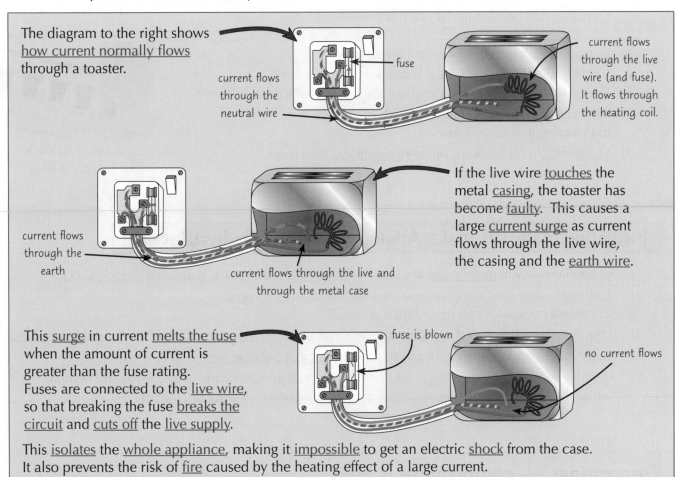

The diagram to the right shows <u>how current normally flows</u> through a toaster.

current flows through the neutral wire

fuse

current flows through the live wire (and fuse). It flows through the heating coil.

If the live wire <u>touches</u> the metal <u>casing</u>, the toaster has become <u>faulty</u>. This causes a large <u>current surge</u> as current flows through the live wire, the casing and the <u>earth wire</u>.

current flows through the earth

current flows through the live and through the metal case

This <u>surge</u> in current <u>melts the fuse</u> when the amount of current is greater than the fuse rating. Fuses are connected to the <u>live wire</u>, so that breaking the fuse <u>breaks the circuit</u> and <u>cuts off</u> the <u>live supply</u>.

fuse is blown

no current flows

This <u>isolates</u> the <u>whole appliance</u>, making it <u>impossible</u> to get an electric <u>shock</u> from the case. It also prevents the risk of <u>fire</u> caused by the heating effect of a large current.

4) As well as the fuses in plugs, there are also <u>household fuses</u> (these are the ones that blow when a light bulb goes). These work in the <u>same way</u>, but protect the <u>wiring in the house</u>, not just in an appliance.

# Electrical Safety

*Fuses and **circuit breakers** are super important. And questions on them **cover a whole barrel of fun** — electrical current, resistance, potential difference... Read this page and make sure you've got it sussed.*

## A **Fuse Rating** is the **Minimum Current** needed to **Break** a Fuse

1) Fuses should be rated as near as possible but just higher than the normal operating current.
2) The larger the current, the thicker the cable you need to carry it (to stop the cable getting too hot and melting). That's why the fuse rating needed for cables usually increases with cable thickness.

> **EXAMPLE**
>
> **A 1 kW hair dryer is connected to a 230 V supply.**
> **Suggest whether a 3 A, a 5 A or a 13 A fuse is needed.**
>
> 1) Convert from kilowatts to watts.  $1 \text{ kW} = 1000 \text{ W}$
> 2) Then rearrange $P = I \times V$ (p.146) for $I$.  $I = P \div V$
> 3) Substitute into the rearranged equation.  $I = 1000 \div 230 = 4.3... \text{ A}$
> 4) Choose the fuse with the rating just higher than the calculated current.  So a 5 A fuse is needed.

## Circuit Breakers are Even Safer Than Fuses

Circuit breakers can be used in the place of household fuses.

1) Instead of melting a fuse, a large current may instead 'trip' (turn off) a circuit breaker.
2) Circuit breakers turn off quicker than the time taken for a fuse to melt.
3) They can also be reset, which is much easier than having to replace a fuse.
4) However, circuit breakers are more expensive than fuses.

Household circuit breaker switches.

## Insulating Materials Make Appliances "Double Insulated"

1) All appliances with metal cases are usually "earthed" to reduce the danger of electric shock.
2) "Earthing" just means the case must be attached to an earth wire. An earthed conductor can never become live.
3) If the appliance has a plastic casing and no metal parts showing then it's said to be double insulated.
4) Plastic can't conduct electricity and so the casing can't become live.
5) Anything with double insulation like that doesn't need an earth wire — just a live and neutral. Cables that only carry the live and neutral wires are known as two-core cables.

---

## Fuse ratings — compromise is key...

You want to be sure a fuse will melt if there's a surge in current, so the rating can't be too high. On the other hand you don't want it to be so low that it will blow whilst the appliance is functioning safely.

# Warm-Up & Exam Questions

Time to see if you've been paying close attention to the last three pages — have a go at these delightful warm-up and exam questions. If you get any wrong, look back for a quick recap.

## Warm-Up Questions

1) Is the electricity supplied by a battery alternating current or direct current?
2) Explain the function of the neutral wire in mains wiring.
3) What is the p.d. between the live wire and the neutral wire in mains wiring?
4) Which wire should a fuse be fitted to in mains wiring?
5) True or false? It is best to use a fuse with a rating that is much lower than the appliance's normal operating current.

## Exam Questions

1 Appliances with a metal casing are usually connected to the mains using a three-core cable.

(a) Mains electricity provides alternating current.
State what is meant by alternating current.

*[1 mark]*

**Figure 1**

(b) **Figure 1** shows an electrical cable that has become frayed so that the metal part of the live wire is exposed. Explain why you would get an electric shock if you touched the exposed wire.

*[3 marks]*

2 A kettle is connected to the mains electricity supply.

The kettle develops a fault so that the live wire is in contact with the kettle's metal casing, causing it to become live.

(a) Explain how the earth wire and the fuse isolate the kettle in this situation.

*[3 marks]*

(b) Give an alternative to using a fuse to isolate a faulty appliance.

*[1 mark]*

(c) An appliance has a casing that is made entirely from plastic, and has no metal parts showing. Explain why the appliance does not need an earth wire.

*[1 mark]*

# Revision Summary for Section 7

Well that's all for <u>Section 7</u> folks — try out these revision summary questions to see how much you've learnt.

* Try these questions and <u>tick off each one</u> when you <u>get it right</u>.
* When you're <u>completely happy</u> with a sub-topic, tick it off.

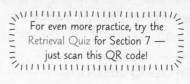 For even more practice, try the Retrieval Quiz for Section 7 — just scan this QR code!

 Section 7 Quiz

## Circuit Basics (p.133-138) ☑

1) Draw the circuit symbols for: a cell, a filament lamp, a diode, a motor and an LDR. ☑
2) What is meant by the potential difference in a circuit? ☑
3) What is meant by the resistance of a circuit? ☑
4) Define current and state an equation that links charge, current and time, with units for each. ☑
5) What is the equation that links potential difference, current and resistance? ☑
6) Describe how the resistance of a fixed resistor varies with temperature. ☑
7) True or false? To measure the current through a component, an ammeter must be connected in parallel with the component. ☑
8) Explain how you would investigate how the current through a component affects its resistance. ☑
9) Sketch the *I-V* graph for a diode. ☑
10) Describe how the resistance of an LDR varies with light intensity. ☑
11) Give one everyday use of an LDR. ☑

## Series and Parallel Circuits (p.140-142) ☑

12) True or false? Potential difference is shared between components in a series circuit. ☑
13) True or false? Adding resistors in series increases the total resistance of the circuit. ☑
14) Give one difference between series and parallel circuits. ☑
15) Does adding two resistors in parallel increase or decrease the total resistance of a circuit? ☑

## Power and Energy Transfers in Circuits (p.144-146) ☑

16) Give two disadvantages of the heating effect in an electrical circuit. ☑
17) What is a power rating? ☑
18) State the equation that links power, energy transferred and time. ☑

## Electricity in the Home and Electrical Safety (p.148-150) ☑

19) True or false? Mains supply electricity is an alternating current. ☑
20) What is the frequency of the UK mains supply? ☑
21) Give the potential difference between the live wire and the earth wire in mains wiring. ☑
22) Which wire is connected to the metal casing of an appliance in order to make the appliance safe to use? ☑
23) True or false? Circuit breakers must be replaced each time they 'trip'. ☑

## Static Electricity

*Static electricity builds up on **insulating** materials. This is due to the **transfer of electrons**.*

### Build-up of **Static** is Caused by **Friction**

1) When certain insulating materials are rubbed together, negatively charged electrons will be scraped off one and dumped on the other.

2) As the materials are insulators, these electrons are not free to move — this build up of charge is static electricity.

3) The materials become electrically charged, with a positive static charge on the one that has lost electrons and an equal negative static charge on the other.

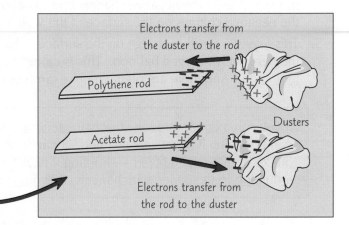

4) Which way the electrons are transferred depends on the two materials involved.

5) But whether an object has a positive or negative charge, it's always the negative electrons that have moved.

6) The classic examples are polythene and acetate rods being rubbed with a cloth duster.

### **Like** Charges **Repel**, **Opposite** Charges **Attract**

1) Electrically charged objects exert a force on one another.

2) Two things with opposite electric charges are attracted to each other, while two things with the same electric charge will repel each other.

3) These forces get weaker the further apart the two things are.

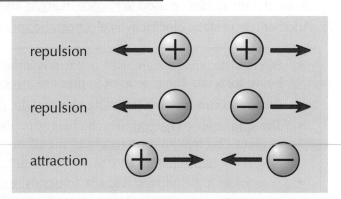

- One way to see these forces is to suspend a rod with a known charge from a piece of string (so it is free to move).
- Placing an object with the same charge nearby will repel the rod — the rod will move away from the object.
- An oppositely-charged object will attract the rod, causing it to move towards the object.

## Static builds up as electrons are transferred between two materials...

The material that the electrons have been transferred to will end up with a negative static charge, and the material the electrons have been transferred from will end up with a positive static charge.

# Applications of Static Electricity

*Static electricity can be pretty **useful**, especially in **industry**. First up though, I'll be explaining why **balloons** can **stick to walls**. Unfortunately, it's **not** as magical as it seems.*

## Electrically Charged Objects can Attract Uncharged Objects

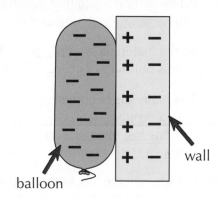

1) Rubbing a balloon against your hair or clothes transfers electrons to the balloon, leaving it with a negative charge. If you then hold the balloon against a wall it will stick, even though the wall isn't charged.

2) That's because the charges on the surface of the wall can move a little — the negative charges on the balloon repel the negative charges on the surface of the wall.

3) This leaves a positive charge on the surface, which attracts the negatively charged balloon. This is called attraction by induction. And there are plenty more examples of it, too...

> If you run a comb through your hair, electrons will be transferred to the comb making it negatively charged. It can then be used to pick up little pieces of uncharged paper — holding it near the little pieces of paper causes induction in the paper, which means they jump up and stick to the comb.

## Static Electricity is Used in Industry

1) Photocopiers use static electricity to copy images onto a charged plate before printing them.

2) Static electricity can be used to reduce the dust and smoke that rises out of industrial chimneys.

3) Another use of static electricity is electrostatic sprayers:

- Electrostatic sprayers are used in various industries to give a fine, even coat of whatever's being sprayed. The classic examples are insecticide sprayers and paint sprayers.

- Bikes and cars are painted using electrostatic paint sprayers.

- The spray gun is charged, which charges up the small drops of paint. Each paint drop repels all the others, since they've all got the same charge, so you get a very fine, even spray.

- The object to be painted is given an opposite charge to the gun. This attracts the fine spray of paint.

- This method gives an even coat and hardly any paint is wasted. In addition, parts of the bicycle or car pointing away from the spray gun still receive paint, i.e. there are no paint shadows.

- Insecticide sprayers work in a similar way, except the crops to be sprayed aren't given an opposite charge — the plants charge by induction as the insecticide droplets come near them (see above).

## Static electricity is used in a lot of places...

An exam question might ask you to explain how a bit of equipment (that you may not have met before) uses static electricity. Sounds tough, I know. But the answer will probably boil down to the fact that opposite charges attract and like charges repel. Using this and the information in the question, you should be able to figure out how static charge helps the product to function properly.

# Dangers of Static Electricity

*If enough **static electricity** builds up, **sparks** can be produced, which can be pretty **dangerous**.*

## Too Much Static Causes **Sparks**

1) As electric charge builds on an object, the potential difference between the object and the earth (which is at underline{0 V}) increases.

For more on how sparks actually jump across gaps, see page 156.

2) If the potential difference gets large enough, electrons can jump across the gap between the charged object and the earth — this is the spark.

3) They can also jump to any earthed conductor that is nearby — which is why you can get static shocks from clothes, or getting out of a car.

4) This usually happens when the gap is fairly small.  (But not always — lightning is just a really big spark.)

## Static Electricity Can be **Dangerous**

Static electricity can be inconvenient and sometimes even dangerous.

Refueling cars — as fuel flows out of a filler pipe, e.g. into an aircraft or tanker, then static can build up.  This can easily lead to a spark which might cause an explosion in dusty or fumey places — like when filling up a car with fuel at a petrol station.

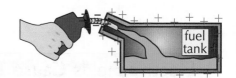

Static on airplanes — as planes fly through the air, friction between the air and the plane causes the plane to become charged. This build up of static charge can interfere with communication equipment.

Lightning — raindrops and ice bump together inside storm clouds, leaving the top of the cloud positively charged and the bottom of the cloud negative.  This creates a huge voltage and a big spark, which can damage homes or start fires when it strikes the ground.

You can reduce some of these dangers by earthing charged objects (see below).

## Objects Can be **Earthed** to Stop **Static Charge Building Up**

1) Dangerous sparks can be prevented by connecting a charged object to the ground using a conductor (e.g. a copper wire) — this is called earthing.

2) Earthing provides an easy route for the static charges to travel into the ground. This means no charge can build up to give you a shock or make a spark.

3) The electrons flow down the conductor to the ground if the charge is negative and flow up the conductor from the ground if the charge is positive.

4) Fuel tankers must be earthed to prevent any sparks that might cause the fuel to explode.

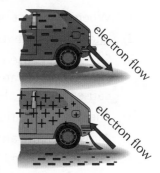

## A spark can occur if enough static charge builds up on an object

Sparks can be dangerous, especially when flammable materials such as fuels are involved. Luckily, we can prevent sparks from occurring by earthing the objects where static charge would normally build up, like the fuel pump and fuel tank when filling up a vehicle.

# Electric Fields

*Electric fields* are produced by all **charged objects**, and can be shown with **field lines**. It's not just **electric** fields that you need to know about though — you'll come across **magnetic** fields and their field lines on p.158.

## Electric **Charges** Create an **Electric Field**

1) An electric field is created around any electrically charged object.
   It's the region around a charged object where, if a second charged object was
   placed inside it, a force would be exerted on both of the charges (see below).

2) The closer to the object you get, the stronger the field is. (And the further from it, the weaker it is.)

3) You can show an electric field around an object using field lines. For example, you can
   draw the field lines for an isolated (i.e. not interacting with anything) point charge:

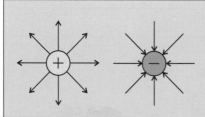

- Electric field lines go from positive to negative.
- They're always at a right angle to the surface.
- The closer together the lines are, the stronger the field is — you can see that the further from a charge you go, the further apart the lines are and so the weaker the field is.

*If you need to draw field lines around a point charge, you should draw at least eight equally spaced field lines.*

## Electric Fields Cause **Electrostatic Forces**

1) When a charged object is placed in an electric field, it feels a force.
   This force is caused by the electric fields around two charged objects interacting.

2) If the field lines between the charged objects point in the same direction,
   the field lines 'join up' and the objects are attracted to each other.

3) When the field lines between the charged objects point in opposite directions,
   the field lines 'push against' each other and the objects repel each other.

4) Between two oppositely-charged parallel plates,
   you get a uniform field that looks like this.

5) The strength and direction of the field is
   the same anywhere between the two plates
   (it's only different at the very ends).

*If you need to draw electric fields, don't forget the arrows on your field lines.*

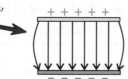

*When you're drawing a uniform field, you need to show at least three field lines, parallel and all the same distance apart.*

## **Sparking** Can be **Explained** by **Electric Fields**

1) When an object becomes statically charged, it generates its own electric field.

2) Interactions between this field and other objects are the cause of events like sparking.

3) Sparks are caused when there is a high enough potential difference between a
   charged object and the earth (or an earthed object). A high potential difference
   causes a strong electric field between the charged object and the earthed object.

4) The strong electric field causes electrons in the air particles to be removed (known as ionisation).

5) Air is normally an insulator, but when it is ionised it is much more
   conductive, so a current can flow through it. This is the spark.

---

## Electric field lines always go from positive to negative...

Electric fields may seem a bit weird at first — but the good news is they're <u>very similar</u> to
magnetic fields (on page 158), so if you <u>understand one</u> of them, you can understand them <u>both</u>.

Q1 Video Solution

Q1    An isolated, uniform, positively-charged sphere can be assumed to have the same
electric field as a positive point charge. Draw the field lines surrounding the sphere. [3 marks]

# Warm-Up & Exam Questions

Have you been paying close attention to the last few pages?  Only one way to tell really — have a go at these delightful warm-up and exam questions.  If you get any wrong, go back and read it all again.

## Warm-Up Questions

1) Two insulators are rubbed together and become charged.
   What particles move to cause the objects to become charged?

2) Do opposite charges attract or repel each other?

3) When spray painting a bike, the paint droplets are each given a negative charge and the bike is given a positive charge.  Explain why this gives an even coat of paint on the bike.

4) Explain how earthing an object helps to prevent a spark from occurring.

5) What is an electric field?

6) Sketch the electric field around a negative point charge.

7) How does the strength of an electric field produced by a charged object change with distance from the charged object?

## Exam Questions

1   A student rubbed a plastic sphere with a cloth, and the sphere became negatively charged.

(a)   Describe the movement of charge which caused the sphere to become charged.

*[1 mark]*

An image of the charged sphere is shown in **Figure 1**.

**A**                                **B**  ⊖                            **C**

**Figure 1**

(b)   Give the position (A, B or C) where a point charge would feel the greatest force.

*[1 mark]*

(c)   Draw an arrow to show the direction of the force a negative point charge would feel at that point due to the charged sphere.

*[1 mark]*

(d)   An earthed conductor is brought near to the sphere, causing a spark to jump between the conductor and the sphere.  Explain how the presence of the sphere's electric field led to a spark.

*[2 marks]*

2   A student hangs an uncharged balloon from a thread.  She brings a negatively charged polythene rod towards the balloon.
**Figure 2** shows how the positive charges in the balloon rearrange themselves when she does this.

The diagram is labelled with three different positions, A, B and C.  State and explain which of these positions the student held the rod in.

*[3 marks]*

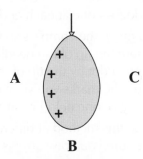

**Figure 2**

# Magnets and Magnetic Fields

*Just as electric fields are produced by charges, **magnetic fields** are **produced** by **magnets**. Well that was easy.*

## Magnets Produce **Magnetic Fields**

1) All magnets have two poles — north and south.

2) All magnets produce a magnetic field — a region where other magnets or magnetic materials (see next page) experience a force.

3) You can show a magnetic field by drawing magnetic field lines.

4) The lines always go from north to south and they show which way a force would act on a north pole at that point in the field.

5) The closer together the lines are, the stronger the magnetic field.

6) The further away from a magnet you get, the weaker the field is.

7) The magnetic field is strongest at the poles of a magnet. This means that magnetic forces are also strongest at the poles.

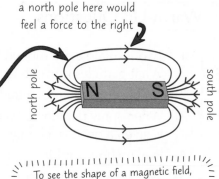

a north pole here would feel a force to the right

north pole
south pole

To see the shape of a magnetic field, place a piece of card over a magnet and sprinkle iron filings onto it. The filings line up with the field lines — but they won't show you the direction of the field.

## Magnetic Fields Cause **Forces** between **Magnets**

1) Between two magnets there is a magnetic force that can be attractive or repulsive. Two poles that are the same (these are called like poles) will repel each other. Two unlike poles will attract each other.

2) Placing the north and south poles of two bar magnets near each other creates a uniform field between the two poles. The magnetic field is the same strength everywhere between the poles.

3) If you're asked to draw a uniform magnetic field, you need to draw at least three field lines, parallel to each other and all the same distance apart.

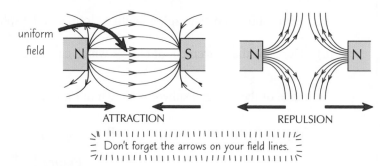

uniform field

ATTRACTION

REPULSION

Don't forget the arrows on your field lines.

## **Plotting Compasses** Show the **Directions** of Magnetic Fields

1) Inside a compass is a tiny bar magnet called a needle. A compass needle always lines up with the magnetic field it's in.

2) You can use a compass to build up a picture of what the field around a magnet looks like:

   • Put the magnet on a piece of paper and draw round it.

   • Place the compass on the paper near the magnet. The needle will point in the direction of the field line at this position.

   • Mark the direction of the compass needle by drawing two dots — one at each end of the needle.

   • Then move the compass so that the tail end of the needle is where the tip of the needle was in the previous position and put a dot by the tip of the needle. Repeat this and then join up the marks you've made — you'll end up with a drawing of one field line around the magnet.

   • Repeat this method at different points around the magnet to get several field lines. Make sure you draw arrows from north to south on your field lines.

3) When they're not near a magnet, compasses always point towards the Earth's North Pole. This is because the Earth generates its own magnetic field (and the North Pole is actually a magnetic south pole). This shows the inside (core) of the Earth must be magnetic.

The compass follows the field lines and points towards the south pole of the bar magnet.

# Permanent and Induced Magnets

*Magnetic fields don't just affect **magnets** — they affect a few special **magnetic materials** too.*

## Very Few Materials are Magnetic

1) The main <u>three</u> magnetic elements are <u>iron</u>, <u>nickel</u> and <u>cobalt</u>.

2) Some alloys and compounds of these metals are also magnetic.
For example, <u>steel</u> is magnetic because it contains <u>iron</u>.

3) If you put a magnetic material near a magnet, it is <u>attracted</u> to that magnet.
The magnetic force between a magnet and a magnetic material is <u>always</u> attractive.

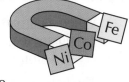

## Magnets Can be Permanent or Induced

1) <u>Permanent</u> magnets (e.g. bar magnets) produce their own magnetic field <u>all the time</u>.

2) <u>Induced</u> (or <u>temporary</u>) magnets only produce a magnetic field while they're <u>in</u> another <u>magnetic field</u>.

3) If you put any <u>magnetic material</u> into a magnetic field, it becomes an <u>induced</u> magnet.

4) This <u>magnetic induction</u> explains why the force between a magnet and a magnetic material is always <u>attractive</u> — the south pole of the magnet induces a north pole in the material, and vice versa.

5) When you <u>take away</u> the magnetic field, induced magnets return to normal and <u>stop producing</u> a magnetic field. How <u>quickly</u> they lose their magnetism depends on the material they're made from.

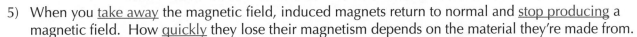

The <u>magnetic material</u> becomes <u>magnetised</u> when it is brought near the <u>bar magnet</u>. It has its own <u>poles</u> and <u>magnetic field</u>:

induced poles

- Magnetically '<u>soft</u>' materials, e.g. pure <u>iron</u> and <u>nickel-iron alloys</u>, lose their magnetism very quickly.
- Magnetically '<u>hard</u>' materials, e.g. <u>steel</u>, lose their magnetism more slowly. <u>Permanent magnets</u> are made from magnetically hard materials.

## Magnetic Materials have Lots of Uses

There are many different <u>uses</u> of <u>magnetic materials</u>, the number of which has grown since the invention of <u>electromagnets</u> (p.163). For example:

1) <u>Fridge doors</u> — there is a <u>permanent</u> magnetic strip in your fridge door to keep it closed.

2) <u>Cranes</u> — these use <u>induced</u> electromagnets to <u>attract</u> and <u>move</u> magnetic materials — e.g. moving <u>scrap metal</u> in scrap yards.

3) <u>Maglev trains</u> — these use <u>magnetic repulsion</u> to make trains <u>float</u> slightly above the track (to reduce losses from <u>friction</u>) and to <u>propel</u> them along.

4) <u>MRI machines</u> — these use magnetic fields to create <u>images</u> of the inside of your body without having to use <u>ionising radiation</u> (like X-rays, p.81).

5) <u>Speakers and microphones</u> — there's more about these on page 167.

## Magnets attract magnetic materials due to magnetic induction...

However, once the permanent magnet is <u>removed</u>, the <u>induced magnet</u> becomes <u>unmagnetised</u> again.

# Electromagnetism and The Motor Effect

*A **magnetic field** can be produced by a **current passing through a wire**. This can result in something called the **motor effect** if the current-carrying **wire** is placed in an **external magnetic field** (e.g. of a bar magnet).*

## A **Moving Charge** Creates a Magnetic Field

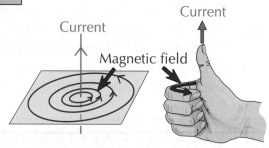

1) When a current flows through a long, straight conductor (e.g. a wire) a magnetic field is created around it.

2) The field is made up of concentric circles perpendicular to the wire, with the wire in the centre.

3) Changing the direction of the current changes the direction of the magnetic field — use the right-hand thumb rule to work out which way it goes.

4) In experiments, you can use a plotting compass to find its direction (see p.158).

5) The larger the current through the wire, or the closer to the wire you are, the stronger the field is.

> The Right-Hand Thumb Rule
> Using your right hand, point your thumb in the direction of current and curl your fingers. The direction of your fingers is the direction of the field.

## A **Current** in a **Magnetic Field** Experiences a **Force**

1) When a current-carrying conductor (e.g. a wire) is put between magnetic poles, the two magnetic fields interact. The result is a force on the wire. This is known as the motor effect.

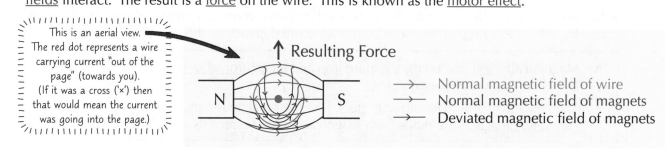

This is an aerial view. The red dot represents a wire carrying current "out of the page" (towards you). (If it was a cross ('×') then that would mean the current was going into the page.)

↑ Resulting Force

→ Normal magnetic field of wire
→ Normal magnetic field of magnets
→ Deviated magnetic field of magnets

2) To experience the full force, the wire has to be at 90° (right angles) to the magnetic field. If the wire runs along the magnetic field, it won't experience any force at all. At angles in between, it'll feel some force.

3) The force always acts in the same direction relative to the magnetic field and the direction of the current in the wire. So changing the direction of either the magnetic field or the current will change the direction of the force.

> The wire also exerts an equal and opposite force on the magnet (from Newton's Third Law, see p.26) but we're just looking at the force on the wire.

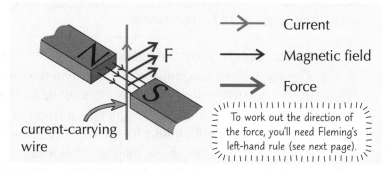

current-carrying wire

→ Current
→ Magnetic field
→ Force

> To work out the direction of the force, you'll need Fleming's left-hand rule (see next page).

## Just point your thumb in the direction of the current...

... and your fingers show the direction of the field it produces. Remember, it's always your right thumb. Not your left. You'll use your left hand on the next page though, so it shouldn't feel left out...

# The Motor Effect

*So you know that a **current-carrying wire** experiences a **force** in a **magnetic field**.*
*Time now to see how to find the **size** and the **direction** of this force.*

## You Can Find the **Size** of the **Force**...

The size of the <u>force</u> acting on a <u>conductor</u> in a <u>magnetic field</u> depends on three things:

1) The <u>magnetic flux density</u> — how many <u>field</u> (<u>flux</u>) lines there are in a <u>region</u>. This shows the <u>strength</u> of the magnetic field (p.158).

2) The size of the <u>current</u> through the conductor.

3) The <u>length</u> of the conductor that's <u>in</u> the magnetic field.

When the current is at <u>90°</u> to the magnetic field it is in, the <u>force</u> acting on it can be found using the equation:

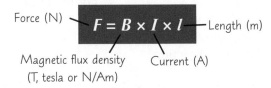

Force (N) — $F = B \times I \times l$ — Length (m)

Magnetic flux density (T, tesla or N/Am)   Current (A)

## ... and **Which Way** it's Acting

You can find the direction of the force on a current-carrying conductor with <u>Fleming's left-hand rule</u>.

1) Using your <u>left hand</u>, point your **First finger** in the direction of the magnetic **Field**.

2) Point your <u>seCond</u> finger in the direction of the <u>Current</u>.

3) Your <u>thuMb</u> will then point in the direction of the <u>force</u> (**Motion**).

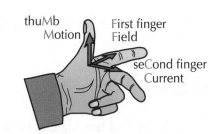

thuMb Motion   First finger Field   seCond finger Current

**EXAMPLE**

**In the diagram on the right, in which direction does the force act on the wire?**

1) Draw in current arrows (positive to negative).

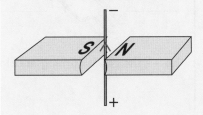

2) Use <u>Fleming's LHR</u>.

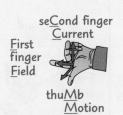

seCond finger Current / First finger Field / thuMb Motion

3) Draw in <u>direction of force</u> (motion).

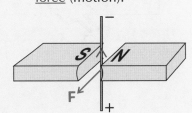

## Fleming's left-hand rule can really come in handy...

Use the left-hand rule in the <u>exam</u>. You might look a bit silly, but as long as you remember <u>which digit</u> corresponds to <u>motion</u>, <u>field</u> and <u>current</u>, it makes getting those marks so much easier.

Q1   A section of a current-carrying wire is in a magnetic field, as shown in the diagram. The wire is at 90° to the magnetic field. Find the direction of the force acting on the wire.

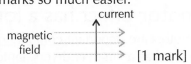

current / magnetic field   [1 mark]

Q1 Video Solution

# Motors

*Electric motors* use the *motor effect* (see the previous two pages) to get them (and keep them) *moving*. This is one of the favourite exam topics of all time. Read it. Understand it. Learn it. Lecture over.

## A Current-Carrying **Coil** of Wire Can **Rotate** in a Magnetic Field

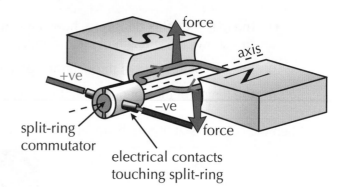

1) The diagram on the right shows a <u>basic d.c. motor</u>. <u>Forces</u> act on the two <u>side arms</u> of a <u>coil</u> of wire that's carrying a <u>current</u>.

2) These forces are just the <u>usual forces</u> which act on <u>any current</u> in a <u>magnetic field</u> (p.160).

3) These forces act in <u>opposite directions</u> on each side, so the coil <u>rotates</u>.

4) The <u>split-ring commutator</u> is a clever way of <u>swapping</u> the contacts <u>every half turn</u> to keep the motor rotating in the <u>same direction</u>.

5) The direction of the motor can be <u>reversed</u> either by swapping the <u>polarity</u> of the <u>d.c. supply</u> (reversing the <u>current</u>) or swapping the <u>magnetic poles</u> over (reversing the <u>field</u>).

6) You can use <u>Fleming's left-hand rule</u> to work out which way the coil will <u>turn</u>.

**EXAMPLE**

**Is the coil turning clockwise or anticlockwise?**

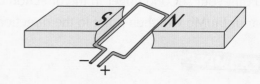

1) Draw in <u>current arrows</u> (positive to negative, p.133).

2) Use <u>Fleming's left-hand rule</u> on <u>one</u> branch (here, I've picked the right-hand branch).

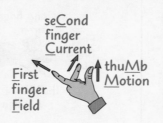

seCond finger
Current

thuMb
Motion

First finger
Field

3) Draw in <u>direction of force</u> (motion).

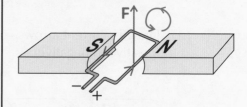

So — the coil is turning anticlockwise.

## The motor effect has a lot of important applications...

Electric motors are <u>important components</u> in a lot of <u>everyday items</u>. Food mixers, DVD players, and anything that has a fan (hair dryers, laptops, etc) use electric motors to keep things turning.

# Solenoids

*A **solenoid** is a fancy way of saying **coils of wire** with a **current** flowing through them. The cur...
that solenoids produce a **magnetic field** which, as it turns out, is **similar** to the **field** around a ba...*

## A **Solenoid** is a **Long Coil** of Wire

1) Around a <u>single loop</u> of current-carrying wire, the magnetic field looks like this:

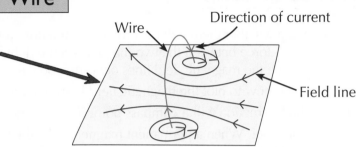

Wire — Direction of current

Field line

2) You can <u>increase</u> the <u>strength</u> of the magnetic field produced by a length of wire by <u>wrapping</u> it into a <u>long coil</u> with <u>lots</u> of loops, called a <u>solenoid</u>.

3) The <u>field lines</u> around each separate loop of wire <u>line up</u>.

   • <u>Inside</u> the solenoid, you get <u>lots</u> of field lines <u>pointing in the same direction</u>. The magnetic field is <u>strong</u> and almost <u>uniform</u>.

   • <u>Outside</u> the coil, the <u>overlapping</u> field lines <u>cancel each other out</u> — so the field is <u>weak</u> apart from at the <u>ends</u> of the solenoid.

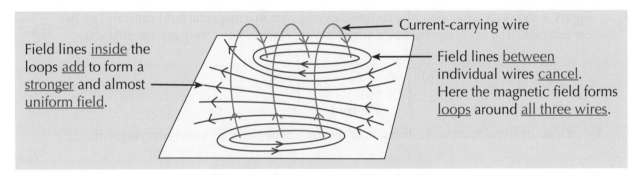

Field lines <u>inside</u> the loops <u>add</u> to form a <u>stronger</u> and almost <u>uniform field</u>.

Current-carrying wire

Field lines <u>between</u> individual wires <u>cancel</u>. Here the magnetic field forms <u>loops</u> around <u>all three wires</u>.

4) You end up with a field that looks like the one around a <u>bar magnet</u>. The <u>direction</u> of the field depends on the <u>direction of the current</u> (p.160).

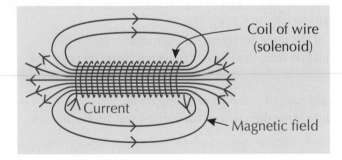

Coil of wire (solenoid)

Current

Magnetic field

5) A <u>solenoid</u> is an <u>example</u> of an <u>ELECTROMAGNET</u> — a magnet with a magnetic field that can be turned <u>on</u> and <u>off</u> using an <u>electric current</u>.

6) You can <u>increase</u> the field strength of the solenoid <u>even more</u> by putting a block of <u>iron</u> in the <u>centre</u> of the coil. This <u>iron core</u> becomes an <u>induced magnet</u> (see p.159) whenever current is flowing.

## The fields around bar magnets and solenoids are the same shape...

The main <u>advantage</u> of using an <u>electromagnet</u> (such as a <u>solenoid</u>) rather than a bar magnet is that the <u>magnetic field</u> can be <u>turned on</u> and <u>off</u> with the <u>current</u>. This makes an electromagnet pretty <u>handy</u> — for example, they're used in <u>microphones</u> and <u>loudspeakers</u>, but we'll come onto these in a few pages time.

# Warm-Up & Exam Questions

It's time for another page of questions to see how much you've absorbed. If you can do the warm-up questions without breaking into a sweat, then see how you get on with the exam questions below.

## Warm-Up Questions

1) a)  State whether there will be a force of attraction, repulsion, or no force between the two magnets on the right.
   b)  Sketch the magnetic field lines occurring between the two bar magnets.
2)  Describe how to plot the magnetic field lines of a bar magnet using a compass.
3)  In which direction will a compass point if it is not near any magnets?
4)  True or false? When a permanent magnet is placed next to a magnetic material, the magnetic material becomes an induced magnet that repels the permanent magnet.
5)  What is the role of a split-ring commutator in a d.c. motor?

## Exam Questions

1   **Figure 1** shows an aerial view of a current-carrying wire in a magnetic field generated by two bar magnets. The circle represents the wire carrying current out of the page, towards you.

N   ○   S

**Figure 1**

(a)  Draw an arrow to show the direction of the force acting on the current-carrying wire.

*[1 mark]*

(b)  Explain what causes the force to act on the current-carrying wire.

*[1 mark]*

(c)  The magnetic field strength of the field generated by the bar magnets is 0.028 T.
7.0 cm of the current-carrying wire lies within the magnetic field of the bar magnets.
The current through the wire is 5.5 A.
Calculate the size of the force acting on the current-carrying wire.
Use the correct equation from the Physics Equation Sheet on page 268.

*[2 marks]*

(d)  Describe what would happen to the force acting on the current-carrying wire if the direction of the current was reversed.

*[1 mark]*

2   A student makes an electromagnet by wrapping a current-carrying wire into a solenoid around a nail. When the nail is brought close to some paperclips, the paperclips are attracted to the nail.

(a)  Explain why a strong uniform field is created within the coils of the solenoid.

*[2 marks]*

(b)  Suggest an element that the nail might contain.

*[1 mark]*

(c)  The student wants to increase the magnetic field strength of the electromagnet.
State **one** way in which he could do this.

*[1 mark]*

# Electromagnetic Induction

*Electromagnetic induction* — *sounds scary, but read this page **carefully** and it shouldn't be too complicated.*

## A **Changing** Magnetic Field Induces a **Potential Difference** in a **Wire**

Electromagnetic Induction:  The induction of a potential difference (and current if there's a complete circuit) in a wire which is experiencing a change in magnetic field.

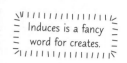
Induces is a fancy word for creates.

1) There are two different situations where you get electromagnetic induction. The first is if an electrical conductor (e.g. a coil of wire) and a magnetic field move relative to each other:

- You can do this by moving/rotating either a magnet in a coil of wire OR a conductor (wire) in a magnetic field (the conductor "cuts through" the magnetic field lines).

Voltmeter

- If you move or rotate the magnet (or conductor) in the opposite direction, then the potential difference/current will be reversed. Likewise if the polarity of the magnet is reversed (by turning the magnet around), then the potential difference/current will be reversed too.

- If you keep the magnet (or the coil) moving backwards and forwards, or keep it rotating in the same direction, you produce an alternating current (p.148).

2) You also get an induced p.d. when the magnetic field through an electrical conductor changes (gets bigger or smaller or reverses).  This is what happens in a transformer (p.168).

3) You can increase the size of the induced p.d. by increasing the STRENGTH of the magnetic field, increasing the SPEED of movement/change of field or having MORE TURNS PER UNIT LENGTH on the coil of wire.

## Induced Current **Opposes** the Change that Made It

1) So, a change in magnetic field can induce a current in a wire.  But, as you saw on page 160, when a current flows through a wire, a magnetic field is created around the wire. (Yep, that's a second magnetic field — different to the one whose field lines were being cut in the first place.)

2) The magnetic field created by an induced current always acts against the change that made it (whether that's the movement of a wire or a change in the field it's in). Basically, it's trying to return things to the way they were.

3) This means that the induced current always opposes the change that made it.

---

## Electromagnetic induction works whether the coil or the field moves

Electromagnetic induction may seem like a difficult concept to grasp, but there are really only a couple of key things to remember.  It doesn't matter what's moving, electromagnetic induction occurs as long as field lines are being 'cut'.  And the current that's induced will oppose the change that generated it.

# Dynamos and Alternators

*Generators make use of **electromagnetic induction** from the previous page to induce a current. Whether this current is **alternating** or **direct** depends on how the generator's put together.*

## Dynamos Generate Direct Current

1) Generators <u>apply a force</u> to <u>rotate a coil</u> in a <u>magnetic field</u> (or a magnet in a coil) — their <u>construction</u> is a lot like a <u>motor</u>.

2) As the <u>coil</u> (or <u>magnet</u>) spins, a <u>current</u> is <u>induced</u> in the coil. This current <u>changes direction</u> every half turn.

3) <u>Dynamos</u> are d.c. generators. They have a <u>split-ring commutator</u> (like a d.c. motor, p.162).

4) This <u>swaps the connection</u> every half turn to keep the <u>current</u> flowing in the <u>same direction</u>.

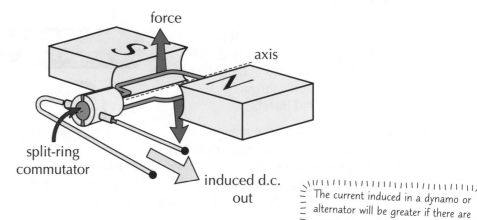

force

axis

split-ring
commutator

induced d.c.
out

*The current induced in a dynamo or alternator will be greater if there are more turns of wire in the coil, the magnetic flux density is increased or if the speed of rotation is increased.*

## Alternators Generate Alternating Current

1) <u>Alternators</u> work in the same way as dynamos, apart from one important difference.

2) Instead of a <u>split-ring commutator</u>, a.c. generators have <u>slip rings</u> and <u>brushes</u> so the contacts <u>don't swap</u> every half turn.

3) This means an alternator produces an <u>alternating p.d.</u> and therefore an <u>alternating current (a.c.)</u> if the coil is part of a complete circuit.

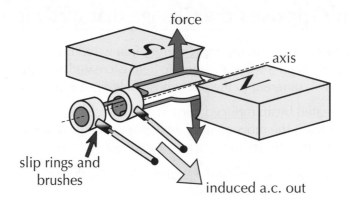

force

axis

slip rings and
brushes

induced a.c. out

## Don't get your dynamos and your alternators mixed up...

There's an easy way to remember the difference — **d**ynamos produce a **d**irect current, **alternat**ors produce an **alternat**ing current. Other than that, they can both be used to do the same thing — convert the <u>rotational motion</u> of a <u>coil</u> or <u>magnet</u> into an <u>electric current</u>.

# Microphones and Loudspeakers

*You may have wondered how **microphones** and **loudspeakers work** — it's all down to **electromagnetism**.*

## Microphones Generate Current From Sound Waves

1) Microphones use <u>electromagnetic induction</u> to generate an electrical signal.

2) <u>Sound waves</u> hit a flexible <u>diaphragm</u> that is attached to a coil of wire. The coil of wire <u>surrounds one pole</u> of a <u>permanent magnet</u> and is <u>surrounded by the other pole</u>.

3) This means as the <u>diaphragm</u> (and so the <u>coil</u>) moves, a <u>current is generated</u> in the coil.

4) The <u>movement</u> of the coil (and so the generated current) depends on the properties of the sound wave (<u>louder</u> sounds make the diaphragm move <u>further</u>).

5) This is how microphones can <u>convert</u> the <u>pressure</u> variations of a sound wave into variations in <u>current</u> in an electric circuit.

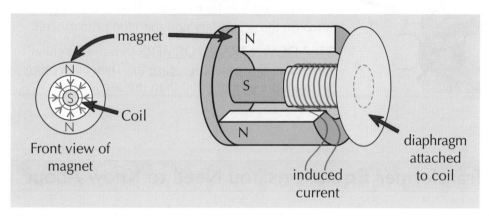

Front view of magnet

magnet · Coil · N · S · N

diaphragm attached to coil

induced current

## Loudspeakers are like Microphones in Reverse

1) In a <u>loudspeaker</u>, the diaphragm is replaced with a <u>paper cone</u>.

2) The coil is wrapped around one pole of a <u>permanent magnet</u>, so the a.c. signal causes a <u>force</u> on the coil, which <u>moves the cone</u>. (This is the <u>motor effect</u> — see page 160.)

3) When the current is <u>reversed</u>, the force acts in the <u>opposite direction</u>.

4) These movements make the cone <u>vibrate</u>, which makes the air around the cone vibrate and creates the variations in <u>pressure</u> that cause a <u>sound wave</u> (p.66).

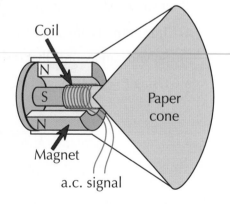

Coil

Paper cone

Magnet

a.c. signal

## Microphones and loudspeakers have a lot of similarities...

...one is basically the other in <u>reverse</u>. <u>Microphones</u> turn <u>sound waves</u> into <u>alternating current</u>, while loudspeakers turn an <u>alternating current</u> into <u>sound waves</u>. The main difference is that microphones use <u>electromagnetic induction</u>, but loudspeakers use the <u>motor effect</u>. Splendid — next up, it's <u>transformers</u>.

# Transformers

*Transformers are yet another **application** of **electromagnetic induction** for you to sink your teeth into.*

## Transformers Change the p.d. — but Only for **Alternating** Current

1) Transformers use <u>induction</u> to change the size of the <u>potential difference</u> of an <u>alternating</u> current.
2) They all have two coils of wire, the <u>primary</u> and the <u>secondary</u> coils, joined with an <u>iron core</u>.
3) When an <u>alternating</u> p.d. is applied across the <u>primary coil</u>, it produces an <u>alternating magnetic field</u>.
4) The iron in the <u>core</u> is a <u>magnetic material</u> (see p.159) that is <u>easily magnetised</u> and <u>demagnetised</u>. Because the coil is producing an <u>alternating magnetic field</u>, the <u>magnetisation</u> of the core also <u>alternates</u>.
5) This <u>changing</u> magnetic field <u>induces a p.d.</u> in the <u>secondary coil</u>.

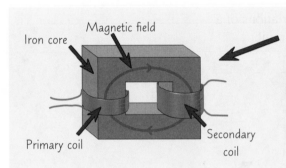

STEP-UP TRANSFORMERS step the potential difference <u>up</u> (i.e. <u>increase</u> it). They have <u>more</u> turns on the <u>secondary</u> coil than the primary coil.

STEP-DOWN TRANSFORMERS step the potential difference <u>down</u> (i.e. <u>decrease</u> it). They have <u>more</u> turns on the <u>primary</u> coil than the secondary.

## There are **Two** Transformer **Equations** You Need to Know About

1) The <u>ratio</u> between the <u>potential differences</u> in the primary and secondary coils of a transformer is the <u>same</u> as the ratio between the number of <u>turns</u> on the coils.

2) So as long as you know the <u>input</u> p.d. and the <u>number of turns</u> on each coil, you can <u>calculate</u> the <u>output</u> p.d. from a transformer using the <u>transformer equation</u>:

Input p.d. (V) ⟶     Output p.d. (V) ⟶ $$\frac{V_p}{V_s} = \frac{N_p}{N_s}$$ ⟵ Number of turns on primary coil    ⟵ Number of turns on secondary coil

3) It works <u>either way up</u>, so $\frac{V_s}{V_p} = \frac{N_s}{N_p}$ works just as well.

4) Transformers are <u>almost 100% efficient</u>.

5) So you can assume that the <u>input power</u> is <u>equal</u> to the <u>output power</u>.

6) Using $P = I \times V$ (page 146), you can write this as:

p.d. across primary coil (V) ⟶ $$V_p \times I_p = V_s \times I_s$$ ⟵ Current through secondary coil (A)

Current through primary coil (A)     p.d. across secondary coil (V)

7) $V_p \times I_p$ is the <u>power input</u> at the primary coil. $V_s \times I_s$ is the <u>power output</u> at the secondary coil.

## Step-up transformers increase the potential difference...

To help remember the <u>difference</u> between <u>step-up</u> and <u>step-down transformers</u>, try to think about what's changing from the <u>primary coil</u> to the <u>secondary coil</u>. If the number of <u>turns</u> is <u>increasing</u>, the <u>p.d.</u> will also <u>increase</u> — <u>both</u> things have been "stepped up", so it's a <u>step-up</u> transformer.

Q1 Video Solution

Q1    A transformer has an input p.d. of 1.6 V. The output power is 320 W. Find the input current.      [2 marks]

# Generating and Distributing Electricity

*Now it's time for the big leagues — how electricity is **generated** and **distributed** on a **national** scale.*
*And for this, you'll need your good ol' friends the **generator** and the **transformer**.*

## A **Power Station** Uses a Turbine to Turn a **Huge Generator**

1) Most of the electricity we use is generated from burning <u>fuels</u>
   (coal, oil, gas or biomass) in the <u>boilers</u> of big power stations.

2) The burning fuel is used to heat <u>water</u> and convert it to <u>steam</u>, which turns a <u>turbine</u>.

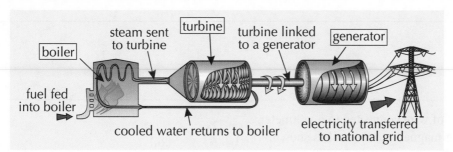

steam sent to turbine | turbine | turbine linked to a generator | generator
boiler
fuel fed into boiler
cooled water returns to boiler
electricity transferred to national grid

3) The turbine is connected to a generator — a powerful <u>magnet</u> (usually an <u>electromagnet</u>,
   see p.163) inside a huge cylinder wound with <u>coils</u> of copper wire.

4) As the turbine spins, the magnet spins with it, inducing a <u>large p.d.</u> and <u>alternating current</u> in the coils.

5) The coils are joined together <u>in parallel</u> (see p.141) to produce a <u>single output</u> from the generator.

6) A similar set-up is used for most <u>other types</u> of electricity generation as well. In <u>hydroelectric</u>, <u>tidal</u> and
   <u>wind</u> power (see p.50-51) the turbine is turned <u>directly</u>, without needing to turn water into steam first.

7) The only type of power generation that <u>doesn't</u> use a turbine and generator system is <u>solar</u> (p.50).

## The **National Grid** Uses a **High p.d.** and a **Low Current**

1) Once the electricity has been generated, it goes into the <u>national grid</u> — a network of <u>wires</u>
   and <u>transformers</u> that connects UK <u>power stations</u> to <u>consumers</u> (anyone who uses electricity).

2) The national grid has to transfer <u>loads of energy each second</u>, which means it transmits
   electricity at a <u>high power</u> (as <u>power = energy transferred ÷ time taken</u>, $P = E \div t$, p.146).

3) <u>Electrical power = current × potential difference</u> ($P = I \times V$, p.146), so to transmit the huge
   amounts of power needed, you either need a <u>high potential difference</u> or a <u>high current</u>.

4) But a <u>high current</u> makes wires <u>heat up</u>, so loads of energy is <u>wasted to thermal energy stores</u>. The <u>power
   lost</u> due to <u>resistive heating</u> is found using <u>electrical power = current² × resistance</u> ($P = I^2 \times R$, p.146).

5) So to <u>reduce these losses</u> and make the national grid <u>more efficient</u>, high-potential difference,
   <u>low-resistance cables</u>, and <u>transformers</u> are used. You saw on the previous page that transformers are
   (almost) 100% efficient, so the <u>input power</u> is <u>equal</u> to the <u>output power</u>. For a <u>given power</u>, as you
   increase the <u>potential difference</u> across a coil, you <u>decrease</u> the <u>current</u> through it ($V_p \times I_p = V_s \times I_s$).

6) <u>Step-up transformers</u> at <u>power stations</u> boost the p.d. up <u>really high</u> (400 000 V) and keep the current <u>low</u>.
   <u>Step-down transformers</u> then bring it back down to <u>safe</u>, <u>usable levels</u> at the consumers' end.

## The national grid — it's a powerful thing...

Electricity is transmitted across the national grid with a <u>high p.d.</u> in order to transmit <u>large</u> amounts of <u>power</u>.
It's also transmitted at a <u>low current</u> to reduce <u>energy losses by heating</u>. To get this high p.d. and low current,
a <u>step-up transformer</u> is used to transfer the electricity from the power station to the national grid.

# Warm-Up & Exam Questions

There were lots of new ideas in that section, not to mention those equations on page 168. Better have a go at these questions so you can really see what's gone in and what you might need to go over again.

## Warm-Up Questions

1) How does the electricity generated by a dynamo differ to that generated by an alternator?

2) Do step-up transformers have more turns on their primary or secondary coil?

3) Why is a high current not used to transmit large amounts of power across the national grid?

## Exam Questions

1   **Figure 1** shows a coil of wire connected to a voltmeter. A student moves a bar magnet into the coil as shown. The pointer on the voltmeter moves to the left.

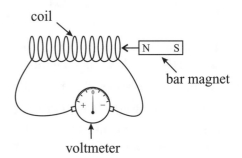

(a)   Explain why the pointer moves.

*[1 mark]*

(b)   State how the student could get the voltmeter's pointer to move to the right.

*[1 mark]*

(c)   State how he could get a larger reading on the voltmeter.

*[1 mark]*

**Figure 1**

(d)   State what reading the voltmeter will show if the student holds the magnet still inside the coil.

*[1 mark]*

2   A student is trying to test a transformer that has a d.c. power supply connected to the primary coil.

(a)   Explain why the voltmeter connected to the secondary coil reads 0 V.

*[2 marks]*

The student connects a power source with an alternating current of 2.5 A and a potential difference of 12 V to the primary coil. The potential difference across the secondary coil is 4 V.

(b)   Calculate the current in the secondary coil, $I_S$.
Use the correct equation from the Physics Equation Sheet on page 268.

*[2 marks]*

(c)   The primary coil has 15 turns. Determine how many turns there must be on the secondary coil.
Use the correct equation from the Physics Equation Sheet on page 268.

*[2 marks]*

3   **Figure 2** shows the parts inside an earphone. Sound waves are caused by mechanical vibrations.

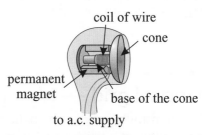

Explain how the earphone uses an a.c. supply to produce sound waves.

*[4 marks]*

**Figure 2**

# Revision Summary for Section 8

Congratulations — you've battled to the end of <u>Section 8</u>.
Now put your knowledge to the test.

For even more practice, try the Retrieval Quiz for Section 8 — just scan this QR code!

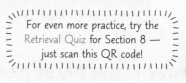 

Section 8 Quiz

- Try these questions and <u>tick off each one</u> when you <u>get it right</u>.
- When you're <u>completely happy</u> with a sub-topic, tick it off.

## Static Electricity and Electric Fields (p.153-156) ☐

1) How does static electricity build up when two insulating materials are rubbed together? ☐
2) Explain why a charged rod will attract small pieces of paper. ☐
3) Explain how an electrostatic sprayer works. ☐
4) Give an example of a situation where a build up of static electricity can be dangerous. ☐
5) Sketch the electric field between two oppositely-charged straight, parallel plates. ☐

## Magnetism (p.158-159) ☐

6) What is a magnetic field? In which direction do magnetic field lines point? ☐
7) Sketch the magnetic field lines around a bar magnet. ☐
8) Explain why a plotting compass points north when it is far away from a magnet. ☐
9) Give three examples of magnetic materials. ☐
10) What is the difference between a permanent magnet and an induced magnet? ☐

## Electromagnetism and the Motor Effect (p.160-163) ☐

11) Describe the magnetic field around a current-carrying wire. ☐
12) What is Fleming's left-hand rule? ☐
13) Name two ways you could decrease the force on a current-carrying wire in a magnetic field. ☐
14) Explain how a basic d.c. motor works. ☐
15) What is meant by an electromagnet? ☐

## Electromagnetic Induction and Transformers (p.165-169) ☐

16) Describe how you can induce a current in a coil of wire. ☐
17) Give two ways you could reverse the direction of an induced current. ☐
18) True or false? Induced currents create magnetic fields that oppose the change that made them. ☐
19) What kind of current do dynamos produce? ☐
20) Explain how microphones translate sound waves into electrical signals. ☐
21) What kind of current are transformers used with? ☐
22) True or false? Step-down transformers have more coils on their primary coil than on their secondary. ☐
23) A transformer has an input p.d. of 100 V and an output p.d. of 20 V. What kind of transformer is it? ☐
24) Describe how a fossil fuel power station generates electricity. ☐
25) Explain how transformers are used to improve efficiency when transmitting electricity across the national grid. ☐

# Density

Density tells you how much **mass** is packed into a given **volume** of space. You need to be able to work it out, as well as carry out **practicals** to work out the densities of liquids and solids. Lucky you.

## Density is the Mass per Unit Volume of a Substance

Density is a measure of the 'compactness' of a substance. It relates the <u>mass</u> of a substance to how much <u>space</u> it takes up (i.e. it's a substance's <u>mass</u> per <u>unit volume</u>).

$$\text{Density} = \frac{\text{Mass}}{\text{Volume}}$$

$$\frac{m}{\rho \times V}$$

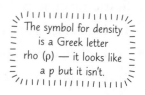
The symbol for density is a Greek letter rho (ρ) — it looks like a p but it isn't.

1) The <u>units</u> of <u>density</u> can be <u>kg/m³</u> (where the <u>mass</u> is in <u>kg</u> and the <u>volume</u> is in <u>m³</u>) or <u>g/cm³</u> (where the mass is in g and the volume is in <u>cm³</u>). 1 g/cm³ = 1000 kg/m³.

2) The <u>density</u> of an <u>object</u> depends on what it's <u>made of</u>. Density <u>doesn't vary</u> with <u>size</u> or <u>shape</u>.

3) The average <u>density</u> of an object determines whether it <u>floats</u> or <u>sinks</u> — a solid object will <u>float</u> on a fluid if it has a <u>lower average density</u> than the fluid (p.184).

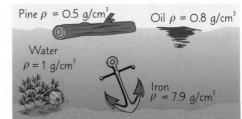
Pine ρ = 0.5 g/cm³    Oil ρ = 0.8 g/cm³
Water ρ = 1 g/cm³
Iron ρ = 7.9 g/cm³

## You Need to be Able to Measure Density in Different Ways

### To Find the Density of a Liquid

**PRACTICAL**

1) Place a <u>measuring cylinder</u> on a balance and <u>zero</u> the balance (see p.191).

2) Pour <u>10 ml</u> of the liquid into the measuring cylinder and record the liquid's <u>mass</u>.

3) Pour <u>another 10 ml</u> into the measuring cylinder and record the <u>total volume</u> and <u>mass</u>. Repeat this process until the measuring cylinder is <u>full</u>.

4) For each measurement, use the <u>formula</u> to find the <u>density</u>. (Remember that 1 ml = 1 cm³.)

5) Finally, take an <u>average</u> of your calculated densities to get an accurate value for the <u>density</u> of the <u>liquid</u>.

### To Find the Density of a Solid Object

**PRACTICAL**

1) Use a <u>balance</u> to measure its <u>mass</u> (see p.191).

2) For some solid shapes, you can find the <u>volume</u> using a <u>formula</u>. E.g. the volume of a cube is just width × height × length.

Make sure you know the formulas for the volumes of basic shapes.

3) For a trickier shaped-solid, you can find its volume by <u>submerging</u> it in a <u>eureka can</u> filled with water. The water <u>displaced</u> by the object will be <u>transferred</u> to the <u>measuring cylinder</u>:

4) Record the <u>volume</u> of water in the measuring cylinder. This is the <u>volume</u> of the <u>object</u>.

5) Plug the object's <u>mass</u> and <u>volume</u> into the <u>formula</u> above to find its <u>density</u>.

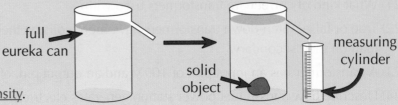
full eureka can    solid object    measuring cylinder

## Light objects with large volumes aren't very dense...

Remember — density is all about how <u>tightly packed</u> the <u>particles</u> in a substance are.

Q1   A cube has edges of length 1.5 cm and an average density of 3500 kg/m³. What is its mass? [3 marks]

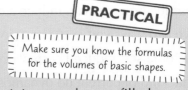
Q1 Video Solution

# Kinetic Theory and States of Matter

*You've definitely met a lot of the terms on this page before, but that **doesn't** mean you can skip it...*

## Kinetic Theory is a Way of Explaining Matter

1) In kinetic theory, you can think of the particles that make up matter as <u>tiny balls</u>.

2) You can explain the ways that matter behaves in terms of how these balls <u>move</u>, and the <u>forces</u> between them. For example, kinetic theory is used to describe the <u>states of matter</u>.

## Matter Can Be In Different States

1) <u>Three states of matter</u> are <u>solid</u> (e.g. ice), <u>liquid</u> (e.g. water) and <u>gas</u> (e.g. water vapour).

2) The <u>particles</u> of a substance in each state are <u>the same</u>
— only the <u>arrangement</u> and <u>energy</u> of the particles are <u>different</u>.

### Solids

1) <u>Strong forces</u> of attraction hold the particles <u>close together</u> in a <u>fixed</u>, <u>regular</u> arrangement.

2) The particles don't have much <u>energy</u> in their <u>kinetic energy stores</u> so they can only <u>vibrate</u> about their <u>fixed</u> positions.

### Liquids

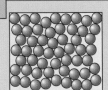

1) The forces of attraction between the particles are <u>weaker</u>.

2) The particles are <u>close together</u>, but can <u>move past each other</u> and form <u>irregular</u> arrangements.

3) They have <u>more energy</u> in their <u>kinetic energy stores</u> than the particles in a <u>solid</u> — they move in <u>random directions</u> at <u>low speeds</u>.

### Gases

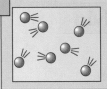

1) There are <u>almost no</u> forces of attraction between the particles.

2) For any given substance, in the gas state its particles will have <u>more energy</u> than in the solid state or the liquid state.

3) They are <u>free to move</u>, and travel in <u>random directions</u> and at <u>high speeds</u>.

## You Need to Know the Changes of State

*The energy transfers that take place during a change in state are covered on p.178.*

1) You need to know the names of the different <u>changes of state</u>:
- <u>melting</u> — solid to liquid
- <u>condensing</u> — gas to liquid
- <u>sublimating</u> — solid to gas
- <u>freezing</u> — liquid to solid
- <u>evaporating/boiling</u> — liquid to gas

2) If you <u>reverse</u> a change of state, the particles <u>go back</u> to how they were before.

3) So changes of state are <u>physical changes</u> (only the <u>form</u> of a substance changes).
These are <u>different</u> from <u>chemical reactions</u>, where <u>new substances</u> are created by the reaction.

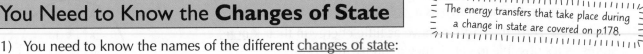

1) Provided you're working with a <u>closed system</u> (i.e. no particles can escape, and no new particles can get in) the <u>mass</u> of a substance <u>isn't affected</u> when it changes <u>state</u>.

2) This makes sense — the <u>mass of a substance</u> is the <u>mass of its particles</u>, and the particles aren't changing, they're just being rearranged.

3) However, when a substance changes state its <u>volume does change</u>. The particles in most substances are <u>closer together</u> when they're a <u>solid</u> than a <u>liquid</u> (ice and water are an exception), and are closer together when they're a <u>liquid</u> than a <u>gas</u> (see the diagrams above).

4) Since <u>density = mass ÷ volume</u> (p.172), then density must change too. Generally, substances are <u>most dense</u> when they're <u>solids</u> and <u>least dense</u> when they're <u>gases</u>.

# Internal Energy and Absolute Zero

*According to kinetic theory, everything is made of **tiny little particles**.*
*The **energy** of a **system** is determined by the energy of the **particles** that make it up.*

## Internal Energy is Stored by the Particles That Make Up a System

1) The particles in a system vibrate or move around — they have energy in their kinetic energy stores. The more energy they have in their kinetic energy stores, the faster the particles move.

2) They also have energy in their potential energy stores due to their positions. Usually, the further apart they are from each other, the more energy the particles have in this store.

3) The energy stored in a system is stored by its particles.

4) The internal energy of a system is the total energy that its particles have in their kinetic and potential energy stores.

5) The energy in the thermal energy store of a system is the energy in just the kinetic energy stores of its particles.

6) Heating a system transfers energy to its particles, so heating a system always increases its internal energy.

7) This leads to a change in temperature (when energy is transferred to the kinetic energy stores of the particles) or a change in state (when energy is transferred to the potential energy stores of the particles — see p.178).

## Absolute Zero is as Cold as Stuff Can Get — 0 kelvin

1) If you increase the temperature of something, you give its particles more energy — they move about more quickly or vibrate more. In the same way, if you cool a substance down, you're reducing the energy of the particles.

2) In theory, the coldest that anything can ever get is –273 °C — this temperature is known as absolute zero.

3) At absolute zero, the particles have as little energy in their kinetic stores as it's possible to get — they're pretty much still.

4) Absolute zero is the start of the Kelvin scale of temperature.

5) A temperature change of 1 °C is also a change of 1 kelvin. The two scales are pretty similar — the only difference is where the zero occurs.

6) To convert from degrees Celsius to kelvins, just add 273.

7) And to convert from kelvins to degrees Celsius, just subtract 273.

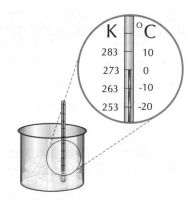

## You can't get colder than absolute zero...

Always double check that your answer seems sensible in the exam. For example, nothing can get colder than 0 K or –273 °C, so if your answer is below that, you've done something wrong in your calculations.

# Warm-Up & Exam Questions

Time to try your hand at some questions, before getting to grips with the rest of the section.

## Warm-Up Questions

1) What is density a measure of?
2) In what state can the particles in a substance move in random directions at high speeds?
3) Name the change of state for a solid changing into a gas.
4) Are changes of state chemical or physical changes?
5) How does cooling a system affect its internal energy?
6) State the temperature of absolute zero in degrees Celsius.
7) How do you convert a temperature value from kelvin to degrees Celsius?

## Exam Questions

**1** A block of lead is solid at room temperature. Grade 4-6

(a) Describe the arrangement and movement of the particles in a solid.

*[2 marks]*

(b) The lead block has a mass of 850.5 g and a volume of 75.0 $cm^3$.
Calculate the density of the lead block. Give your answer in $g/cm^3$.

*[2 marks]*

(c) If the lead block is heated to 327.5 °C, it can change from a solid to a liquid.
Give the name of this process.

*[1 mark]*

**PRACTICAL**

**2** A student has a collection of metal toy soldiers, each made from the same metal. Grade 6-7
Each toy soldier has a different volume.

(a) Which of the following statements about the toy soldiers is true?

☐ **A** The masses and densities of each of the toy soldiers are the same.

☐ **B** The masses of each of the toy soldiers are the same, but their densities will vary.

☐ **C** The densities of each of the toy soldiers are the same, but their masses will vary.

☐ **D** The densities and masses of each toy soldier will vary.

*[1 mark]*

(b) The student wants to measure the density of one of the toy soldiers.
He has a eureka can (a beaker with a spout in the side, as shown in **Figure 1**), a measuring cylinder, a mass balance and some water.
State the **two** quantities the student must measure in order to calculate the density of the toy soldier.

*[2 marks]*

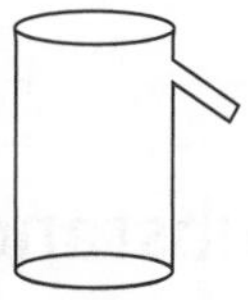

**Figure 1**

*(c) Describe the steps the student could take to find the density of the toy soldier using the equipment he has.

*[6 marks]*

# Specific Heat Capacity

*Specific heat capacity is really just a sciencey way of saying **how hard** it is to **heat** something up.*

## Specific Heat Capacity Relates Temperature and Energy

1) It takes <u>more energy</u> to <u>increase the temperature</u> of some materials than others.

2) For example, you need <u>4200 J</u> to warm 1 kg of <u>water</u> by 1 °C, but only <u>139 J</u> to warm 1 kg of <u>mercury</u> by 1 °C.

3) Materials that need to <u>gain</u> lots of energy to <u>warm up</u> also <u>release</u> loads of energy when they <u>cool down</u> again. They <u>store</u> a lot of energy for a given change in temperature.

4) The <u>change in the energy</u> stored in a substance when you heat it is related to the change in its <u>temperature</u> by its <u>specific heat capacity</u>.

5) The <u>specific heat capacity</u> of a substance is the <u>change in energy</u> in the substance's thermal energy store needed to raise the temperature of <u>1 kg</u> of that substance by <u>1 °C</u>.

6) You need to know how to use the <u>equation</u> relating energy, mass, specific heat capacity and temperature.

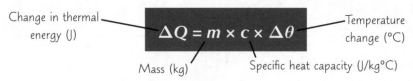

Change in thermal energy (J) ⟶ $\Delta Q = m \times c \times \Delta\theta$ ⟵ Temperature change (°C)

Mass (kg) — Specific heat capacity (J/kg°C)

7) The Δs in the <u>equation</u> just mean '<u>change in</u>'.

## You can Find the Specific Heat Capacity of Water

**PRACTICAL**

You can use the experiment below to find the <u>specific heat capacity</u> of <u>water</u> — or any <u>liquid</u> for that matter. In the experiment, an <u>electric immersion heater</u> is used to heat a container full of water. It is <u>assumed</u> that <u>all</u> of the energy transferred to the heater from its power supply is transferred <u>usefully</u> to the water — i.e. all of the energy transferred heats the water.

*You can use this set up with solid blocks to find the SHC of solids.*

1) First, place your container on a <u>mass balance</u>.

2) <u>Zero</u> the balance and fill the container with water. Record the <u>mass</u> of the water.

3) Set up the experiment as shown — make sure the joulemeter reads <u>zero</u> and place a <u>lid</u> on the container if you have one.

4) Measure the <u>temperature</u> of the water, then turn on the power.

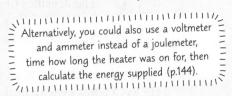

electric immersion heater

joulemeter

to power supply

thermometer

water

container

5) Keep an eye on the <u>thermometer</u>. When the temperature has increased by e.g. <u>ten degrees</u>, stop the experiment and record the <u>energy</u> on the joulemeter, and the <u>increase in temperature</u>.

6) You can then calculate the specific heat capacity of the water by <u>rearranging</u> $\Delta Q = m \times c \times \Delta\theta$ to give you $c = \Delta Q \div (m \times \Delta\theta)$ and plugging in your measurements.

*Alternatively, you could also use a voltmeter and ammeter instead of a joulemeter, time how long the heater was on for, then calculate the energy supplied (p.144).*

7) <u>Repeat</u> the whole experiment at least three times, then calculate an <u>average</u> of the specific heat capacity (p.9).

---

## Some substances can store more energy than others...

Learn the <u>definition</u> of specific heat capacity and make sure you know how to use the <u>formula</u> above.

Q1 Find the final temperature of 5 kg of water, at an initial temperature of 5 °C, after 50 kJ of energy has been transferred to it. The specific heat capacity of water is 4200 J/kg°C.

[3 marks]

Q1 Video Solution

# Specific Latent Heat

*The **energy needed** to change the state of a substance is called **specific latent heat**. But first, insulation...*

## Use **Thermal Insulation** to get More **Accurate** Results

1) During <u>any</u> process, some energy is always <u>wasted</u>.

2) So in the experiment on the previous page, not <u>all</u> of the energy transferred from the power supply is used to heat the water (although we assume it's true to make calculations easier).

3) Some is <u>lost</u> heating up the wires of the immersion heater and some is transferred by heating to the container and the air around it.

4) To <u>reduce</u> these <u>unwanted energy transfers</u> and make your result more <u>accurate</u> (p.7), you should wrap the container in a <u>thermally insulating</u> material (e.g. cotton wool) and place it on an <u>insulating surface</u>, like a cork mat.

5) <u>Thermal insulators</u> reduce the <u>rate</u> at which energy is transferred by <u>heating</u>, which means that <u>less energy</u> is transferred to the thermal energy stores of the surroundings. There's more about thermal insulation on page 48.

## **Specific Latent Heat** is the **Energy Needed** to **Change State**

1) The <u>specific latent heat</u> (SLH) of a <u>change of state</u> of a substance is the <u>amount of energy</u> needed to <u>change 1 kg</u> of it from <u>one state to another without changing its temperature</u>.

2) For <u>cooling</u>, specific latent heat is the energy <u>released</u> by a change in state.

3) Specific latent heat is <u>different</u> for <u>different materials</u>, and for changing between <u>different states</u>.

> The specific latent heat for changing between a <u>solid</u> and a <u>liquid</u> (<u>melting</u> or <u>freezing</u>) is called the <u>specific latent heat of fusion</u>. The specific latent heat for changing between a <u>liquid</u> and a <u>gas</u> (<u>evaporating</u>, <u>boiling</u> or <u>condensing</u>) is called the <u>specific latent heat of vaporisation</u>.

4) You can work out the <u>energy needed</u> (or <u>released</u>) when a substance of mass $m$ changes state using this <u>formula</u>:

**Thermal energy (J) = Mass (kg) × Specific Latent Heat (J/kg)**

$$\frac{Q}{m \times L}$$

 **EXAMPLE**

**The specific latent heat of vaporisation for water (boiling) is 2 260 000 J/kg. How much energy is needed to completely boil 1.50 kg of water at 100 °C?**

1) Just plug the numbers into the <u>formula</u>.

$Q = m \times L$
= 1.50 × 2 260 000

2) The units are <u>joules</u> because it's <u>energy</u>.

= 3 390 000 J

## Different changes of state mean different specific latent heats...

When it comes to the specific latent heat of <u>vaporisation</u> and <u>fusion</u>, the formula's the same, but the process is different. Make sure you understand which process you're actually looking at.

Q1 The SLH of fusion for a particular substance is 120 000 J/kg. How much energy is needed to melt 250 g of the substance when it is already at its melting temperature? [2 marks]

# Investigating Water

o **investigate** what happens to the **temperature** of water during a **change of state**.

## You Need to **Put In Energy** to **Break Bonds Between Particles**

1) When a system is <u>heated</u> and its <u>state changes</u> (e.g. melting, boiling), <u>energy</u> is <u>transferred</u> to the <u>potential energy stores</u> of the particles instead of to their kinetic energy stores.

2) The <u>particles</u> in the system <u>move apart</u> from each other and the <u>intermolecular forces</u> between the particles get <u>weaker</u> (see p.173).

3) Because the amount of energy in the particles' <u>kinetic energy stores</u> stays the <u>same</u>, the <u>average speed</u> of the particles and the <u>temperature</u> of the system remain <u>constant</u> whilst the substance <u>changes state</u>.

4) During a change of state due to <u>cooling</u>, the particles <u>lose energy</u> from their <u>potential energy stores</u>. They move <u>closer together</u> and the <u>intermolecular forces</u> between them get <u>stronger</u>. Their <u>average speed</u> still doesn't change though (so the <u>temperature</u> still remains <u>constant</u>).

5) You can see this by doing this simple <u>experiment</u>:

**PRACTICAL**

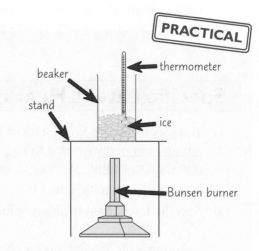

1) Fill a <u>beaker</u> with <u>crushed ice</u>, and place a <u>thermometer</u> into the beaker to record the <u>temperature</u> of the ice.

2) Start a stopwatch and <u>gradually heat</u> the beaker full of ice using a Bunsen burner.

3) Every twenty seconds, record the <u>temperature</u> and the <u>current state</u> of the ice (e.g. partially melted, completely melted).

4) Continue this process until all of the ice has turned into water and the water begins to <u>boil</u>.

5) <u>Stop</u> the stopwatch and <u>turn off</u> the Bunsen burner.

6) Plot a graph of <u>temperature against time</u> for your experiment.

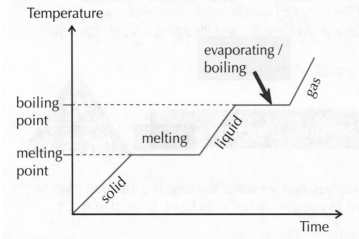

7) You should get a graph similar to the <u>blue</u> sections in the graph on the left.

8) The <u>purple line</u> shows what your graph would look like if you were able to trap and <u>heat</u> the <u>water vapour</u> produced.

9) Comparing the graph to your measurements, you should see that the <u>flat spots</u> occur when there is a <u>change of state</u>.

10) Energy is being transferred to the <u>potential</u> energy stores of the water particles at these points, so the temperature <u>doesn't change</u>.

11) If you carried out an experiment for <u>cooling water</u> instead of heating it, you would get a <u>similar</u> graph. However, the <u>temperature-time</u> graph for a substance <u>cooled</u> from a gas has a <u>negative</u> gradient and <u>flat spots</u> where the substance is condensing or freezing.

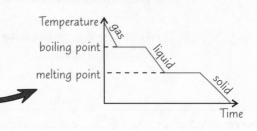

---

## The temperature of a substance is constant as it changes state...

Energy isn't transferred to the particles' kinetic energy stores for a <u>change of state</u>, so the <u>temperature</u> of the substance stays the <u>same</u> and you get <u>flat spots</u> on a temperature-time graph. Learn that, and understand it.

# Warm-Up & Exam Questions

Time to test yourself on specific heat capacity and specific latent heat.  There's no escaping it, get going.

## Warm-Up Questions

1) What is the specific heat capacity of a material?

2) In an experiment to find the specific heat capacity of water, a container of water is wrapped in a thermally insulating material and heated. Explain how this improves the results of the experiment.

3) What are the units of specific latent heat?

4) Sketch a temperature-time graph for water turning into ice.

## Exam Questions

**1** 47 100 J of energy is required to convert 40.8 g of liquid methanol to gaseous methanol without changing its temperature.  *Grade 4-6*

Calculate the specific latent heat of vaporisation of methanol.  Give your answer in J/kg. Use the correct equation from the Physics Equation Sheet on page 268.

*[2 marks]*

**2** 36 000 J of energy is transferred to a 0.5 kg concrete block. The block increases in temperature from 20 °C to 100 °C.  *Grade 6-7*

(a) Calculate the specific heat capacity of the concrete block. Use the correct equation from the Physics Equation Sheet on page 268.

*[2 marks]*

(b) **Figure 1** shows a storage heater in a room.  Energy is transferred to the thermal energy store of the electric storage heater at night, and then transferred away to the thermal energy stores of the surroundings during the day. Lead has a specific heat capacity of 126 J/kg°C.

Using your answer to (a), explain why concrete blocks are used in storage heaters rather than lead blocks.

*[3 marks]*

**Figure 1**

PRACTICAL

**3** A student uses an electrical immersion heater to transfer energy to a beaker containing 1.0 kg of water. She produces a graph of the energy supplied against the increase in temperature of the water, shown in **Figure 2**.  *Grade 7-9*

(a) Use the gradient of the line of best fit in **Figure 2** to determine a value for the specific heat capacity of water in J/kg°C.

*[3 marks]*

(b) State and explain whether you would you expect the true value for the specific heat capacity of water to be higher or lower than the value found in this experiment.

*[2 marks]*

**Figure 2**

*(Graph: Temperature change in °C (y-axis, 0 to 0.75) against Energy in kJ (x-axis, 0 to 3))*

# Gas Pressure

*Kinetic theory* helps explain how **temperature**, **pressure**, **volume** and the **energy in kinetic stores** are all related.

## The **Average Speed** of Particles **Increases** With **Temperature**

1) According to kinetic theory, the particles in a gas are constantly moving with random directions and speeds (see p.173).

2) If you increase the temperature of a gas, you transfer energy into the kinetic energy stores of its particles (see page 174).

3) So as you increase the temperature of a gas, the average speed of its particles increases. This is because the energy in the particles' kinetic energy stores is $\frac{1}{2} \times m \times v^2$ — p.42.

## **Colliding** Gas Particles Create **Pressure**

1) Particles in a gas hardly take up any space. Most of the gas is empty space.

2) As gas particles move about at high speeds, they bang into each other and whatever else happens to get in the way. When they collide with something, they exert a force (and so a pressure — p.182) on it.

3) In a sealed container, the outward gas pressure is the total force exerted by all of the particles in the gas on a unit area of the container walls.

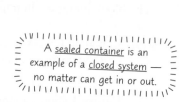
A sealed container is an example of a closed system — no matter can get in or out.

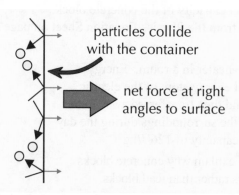
particles collide with the container

net force at right angles to surface

4) The higher the temperature of the gas, the faster the particles move and the more often they collide with the container.

5) The force exerted by each particle during a collision also increases as the temperature increases.

6) So increasing the temperature of a fixed volume of gas increases its pressure.

7) Alternatively, if temperature is constant, increasing the volume of a gas means the particles get more spread out and hit the walls of the container less often. The gas pressure decreases.

8) Pressure and volume are inversely proportional — at a constant temperature, when volume goes up, pressure goes down (and when volume decreases, pressure increases).

9) For a gas of fixed mass at a constant temperature, the relationship is:

$$P_1 \times V_1 = P_2 \times V_2$$

where $P_1$ is the pressure at a volume $V_1$ and $P_2$ is the pressure at a volume $V_2$. Pressure is in Pa (or N/m$^2$) and volume is in m$^3$.

# Gas Pressure

*So you've had a whole page on **particle motion in gases** and even an equation to boot.  Unfortunately you're not done with gas pressure yet — but there are **balloons** on this page, so it's sort of like a party.*

## A Change in **Pressure** Can Cause a Change in **Volume**

1) You saw on the previous page that the <u>pressure</u> of a gas causes a <u>net outwards force</u> at right angles to the surface of its container.

2) Unless it's in a <u>vacuum</u>, the <u>outside</u> of a gas container will also be under <u>pressure</u> from <u>whatever's around it</u> — e.g. <u>atmospheric pressure</u> from the air (p.183).

3) For containers <u>without a fixed volume</u> (e.g. a balloon) the <u>volume</u> of the container (and so the volume of the gas inside) is only <u>constant</u> (it isn't expanding or contracting) when the <u>pressure</u> of the gas <u>inside pushing outwards</u> is <u>equal to</u> the <u>pressure</u> of the air <u>outside pushing inwards</u>.

4) You can change the <u>volume of a gas</u> in a <u>container that doesn't have a fixed volume</u> by changing <u>either</u> the <u>internal</u> (<u>outward</u>) or <u>external</u> (<u>inward</u>) <u>pressure</u> on the container:

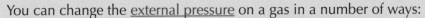

> You can change the <u>external pressure</u> on a gas in a number of ways:
> - For a gas in an air-tight <u>syringe</u>, pushing hard on the <u>plunger</u> increases the <u>inward</u> pressure on the gas, so that it is larger than the outward pressure.  This causes the gas inside of the syringe to be <u>compressed</u>.
> - <u>Atmospheric pressure</u> (p.183) decreases as altitude increases, so as a container of gas <u>rises</u>, the <u>inward</u> pressure <u>decreases</u>. This causes the gas to <u>expand</u> as the altitude increases.

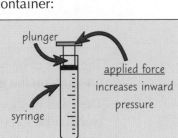

> You can change the <u>pressure</u> of a gas inside a container (e.g. a balloon) by <u>heating</u> or <u>cooling</u>:
> - If a balloon is <u>heated</u>, the gas particles <u>inside it</u> gain <u>energy</u> and move around <u>quicker</u>.  This <u>increases the pressure</u> of the gas inside the balloon.
> - The <u>outward</u> pressure of the gas inside the balloon is now <u>larger</u> than the <u>inward</u> pressure caused by the <u>surroundings</u>.  The <u>balloon</u> (and so the volume of the gas) <u>expands</u> until the pressures are <u>equal</u> once more.
>
> *Cooling the gas in the balloon has the opposite effect — the outward pressure is smaller than the inward pressure, so the balloon shrinks.*

## **Doing Work** on a Gas Can Increase its **Temperature**

1) <u>Doing work</u> on a gas can increase its <u>internal energy</u> (p.174), which increases its <u>temperature</u>.

2) You do work on a gas when you <u>heat it</u> up. You can also do work on a gas <u>mechanically</u>, e.g. with a <u>bike pump</u>.

*There's more about doing work on p.123.*

3) The gas <u>exerts pressure</u> on the <u>plunger</u> of the pump, and so exerts a <u>force</u> on it.  Work has to be done <u>against this force</u> to push down the plunger.

4) This transfers energy to the <u>kinetic energy stores</u> of the gas particles, which means the <u>temperature</u> of the gas <u>increases</u>.  (Remember, the higher the temperature of a gas, the <u>faster</u> its particles move — see previous page.)

5) If the pump is connected to e.g. a tyre, some of this energy is <u>transferred</u> from the gas to the <u>thermal energy store</u> of the tyre, and you'll feel the tyre getting <u>warmer</u> as you pump it up.

---

## Gases can be compressed or expanded by pressure changes...

You should be able to explain how doing <u>work</u> on a <u>gas</u> that's <u>enclosed</u> will lead to an <u>increase</u> in <u>temperature</u> of the gas.  It helps if you understand that work is just the <u>transfer of energy</u> by a force.

**Q1** Explain how a gas exerts pressure on its container. [2 marks]

**Q2** 3.5 m³ of a gas is at a pressure of 520 Pa.  It is compressed to a volume of 1 m³ at a constant temperature.  What is the new pressure of the gas? [3 marks]

# Pressure and Fluid Pressure

*Right, time for an equation for calculating **pressure**. Once you've got that under your belt, we'll have a look at **two factors** that affect the **amount of pressure** in a **fluid** — density and depth.*

## Pressure is the Force per Unit Area

Pressure is the <u>force per unit area</u>. The following equation can be used for <u>solids</u>, <u>liquids</u> and <u>gases</u>:

Pressure in pascals (Pa) $\longrightarrow$ $$P = \frac{F}{A}$$ $\longrightarrow$ Force normal to a surface (N)
$\longrightarrow$ Area of that surface (m²)

### EXAMPLE

**The point of a drawing pin has a surface area of $2 \times 10^{-8}$ m². It is pushed into a notice board with a force of 12 N. Calculate the pressure that the pin exerts on the notice board.**

$P = F \div A = 12 \div (2 \times 10^{-8}) = 6 \times 10^{8}$ Pa

The soles of <u>high-heeled shoes</u> have a <u>small area</u>, so they exert a <u>large pressure</u> on the ground, which can damage some types of flooring.

The soles of <u>snowshoes</u> have very <u>large</u> areas, which 'spread out' your weight (the force) and stop you sinking into snow as you walk.

## Gases and Liquids are Fluids

1) <u>Gases</u> and <u>liquids</u> are both <u>fluids</u> (their particles are free to move, or '<u>flow</u>').
2) <u>Fluid pressure</u> is the pressure caused by the <u>collisions</u> of <u>gas</u> or <u>liquid</u> particles <u>on a given surface</u>.
3) Fluid pressure always exerts a <u>force</u> at <u>right angles</u> (<u>normal</u>) to any <u>surface</u> in contact with the fluid (p.180).
4) The <u>force</u> on a <u>surface</u> due to fluid pressure depends on the <u>area</u> of the object the fluid is in contact with.
5) The <u>properties</u> of a fluid and the <u>atmospheric pressure</u> surrounding the fluid affect fluid pressure (see next page).

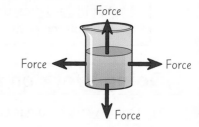

## Fluid Pressure Depends on Density and Depth

1) <u>Density</u> is a measure of how <u>close together</u> the particles in a substance are (p.172).
2) For a given <u>liquid</u>, the <u>density</u> is <u>uniform</u> (the <u>same everywhere</u>) and it <u>doesn't vary</u> with <u>shape</u> or <u>size</u>.
3) The density of a <u>gas</u> can vary though.
4) Assuming their particles have the <u>same mass</u>, a <u>denser</u> fluid has <u>more particles</u> in a certain space than a <u>less dense</u> one.
5) This means there are more particles that are able to <u>collide</u>, so the <u>pressure is higher</u> in the denser fluid.
6) As the <u>depth</u> of a fluid increases, the number of particles <u>above</u> that point increases.
7) The <u>weight</u> of these particles adds to the pressure felt at that point, so <u>fluid pressure</u> increases with depth.

## Fluid pressure increases as density and depth increase...

Make sure you can explain <u>why</u> this is the case in terms of <u>particles</u> and <u>kinetic theory</u>. Once you've got that sussed, there's another <u>pressure equation</u> waiting for you on the next page.

# Fluid Pressure

*And there's still more to learn about **pressure**, including how to use a fairly tricky-looking **equation**.*

## You Can **Calculate** the **Pressure** Due to a **Liquid**

You can calculate the <u>pressure</u> due to a <u>column</u> of liquid <u>above</u> a certain <u>depth</u> using:

Pressure due to a column of liquid (Pa) ⎯ Height of the column (the depth) in m ⎯ Density of the liquid (kg/m³) ⎯ Gravitational field strength (N/kg)

$$P = h \times \rho \times g$$

**EXAMPLE**

**Calculate the change in pressure between a point 20 m below the surface of water and a point 40 m below the surface. The density of water is 1000 kg/m³. The gravitational field strength of the Earth is 10 N/kg.**

1) Calculate the <u>pressure</u> caused by the water at a depth of <u>20 m</u>.

$P = h \times \rho \times g = 20 \times 1000 \times 10$
$= 200\ 000$ Pa

2) Do the same for a depth of <u>40 m</u>.

$P = h \times \rho \times g = 40 \times 1000 \times 10$
$= 400\ 000$ Pa

3) <u>Take away</u> the pressure at <u>20 m</u> from the pressure at <u>40 m</u>.

$400\ 000 - 200\ 000$
$= 200\ 000$ Pa (200 kPa)

*Check your answer makes sense (you can't get negative pressure).*

## **Atmospheric Pressure** Decreases with **Height**

1) The <u>atmosphere</u> is a <u>layer</u> of <u>air</u> that surrounds Earth. It is <u>thin compared</u> to the size of the <u>Earth</u>.

2) <u>Atmospheric pressure</u> is created on a surface by <u>air molecules</u> colliding with the surface.

3) As the <u>altitude</u> (<u>height</u> above Earth) <u>increases</u>, atmospheric pressure <u>decreases</u> — as shown on the graph.

4) The graph is <u>curved</u> because atmospheric pressure is affected by the <u>density</u> of the atmosphere, which also <u>varies with height</u>.

5) As the altitude increases, the atmosphere gets <u>less dense</u>, so there are <u>fewer air molecules</u> that are able to collide with the surface.

6) There are also <u>fewer</u> air molecules <u>above</u> a surface as the height increases.

7) This means that the <u>weight</u> of the air <u>above</u> it, which contributes to atmospheric pressure, <u>decreases</u> with altitude.

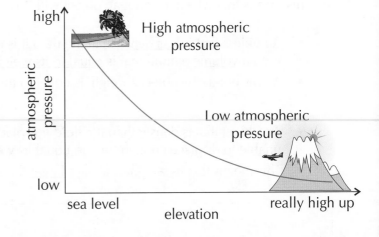

## Make sure you always show your working...

Especially when you're working with more <u>complicated equations</u>, like that pressure one above. Writing out <u>each step</u> means you're <u>less likely to make mistakes</u> when rearranging and substituting, and it'll usually bag you a <u>mark or two</u> in the <u>exam</u> if you end up getting the final answer wrong.

Q1 Video Solution

Q1 At a point 5 cm below the surface of a jug of olive oil, the pressure is 450 Pa. Calculate the density of olive oil. The gravitational field strength of Earth is 10 N/kg.

[2 marks]

# Upthrust

*Fluid pressure* can explain why potatoes **sink** and apples **float**. *Because you've been dying to know...*

## Objects in Fluids Experience Upthrust

1) When an object is submerged <u>in</u> a fluid (either partially or completely), the <u>pressure</u> of the fluid exerts a <u>force</u> on it from <u>every direction</u>.

2) Pressure <u>increases with depth</u>, so the force exerted on the <u>bottom</u> of the object is <u>larger than</u> the force acting on the <u>top</u> of the object.

3) This causes a <u>resultant force</u> (p.127) upwards, known as <u>upthrust</u>.

4) The upthrust is <u>equal</u> to the <u>weight</u> of fluid that has been <u>displaced</u> by the object (e.g. the upthrust on a spoon in water is equal to the <u>weight</u> of a <u>spoon-shaped volume</u> of water).

Pressure

Spoon displaces this much water.

Upthrust is equal to the weight of this amount of water.

## An Object Floats if its Weight = Upthrust

1) If the <u>upthrust</u> on an object is <u>equal to</u> the object's <u>weight</u>, then the forces <u>balance</u> and the object <u>floats</u>.

2) If an object's <u>weight</u> is <u>more than</u> the <u>upthrust</u>, the object <u>sinks</u>.

3) This means that whether or not an object will float depends on its <u>density</u>.

- An object that is <u>less dense</u> than the fluid it is placed in <u>displaces</u> (pushes out of the way) a <u>volume</u> of fluid that is <u>equal to its weight</u> before it is <u>completely submerged</u>.
- At this point, the object's weight is <u>equal</u> to the upthrust, so the object <u>floats</u>.

- An object that is <u>denser</u> than the fluid it is placed in is <u>unable</u> to displace enough fluid to equal its weight.
- This means that its weight is always <u>larger</u> than the upthrust, so it <u>sinks</u>.

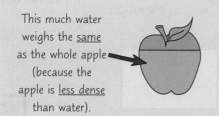

This much water weighs the <u>same</u> as the whole apple (because the apple is <u>less dense</u> than water).

The apple has displaced a volume of water <u>equal</u> to its weight so it floats.

This much water weighs <u>less</u> than a potato (because the potato is <u>denser</u> than water).

The potato can <u>never</u> displace a volume of water equal to its weight so it sinks.

Submarines make use of <u>upthrust</u>. To <u>sink</u>, large tanks are <u>filled with water</u> to increase the <u>weight</u> of the submarine so that it is <u>more than</u> the upthrust. To rise to the surface, the tanks are filled with <u>compressed air</u> to reduce the weight so that it's <u>less than</u> the upthrust.

# Warm-Up & Exam Questions

You should know the drill by now — some warm up questions to get you started, then some exam practice.

## Warm-Up Questions

1) If a gas is kept at a constant volume, explain why increasing the temperature of the gas causes the gas pressure to increase.

2) Explain how the pressure inside and outside a helium balloon changes if it's released and floats upwards in the atmosphere.

3) Explain why the air inside a bicycle tyre becomes warmer when work is done to pump up the tyre.

4) Define the term pressure.

5) Explain why fluid pressure is greater in a denser fluid.

6) An object with a weight of 3.5 N is floating in a bucket of water.
   Give the size of the upthrust acting on the object.

## Exam Questions

**1**   A student places a ball into a bucket of water
and it sinks to the bottom, as shown in **Figure 1**.
The water is 50 cm deep, and the ball has a diameter of 8 cm.

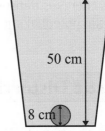

(a)   State a conclusion that can be made about the density of the ball.

*[1 mark]*

(b)   Water has a density of 1000 kg/m³.  The gravitational field strength
is 10 N/kg.  Calculate the pressure on the top of the ball due to the
column of water.  Use the correct equation from the Physics
Equation Sheet on page 268.

**Figure 1**

*[3 marks]*

**2**   **Figure 2** shows a simple hydraulic
system containing a liquid.

In a hydraulic system, pressure is transmitted from
one piston to another through the liquid.

The liquid cannot be compressed, so the pressure
is the same at all points in the liquid.

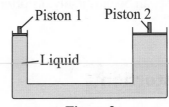

**Figure 2**

(a)   A force of 175 N is applied to piston 1, which has a cross-sectional area of 0.25 m².
Calculate the pressure created at piston 1 due to the liquid.

*[2 marks]*

(b)   Piston 2 has a cross-sectional area of 1.3 m².
Calculate the force acting on piston 2 due to the liquid.

*[3 marks]*

**3**   A sealed balloon contains 0.034 m³ of air at a pressure of 98 kPa.  The balloon is
compressed to 0.031 m³.  The temperature of the air inside it remains constant.
Calculate the air pressure inside the balloon after the compression.
Give your answer in kPa and to 2 significant figures.
Use the correct equation from the Physics Equation Sheet on page 268.

*[4 marks]*

# Elasticity

*Forces don't just make objects **move**, they can also make them **change shape**. Whether they change shape **temporarily** or **permanently** depends on **the object** and the forces applied.*

## Stretching, Compressing or Bending Transfers Energy

1) When you apply a force to an object you may cause it to <u>bend</u>, <u>compress</u> or <u>stretch</u>.

2) To do this, you need <u>more than one</u> force acting on the object — otherwise the object would simply <u>move</u> in the direction of the <u>applied force</u>, instead of changing shape.

3) <u>Work is done</u> when a force stretches or compresses an object and causes energy to be transferred to the <u>elastic potential energy</u> store of the object.

4) If it is <u>elastically distorted</u> (see below), <u>ALL</u> this energy is transferred to the object's <u>elastic potential energy store</u> (see p.42).

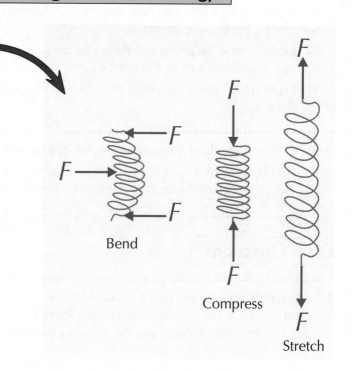

Bend

Compress

Stretch

## Elastic Distortion

1) An object has been <u>elastically distorted</u> if it can <u>go back</u> to its <u>original shape</u> and <u>length</u> after the force has been removed.

2) Objects that can be elastically distorted are called <u>elastic objects</u> (e.g. a spring).

## Inelastic Distortion

1) An object has been <u>inelastically distorted</u> if it <u>doesn't</u> return to its <u>original shape</u> and <u>length</u> after the force has been removed.

2) The <u>elastic limit</u> is the point where an object <u>stops</u> distorting <u>elastically</u> and <u>begins</u> to distort <u>inelastically</u>.

---

REVISION TIP

## Elastic objects are only elastic up to a certain point...

Remember the difference between <u>elastic distortion</u> and <u>inelastic distortion</u>. If an <u>object</u> has been <u>elastically distorted</u>, it will <u>return</u> to its <u>original shape</u> when you <u>remove the force</u>. If it's been <u>inelastically distorted</u>, its shape will have been <u>changed permanently</u> — for example, an over-stretched spring will stay stretched even after you remove the force.

# Elasticity

*Springs obey a really handy little **equation** that relates the **force** on them to their **extension** — for a while at least. Thankfully, you can **plot a graph** to see where this equation is **valid**.*

## Extension is Directly Proportional to Force...

If a spring is supported at the top and a weight is attached to the bottom, it <u>stretches</u>.

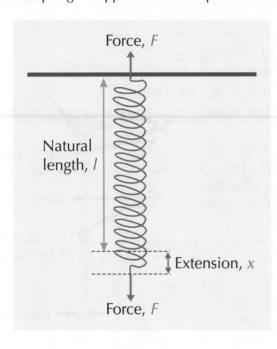

Force, F

Natural length, l

Extension, x

Force, F

1) The <u>extension</u> of a stretched spring (or certain other elastic objects) is <u>directly proportional</u> to the load or <u>force</u> applied — so $F \propto x$.

2) This means that there is a <u>linear</u> relationship between force and extension. (If you plotted a <u>force-extension</u> graph for the spring, it would be a <u>straight line</u>.)

3) This is the equation:

Applied force (N)

Spring constant (N/m)

$$F = k \times x$$

Extension (m)

4) For a <u>linear relationship</u>, the <u>gradient</u> of an object's force-extension graph is equal to its <u>spring constant</u>.

5) The <u>spring constant</u>, depends on the <u>material</u> that you are stretching — a <u>stiffer</u> spring has a <u>greater</u> spring constant.

6) The equation also works for <u>compression</u> (where x is just the <u>difference</u> between the <u>natural</u> and <u>compressed</u> lengths — the <u>compression</u>).

## ...But this Stops Working when the Force is Great Enough

There's a <u>limit</u> to the amount of force you can apply to an object for the extension to keep on increasing <u>proportionally</u>.

1) The graph shows <u>force against extension</u> for an elastic object.

2) There is a <u>maximum</u> force above which the graph <u>curves</u>, showing that extension is <u>no longer</u> proportional to force.

3) The relationship is now <u>non-linear</u> — the object <u>stretches more</u> for each unit increase in force. This point is known as the <u>limit of proportionality</u> and is shown on the graph at the point marked P.

4) The <u>elastic limit</u> (see previous page) is marked as E. Past this point, the object is <u>permanently stretched</u>.

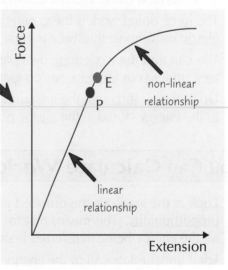

Force

E

P

non-linear relationship

linear relationship

Extension

## The spring constant is measured in N/m...

Be careful with <u>units</u> when doing calculations with springs. Some exam questions might have the extension in <u>centimetres</u>, but the <u>spring constant</u> is measured in <u>newtons per metre</u>. So <u>convert</u> the extension into metres <u>before</u> you do any calculations, or you'll get the wrong answer.

Q1 Video Solution

Q1    A spring is fixed at one end and a force of 1 N is applied to the other end, causing it to stretch. The spring extends by 2 cm. Calculate the spring constant of the spring.    [2 marks]

# Investigating Elasticity

*...easy **experiment** to see exactly how adding **masses** to a spring causes it to **stretch**.*

## You Can **Investigate** the Link Between **Extension and Work Done**

Set up the apparatus as shown in the diagram. Make sure you have plenty of extra masses, then measure the <u>mass</u> of each (with a mass balance) and calculate its <u>weight</u> (the <u>force</u> applied) using $W = m \times g$ (p.30).

**PRACTICAL**

You could do a quick <u>pilot experiment</u> first to find out what size masses to use.

* Using an <u>identical spring</u> to the one you will be testing, <u>load</u> it with <u>masses</u> one at a time and record the <u>force</u> (weight) and <u>extension</u> each time.
* Plot a <u>force-extension</u> graph and check that you get a nice <u>straight line</u> for at least the <u>first 6 points</u>. If it curves <u>too early</u>, you need to use <u>smaller masses</u>.

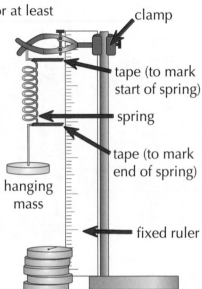

clamp

tape (to mark start of spring)

spring

tape (to mark end of spring)

hanging mass

fixed ruler

extra masses   weighted stand

1) Measure the <u>natural length</u> of the spring (when <u>no load</u> is applied) with a <u>millimetre ruler</u> clamped to the stand. Make sure you take the reading at eye level and add <u>markers</u> (e.g. thin strips of tape) to the <u>top</u> and <u>bottom</u> of the spring to make the reading more accurate.

2) Add a mass to the spring and allow the spring to come to <u>rest</u>. Record the mass and measure the new <u>length</u> of the spring. The <u>extension</u> is the change in length.

3) <u>Repeat</u> this process until you have enough measurements (no fewer than 6).

4) <u>Plot</u> a <u>force-extension graph</u> of your results. It will only start to <u>curve</u> if you <u>exceed</u> the <u>limit of proportionality</u>, but don't worry if yours doesn't (as long as you've got the straight line bit).

1) You should find that a <u>larger force</u> causes a <u>bigger extension</u>.

2) You can also think of this as <u>more work</u> needing to be done to cause a larger extension.

3) The <u>force</u> doing work is the <u>gravitational force</u> and for <u>linear elastic</u> distortions, this force is <u>equal</u> to $F = k \times x$.

4) You can find the <u>work done</u> by a particular force by calculating the <u>area</u> under your <u>force-extension</u> graph <u>up to</u> that value of force.

5) Up to the <u>elastic limit</u>, the area under the graph (work done) is <u>also equal to</u> the energy stored in the <u>elastic potential energy store</u> (see below).

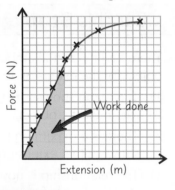

Force (N)

Work done

Extension (m)

## You Can **Calculate Work Done** for **Linear** Relationships

1) Look at the graph on the previous page. The <u>elastic limit</u> is always <u>at</u> or <u>beyond</u> the <u>limit of proportionality</u>. This means that for a <u>linear relationship</u>, the distortion is always <u>elastic</u> — all the energy being transferred is stored in the spring's <u>elastic potential energy store</u>.

2) For a linear relationship, the <u>energy</u> in the <u>elastic potential energy store</u> (and so the <u>work done</u>) can be found using:

$$E = \tfrac{1}{2} \times k \times x^2$$

Extension² (m²)

Spring constant (N/m)

Energy transferred in stretching (J)

## Take care when setting up to get more accurate measurements...

Make sure the ruler is <u>vertical</u> before you begin, otherwise you will have more <u>error</u> in your results.

Q1    A spring with a spring constant of 40 N/m extends elastically by 2.5 cm. Calculate the amount of energy stored in its elastic potential energy store.    [2 marks]

Q1 Video Solution

# Warm-Up & Exam Questions

Time to do some work and stretch yourself with these questions.

## Warm-Up Questions

1) True or false? You can stretch a spring by only applying one force to it.
2) What is meant by elastic distortion?
3) State the formula linking force, spring constant and extension.

## Exam Questions

**PRACTICAL**

1 A student investigates the relationship between the force applied to a spring and its extension.

**Figure 1** shows the force-extension graph of his results.

Calculate the work done to stretch the spring by 4 cm.

*[2 marks]*

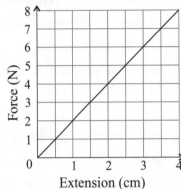

**Figure 1**

**PRACTICAL**

2 A teacher shows his students an experiment to show how a spring extends when masses are hung from it. He hangs a number of 90 g masses from a 50 g hook attached to the base of the spring. He records the extension of the spring and the total weight of the masses and hook each time he adds a mass to the bottom of the spring.

(a) Give the independent variable in this experiment

*[1 mark]*

(b) Give **one** control variable in this experiment.

*[1 mark]*

(c) When a force of 4 N is applied to the spring, the spring extends elastically by 2.5 cm. Calculate the spring constant of the spring.

*[3 marks]*

(d) The teacher applies a 15 N force to the spring. When he removes the force, the spring is 7 cm long. The original length of the spring was 5 cm. Describe what has happened to the spring.

*[1 mark]*

3 A spring is compressed linearly and elastically. It takes 36 J of energy to compress the spring. The original length of the spring is 1.20 m. The spring has a spring constant of 400 N/m. Calculate the length of the spring after it has been compressed. Use the correct equation from the Physics Equation Sheet on page 268.

*[3 marks]*

# Revision Summary for Section 9

Phew, that's the end of <u>Section 9</u> — the last one in the book. Test yourself before you celebrate.

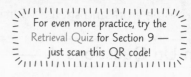 

For even more practice, try the Retrieval Quiz for Section 9 — just scan this QR code!

Section 9 Quiz

- Try these questions and <u>tick off each one</u> when you <u>get it right</u>.
- When you're <u>completely happy</u> with a sub-topic, tick it off.

## Density and the Kinetic Theory of Matter (p.172-178) ☑

1) What is the formula for density? What are the units of density?
2) Briefly describe an experiment to find the density of a liquid.
3) For each state of matter, describe the arrangement of the particles.
4) Name five changes of state.
5) True or false? Mass stays the same when a substance changes state.
6) What is absolute zero? What value does it have in kelvin?
7) What are the units of specific heat capacity?
8) Define specific latent heat.
9) Describe an experiment that could be used to plot a temperature-time graph for ice melting into water.

## Pressure and Upthrust (p.180-184) ☐

10) Describe how a gas exerts a pressure on the walls of its container.
11) What happens to the pressure of a gas in a sealed container of fixed volume when it is heated?
12) True or false? Doing work on a gas can cause an increase in its temperature.
13) State the equation linking pressure, force and area.
14) True or false? Gases are fluids.
15) Explain how the pressure in a liquid varies with the density of the liquid.
16) True or false? Pressure in a liquid decreases with depth.
17) What is atmospheric pressure?
18) True or false? Atmospheric pressure decreases as altitude increases.
19) Explain the cause of upthrust.
20) In what conditions will an object float?

## Stretching, Compressing and Bending (p.186-188) ☐

21) Explain why you need more than one force acting on an object to cause it to stretch.
22) What is the difference between an elastic and an inelastic distortion?
23) How do you find the spring constant from a linear force-extension graph?
24) Draw a typical force-extension graph for an elastic object being stretched past its elastic limit.
25) Describe an experiment that could be used to investigate the relationship between the applied force on a spring and the extension of the spring.

# Apparatus and Techniques

This section covers <u>practical skills</u> you'll need to know about for your course.

- You'll have to do <u>8 core practicals</u> (experiments). These are covered earlier in the book and they're <u>highlighted</u> with <u>practical stamps</u> like this one. ➡ **PRACTICAL**
- The following pages of this section cover some <u>extra bits and bobs</u> you need to know about practical work. First up, using apparatus to take measurements...

## **Mass** Should Be Measured Using a **Balance**

1) For a <u>solid</u>, set the balance to <u>zero</u> and then place your object onto the scale and read off the mass.

2) If you're measuring the mass of a <u>liquid</u>, start by putting an empty <u>container</u> onto the <u>balance</u>. Next, <u>reset</u> the balance to zero.

3) Then just pour your <u>liquid</u> into the container and record the mass displayed.

## Measure **Most Lengths** with a **Ruler**

1) In most cases a bog-standard <u>centimetre ruler</u> can be used to measure <u>length</u>. It depends on what you're measuring though — <u>metre rulers</u> or long <u>measuring tapes</u> are handy for <u>large</u> distances, while <u>micrometers</u> are used for measuring tiny things like the <u>diameter of a wire</u>.

2) The ruler should always be <u>parallel to</u> what you want to measure.

3) If you're dealing with something where it's <u>tricky</u> to measure just <u>one</u> accurately (e.g. water ripples, p.58), you can measure the length of <u>some</u> of them and then <u>divide</u> to find the <u>length of one</u>.

4) If you're taking <u>multiple measurements</u> of the <u>same</u> object (e.g. to measure changes in length) then make sure you always measure from the <u>same point</u> on the object. It can help to draw or stick a small <u>marker</u> onto the object, and <u>line it up</u> with the ruler so that the measurement is always read from the marker.

5) Make sure the ruler and the object are always at <u>eye level</u> when you take a reading. This stops <u>parallax</u> affecting your results, e.g. if you're investigating the link between <u>force</u> and the <u>extension</u> of a spring (p.188).

<u>Parallax</u> is where a measurement appears to <u>change</u> based on <u>where you're looking from</u>.

The <u>blue line</u> is the measurement taken when the spring is at <u>eye level</u>. It shows the correct length of the spring.

If the eye <u>isn't level</u> with this line, it looks like the spring is <u>too long</u> or <u>too short</u>.

## Use a **Protractor** to Find **Angles**

1) First align the <u>vertex</u> (point) of the angle with the mark in the <u>centre</u> of the protractor.

2) Line up the <u>base line</u> of the protractor with one line that forms the <u>angle</u> and then measure the angle of the other line using the scale on the <u>protractor</u>.

3) If the lines creating the angle are very <u>thick</u>, align the protractor and measure the angle from the <u>centre</u> of the lines. Using a <u>sharp pencil</u> to trace light rays or draw diagrams helps to <u>reduce errors</u> when measuring angles.

4) If the lines are <u>too short</u> to measure easily, you may have to <u>extend</u> them. Again, make sure you use a <u>sharp pencil</u> to do this.

# Apparatus and Techniques

## ...emperature Accurately with a **Thermometer**

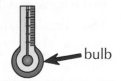

1) Make sure the <u>bulb</u> of your thermometer is <u>completely submerged</u> in any substance you're measuring the temperature of.

2) Wait for the temperature reading to <u>stabilise</u> before you take your initial reading.

3) Again, read your measurement off the <u>scale</u> on a thermometer at <u>eye level</u>.

bulb

## **Measuring Cylinders** and **Pipettes** Measure **Liquid Volumes**

1) <u>Measuring cylinders</u> are the most common way to measure a liquid.

2) They come in all different <u>sizes</u>. Make sure you choose one that's the <u>right size</u> for the measurement you want to make. It's no good using a huge 1 dm³ cylinder to measure out 2 cm³ of a liquid — the graduations (markings for scale) will be <u>too big</u> and you'll end up with <u>massive errors</u>. It'd be much better to use one that measures up to 10 cm³.

3) You can also use a <u>pipette</u> to measure volume. <u>Pipettes</u> are used to suck up and <u>transfer</u> volumes of liquid between containers.

4) <u>Graduated pipettes</u> are used to transfer accurate volumes. A <u>pipette filler</u> is attached to the end of a graduated pipette to <u>control</u> the amount of liquid being drawn up.

5) Whichever method you use, always read the volume from the <u>bottom of the meniscus</u> (the curved upper surface of the liquid) when it's at <u>eye level</u>.

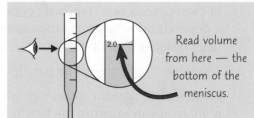

Read volume from here — the bottom of the meniscus.

## You May Have to Measure the **Time Taken** for a Change

1) You should use a <u>stopwatch</u> to <u>time</u> most experiments — they're more <u>accurate</u> than regular watches.

2) Always make sure you <u>start</u> and <u>stop</u> the stopwatch at exactly the right time. Or alternatively, set an <u>alarm</u> on the stopwatch so you know exactly when to stop an experiment or take a reading.

3) You might be able to use a <u>light gate</u> instead (see below). This will <u>reduce the errors</u> in your experiment.

## **Light Gates** Measure **Speed** and **Acceleration**

1) A <u>light gate</u> sends a <u>beam</u> of light (or sometimes infrared) from one side of the gate to a <u>detector</u> on the other side. When something passes through the gate, the beam of light is <u>interrupted</u>. The light gate then measures <u>how long</u> the beam was undetected for.

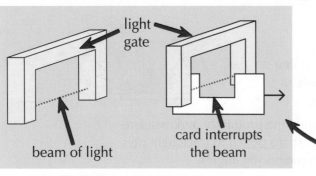

light gate

beam of light

card interrupts the beam

Have a look at page 28 for an example of a light gate being used.

2) To find the <u>speed</u> of an object, connect the light gate to a <u>computer</u>. Measure the <u>length</u> of the object and <u>input</u> this using the software. It will then <u>automatically calculate</u> the speed of the object as it passes through the beam.

3) To measure <u>acceleration</u>, use an object that interrupts the signal <u>twice</u> in a <u>short</u> period of time, e.g. a piece of card with a gap cut into the middle.

4) The light gate measures the speed for each section of the object and uses this to calculate its <u>acceleration</u>. This can then be read from the <u>computer screen</u>.

# Working With Electronics

*Electrical devices* *are used in a bunch of* *experiments*, *so make sure you know how to use the*

## You Have to Interpret **Circuit Diagrams**

Before you get cracking on an experiment involving any kind of electrical devices, you
have to plan and build your circuit using a <u>circuit diagram</u>.  Make sure you know all
of the <u>circuit symbols</u> on page 133 so you're not stumped before you've even started.

## You Can Measure **Potential Difference** and **Current**

### Voltmeters Measure Potential Difference

1) If you're using an <u>analogue voltmeter</u>, choose the voltmeter
   with the <u>most appropriate unit</u> (e.g. V or mV).
2) If you're using a <u>digital</u> voltmeter, you'll most likely be able to <u>switch</u> between them.
3) Connect the voltmeter in <u>parallel</u> (p.141) across the component you want to test.
4) The wires that come with a voltmeter are usually <u>red</u> (positive) and <u>black</u> (negative).
   These go into the red and black coloured <u>ports</u> on the voltmeter.
5) Then simply read the potential difference from the <u>scale</u> (or from the <u>screen</u> if it's digital).

### Ammeters Measure Current

1) Just like with voltmeters, choose the <u>ammeter</u> with the most appropriate <u>unit</u>.
2) Connect the ammeter in <u>series</u> (p.140) with the component you want to
   test, making sure they're both on the <u>same branch</u>.  Again, they usually
   have <u>red</u> and <u>black</u> ports to show you where to connect your wires.
3) Read off the current shown on the <u>scale</u> or by the <u>screen</u>.

> Turn your circuit off between
> readings to prevent wires
> overheating and affecting
> your results (p.135).

### Multimeters Measure Both

1) Instead of having a <u>separate</u> ammeter and voltmeter, many circuits
   use <u>multimeters</u>.  These are devices that measure a range of
   properties — usually potential difference, current and resistance.
2) If you want to find <u>potential difference</u>, make sure the
   <u>red</u> wire is plugged into the port that has a '<u>V</u>' (for volts).
3) To find the <u>current</u>, use the port labelled '<u>A</u>' or '<u>mA</u>' (for amps).
4) The <u>dial</u> on the multimeter should then be turned to the
   <u>relevant section</u>, e.g. to 'A' to measure <u>current</u> in <u>amps</u>.
   The <u>screen</u> will display the value you're measuring.

---

## Don't get your wires in a tangle when you're using circuits...

When you're dealing with <u>voltmeters</u>, <u>ammeters</u> and <u>multimeters</u>, you need to make sure that you
<u>wire</u> them into your circuit correctly, otherwise you could mess up your readings.  Just remember,
the <u>red wires</u> should go into the <u>red ports</u> and the <u>black wires</u> should go into the <u>black ports</u>.

# Safety Precautions

*There's **danger** all around, particularly in science experiments. But don't let this put you off. Just be aware of the **hazards** and take **sensible precautions**. Read on to find out more...*

## Be **Careful** When You Do Experiments

1) There are always hazards in any experiment, so before you start an experiment you should read and follow any safety precautions to do with your method or the apparatus you're using.

2) Stop masses and equipment falling by using clamp stands.

3) Make sure any masses you're using in investigations are of a sensible weight so they don't break the equipment they're used with. Also, make sure strings used in pulley systems are of a sensible length. That way, any hanging masses won't hit the floor or the table during the experiment.

4) When heating materials, make sure to let them cool before moving them, or wear insulated gloves while handling them. If you're using an immersion heater to heat liquids, you should always let it dry out in air, just in case any liquid has leaked inside the heater.

5) If you're using a laser, there are a few safety rules you must follow. Always wear laser safety goggles and never look directly into the laser or shine it towards another person. Make sure you turn the laser off if it's not needed to avoid any accidents.

6) When working with electronics, make sure you use a low enough voltage and current to prevent wires overheating (and potentially melting) and also to avoid damaging components, e.g. blowing a filament bulb.

7) You also need to be aware of general safety in the lab — handle glassware carefully so it doesn't break, don't stick your fingers in sockets and avoid touching frayed wires. That kind of thing.

## BEWARE — hazardous physics experiments about...

Before you carry out an experiment, it's important to consider all of the hazards. Hazards can be anything from lasers to electrical currents, or weights to heating equipment. Whatever the hazards, make sure you know all the safety precautions you should follow to keep yourself safe.

## Practice Exams

Once you've been through all the questions in this book, you should feel pretty confident about the exams.
As final preparation, here is a set of **practice exams** to really get you set for the real thing. The time allowed for
each paper is 1 hour 45 minutes. These papers are designed to give you the best possible preparation for your exams.

# GCSE Physics

## Paper 1

## *Higher Tier*

In addition to this paper you should have:
• A ruler.
• A calculator.

| Centre name | | | |
|---|---|---|---|
| Centre number | | | |
| Candidate number | | | |

**Time allowed:**
• 1 hour 45 minutes

| Surname | |
|---|---|
| Other names | |
| Candidate signature | |

**Instructions to candidates**
• Write your name and other details in the spaces provided above.
• Answer **all** questions in the spaces provided.
• Do all rough work on the paper.
• Cross out any work you do not want to be marked.
• You are allowed to use a calculator.

**Information for candidates**
• The marks available are given in brackets at the end of each question.
• There are 100 marks available for this paper.
• You should use good English and present your answers in a
clear and organised way.
• For questions marked with an asterisk (*) ensure that your answers
have a logical structure with points that link together clearly, and
include detailed, relevant information.

**For examiner's use**

| Q | Attempt Nº | | | Q | Attempt Nº | | |
|---|---|---|---|---|---|---|---|
| | 1 | 2 | 3 | | 1 | 2 | 3 |
| 1 | | | | 6 | | | |
| 2 | | | | 7 | | | |
| 3 | | | | 8 | | | |
| 4 | | | | 9 | | | |
| 5 | | | | 10 | | | |
| | | | | Total | | | |

**Advice to candidates**
• In calculations show clearly how you worked out your answers.
• Read each question carefully before answering it.
• Check your answers if you have time.

**1** A group of students are investigating different types of energy transfer.

**(a)** One student heats a metal spoon over a Bunsen burner.

**(i)** Explain why the amount of energy transferred to the spoon and its surroundings cannot be greater than the amount of energy transferred from the Bunsen burner.

.................................................................................................................................

.................................................................................................................................

*[1 mark]*

**(ii)** Which energy store of the gas is energy being transferred from as the Bunsen is used?

☐ **A** Nuclear

☐ **B** Electrostatic

☐ **C** Chemical

☐ **D** Kinetic

*[1 mark]*

The student then uses tongs to place the hot spoon into an insulated flask full of cold water, like the one shown in **Figure 1**.
The insulated flask is then sealed.

**Figure 1**

**(iii)** The sealed flask can be treated as a closed system.
Which of the following statements is **true** for a closed system?

☐ **A** The net change in the energy of the system is always positive.

☐ **B** The net change in the energy of the system is always negative.

☐ **C** The net change in the energy of the system is always zero.

☐ **D** The net change in the energy of the system may be positive or negative.

*[1 mark]*

**(b)** Another student is investigating how much a rubber ball heats up when it is bounced. During the experiment:

1. The ball is thrown horizontally at a wall.
2. The ball hits the wall, causing it to deform and heat up.
3. The ball bounces back to the student.
4. The student repeatedly throws the ball at the wall.
5. Every 20 seconds, the student uses a thermometer to measure the temperature of the ball's surface.

**(i)** Suggest **one** way to improve the student's experiment.

.................................................................................................................................
*[1 mark]*

**(ii)** Describe the energy transfers that occur as the ball collides with the wall and moves away from the wall.

.................................................................................................................................

.................................................................................................................................

.................................................................................................................................

.................................................................................................................................

.................................................................................................................................

.................................................................................................................................

.................................................................................................................................
*[4 marks]*

**(c)** The experiment is changed so that now the ball is released from a height of 1.75 metres and allowed to fall vertically. The ball has a mass of 30 grams. The gravitational field strength of Earth is 10 N/kg.

Calculate the energy transferred from the GPE store as the ball falls 1.75 m. Use the equation:

change in GPE = mass × gravitational field strength × change in vertical height

Energy = .......................... J
*[2 marks]*
*[Total 10 marks]*

**Turn over for the next question**

**Turn over ▶**

**2**   A home owner would like to make her home more energy efficient in order to reduce her impact on the environment.

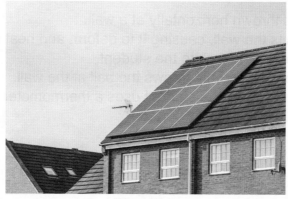

**Figure 2**

(a) **Figure 2** shows the solar panels the home owner has fitted to the roof to generate electricity.  Solar panels are an example of a renewable energy resource.

   **(i)**   Give **one** other example of a renewable energy resource.

......................................................................................................................................................
*[1 mark]*

Each hour the Sun's rays transfer 1.2 MJ of energy to the solar panels' surfaces. Of this energy, 0.2 MJ is transferred away usefully.

   **(ii)**  State the equation relating efficiency, total energy supplied to a device and useful energy transferred by the device.

......................................................................................................................................................
*[1 mark]*

   **(iii)** Calculate the efficiency of the home owner's solar panels.

Efficiency = .........................
*[2 marks]*

(b) **Figure 3** shows a country's total energy use per year over 15 years.

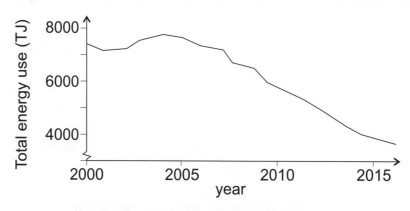

**Figure 3**

**(i)** Describe how the amount of energy used by the country has changed over time. Suggest **one** reason for this.

...................................................................................................................

...................................................................................................................

...................................................................................................................
*[2 marks]*

The overall use of renewable resources in the country has increased over time.

**(ii)** Suggest **two** factors which might limit the use of renewable energy resources.

1. ...............................................................................................................

2. ...............................................................................................................
*[2 marks]*

**(c)** The home owner wants to build an extension.
The extension will be built with walls that are a single brick thick.
The home owner is trying to decide which type of brick to use to build the extension walls. **Figure 4** shows some types of brick that could be used.

| Brick | Volume (cm³) | Thickness (cm) | Thermal Conductivity (W/mK) |
|-------|-------------|----------------|------------------------------|
| Brick X | 150 | 8 | 0.84 |
| Brick Y | 150 | 12 | 0.62 |
| Brick Z | 150 | 10 | 0.84 |

**Figure 4**

Suggest which type of brick the home owner should use to minimise the rate of cooling of the extension. Justify your answer.

...................................................................................................................

...................................................................................................................

...................................................................................................................

...................................................................................................................

...................................................................................................................
*[3 marks]*

*[Total 11 marks]*

**Turn over for the next question**

**Turn over ▶**

**3** **Figure 5** shows a couple doing a dance routine on an ice rink.

**Figure 5**

At the start of the routine, the first skater is at the entrance to the ice rink.

**Figure 6** shows the first skater's distance-time graph for the first 35 seconds of the routine.

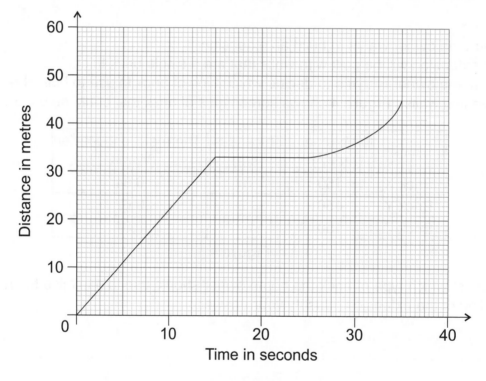

**Figure 6**

**(a)** Describe the motion of the first skater during the first 35 seconds of the routine.

...................................................................................................................................................

...................................................................................................................................................

...................................................................................................................................................

...................................................................................................................................................

*[3 marks]*

**(b)** After travelling 33 m the first skater arrives at the centre of the rink. Use **Figure 6** to determine the speed of the first skater as she travels to the centre of the rink.

Speed = ........................ m/s

*[2 marks]*

The second skater is travelling at a constant speed of 3.5 metres per second.

**(c) (i)** State the equation relating speed, distance and time.

*[1 mark]*

**(ii)** Calculate the time it will take the second skater to travel a distance of 14 metres.

Time = ........................ s

*[3 marks]*

**(d)** The second skater then comes to a complete stop in 7 seconds.

**(i)** Which of the following options is the correct value of his average deceleration?

- [ ] **A** 0.5 m/s²
- [ ] **B** 7 m/s²
- [ ] **C** 10 m/s²
- [ ] **D** 24.5 m/s²

*[1 mark]*

**(ii)** Compare the magnitudes of the driving forces and the frictional forces acting on the second skater as he decelerates.

.................................................................................................................................

.................................................................................................................................

*[1 mark]*

*[Total 11 marks]*

**Turn over for the next question**

**Turn over ▶**

**4** The Sun is a main sequence star.

**(a)** Stars are held together by gravitational attraction.
Explain how the Sun remains stable and does not collapse under gravity.

......................................................................................................................................................

......................................................................................................................................................

*[2 marks]*

**(b)** Explain why the mass of a main sequence star decreases over time.

......................................................................................................................................................

......................................................................................................................................................

*[2 marks]*

**(c)** The Sun will eventually become a red giant star.
What will the Sun become immediately after its red giant stage?

☐ **A** Nebula

☐ **B** White dwarf

☐ **C** Neutron star

☐ **D** Red supergiant

*[1 mark]*

**Figure 7** provides data concerning Earth and Venus.

| | Mass in kg | Diameter in km | Orbital radius in km | Orbital speed in km/s | Gravitational field strength in N/kg |
|---|---|---|---|---|---|
| **Venus** | $5 \times 10^{24}$ | 12 000 | $1.1 \times 10^8$ | .................... | 9 |
| **Earth** | $6 \times 10^{24}$ | 13 000 | $1.5 \times 10^8$ | 30 | 10 |

**Figure 7**

**(d)** Using the data from **Figure 7**, what is the orbital speed of Venus?

☐ **A** 20 km/s      ☐ **B** 35 km/s      ☐ **C** 30 km/s      ☐ **D** 25 km/s

*[1 mark]*

**(e)** Calculate the weight of a 1400 kg object on the surface of Venus.

Weight = ........................ N

*[2 marks]*

*[Total 8 marks]*

5   A student wants to investigate how much different transparent materials will refract a beam of light. The student has three rectangular blocks made out of different transparent materials, similar to the one shown in **Figure 8**.

**Figure 8**

(a) Describe an experiment the student could carry out in order to investigate this.

...............................................................................................................................................

...............................................................................................................................................

...............................................................................................................................................

...............................................................................................................................................

*[3 marks]*

(b) (i) Name a piece of equipment that the student could use to create a thin beam of light.

...............................................................................................................................................

*[1 mark]*

(ii) Explain **one** advantage of using a thin beam of light.

...............................................................................................................................................

...............................................................................................................................................

*[1 mark]*

**Question 5 continues on the next page**

**Turn over ▶**

**(c)** **Figure 9** shows the angles of refraction for three different materials, for a fixed angle of incidence.

| Material | Angle of refraction (°) |
|---|---|
| Ice | 37 |
| Flint glass | 24 |
| Acrylic | 31 |

**Figure 9**

(i) State the material in which light travels the slowest.

.......................................................................................................................................

*[1 mark]*

(ii) Explain your answer to part **(i)**.

.......................................................................................................................................

.......................................................................................................................................

*[2 marks]*

**(d)** When light of frequency $5.1 \times 10^{14}$ Hz is travelling through flint glass, the wavelength of the light is 353 nm.

Calculate the speed of light in flint glass.

Speed of light in flint glass = ....................... m/s

*[2 marks]*

*[Total 10 marks]*

6 *(a) Models of the atom have developed over time.

Figure 10 shows an early model of the atom, Model X, and a currently used model of the atom, Model Y.

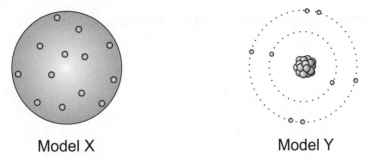

Model X                                      Model Y

Figure 10

Explain how experiments and scientific discoveries caused our understanding of the atom to develop from Model X to Model Y.
Your answer should include descriptions of the models shown in Figure 10.

.......................................................................................................................................................

.......................................................................................................................................................

.......................................................................................................................................................

.......................................................................................................................................................

.......................................................................................................................................................

.......................................................................................................................................................

.......................................................................................................................................................

.......................................................................................................................................................
[6 marks]

(b) (i) An unstable atom will emit radiation.

A student places a detector next to a radioactive sample of bismuth-212.
The student records the count-rate measured by the detector every 10 seconds.

Name a detector that the student could use to measure the count-rate.

.......................................................................................................................................................
[1 mark]

**Question 6 continues on the next page**

**Turn over ▶**

**(ii)** Bismuth-212 can decay by beta-minus emission to form an isotope of polonium (Po). **Figure 11** shows an incomplete nuclear equation showing this decay.

$$^{212}_{83}\text{Bi} \rightarrow \, ^{212}_{A}\text{Po} \, + \, ^{0}_{B}\beta$$

**Figure 11**

Determine the atomic number, A, of the polonium atom.

A = ........................
*[1 mark]*

**(iii)** The student plots a graph of the count-rate of the bismuth-212 sample against time.

**Figure 12** shows the student's graph.

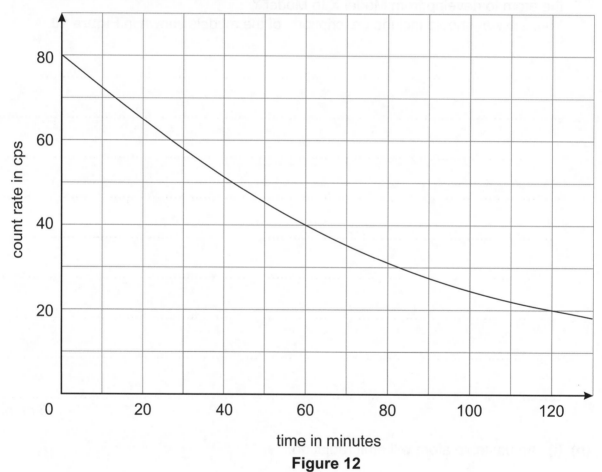

time in minutes

**Figure 12**

Use **Figure 12** to calculate the half-life of bismuth-212.
Give your answer in minutes.

Half-life = ........................ minutes
*[2 marks]*

**(c)** Another radioactive isotope, iodine-131, emits gamma rays.

Iodine-131 is typically stored in a lead-lined box.

**Figure 13** shows the radiation detected outside the box against the thickness of the box's lead lining.

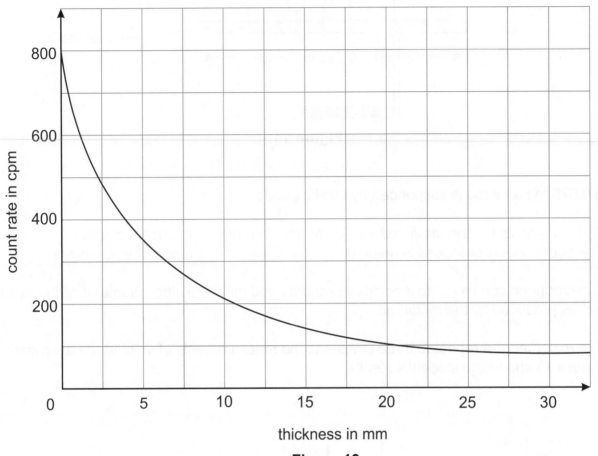

**Figure 13**

Using **Figure 13**, describe how the thickness of the box's lead lining affects the safety of people near to the box.

.......................................................................................................................................

.......................................................................................................................................

.......................................................................................................................................

*[2 marks]*

*[Total 12 marks]*

**Turn over for the next question**

**Turn over ▶**

7   A student is investigating sound waves. The experimental set-up is shown in **Figure 14**.

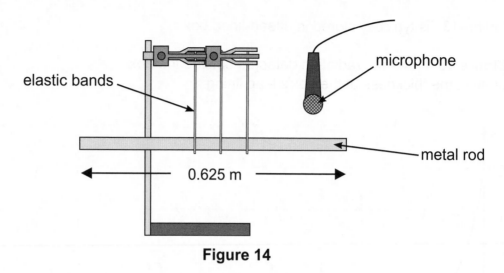

**Figure 14**

A 0.625 m metal rod is suspended by elastic bands.

The student strikes the metal rod with a hammer in order to produce a sound.
The sound that is produced is made up of sound waves of a range of frequencies.

A microphone connected to a computer records and measures the volume of all the sound waves produced by the metal rod.

The experiment is repeated three times and the measurements of volume are averaged.
**Figure 15** shows the student's results.

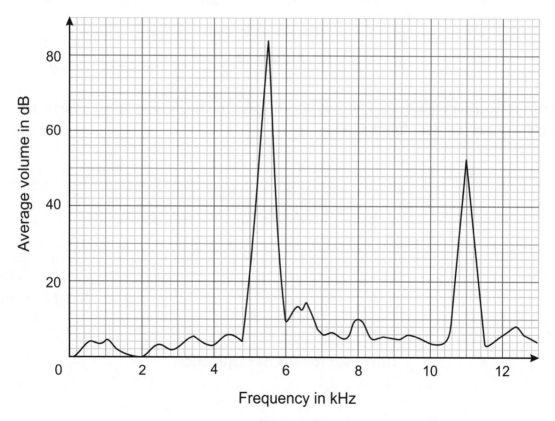

**Figure 15**

**(a)** What was the average volume of the 8 kHz sound wave produced by the rod?

Volume = ........................ dB

*[1 mark]*

**(b)** The frequency of the sound wave with the highest volume is known as the 'peak frequency'. The rod's peak frequency is 5500 Hz.

The wave in the rod that produced this peak frequency has a wavelength equal to twice the length of the rod.

Calculate the speed of this wave.
Give you answer to 2 significant figures.

Wave speed = ........................ m/s

*[4 marks]*

**(c)** The student carried out the experiment with a window open. As a result, the microphone also recorded background noise from the street outside.

What type of error did this introduce to the experiment?

☐ **A** Random error

☐ **B** Zero error

☐ **C** Systematic error

☐ **D** Anomalous error

*[1 mark]*

*[Total 6 marks]*

**Turn over for the next question**

**Turn over ▶**

**8**   A vehicle's total mass is increased by loading it with crash test dummies.
**Figure 16** lists the braking distance of the vehicle as its total mass increases.

| Total Mass of Vehicle (kg) | Braking Distance (m) |
|---|---|
| 1200 | 83 |
| 1300 | 89 |
| 1400 | 97 |
| 1500 | 103 |
| 1600 | 110 |
| 1700 | 119 |

**Figure 16**

**Figure 17** shows an incomplete plot of the data in **Figure 16**.

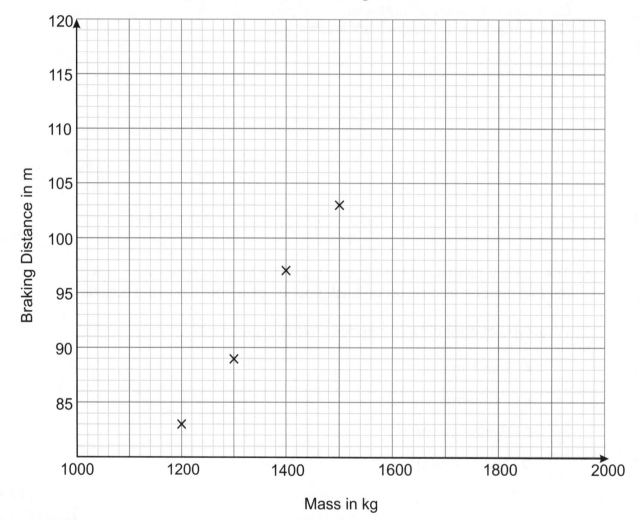

Mass in kg

**Figure 17**

**(a) (i)**   Complete **Figure 17** by plotting the missing points and drawing a line of best fit.

*[2 marks]*

**(ii)**   Describe the relationship between vehicle mass and braking distance.

..................................................................................................................................................
*[1 mark]*

**(b)** A small car has a total mass of 1100 kg.
Whilst travelling through a flat, built-up area the car performed an emergency stop.

Its brakes provided a constant force of 7000 N.  It stopped after braking for 18 m.

**(i)** Calculate the work done by the brakes to stop the car.
Use the equation:

work done = force × distance moved in the direction of the force

Work done = ........................J
*[2 marks]*

**(ii)** Calculate the speed at which the car was travelling before performing the emergency stop.

Speed = ........................m/s
*[3 marks]*

**(iii)** Calculate the deceleration of the car.

Deceleration = ........................m/s²
*[2 marks]*
*[Total 10 marks]*

**Turn over for the next question**

**Turn over ▶**

**9** A student carries out an investigation into the use of different materials in crumple zones. The set-up used is shown in **Figure 18**.

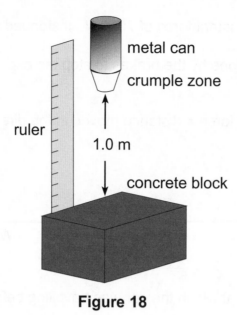

**Figure 18**

This is the student's method:

* A material is attached to the bottom of a hollow metal can to create a crumple zone.
* The total mass of the can and crumple zone is measured.
* Masses are added to the can until the total mass of the can and the crumple zone is 1 kg.
* The can is dropped from a height of 1 m onto a concrete block.
* A video of the can's fall and collision is recorded.
* The steps are repeated for a new material. The size of the crumple zone is kept constant for each material.

**(a)** Explain the importance of ensuring that the total mass of the can and the crumple zone is the same for each drop.

......................................................................................................................................................

......................................................................................................................................................

*[1 mark]*

**(b)** The student uses the footage to determine that in all the tests, the can is travelling at 4.4 m/s just before it hits the block.

Describe how the student could also use the recorded footage to calculate the deceleration of the can when it collides with the concrete block.

......................................................................................................................................................

......................................................................................................................................................

......................................................................................................................................................

......................................................................................................................................................

*[3 marks]*

The student tests three different materials as crumple zones. Each crumple zone is tested three times and a mean is taken. The results are displayed in **Figure 19**.

| | Deceleration (m/s$^2$) | | | |
| --- | --- | --- | --- | --- |
| | Test 1 | Test 2 | Test 3 | Mean |
| Material A | 110 | 102 | 104 | 105 |
| Material B | 27 | 28 | 27 | 27 |
| Material C | 7 | 10 | 10 | |

**Figure 19**

**(c) (i)** Calculate the mean deceleration experienced by the can when it was fitted with a crumple zone made out of material C.

Deceleration = .........................m/s$^2$

*[2 marks]*

**(ii)** Select the material which would be most suitable for use in a crumple zone. Justify your answer.

......................................................................................................................................

......................................................................................................................................

......................................................................................................................................

*[2 marks]*

**(d)** Seat belts are also used to improve vehicle safety.

A 60 kg driver undergoes a collision while wearing a seat belt.
He decelerates from 3.0 m/s to rest in 0.40 s.

Calculate the size of the force experienced by the driver.
Use the correct equation from the Physics Equation Sheet on page 268.

Force = ......................... N

*[2 marks]*

*[Total 10 marks]*

**Turn over for the next question**

**Turn over ▶**

**10** **Figure 20** shows the amount that different electromagnetic waves from space are absorbed by the Earth's atmosphere.

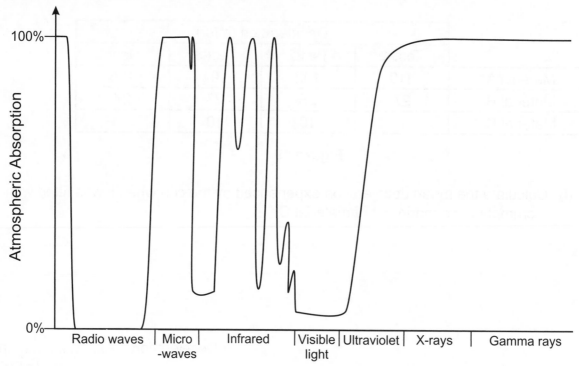

**Figure 20**

(a) Using **Figure 20**, explain **one** way in which Earth's atmosphere protects humans.

.......................................................................................................................................................

.......................................................................................................................................................

.......................................................................................................................................................

.......................................................................................................................................................

*[2 marks]*

*(b) Radio waves and microwaves are used by communications satellites
to transfer information.
Use **Figure 20** to explain why radio waves are a suitable type
of electromagnetic wave for use by communications satellites.
Describe how radio waves can be produced and received by a satellite.

...............................................................................................................................

...............................................................................................................................

...............................................................................................................................

...............................................................................................................................

...............................................................................................................................

...............................................................................................................................

...............................................................................................................................

...............................................................................................................................

...............................................................................................................................

...............................................................................................................................

*[6 marks]*

(c) The local temperature of a point on the Earth decreases at night.
Explain why the local temperature decreases less during cloudy nights
than during clear nights.

...............................................................................................................................

...............................................................................................................................

...............................................................................................................................

...............................................................................................................................

...............................................................................................................................

...............................................................................................................................

*[4 marks]*

*[Total 12 marks]*

**END OF QUESTIONS**

# GCSE Physics

## Paper 2

## *Higher Tier*

In addition to this paper you should have:
- A ruler.
- A calculator.
- A protractor.

| Centre name | | | | |
|---|---|---|---|---|
| Centre number | | | | |
| Candidate number | | | | |

**Time allowed:**
- 1 hour 45 minutes

| Surname | |
|---|---|
| Other names | |
| Candidate signature | |

**Instructions to candidates**
- Write your name and other details in the spaces provided above.
- Answer **all** questions in the spaces provided.
- Do all rough work on the paper.
- Cross out any work you do not want to be marked.
- You are allowed to use a calculator.

**Information for candidates**
- The marks available are given in brackets at the end of each question.
- There are 100 marks available for this paper.
- You should use good English and present your answers in a clear and organised way.
- For questions marked with an asterisk (*) ensure that your answers have a logical structure with points that link together clearly, and include detailed, relevant information.

**Advice to candidates**
- In calculations show clearly how you worked out your answers.
- Read each question carefully before answering it.
- Check your answers if you have time.

**For examiner's use**

| Q | Attempt Nº | | | Q | Attempt Nº | | |
|---|---|---|---|---|---|---|---|
| | 1 | 2 | 3 | | 1 | 2 | 3 |
| 1 | | | | 6 | | | |
| 2 | | | | 7 | | | |
| 3 | | | | 8 | | | |
| 4 | | | | 9 | | | |
| 5 | | | | 10 | | | |
| | | | | Total | | | |

1 **Figure 1** shows a kettle that uses electricity to boil water.

**Figure 1**

(a) **(i)** Which of the following equations correctly relates charge, current and time?

☐ **A** charge = current × time

☐ **B** charge = ½ × current × time

☐ **C** charge = current ÷ time

☐ **D** charge = time ÷ current

*[1 mark]*

**(ii)** The current through the kettle is 12 A.
Calculate the time taken for 1440 C to pass through the kettle.

Time = ..................... s

*[3 marks]*

(b) The kettle has a power rating of 3000 W.
Explain what the term power rating means.

...................................................................................................................................

...................................................................................................................................

...................................................................................................................................

*[1 mark]*

**Question 1 continues on the next page**

**Turn over ▶**

**(c)** When the kettle is heating water, energy is transferred electrically from the mains to the heating element of the kettle.

Describe the energy transfer that occurs between the heating element and the water in the kettle.

..................................................................................................................................

..................................................................................................................................

..................................................................................................................................

..................................................................................................................................

..................................................................................................................................

*[3 marks]*

**(d)** To bring a full kettle of water to the boil, 740 kJ of energy is transferred to the kettle. 680 kJ of this energy is usefully transferred to the water.

Using this information, complete the energy transfer diagram in **Figure 2** for bringing a full kettle of water to the boil.

Label the diagram with the correct values for the energy transferred.

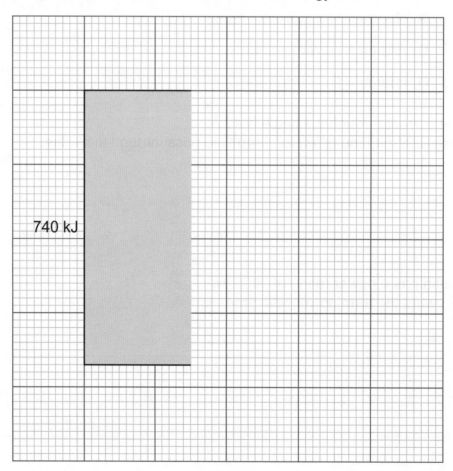

740 kJ

**Figure 2**

*[2 marks]*

*[Total 10 marks]*

**2**   A scientist is investigating how the pressure of a gas depends on its volume.

The scientist uses a syringe that initially contains 50 ml of a gas.
The syringe is sealed so that the gas cannot escape.
The scientist connects a pressure sensor to the syringe to measure the gas pressure in the syringe.
This set-up is shown in **Figure 3**.

The scientist uses the following method:

1.   Measure the initial gas pressure.
2.   Compress the gas in the syringe to 40 ml.
3.   Immediately take a gas pressure reading using the pressure sensor.
4.   Repeat steps 2 and 3 for 30 ml, 20 ml and 10 ml volumes of gas.
5.   Repeat the investigation two more times, and calculate
     a mean pressure for each volume of gas.

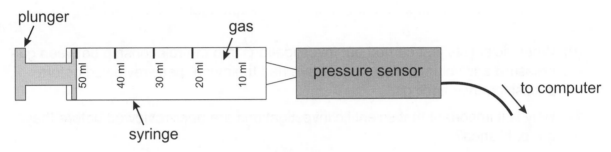

**Figure 3**

**(a)** Give **one** reason why it is a good idea for the scientist to repeat the experiment.

.................................................................................................................................

.................................................................................................................................
*[1 mark]*

**(b)** The temperature of a gas can increase when its volume is decreased.
This increases the gas pressure.

Suggest an improvement that the scientist could make to the experimental method given in the question to ensure this doesn't affect the results of the experiment.

.................................................................................................................................

.................................................................................................................................
*[1 mark]*

**Question 2 continues on the next page**

**Turn over ▶**

**(c)** State and explain what would have happened to the gas pressure when its volume was decreased, if the temperature of the gas had been kept constant.
Use ideas about particles in your answer.

..................................................................................................................................................

..................................................................................................................................................

..................................................................................................................................................

..................................................................................................................................................

..................................................................................................................................................

..................................................................................................................................................

*[3 marks]*

**(d)** When scientists first carried out investigations into the relationship between gas pressure and volume, they would have had their work peer-reviewed before publishing their findings.

Why is it important that scientific investigations are peer-reviewed before they are published?

☐  **A**  To make the investigation more biased.

☐  **B**  To reduce the risk of hazards in the investigation.

☐  **C**  So that other scientists can use the results in their own work.

☐  **D**  So that other scientists can check that the experimental methods used are sensible.

*[1 mark]*

*[Total 6 marks]*

3   A student is given a set of apparatus, set up as shown in **Figure 4**.
    The hook is assumed to have zero mass.

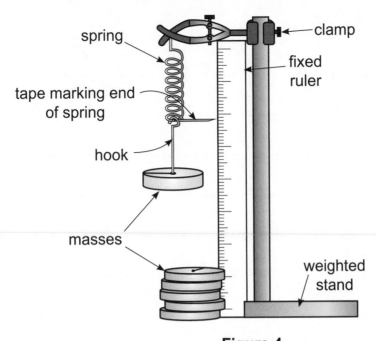

**Figure 4**

(a) (i) Placing one of the masses on the hook exerts a force of 1 N on the bottom
        of the spring.

A force is exerted by the clamp on the other end of the spring.

What is the size of the force exerted on the spring by the clamp?

☐  **A**  0.5 N

☐  **B**  1 N

☐  **C**  1.5 N

☐  **D**  2 N

[1 mark]

(ii) Explain why more than one force is needed to deform a spring.

.............................................................................................................................

.............................................................................................................................

[1 mark]

(b) Name the type of error which may be reduced by the use of the tape marker
    at the end of the spring.

☐  **A**  zero error

☐  **B**  anomalous error

☐  **C**  systematic error

☐  **D**  random error

[1 mark]

**Question 3 continues on the next page**

**Turn over ▶**

*(c) Describe how the student could use the experimental set-up in **Figure 4** to find the spring constant of the spring.

...........................................................................................................................................................

...........................................................................................................................................................

...........................................................................................................................................................

...........................................................................................................................................................

...........................................................................................................................................................

...........................................................................................................................................................

...........................................................................................................................................................

...........................................................................................................................................................

...........................................................................................................................................................

...........................................................................................................................................................

...........................................................................................................................................................

...........................................................................................................................................................

*[6 marks]*

(d) The student used the apparatus in **Figure 4** to produce the graph shown in **Figure 5**.

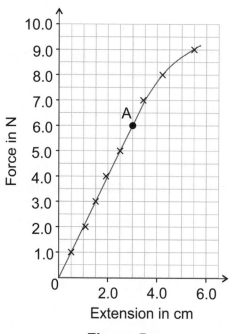

Figure 5

Calculate the work done to stretch the spring to point A.

Work done = ........................ J

*[3 marks]*

**(e)** The student then decided to use the apparatus to create a force-extension graph for a rubber band. The student's graph is shown in **Figure 6**.

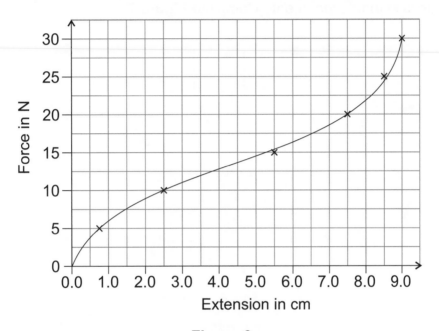

**Figure 6**

Before the experiment, the student made the following statement:

"I think that rubber bands will behave elastically when stretched.
I also think the relationship between force and extension will be linear."

After the experiment, the rubber band returned to its original shape and size.

Discuss the extent to which the student's statement is supported by the results of the experiment.

..................................................................................................................................................

..................................................................................................................................................

..................................................................................................................................................

..................................................................................................................................................

..................................................................................................................................................

*[2 marks]*

*[Total 14 marks]*

**Turn over for the next question**

**Turn over ▶**

**4** A student wants to investigate the relationship between current and potential difference for a fixed resistor.

The student has:

- a battery
- a fixed resistor
- a variable resistor
- an ammeter
- a voltmeter

**(a)** **Figure 7** is an incomplete circuit diagram of the circuit the student uses in their experiment. Complete **Figure 7**.

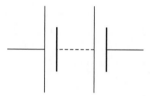

**Figure 7**

*[3 marks]*

**(b)** The student carries out the experiment three times.
**Figure 8** is a table of the student's measurements.

| Potential Difference across resistor (V) | Current through resistor (A) | | |
|---|---|---|---|
| | Test 1 | Test 2 | Test 3 |
| 0.0 | 0.00 | 0.00 | 0.00 |
| 1.0 | 0.52 | 0.51 | 0.50 |
| 2.0 | 0.99 | 0.99 | 1.00 |
| 3.0 | 1.52 | 1.50 | 1.50 |
| 4.0 | 1.98 | 1.99 | 1.99 |
| 5.0 | 2.53 | 2.52 | 2.51 |

**Figure 8**

Calculate the mean current flowing through the resistor when the potential difference across it was 5.0 V.

Current = ........................ A

*[1 mark]*

**(c)** The student notices that over time, the resistor being tested feels warm.
This is because energy is transferred when work is done against electrical resistance.

In terms of electrons and ions, explain the cause of this energy transfer in the resistor.

..................................................................................................................................

..................................................................................................................................

..................................................................................................................................

..................................................................................................................................

..................................................................................................................................

*[2 marks]*

**(d)** The student tests another fixed resistor, which has a resistance of 2 Ω.
Calculate the potential difference that needs to be applied across the resistor to cause a current of 5 A to flow through the resistor.

Potential difference = ........................ V

*[2 marks]*

**Question 4 continues on the next page**

**Turn over ▶**

**(e)** The student uses a similar experiment to investigate the relationship between current and potential difference in a filament lamp.

The student then plots the results on a graph of current against potential difference.

What should the graph look like?

A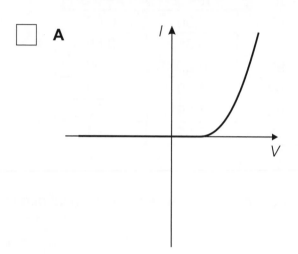

B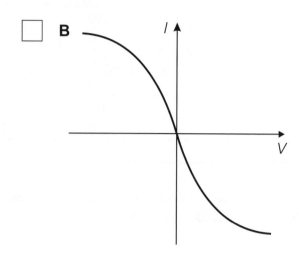

C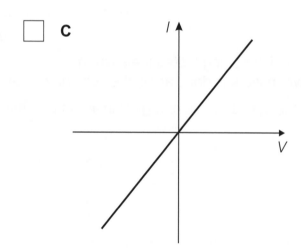

D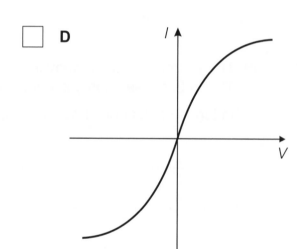

*[1 mark]*

*[Total 9 marks]*

**5** Transformers are used to change the size of potential differences in the national grid.

**(a)** Which of the following graphs shows the current that is needed for a transformer to work?

☐ **A**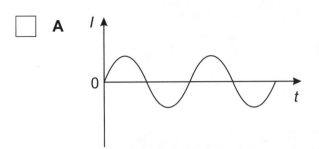

☐ **B**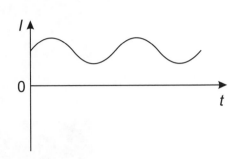

☐ **C**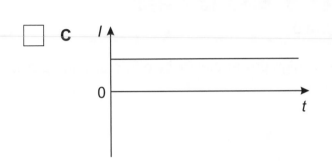

☐ **D**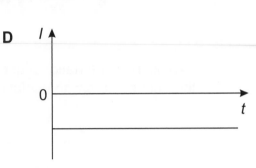

[1 mark]

**(b)** A transformer is made up of a primary and secondary coil of wire, joined with an iron core.

Explain how a potential difference across the primary coil of the transformer can create a potential difference across the secondary coil.

.............................................................................................................................................

.............................................................................................................................................

.............................................................................................................................................

.............................................................................................................................................

[3 marks]

**(c)** The primary coil of a transformer in the national grid has 5000 turns and a potential difference of 25 kV across it.

The secondary coil has a potential difference of 400 kV across it.

Calculate how many turns there must be on the secondary coil.
Use the correct equation from the Physics Equation Sheet on page 268.

Number of turns = .............................

[3 marks]

**Question 5 continues on the next page**

**Turn over ▶**

*(d) The national grid is a network of cables and transformers that transmits electricity across the UK. **Figure 9** shows a part of the national grid.

**Figure 9**

Explain how the national grid can transmit high power electricity efficiently, and provide their consumers with useful electric power.

.......................................................................................................................................................

.......................................................................................................................................................

.......................................................................................................................................................

.......................................................................................................................................................

.......................................................................................................................................................

.......................................................................................................................................................

.......................................................................................................................................................

.......................................................................................................................................................

.......................................................................................................................................................

.......................................................................................................................................................

.......................................................................................................................................................

.......................................................................................................................................................

.......................................................................................................................................................

.......................................................................................................................................................

*[6 marks]*

*[Total 13 marks]*

**6** A factory worker is wearing polyester overalls. When the worker removes his hood, his hair stands on end because his hair has become positively charged.

**(a)** Explain how the worker's hair has become positively charged in terms of the movement of charges.

.......................................................................................................................

.......................................................................................................................
*[2 marks]*

**(b)** The worker goes to open a door.
A small spark jumps between the metal door handle and the worker's hand, giving him a small electric shock.

Explain why a spark is created between the worker's hand and the door handle.

.......................................................................................................................

.......................................................................................................................

.......................................................................................................................

.......................................................................................................................
*[3 marks]*

**(c)** The charge which had built up on the worker was 12 µC.
The potential difference between the worker's hand and the door handle was 10 kV.

Calculate the energy transferred by the spark.

Energy transferred = ........................ J
*[3 marks]*

**(d)** Sparks can also be generated when aircraft are being refuelled.

This is because a static charge can build up as fuel flows through the filler pipe and into the fuel tank.

**(i)** Explain why a spark could be dangerous when refuelling aircraft.

.......................................................................................................................

.......................................................................................................................
*[1 mark]*

**(ii)** State one way in which a spark could be prevented from forming during refuelling.

.......................................................................................................................
*[1 mark]*
*[Total 10 marks]*

**Turn over for the next question**

**Turn over ▶**

**7** A student is investigating the energy needed to boil different masses of water.
This is their method:

1. Place an empty beaker on a mass balance and zero the balance.
2. Add 0.25 kg of water to the beaker.
3. Use a clamp and stand to hold an electric immersion heater and a thermometer in the water.
4. Keeping the beaker on the mass balance, switch on the heater.
5. Record the current through and potential difference across the heater using an ammeter and a voltmeter.
6. Wait for the temperature of the water to reach 100 °C.
7. Start a stopwatch and record how long it takes the heater to boil off 0.025 kg of water.
8. Continue boiling the water, and record how long it takes to boil off the next 0.025 kg. Repeat the process until 0.05 kg of water remains in the beaker.
9. Calculate the energy transferred by the heater to boil the water using:
energy transferred = current × potential difference × time.

**(a) (i)** Suggest **one** safety precaution that should be taken during this experiment.

.................................................................................................................................

*[1 mark]*

**(ii)** Suggest **one** piece of equipment the student could use instead of the ammeter and voltmeter.

.................................................................................................................................

*[1 mark]*

**Figure 10** shows a graph of the student's results.

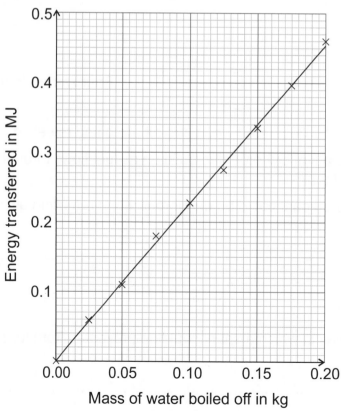

**Figure 10**

**(b)** Use **Figure 10** to determine the specific latent heat of vaporisation for water.

Specific latent heat = .................... MJ/kg

*[2 marks]*

**(c)** The electric immersion heater had a potential difference of 12 V across it.
The current through the heater was 8 A.

Using **Figure 10**, how long had the water been boiling for when 0.185 kg of water had boiled off?

You can assume that no energy was transferred from the water to the surroundings, and that the immersion heater was 100% efficient.

Use the correct equation from the Physics Equation Sheet on page 268.

☐ **A** 4375 s

☐ **B** 4271 s

☐ **C** 40 s

☐ **D** 35 000 s

*[1 mark]*

**(d)** Describe **one** difference between particles in liquid water and particles in water vapour.

...................................................................................................................................................

...................................................................................................................................................

*[1 mark]*

*[Total 6 marks]*

**Turn over for the next question**

**8**  A student has a length of wire.

**(a)** Which of the following shows the magnetic field around the wire when a current flows through the wire? The current is flowing into the paper.

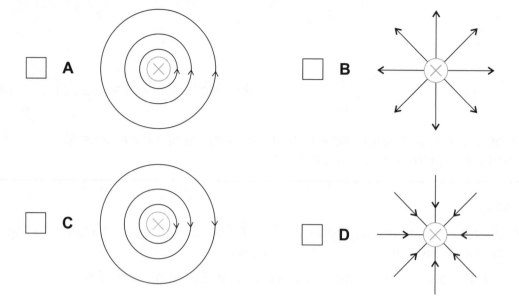

☐ **A**

☐ **B**

☐ **C**

☐ **D**

[1 mark]

**(b)** The current flowing through the wire is 3 A.

How much charge will have flowed through the wire in 30 minutes?

☐ **A** 600 C

☐ **B** 5400 C

☐ **C** 6 C

☐ **D** 90 C

[1 mark]

(c) The student bends the wire into a coil and connects it to a circuit to create a basic motor, as shown in **Figure 11**.

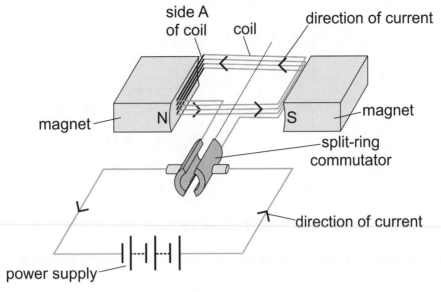

**Figure 11**

State the direction the coil in **Figure 11** will rotate in.

......................................................................................................................................................

*[1 mark]*

(d) The coil is made of 4 loops of wire.
Each side of the coil is 0.050 m long.
The current through the coil is 2.4 A.
The magnetic field between the poles has a magnetic flux density of 0.75 T.

Calculate the size of the force on side A when it is in the position shown in **Figure 11**.

Use the correct equation from the Physics Equation Sheet on page 268.

Force = ......................... N

*[3 marks]*

(e) Suggest **one** way that the student could change the set-up shown in **Figure 11** to increase the size of the force on side A of the coil.

......................................................................................................................................................

......................................................................................................................................................

*[1 mark]*

*[Total 7 marks]*

**Turn over for the next question**

**Turn over ▶**

**9** A student sets up the circuit shown in **Figure 12**.

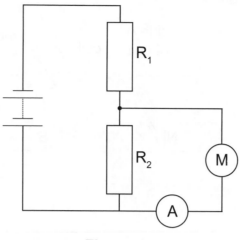

**Figure 12**

**(a) (i)** State the equation that links electrical power, current and potential difference.

..............................................................................................................................................

*[1 mark]*

**(ii)** The battery used in the circuit is a 12 V battery.
The potential difference across $R_1$ is 4.0 V.
The current through $R_1$ is 5.0 A. The current through $R_2$ is 3.0 A.
Calculate the power of the motor.

Power = ........................ W

*[3 marks]*

**(b)** The motor is attached to fan blades.
The student decides to investigate how fast the fan blades will spin when different motors are used.

The student draws a graph of the speed of the blades over time for three different motors, as shown in **Figure 13**. All the motors have the same efficiency.

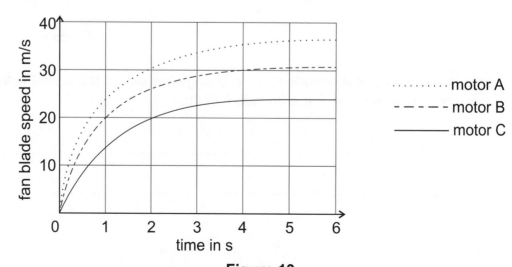

**Figure 13**

**(i)** Explain which motor has the highest power.

..................................................................................................................................

..................................................................................................................................

..................................................................................................................................
*[3 marks]*

**(ii)** Suggest one way to reduce energy losses from the motors.

..................................................................................................................................
*[1 mark]*

**(c)** The student creates a sensing circuit to control an electric heater, as shown in **Figure 14**.

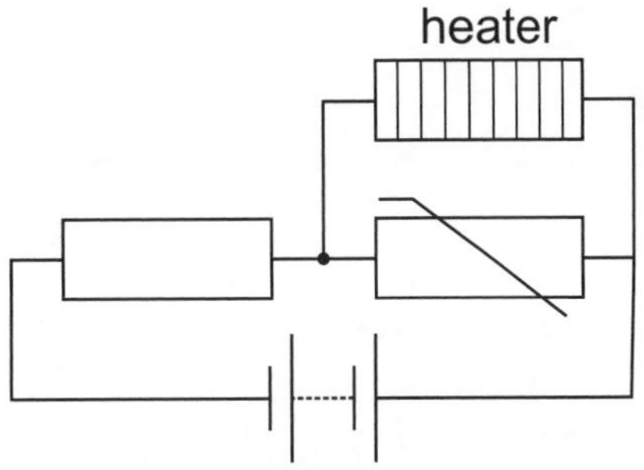

heater

**Figure 14**

Explain what will happen to the potential difference across the heater as the room temperature increases.

..................................................................................................................................

..................................................................................................................................

..................................................................................................................................
*[3 marks]*

**(d)** The electric heater is used to heat 2.1 kg of water.
The water is heated from 16 °C to 65 °C.
The specific heat capacity of water is 4200 J/kg°C.

The heater is 85% efficient.
Calculate the energy transferred to the heater when it is used to heat the water.
Use the correct equation from the Physics Equation Sheet on page 268.

Energy transferred = .................................... J
*[4 marks]*
*[Total 15 marks]*

**Turn over for the next question**

**Turn over ▶**

**10** A scuba diver is travelling out to sea on a boat.

**Figure 15** shows the horizontal forces acting on the boat.

The wind exerts a force of 210 N on the sails of the boat, at an angle of 35° clockwise from North.

The water exerts a force of 90.0 N in a westerly direction on the hull of the boat.

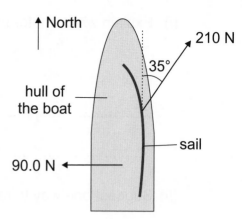

**Figure 15**

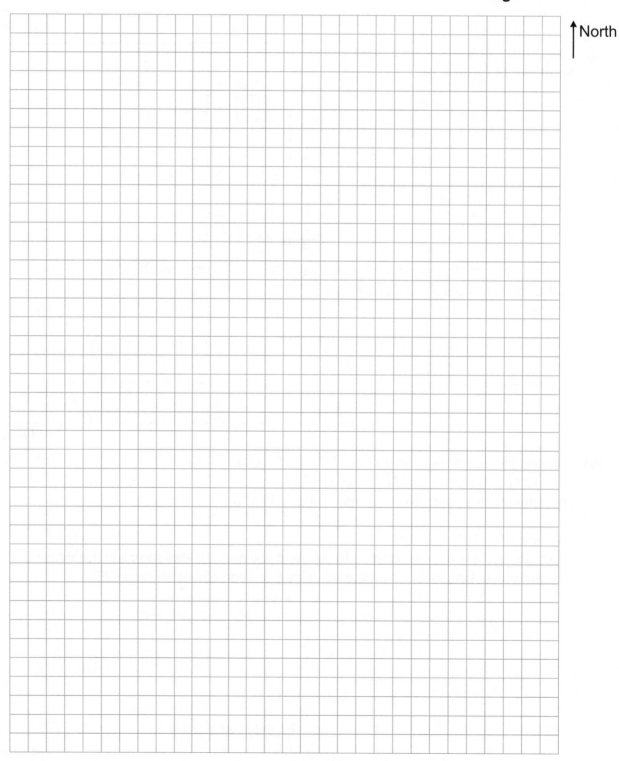

**Figure 16**

**(a) (i)** Draw a vector diagram on the grid in **Figure 16**, showing the horizontal forces and the resultant force acting on the boat.

*[2 marks]*

**(ii)** Use your diagram to determine the magnitude and direction of the resultant force on the sailboat.

Give the direction as a clockwise angle from North.

Magnitude of resultant force = ................................ N

Direction = ................................ °

*[2 marks]*

**(b)** The scuba diver goes on a dive.

As the scuba diver's depth increases, so does the pressure acting on her from the water.

Explain why the pressure acting on the diver increases with her depth.

..................................................................................................................................

..................................................................................................................................

..................................................................................................................................

..................................................................................................................................

..................................................................................................................................

..................................................................................................................................

*[3 marks]*

**(c)** At the deepest point of the dive, the pressure on the diver due to the water is 255 kPa. The density of seawater is 1020 kg/m³ and the gravitational field strength is 10 N/kg.

Calculate the depth of the diver at the deepest point of the dive.
Use the correct equation from the Physics Equation Sheet on page 268.

Depth = ...................... m

*[3 marks]*

*[Total 10 marks]*

**END OF QUESTIONS**

# Answers

## Section 1 — Motion and Forces

### Page 19
#### Speed
Q1   $s = d \div t = 200 \div 25$ *[1 mark]*
   = **8 m/s** *[1 mark]*

### Page 21
#### Acceleration
Q1   $u = 0$ m/s, $v = 5$ m/s, $a = g = 10$ m/s$^2$,
   $x = (v^2 - u^2) \div 2a$
   $= (25 - 0) \div (2 \times 10)$ *[1 mark]*
   = **1.25 m** *[1 mark]*

### Page 22
#### Distance/Time Graphs
Q1   E.g.

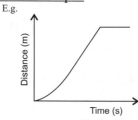

*[1 mark for a curved line with an increasing positive gradient, 1 mark for the line becoming a straight line with a positive gradient, 1 mark for the line then becoming horizontal]*

### Page 23
#### Velocity/Time Graphs
Q1

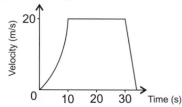

*[1 mark for an upwards curved acceleration line to 20 m/s, 1 mark for a straight line representing steady speed, 1 mark for a straight line representing deceleration]*

### Page 24
#### Warm-Up Questions
1   Speed is scalar, velocity is a vector / velocity has a direction, speed does not.
2 a)   E.g. 3 m/s
  b)   E.g. 250 m/s
  c)   E.g. 340 m/s
*Your answers may be slightly different to these, but as long as they're about the same size, you should be fine to use them in the exam.*
3   Velocity is calculated from the gradient.
4   A straight, horizontal line.

#### Exam Questions
1 a)   The cyclist travels at a constant speed (of 3 m/s) between 5 s and 8 s *[1 mark]*, then decelerates between 8 s and 10 s *[1 mark]*.
  b)   Area of triangle = 0.5 × width × height
     Width = 5 − 2 = 3 s
     Height = 3 m/s
     Distance = 0.5 × 3 × 3 = **4.5 m**
     *[2 marks for correct answer, otherwise 1 mark for a correct method to calculate the area under the graph between 2 and 5 seconds]*
*You can also answer this question by counting the number of squares under the graph between 2 and 5 s — there are 4.5 squares, and the area of one square is equivalent to 1 m (height of one square × width of one square = 1 m/s × 1 s), so the cyclist has travelled 4.5 m.*
  c)   Acceleration is given by the gradient of a velocity-time graph.
     change in $y$ = 3 − 0 = 3 m/s
     change in $x$ = 5 − 2 = 3 s
     acceleration = 3 ÷ 3 = **1 m/s$^2$**
     *[2 marks for correct answer, otherwise 1 mark for a correct method to calculate the gradient of the line between 2 and 5 seconds]*
*You could also have used $a = (v - u) \div t$ here.*

---

d)   average acceleration = change in velocity ÷ change in time /
   $a = (v - u) \div t$
   velocity at 8 s = 3 m/s; velocity at 10 s = 2 m/s
   so $v - u = 2 - 3 = -1$ m/s
   So, $a = -1 \div 2$
      $= -0.5$ m/s$^2$
   So, deceleration = **0.5 m/s$^2$**
   *[3 marks for correct answer, otherwise 1 mark for correct calculation of change in velocity and 1 mark for correct substitution]*
*Your answer should be positive since the question asks for deceleration, rather than acceleration.*
2 a)   E.g. 31 m/s *[1 mark]*
  b) i)   acceleration = change in velocity ÷ change in time
     $a = (v - u) \div t$
     $v - u = 31 - 0 = 31$ m/s
     $a = 31 \div 5$
     $= $ **6.2 m/s$^2$**
     *[2 marks for correct answer, otherwise 1 mark for correct substitution]*
    ii)   $v^2 - u^2 = 2 \times a \times x$
     rearrange for $x$
     $x = (v^2 - u^2) \div (2 \times a)$
     $= (31^2 - 0^2) \div (2 \times 6.2)$
     $= 77.5$ m
     $= $ **78 m (to 2 s.f.)**
     *[3 marks for correct answer, otherwise 1 mark for correct rearrangement and 1 mark for correct substitution]*
*Even if you got the answer to (a) wrong, award yourself the marks for (b) if you did the sums above correctly.*

### Page 25
#### Newton's First and Second Laws
Q1   $F = ma = (80 + 10) \times 0.25$ *[1 mark]*
   = **22.5 N** *[1 mark]*

### Page 26
#### Inertia and Newton's Third Law
Q1   Any one from: e.g the gravitational force of the Earth attracts the car and the gravitational force of the car attracts the Earth *[1 mark]* / the car exerts a normal contact force down against the ground and the normal contact force from the ground pushes up against the car *[1 mark]* / the car (tyres) pushes the road backwards and the road pushes the car (tyres) forwards *[1 mark]*.

### Page 27
#### Warm-Up Questions
1   0 N
2   force = mass × acceleration
*This is Newton's Second Law.*
3   false
4   Boulder B
*Boulder B needs a greater force to accelerate it by the same amount as boulder A.*
5   true
*This is Newton's Third Law.*

#### Exam Questions
1 a)   The ball exerts a force of −500 N on the bat *[1 mark]*, because, from Newton's Third Law, if the bat exerts a force on the ball, the ball exerts an equal force on the bat in the opposite direction *[1 mark]*.
  b)   The acceleration of the ball is greater *[1 mark]* because it has a smaller mass, but is acted on by the same size force (and $F = m \times a$) *[1 mark]*.
2 a)   Force = mass × acceleration / $F = m \times a$
     So, $a = F \div m$
     Set direction of van's motion to be positive, so $F = -200$ N
     $a = -200 \div 2500$
     $= -0.08$ m/s$^2$
     So, deceleration = **0.08 m/s$^2$**
     *[3 marks for correct answer, otherwise 1 mark for correct rearrangement and 1 mark for correct substitution]*
  b)   Force = mass × acceleration / $F = m \times a$
     $F = 4.50 \times 28.0$
     $= $ **126 N**
     *[2 marks for correct answer, otherwise 1 mark for correct substitution]*
  c)   By Newton's Third Law, force on van due to the cone in the collision is −126 N.
     force = mass × acceleration / $F = m \times a$
     So, $a = F \div m$
     $a = -126 \div 2500$
     $= -0.0504$ m/s$^2$
     So deceleration = **0.0504 m/s$^2$**
     *[3 marks for correct answer, otherwise 1 mark for correct rearrangement and 1 mark for correct substitution]*
*You'd still get the marks here, even if you got (b) wrong, as long as your method's correct.*

## Page 30
## Weight
Q1a)    $W = mg = 25 \times 10$ *[1 mark]*
       = **250 N** *[1 mark]*
 b)    $W = 25 \times 1.6$ *[1 mark]*
       = **40 N** *[1 mark]*

## Page 31
## Warm-Up Questions
1    It means that the force due to gravity caused by the hanging mass will be the main cause of the trolley accelerating.
2    Mass is the amount of 'stuff' in an object. Weight is the force acting on an object due to gravity.
3    Newtons

## Exam Questions
1    Weight = mass × gravitational field strength / $W = m \times g$
$W = 80 \times 10$
   = **800 N**
*[2 marks for correct answer, otherwise 1 mark for correct substitution]*
2 a)   mass *[1 mark]*
 b)   acceleration *[1 mark]*
 c)   As the mass increases, the acceleration decreases at a decreasing rate / mass and acceleration are inversely proportional *[1 mark]*.
3 a)   $W = m \times g$, so if the weight of an object on Mars is 0.4 times its weight on Earth, then Mars's gravitational field strength must be 0.4 times Earth's gravitational field strength (since mass is constant).
$0.4 \times 10 = $ **4 N/kg**
*[2 marks for correct answer, otherwise 1 mark for correct reasoning of gravitational field strength being 0.4 times the gravitational field strength on Earth]*
 b)   $W = m \times g$
$m = W \div g$
   $= 3600 \div 4$
   = **900 kg**
*[3 marks for correct answer, otherwise 1 mark for correct rearrangement and 1 mark for correct substitution]*
*Even if you got the answer to (a) wrong, you get full marks for (b) if you did the calculations correctly with your answer for (a).*
4    How to grade your answer:
   Level 0:    There is no relevant information. *[No marks]*
   Level 1:    A simple experiment to investigate force and acceleration which can be performed with the given equipment is partly outlined.
           The answer lacks structure. *[1 to 2 marks]*
   Level 2:    An experiment to investigate force and acceleration which can be performed with the given equipment is outlined in some detail.
           The answer has some structure. *[3 to 4 marks]*
   Level 3:    An experiment to investigate force and acceleration which can be performed with the given equipment is fully described in detail.
           The answer is well structured. *[5 to 6 marks]*
Here are some points your answer may include:
Place all of the masses on the trolley.
Calculate the weight of the hanging hook using $W = m \times g$ — this is the accelerating force.
Place the trolley on the ramp and adjust the height of the ramp until the trolley just starts to move.
Mark a line on the ramp just before the first light gate.
Hold the trolley at the start line and release the trolley, so that it moves through the light gates.
Record the time and velocity as the trolley passes through each light gate.
Calculate and record the trolley's acceleration using $a = (v - u) \div t$.
Take one of the masses from the trolley, and add it to the hook.
Repeat the steps above (starting with calculating the new total weight of the hanging hook) until all the masses from the trolley have been moved to the hook.
Plot the results on a graph of acceleration against accelerating force (the total weight of the hook), and draw a line of best fit.

## Page 33
## Momentum
Q1    $p_{before} = (10 \times 6) + (20 \times 0)$
       = 60 kg m/s *[1 mark]*
$p_{after} = (10 + 20) \times v = 30v$ *[1 mark]*
$p_{before} = p_{after}$
$60 = 30v$
so $v = 60 \div 30 = $ **2 m/s** *[1 mark]*

## Page 34
## Momentum
Q1    First, convert quantities to the correct units: 58 g = 0.058 kg
11.6 ms = 0.0116 s *[1 mark]*
$F = ((m \times v) - (m \times u)) \div t$
   $= ((0.058 \times 34) - (0.058 \times 0)) \div 0.0116$ *[1 mark]*
$F = $ **170 N** *[1 mark]*

## Page 35
## Warm-Up Questions
1    kg m/s
2    In a closed system, the total momentum before an interaction must equal the total momentum after the interaction.
3    The total momentum is zero.
4    It decreases the force.

## Exam Questions
1 a)   momentum = mass × velocity / $p = m \times v$ *[1 mark]*
 b)   $p = 60 \times 5.0$
   = **300 kg m/s**
*[2 marks for correct answer, otherwise 1 mark for correct substitution]*
 c)   force = change in momentum ÷ time / $F = (mv - mu) \div t$
Gymnast comes to a stop, so change in momentum = 300 kg m/s
$F = 300 \div 1.2$
   = **250 N**
*[2 marks for correct answer, otherwise 1 mark for correct substitution]*
2 a)   momentum = mass × velocity / $p = m \times v$
$p = 650 \times 15.0$
   = **9750 kg m/s**
*[2 marks for correct answer, otherwise 1 mark for correct substitution]*
 b)   momentum before = momentum after
momentum of first car = 9750 kg m/s
momentum of second car = $750 \times (-10.0)$
         = –7500 kg m/s
Total momentum before = 9750 + (–7500)
       = 2250 kg m/s
Total momentum after = (mass of car 1 + mass of car 2) × $v$
$2250 = (650 + 750) \times v$
so, $v = 2250 \div (650 + 750)$
   $= 2250 \div 1400$
   = 1.607142...
   = **1.61 m/s (to 3 s.f.)**
*[4 marks for correct answer, otherwise 1 mark for correct calculation of total momentum before the collision, 1 mark for correctly equating momentum before and after the collision and 1 mark for correct unrounded answer]*
3    momentum before = momentum after
momentum of neutron before = $1 \times 14\,000$
         = 14 000
momentum of uranium before = $235 \times 0$
         = 0
momentum of neutron after = $1 \times -13\,000$
         = –13 000
momentum of uranium after = $235 \times v$
So, $14\,000 = -13\,000 + 235 \times v$
so, $v = (14\,000 + 13\,000) \div 235$
   = 114.8936...
   = **115 km/s (to 3 s.f.)**
*[4 marks for correct answer, otherwise 1 mark for correct calculations of momentum, 1 mark for correctly equating momentum before and after the collision and 1 mark for correct unrounded answer]*
*Don't worry too much about the units in this question. The masses given are relative masses, with no units, so we couldn't use the standard units for momentum. As you're only looking for the velocity though, you can just do the calculation as normal, and make sure that the units on your final answer match the units for velocity given in the question.*

## Page 39
## Stopping Safely
Q1    Thinking distance increases linearly with speed, so
      thinking distance = 3 × 6
                        = 18 m *[1 mark]*
      Braking distance increases
      with speed by $3^2$ times.
      So braking distance = $3^2$ × 6 *[1 mark]*
                          = 54 m *[1 mark]*
      Stopping distance = 18 + 54
                        = **72 m** *[1 mark]*

## Page 40
## Warm-Up Questions
1    Get the individual to sit with their arm resting on the edge of a table.
     Hold a ruler end-down so that the 0 cm mark hangs between their thumb
     and forefinger. Drop the ruler without warning. The individual must
     grab the ruler between their thumb and forefinger as quickly as possible.
     Measure the distance at which they have caught the ruler.
     Use $v^2 - u^2 = 2 \times a \times x$ and $a = 10$ m/s$^2$ to calculate $v$,
     and $a = (v - u) \div t$ to calculate the time taken for the ruler
     to fall that distance. This is their reaction time.
2    The thinking distance is the distance travelled during a person's reaction
     time (the time between seeing a hazard, and applying the brakes).
3    The braking distance.
4    Any one from: e.g. poor grip on the roads increases braking
     distance / poor visibility delays when you see the hazard /
     distraction by the weather delays when you see the hazard.
5    Crumple zones increase collision time, which reduces
     the force on the vehicle and passengers (since
     $F = (mv - mu) \div t$). This reduces the risk of harm in a crash.
6    Braking distance will increase by a factor of nine.
*Braking distance increases with the square of the speed — the speed has trebled here, so the braking distance will increase by a factor of $3^2$ (9 times).*

## Exam Question
1 a)  stopping distance = braking distance + thinking distance,
      So, braking distance = stopping distance – thinking distance
      At 40 mph,
      stopping distance = 35 m (accept between 34 m and 36 m)
      thinking distance = 12 m (accept between 11 m and 13 m)
      braking distance = 35 – 12 = **23 m**
      (Accept correct for above readings)
      *[3 marks for correct answer, otherwise 1 mark for*
      *correctly reading stopping and thinking distances from*
      *the graph and 1 mark for correct substitution]*
  b)  braking distance *[1 mark]*
*The stopping distance is over twice as high as the thinking distance at 50 mph, so the braking distance must be bigger than the thinking distance.*
  c)  Stopping distance is not directly proportional to speed. If stopping
      distance and speed were directly proportional, the relationship between
      them would be shown by a straight line / would be linear *[1 mark]*
  d)  If the road were icy, the thinking distance graph would not
      change *[1 mark]* but the stopping distance graph would get
      steeper (as the braking distance would increase) *[1 mark]*.
*The thinking distance graph doesn't change, because the icy road won't change your reaction time. But it will decrease the friction between the car and the road, so the braking distance increases.*

## Section 2 — Conservation of Energy

## Page 42
## Energy Stores
Q1    The change in height is 5 m.
      So the energy transferred from the gravitational potential energy store is:
      $\Delta GPE = m \times g \times \Delta h = 2 \times 10 \times 5$ *[1 mark]*
                 = 100 J *[1 mark]*
      This is transferred to the kinetic energy store of the object,
      so $KE = 100$ J *[1 mark]*
      $KE = \frac{1}{2} \times m \times v^2$
      so $v^2 = (2 \times KE) \div m$
              $= (2 \times 100) \div 2$ *[1 mark]*
              $= 100$ m$^2$/s$^2$
      $v = \sqrt{100} = $ **10 m/s** *[1 mark]*

## Page 44
## Energy Stores and Transfers
Q1    Energy is transferred mechanically *[1 mark]* from the kinetic energy store
      of the wind *[1 mark]* to the kinetic energy store of the windmill *[1 mark]*.

## Page 45
## Warm-Up Questions
1    kinetic energy = $\frac{1}{2}$ × mass × (speed)$^2$ / $KE = \frac{1}{2} \times m \times v^2$
2    A lorry travelling at 60 miles per hour.
3    Any two from: e.g. mechanically (by a force doing work) / electrically
     (work done by a charge) / by heating / by radiation.
4    Energy is transferred by radiation to the thermal energy store of the water.

## Exam Questions
1 a)  Change in gravitational potential energy = mass × gravitational field
      strength × change in height /
      $\Delta GPE = m \times g \times \Delta h$ *[1 mark]*
      So, $\Delta h = \Delta GPE \div (m \times g)$
                   $= 140 \div (20 \times 10)$
                   $= $ **0.7 m**
      *[3 marks for the correct answer, otherwise 1 mark for correct*
      *rearrangement and 1 mark for correct substitution]*
  b)  Energy is transferred from the gravitational potential energy store *[1 mark]*
      to the kinetic energy store of the load *[1 mark]*.
  c)  Some of the energy would also be transferred to the thermal energy store
      of the air (and the thermal energy store of the load) *[1 mark]*.
2 a)  Energy is transferred mechanically from the elastic potential energy store
      of the sling-shot *[1 mark]* to the kinetic energy store of the rock *[1 mark]*.
      This energy is then transferred mechanically to the gravitational potential
      energy store of the rock as it rises *[1 mark]*.
  b)  Kinetic energy = $\frac{1}{2}$ × mass × (speed)$^2$ / $KE = \frac{1}{2} \times m \times v^2$
      $KE = \frac{1}{2} \times 0.06 \times (18)^2$
          $= $ **9.72 J**
          $= $ **9.7 J (to 2 s.f.)**
      *[2 marks for correct answer, otherwise 1 mark for correct substitution]*
  c)  At B all energy from the kinetic store has been transferred to the
      gravitational potential energy store.
      So, $\Delta GPE = 9.72$ J
      $\Delta GPE = m \times g \times \Delta h$
      $\Delta h = \Delta GPE \div (m \times g)$
             $= 9.72 \div (0.06 \times 10)$
             $= $ **16.2 m**
      *[3 marks for the correct answer, otherwise 1 mark for correct*
      *rearrangement and 1 mark for correct substitution]*

## Page 47
## Efficiency
Q1    Useful energy transferred by device
      = 500 – 420 = 80 J *[1 mark]*
      Efficiency = $\dfrac{\text{useful energy transferred by device}}{\text{total energy supplied to device}}$
      = 80 ÷ 500 = 0.16 *[1 mark]*
      0.16 × 100 = **16%** *[1 mark]*

## Page 49
## Warm-Up Questions
1    Thermal energy stores.
2    Some energy is always dissipated, so less than 100% of the energy
     supplied to a device is transferred usefully.
3    E.g. lubrication
4    The higher the thermal conductivity, the greater the rate of the energy
     transfer (i.e. the faster energy is transferred) through it.
5    The thicker the walls, the slower the rate of cooling.

## Exam Questions

1 a) efficiency = useful energy transferred by the device ÷
        total energy supplied to the device *[1 mark]*

  b) efficiency = 480 ÷ 1200
        = **0.4 (or 40%)**
     *[2 marks for correct answer, otherwise 1 mark for correct substitution]*

  c) efficiency = useful energy transferred by the device ÷
        total energy supplied to the device

    total energy supplied to the device
    = useful energy transferred by the device ÷ efficiency
    = 10 ÷ 0.55
    = **18.181... = 18 J (to 2 s.f)**
    *[3 marks for the correct answer, otherwise 1 mark for correct rearrangement and 1 mark for correct substitution]*

  d) Disagree. Torch B has a lower input energy transfer than torch A, i.e. it transfers less energy per minute than torch A (as 18.181... × 60 = 1090.9..., and 1090.9... < 1200) *[1 mark]*.

*Even if you got the answer to (c) wrong, if your conclusion is correct for your answer to (d), you'd get the marks for this question.*

2 Best: C   Second best: B   Worst: A *[1 mark]*
The thicker a sample is, the slower the rate of energy transfer through it so sample B will be a better insulator than sample A *[1 mark]*. Air has a lower thermal conductivity than glass (so it transfers energy at a slower rate than glass does) *[1 mark]* so even though samples B and C are the same thickness, sample C is a better insulator than sample B *[1 mark]*.

## Page 54

### Warm-Up Questions

1 Any three from: coal / oil / natural gas / nuclear fuel (plutonium or uranium).

2 Advantage: e.g. low running costs / won't run out / doesn't create pollution
Disadvantage: e.g. cannot produce energy at night.

3 Any two from: e.g. it releases greenhouse gases and contributes to global warming / it causes acid rain / coal mining damages the landscape.

4 Any two from: e.g. renewable resources don't currently provide enough energy / energy from renewables cannot be relied upon currently / it's expensive to build new renewable power plants / it's impractical to switch to cars running on renewable energy.

### Exam Questions

1 a) Solar *[1 mark]*, bio-fuels *[1 mark]*

  b) E.g. flooding a valley for a dam can destroy habitats for some species *[1 mark]*.

  c) E.g. they cause no pollution *[1 mark]*

2 a) Seconds in 5 hours = 5 × 60 × 60 = 18 000 s
Energy provided by 1 m² solar panel in 5 hours = 200 × 18 000
                        = 3 600 000 J
Number of panels needed = energy needed ÷ energy provided
                        = 32 500 000 ÷ 3 600 000
                        = 9.027... = **10 panels** (to next whole number)
*[4 marks for correct answer, otherwise 1 mark for correct method of calculation of energy provided by one panel, 1 mark for correct value of energy provided by one panel and 1 mark for correct method of calculation of number of panels needed]*

*Remember, because you have to have a set number of whole panels, if you get a decimal answer, you need to round up to the next whole number to be able to provide the right amount of energy.*

  b) Ten 1 m² solar panels are needed, so they will need at least 10 × 1 m² = 10 m² of space. However, they only have 8 m² of space on their roof, so the family cannot install sufficient solar panels *[1 mark]*.

  c) E.g. solar panels are less reliable than coal-fired power stations *[1 mark]*. The energy output of the solar panels will vary based on the number of hours of good sunlight, and may not be able to provide enough energy on a given day *[1 mark]*. The energy output of coal-fired power stations is not influenced by environmental factors like weather, and energy output can be increased to meet demand *[1 mark]*.

## Section 3 — Waves and the Electromagnetic Spectrum

## Page 57

### Transverse and Longitudinal Waves

Q1 7.5 ÷ 100 = 0.075 m
wave speed = frequency × wavelength, so
frequency = wave speed ÷ wavelength *[1 mark]*
    = 0.15 ÷ 0.075 *[1 mark]*
    = **2 Hz** *[1 mark]*

## Page 60

### Warm-Up Questions

1 Waves only transfer energy and information, they do not transfer matter (in this case, the twig and the water particles around the twig).

2 hertz (Hz)

3 e.g. sound / P-waves

4 wave speed = frequency × wavelength / $v = f \times \lambda$

### Exam Questions

1 a) transverse *[1 mark]*

  b) 5 cm *[1 mark]*

  c) 2 m *[1 mark]*

  d) It will halve *[1 mark]*.

*$v = f \times \lambda$, so if f doubles, then λ must halve, so that v stays the same.*

2 a) The distance he measures is 1 wavelength *[1 mark]*.
This can be used, together with the frequency set by the signal generator, in the formula for wave speed,
wave speed = frequency × wavelength / $v = f \times \lambda$ *[1 mark]*.

  b) wave speed = frequency × wavelength / $v = f \times \lambda$
So $v = 50 \times 6.8$
    = **340 m/s**
*[2 marks for correct answer, otherwise 1 mark for correct substitution]*

## Page 62

### Refraction and Ray Diagrams

Q1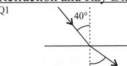

*[1 mark for a correct diagram showing rays and the normal, 1 mark for an angle of incidence of 40°, 1 mark for an angle of refraction greater than 40°]*

## Page 64

### Reflection

Q1

*[1 mark for correct diagram showing straight, correctly drawn rays with consistent arrows and the normal, 1 mark for correct angle of incidence, 1 mark for correct angle of reflection]*

## Page 65

### Warm-Up Questions

1 reflection, transmission and absorption

2 false
*The shorter the wavelength, the more an EM wave will be refracted as it hits a boundary at an angle to the normal.*

3 Away from the normal.

4 e.g. a ray box

5 angle of incidence = angle of reflection

6 false

## Exam Questions

1  a) specular (reflection) *[1 mark]*

   b)

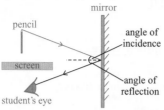

   *[1 mark for line representing reflected ray, 1 mark for the angle of incidence and the angle of reflection being equal, 1 mark for labelling the angle of incidence and the angle of reflection]*

2  a) E.g.

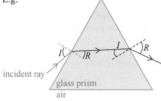

   *[1 mark for refracting the ray towards the normal upon entering the prism, 1 mark for refracting the ray away from the normal as it leaves the prism and 1 mark for correctly labelling all the angles of incidence and refraction]*

   b) E.g. place the prism on a piece of paper and shine a ray of light at the prism. Trace the incident and emergent rays and the boundaries of the prism on the piece of paper *[1 mark]*. Remove the prism and draw in the refracted ray through the prism by joining the ends of the other two rays with a straight line *[1 mark]*. Draw in the normals using a protractor and ruler *[1 mark]* and use the protractor to measure $I$ and $R$ at both boundaries *[1 mark]*.

## Page 68
## Exploring Structures with Waves

Q1  $v = x \div t$,
so $t = x \div v$
$= 2500 \div 1520$ *[1 mark]*
$= 1.64...$ s *[1 mark]*
This is the time it takes for the pulse to reach the seabed. To find the time taken for the sound to return to the submarine, you must double it.
$1.64... \times 2 = 3.28... = 3.3$ s (to 2 s.f.) *[1 mark]*

## Page 70
## Warm-Up Questions

1  longitudinal
2  frequency
3  Human hearing is limited by the size and shape of the eardrum and all the inner parts of the ear that vibrate to transmit the vibrations of the sound wave.
4  infrasound
5  e.g. foetal scanning / sonar / industrial imaging
6  P-waves

## Exam Questions

1  a) 20 kHz / 20 000 Hz *[1 mark]*

   b)

   *[1 mark]*

   c) It will be partially reflected / some of it will be reflected and some will be transmitted into medium 2 *[1 mark]*.

2  $v = x \div t$
It takes 35 μs for the pulse to travel to the crack and back again, so it must take half the time for the pulse to reach the crack.
$t = 35 \div 2 = 17.5$ μs
$x = v \times t$
$= 5800 \times (17.5 \times 10^{-6})$
$= 0.1015$ m
$= 0.10$ m (to 2 s.f.)
*[3 marks for correct answer, otherwise 1 mark for showing that the time taken for the ultrasound to travel to the crack is half the total time and 1 mark for correct substitution]*

3  a) A *[1 mark]*. S-waves only travel through solids *[1 mark]*, and so are stopped by the liquid outer core *[1 mark]*.

   b) When the waves are following curved paths, it shows that the material they are moving through is changing gradually *[1 mark]*. When the waves abruptly change direction, it shows that at that point the material changes suddenly by a larger amount *[1 mark]*, suggesting they have entered a layer of a new material in the Earth's structure *[1 mark]*.

## Page 75
## Lenses and Ray Diagrams

Q1

   *[1 mark for an image at a distance 2F in front of the lens, 1 mark for an inverted image, 1 mark for two correct light rays]*

## Page 76
## Warm-Up Questions

1  It reflects the wavelengths of light corresponding to the red part of the visible spectrum (all other wavelengths are absorbed).
2  The wavelengths reflected from the object (those corresponding to the green part of the visible spectrum) are absorbed by the red filter. The lack of any visible light transmitted is perceived as black, so the object appears black.
3  The distance from the centre of the lens to the principal focus.
4

5  false
*When a virtual image forms the light rays don't actually come together at the point where the image seems to be, so it can't be captured on a screen.*
6  The greater a lens's power, the shorter its focal length.
7  A real, inverted image, the same size as the object will form at a distance of 2F from the lens on the opposite side of the lens to the object.
8  A diverging lens always creates virtual images. A converging lens can create both real and virtual images.

## Exam Questions

1  a) a diverging lens *[1 mark]*

   b)

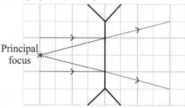

   *[2 marks for correctly identifying the location of the principal focus, otherwise 1 mark for attempting to trace the refracted rays back to a point]*

   c) 10 cm *[1 mark]*
*The focal length is the distance between the centre of the lens and the principal focus. The scale states that 2 squares is equal to 5 cm. The principal focus is 4 squares from the centre of the lens, so the focal length is 5 × 2 = 10 cm.*

2  a) A diverging lens causes parallel rays of light to diverge (spread out) rather than converge (come together) *[1 mark]*. This means that the student's lens cannot focus the sunlight to start a fire *[1 mark]*.

   b)

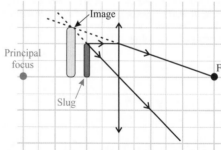

   *[1 mark for showing a ray travelling parallel to the axis of the lens, refracting and going to a correctly positioned principal focus, 1 mark for showing a ray going through the centre of the lens, 1 mark for showing both rays extended backwards (dotted) and the image drawn where they cross]*
*You sometimes need to draw another principal focus on the opposite side of lens, the same distance away from the centre of the lens.*

## Page 83
### Warm-Up Questions
1     transverse
2     false
*All EM waves travel at the same speed in a vacuum.*
3     gamma rays
4     true
5     e.g. communication / broadcasting / satellite transmissions
6     The microwaves penetrate a few centimetres into the food before being absorbed by water molecules in the food. The microwaves transfer their energy to the water molecules, causing the water to heat up. Energy is then transferred from the water to the rest of the food by heating, causing the food to cook.
7     infrared radiation
8     E.g. to sterilise medical equipment / to sterilise food / medical imaging / cancer treatment.
9     true

### Exam Questions
1  a)     X-rays *[1 mark]*
  b)     E.g. could cause cancer / cell mutations / damage cells *[1 mark]*.
2  a)     The incoming wave transfers energy to electrons in the receiver *[1 mark]*. This causes the electrons to oscillate *[1 mark]*, generating an alternating current in the circuit *[1 mark]*.
  b)     The resident shouldn't be concerned as radio waves have a very low frequency so are not dangerous / are not absorbed by the body *[1 mark]*.
3     E.g. ultraviolet radiation is a type of ionising radiation, exposure to this type of radiation can damage skin cells / could lead to skin cancer *[1 mark]*. The damage to cells and risk of developing cancer could be minimised by limiting the patient's exposure to the ultraviolet radiation while still exposing her to enough so that it is an effective treatment for her psoriasis *[1 mark]*. Exposure to ultraviolet radiation could also damage the patient's eyes and cause a variety of eye conditions including blindness *[1 mark]*. The risk of eye damage could be reduced by the patient wearing protective goggles during treatments *[1 mark]*.

## Page 84
### EM Radiation and Temperature
Q1     The second star is cooler *[1 mark]* because it has the longer peak wavelength, and the colder an object is, the longer its peak wavelength *[1 mark]*.

## Page 87
### Warm-Up Questions
1     true
2     The average power emitted by the object will be equal to the average power absorbed by the object.
3     true
4     a matte black surface
5     You could transfer energy by heating to the surfaces at the same rate (e.g. by placing them an equal distance from a Bunsen burner). The surface that is the best absorber will heat up quicker, causing the wax on that surface to melt and the ball bearing to drop first.

### Exam Question
1  a)     Any one from: e.g. place the thermometers at equal distances away from the cube / place the thermometers at the same height as each other / make sure no thermometers are in direct sunlight/a draught *[1 mark]*.
  b)     B *[1 mark]*
  c)     The times recorded would be longer *[1 mark]*. Cooler objects emit a lower intensity of radiation / transfer less energy per second *[1 mark]*.
  d)     E.g. the resolution of the digital thermometer is higher, so there will be less uncertainty in the results (the results will be more accurate) / the student is less likely to misread the temperature (human error is less likely). *[2 marks — 1 mark for each correct answer]*.

## Section 4 — Radioactivity

## Page 92
### Warm-Up Questions
1     The atom consists of a sphere of positive charge throughout which electrons are embedded like fruit in a plum pudding.
2     proton: 1, neutron: 1, electron: 0.0005
3     true
4     In the nucleus.
5     0; an atom has no overall charge.
6     $1 \times 10^{-10}$ m
7     false
*An atom must lose an electron to become a positive ion.*

### Exam Questions
1  a)

|  | Proton | Electron | Neutron |
|---|---|---|---|
| Relative Charge | +1 | -1 | **0** |
| Number Present in Si-28 | 14 | **14** | 14 |

    *[2 marks — 1 mark for each correct answer]*
  b)     Electrons may only occupy fixed energy levels *[1 mark]* at set distances from the nucleus *[1 mark]*.
  c)     $6.9 \times 10^{-19}$ J *[1 mark]*
  d)     +1 *[1 mark]*
2     Most of the alpha particles passed straight through the gold foil *[1 mark]*. However, some were deflected back in the direction they came from *[1 mark]*. He concluded most of the atom is empty space *[1 mark]* whilst positive charge and mass is concentrated in a small nucleus *[1 mark]*.

## Page 95
### Nuclear Equations
Q1     $^{219}_{86}\text{Rn} \rightarrow \,^{215}_{84}\text{Po} + \,^{4}_{2}\alpha$
    *[1 mark for correct layout, 1 mark for correct symbol for an alpha particle, 1 mark for total atomic and mass numbers being equal on both sides]*

## Page 96
### Warm-Up Questions
1     23 – 11 = 12 neutrons
2     false
*Isotopes of an element will have identical atomic numbers and different mass numbers.*
3     Any radiation that can knock electrons from atoms.
4     alpha
5     false
*Gamma rays are stopped by thick sheets of lead or metres of concrete.*
6     The atomic number will decrease by 1.
7     40
*Mass number is unchanged by the emission of gamma radiation.*

### Exam Questions
1     Beta (particles) *[1 mark]*, because the radiation passes through the paper, but not the aluminium, so it is moderately penetrating in comparison to the other two *[1 mark]*.
2  a)     The total number of protons and neutrons in the nucleus/atom. *[1 mark]*
  b)     Atom A and atom B *[1 mark]* because isotopes of the same element have the same atomic number, but different mass numbers *[1 mark]*.
  c)     $X = 94 - 2$
          = **92** *[1 mark]*

## Page 98
### Half-Life
Q1     After one half-life the activity will be
    $40 \div 2 = 20$ Bq *[1 mark]*
    After a second: $20 \div 2 = 10$ Bq
    After a third: $10 \div 2 = 5$ Bq *[1 mark]*
    So the ratio is 5:40 = **1:8** *[1 mark]*

## Page 101

### Warm-Up Questions

1 Any three from: e.g. the air / some foods / building materials / rocks / space / fallout from nuclear explosions / nuclear waste.
2 One decay occurs each second.
3 E.g. a Geiger-Müller tube
4 6 days.
*To decrease by a factor of four, two half-lives must pass. $2 \times 3 = 6$.*
5 Irradiation occurs when an object is exposed to radiation. Contamination occurs when a radioactive source gets onto or into an object.
6 To prevent your hands from becoming contaminated with radioactive materials / to prevent radioactive particles getting stuck to your skin or under your nails.
7 If you are exposed to alpha radiation from an external source (i.e. if you are irradiated), the alpha particles will be blocked by your skin. However, if an alpha source gets inside your body it can do a lot of damage to nearby cells, as it's strongly ionising.

### Exam Questions

1 a) E.g. radiation sickness / cancer.
   *[2 marks — 1 mark for each correct answer]*
  b) Source B, because a longer half-life means its activity will remain at harmful levels for a longer time *[1 mark]*.
  c) E.g. store them in a lead-lined box *[1 mark]*.
2 a) $2 \times 60 = 120$ seconds
   $120 \div 40 = 3$ half-lives
   Activity after 1 half life: $8000 \div 2 = 4000$,
   Activity after 2 half lives: $4000 \div 2 = 2000$,
   Activity after 3 half lives: $2000 \div 2 = \mathbf{1000\ Bq}$
   *[2 marks for correct answer, otherwise 1 mark for correctly calculating the number of half-lives]*
  b) Activity after 1 half life: $8000 \div 2 = 4000$,
   Activity after 2 half lives: $4000 \div 2 = 2000$,
   Activity after 3 half lives: $2000 \div 2 = 1000$,
   Activity after 4 half lives: $1000 \div 2 = 500$,
   Activity after 5 half lives: $500 \div 2 = 250$.
   So it takes **5 half-lives** to drop to 250 Bq
   *[2 marks for correct answer, otherwise 1 mark for attempting to halve values to find number of half-lives]*
  c) $(100 \div 8000) \times 100$ *[1 mark]* = **1.25%** *[1 mark]*

## Page 102

### Uses of Nuclear Radiation

Q1 E.g. Alpha would not be suitable because it is stopped by a few cm of air or a sheet of paper *[1 mark]*. It would not be able to pass through the packaging to sterilise the equipment *[1 mark]*.

## Page 105

### Warm-Up Questions

1 alpha radiation
2 gamma radiation
3 E.g. gamma rays are used to sterilise medical equipment.
4 Alpha radiation is strongly ionising and would not be able to pass out of the body. So the radiation would damage cells and it would not be possible to detect the radiation from outside the body.
5 They have short half-lives. If these isotopes had to be transported over a large distance, their activity could be too low to be useful by the time they arrive at the hospital.
6 E.g. injection / implant.
7 Alpha radiation can't penetrate the skin.

### Exam Questions

1 a) The count-rate would decrease. *[1 mark]*
  b) Gamma radiation is highly penetrating *[1 mark]*,
   so it will easily pass through any thickness of aluminium foil *[1 mark]*.
  c) E.g. locating cracks in underground pipes. *[1 mark]*
2 Technetium-99m *[1 mark]* because it's got a short half-life, which means it won't be very radioactive inside the patient for long *[1 mark]*. It's also a gamma source, which means the radiation will pass out of the patient without causing much damage/ionisation *[1 mark]*.
3 The glucose tracer is taken up by the cancerous cells. The unstable isotopes in the glucose decay, emitting positrons *[1 mark]*. These positrons annihilate with nearby electrons, emitting gamma rays *[1 mark]*. The PET scanner externally detects pairs of gamma rays and uses triangulation to locate the source *[1 mark]*. A high concentration of emitters indicates the presence of a tumour *[1 mark]*.

## Page 109

### Warm-Up Questions

1 true
2 It makes the nucleus more unstable and causes it to split.
3 Daughter nuclei are the smaller nuclei formed when a larger, unstable nucleus splits.
4 The moderator slows down neutrons, so they can be captured by unstable nuclei and trigger fission.
5 false
6 Fusion requires incredibly high temperatures and pressures, which no material can withstand.
7 The energy released by fission is transferred to the thermal energy store of the moderator. This is then transferred to the thermal energy store of the water in a boiler, which causes the water to boil and energy to be transferred to the kinetic energy store of the steam. This energy is then transferred to the kinetic energy store of a turbine and then to the kinetic energy store of a generator. The energy is then transferred away from the generator electrically.
8 E.g. nuclear power stations do not release carbon dioxide.

### Exam Questions

1 a) A uranium-235 nucleus absorbs a neutron *[1 mark]*, splits into two smaller nuclei, and releases 2 or more neutrons *[1 mark]*. These neutrons are slowed down by a moderator and some of them go on to start other fissions, creating a chain reaction *[1 mark]*.
  b) E.g. there could be a meltdown / a runaway fission reaction *[1 mark]*.
  c) Any two from: e.g. negative public perception / high cost of building and decommissioning nuclear power plants / risks associated with disposing of nuclear waste / risk of a major leak at a nuclear power plant.
   *[2 marks — 1 mark for each correct answer]*
2 a) C *[1 mark]*
  b) The positively charged nuclei need to be brought very close together to fuse *[1 mark]*. So, a large amount of energy is required to overcome their electrostatic repulsion *[1 mark]*.
  c) E.g. currently, achieving the conditions for fusion requires more power than fusion can produce / it is expensive and difficult to build a fusion reactor. *[1 mark]*

# Section 5 — Astronomy

## Page 113
### Orbits
Q1 Its orbital speed would be faster *[1 mark]*. The force due to gravity increases the closer you get to the Earth's surface, so if the radius of the Moon's orbit was smaller, the force acting on it would be larger *[1 mark]*. So to remain in a stable orbit, the Moon's instantaneous velocity would need to be larger *[1 mark]*.

## Page 115
### Warm-Up Questions
1 Mercury, Venus, Earth, Mars, Jupiter, Saturn, Uranus, Neptune
2 e.g. dwarf planets/asteroids/comets
3 The Earth is the centre of the Solar System. The Sun and the other planets orbit the Earth in perfect circles.
4 gravity
5 The Earth has a stronger gravitational field strength than the Moon due to its larger mass. The larger the gravitational field strength, the greater the weight of the 1 kg mass.
6 A cloud of dust and gas in space.
7 A red supergiant.

### Exam Questions
1 C *[1 mark]*
2 Satellite A, because it is closer to the Earth *[1 mark]*. The gravitational field strength of Earth is stronger closer to the Earth's surface, so the force due to gravity is stronger on satellite A than on satellite B *[1 mark]*. This means satellite A must travel faster to remain in a stable orbit *[1 mark]*.
3 a) A star forms from a nebula/a cloud of dust and gas which is pulled together by gravitational attraction *[1 mark]*. As the density increases, the temperature rises *[1 mark]*. When the temperature gets high enough, hydrogen nuclei undergo nuclear fusion to form helium nuclei and a huge amount of energy is released, which keeps the core hot *[1 mark]*.
   b) The forces acting on a main sequence star are balanced, so it doesn't collapse or explode *[1 mark]*. The outward pressure from thermal expansion provides an outward force to balance the force of gravity pulling everything inwards *[1 mark]*.
   c) They become unstable and eject their outer layer of dust and gas *[1 mark]*, which leaves a hot, dense, solid core known as a white dwarf *[1 mark]*.
   d) They explode in a supernova *[1 mark]*. The supernova leaves behind a neutron star or a black hole *[1 mark]*.

## Page 120
### Warm-Up Questions
1 red-shift
2 true
3 cosmic microwave background
4 Big Bang theory
5 Increase the size of its aperture. / Use a better quality objective lens.

### Exam Questions
1 a) C *[1 mark]*
   b) B *[1 mark]*
2 E.g. there is no atmosphere to block radiation from reaching the telescope *[1 mark]*. Images are not affected by light pollution *[1 mark]* or air pollution *[1 mark]*.
3 How to grade your answer:
   Level 0: There is no relevant information. *[No marks]*
   Level 1: There is a brief description of red-shift, CMB radiation or the Big Bang theory. The answer lacks structure. *[1 to 2 marks]*
   Level 2: There is a description of the Big Bang theory, and at least one description of red-shift or CMB radiation. There is an explanation of one piece of evidence for the Big Bang theory. The answer has some structure. *[3 to 4 marks]*
   Level 3: There is a description of red-shift, CMB radiation and the Big Bang theory, and a clear and detailed explanation of how observations of red-shift and CMB radiation provide evidence for the Big Bang theory. The answer is well structured. *[5 to 6 marks]*
   Here are some points your answer may include:
   The Big Bang theory states that the universe began as a small region of space that was very hot and dense, which started expanding and has been expanding ever since.
   Red-shift is when the wavelengths of observed light from a source are longer than that of the light emitted by the source.
   This occurs when the source of light is moving away from the observer.
   The light from distant galaxies is observed to be red-shifted.
   This indicates that all of these galaxies are moving away from us and each other.

The light from galaxies that are further away from us is red-shifted more than the light from nearer galaxies.
This indicates that more distant galaxies are moving away faster than nearer galaxies.
This suggests that the Universe is expanding, which supports the Big Bang theory.
CMB radiation is low frequency electromagnetic radiation that can be detected from all parts of the Universe.
The presence of CMB radiation shows that the Universe was once much hotter and denser.
This suggests that the Universe had a beginning, which supports the Big Bang theory.

# Section 6 — Forces and Energy

## Page 123
### Work Done
Q1      First change the distance to metres:
        $20 \div 100 = 0.2$ m
        Then substitute into the equation:
        $E = F \times d = 20 \times 0.2$ *[1 mark]*
                  $= \textbf{4 J}$ *[1 mark]*

## Page 125
### Warm-Up Questions
1      A system is the object or group of objects that you are interested in.
2      true
3      Energy is transferred electrically from the chemical energy store of the battery to the kinetic energy store of the fan's blades.
4      work done = force × distance moved in the direction of the force / $E = F \times d$
5      true
6      watts

### Exam Questions
1   a)      Energy is transferred from the ball's gravitational potential energy store *[1 mark]* to its kinetic energy store *[1 mark]*.
    b)      There will be no change in total energy *[1 mark]*.
*In a closed system, the net change in energy is always zero.*
2   a)   i)    power = work done ÷ time taken / $P = E \div t$ *[1 mark]*
       ii)    $P = 1000 \div 20$
              $= \textbf{50 W}$ *[1 mark]*
    b)      efficiency = useful energy transferred by the device ÷ total energy supplied to the device
        efficiency = $480 \div 1000$
                  $= \textbf{0.48} \ (= \textbf{48\%})$
        *[2 marks for correct answer, otherwise 1 mark for correct substitution]*
    c)      It will be faster / complete the course in less time *[1 mark]* because the motor transfers the same amount of energy, but over a shorter time *[1 mark]*.
3   a)      work done = force × distance moved in the direction of the force / $E = F \times d$
        $E = 42\ 000 \times 700$
           $= 29\ 400\ 000$ J
           $= \textbf{29 400 kJ}$
        *[3 marks for correct answer, otherwise 1 mark for correct substitution and 1 mark for correct answer in J]*
    b)      $KE = \frac{1}{2} \times m \times v^2$
        $v = \sqrt{\dfrac{2 \times KE}{m}}$
        $= \sqrt{\dfrac{2 \times 29\ 400\ 000}{150\ 000}} = 19.79...$ m/s $= \textbf{20 m/s}$ (to 1 s.f.)
        *[3 marks for correct answer, otherwise 1 mark for correct rearrangement and 1 mark for correct substitution]*
*Even if you got the answer to (a) wrong, you get full marks for (b) if you did the calculations correctly with your answer for (a).*

## Page 126
### Forces
Q1      E.g.

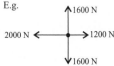

*[2 marks for all forces correctly drawn, 1 mark for three forces correctly drawn — weight and normal contact force arrows should be the same length, the arrow for the driving force should be longer than the weight arrow and the arrow for the resistive force should be shorter]*

## Page 128
### Resolving Forces
Q1      Draw the given forces to scale and tip-to-tail. The third force is found by joining the end of the second force to the start of the first force. E.g.

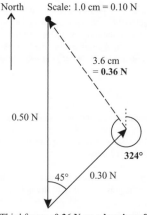

Third force = **0.36 N on a bearing of 324°**.
*[1 mark for a correct scale drawing with a sensible scale, 1 mark for a magnitude between 0.35 and 0.37 N, 1 mark for a bearing between 323 and 325°]*

## Page 129
### Moments
Q1      For forces to balance, anticlockwise moment = clockwise moment *[1 mark]*
        Let your distance = $y$
        So $300 \times 2 = 600 \times y$ *[1 mark]*
        $y = 600 \div 600 = \textbf{1 m}$ *[1 mark]*

## Page 131
### Warm-Up Questions
1      false
*Non-contact forces occur between objects that aren't touching.*
2      The relative magnitude of the forces.
3      A resultant force is the single force obtained by combining all the forces acting on an object. The resultant force has the same effect on the object as all the original forces together.
4      The tip of the last force you draw should end where the tail of the first force you drew began. E.g. for three forces the scale diagram will form a triangle.
5      For an object in equilibrium, the sum of the clockwise moments = the sum of the anticlockwise moments.
6      true
7      false
*Interlocking gears rotate in opposite directions.*

### Exam Questions
1   a)      Total force to the right = $1700 + 300 = 2000$ N
        Total force to the left = 2000 N
        Total horizontal force = $2000 - 2000 = 0$ N
        Resultant force = downwards force − upwards force
                   $= 800 - 300$
                   $= \textbf{500 N downwards}$
        *[3 marks for correct answer, otherwise 1 mark for correctly calculating that the total horizontal force is zero and 1 mark for giving the correct direction of the resultant force]*
    b)      Total vertical force = 0 N
        so, $y = \textbf{400 N}$
        Total horizontal force = 0 N
        so, $x + 500$ N = 2000 N
            $x = 2000 - 500 = \textbf{1500 N}$
        *[2 marks — 1 mark for each correct answer]*
2   a)      distance = 3 cm = 0.03 m
        moment of a force = force × distance
        moment = $15 \times 0.03 = \textbf{0.45 Nm}$
        *[3 marks for correct answer, otherwise 1 mark for correctly converting to metres and 1 mark for correct substitution]*
    b)      distance = 12 cm = 0.12 m
        $M = F \times d = 15 \times 0.12 = \textbf{1.8 Nm}$
        *[3 marks for correct answer, otherwise 1 mark for correctly converting to metres and 1 mark for correct substitution]*
    c)      The B end should be put into the bolt because it produces the greater moment, making the bolt easier to turn when a given force is applied *[1 mark]*.

# Section 7 — Electricity and Circuits

## Page 134
### Circuit Basics
Q1 $Q = It$ so $t = Q \div I$ *[1 mark]*
$\quad = 28\ 800 \div 8$ *[1 mark]*
$\quad = 3600$ s *[1 mark]*
$t = 3600 \div 60 =$ **60 minutes** *[1 mark]*

## Page 135
### Potential Difference and Resistance
Q1 $V = IR$ so $R = V \div I$ *[1 mark]*
$\quad = 230 \div 5.0$ *[1 mark]*
$\quad =$ **46 Ω** *[1 mark]*

## Page 139
### Warm-Up Questions
1

2     ohms
3     false
*Current in metals is the flow of free electrons.*
4     energy transferred = charge moved × potential difference / $E = Q \times V$
5     Electrons collide with the ions in the lattice that make up the resistor as they flow through it. These collisions transfer energy to the kinetic energy store of the ions, causing them to vibrate more (so the energy in the thermal energy store of the resistor will increase).
6     In parallel with the component.
7

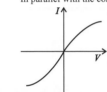

8     It decreases.

### Exam Questions
1 a) i)   $Q = I \times t$
$\quad = 0.30 \times 35$
$\quad =$ **10.5 C**
*[2 marks for correct answer, otherwise 1 mark for correct substitution]*
    ii)   $E = Q \times V$
$\quad = 10.5 \times 1.5$
$\quad =$ **15.75 J**
$\quad =$ **16 J (to 2 s.f.)**
*[2 marks for correct answer, otherwise 1 mark for correct substitution]*
*If you got the answer to (i) wrong, you still get full marks for (ii) if you did the calculations correctly using your answer to (i).*
  b)   It will decrease *[1 mark]*.
2 a)   The temperature of the circuit/diode *[1 mark]*.
  b)   At point A, $V = 6$ V, $I = 3$ A
potential difference = current × resistance / $V = I \times R$
$R = V \div I$
$\quad = 6 \div 3$
$\quad =$ **2 Ω**
*[4 marks for correct answer, otherwise 1 mark for obtaining correct values from the graph, 1 mark for correct rearrangement and 1 mark for correct substitution]*

## Page 140
### Series Circuits
Q1 $R_{total} = 4 + 5 + 6 = 15$ Ω *[1 mark]*
$V = I \times R = 0.6 \times 15$ *[1 mark]*
$\quad =$ **9 V** *[1 mark]*

## Page 141
### Parallel Circuits
Q1   The total current through the circuit decreases *[1 mark]* as there are fewer paths for the current to take *[1 mark]*. The total resistance of the circuit increases *[1 mark]* as, using $V = IR$, a decrease in the total current means an increase in the total resistance *[1 mark]*.

## Page 143
### Warm-Up Questions
1     true
2     The resistances of all the components are added together.
3     3 V
*In a parallel circuit all of the components get the full source potential difference.*
4     Two resistors connected in series.
5     One by one, connect identical resistors in series. Each time a new resistor is added, measure the current passing through the circuit using an ammeter, and then calculate the total resistance using $R = V \div I$, where $V$ is the potential difference of the power supply. Plot a graph of total resistance against number of resistors.

### Exam Questions
1 a)   total resistance $= R_1 + R_2 + R_3$
$\quad = 2 + 3 + 5$
$\quad =$ **10 Ω** *[1 mark]*
  b)   The reading on $A_2$ will be 0.4 A *[1 mark]* because in a series circuit, the same current flows through all parts of the circuit *[1 mark]*.
  c)   $V_3 = V_{supply} - V_1 - V_2$
$\quad = 4 - 0.8 - 1.2$
$\quad =$ **2 V** *[1 mark]*
2 a)   **15 V** *[1 mark]*
*Potential difference is the same across each branch in a parallel circuit.*
  b)   $V = I \times R$
$I = V \div R$
$\quad = 15 \div 3$
$\quad =$ **5 A**
*[3 marks for correct answer, otherwise 1 mark for correct rearrangement and 1 mark for correct substitution]*
  c)   $I_2 = 5 + 3.75$
$\quad =$ **8.75 A** *[1 mark]*
*Even if you got the answer to (b) wrong, you still get full marks for (c) if you did the calculations correctly with your answer to (b).*
  d)   The reading on $A_2$ will decrease *[1 mark]* since current through the branch with two resistors will decrease *[1 mark]*, decreasing the total current in the circuit *[1 mark]*.

## Page 144
### Energy in Circuits
Q1 $t = 60 \times 60$ *[1 mark]*
$E = I \times V \times t$
$\quad = 4.0 \times 230 \times (60 \times 60)$ *[1 mark]*
$\quad = 3\ 312\ 000$ J
$\quad =$ **3 300 000 J** (to 2 s.f.) *[1 mark]*

## Page 146
### Power in Circuits
Q1 $E = P \times t = 250 \times (2 \times 60 \times 60)$
$\quad = 1\ 800\ 000$ J *[1 mark]*
$E = 375 \times (2 \times 60 \times 60)$
$\quad = 2\ 700\ 000$ J *[1 mark]*
So difference in the energy transferred is
$2\ 700\ 000 - 1\ 800\ 000$
$\quad =$ **900 000 J** *[1 mark]*

## Page 147
### Warm-Up Questions
1     energy transferred = current × potential difference × time / $E = I \times V \times t$
2     Energy is transferred electrically from the mains supply to the thermal energy store of the toaster's heating element.
3     E.g. electric heaters/toasters
4     watts
5     The 60 W light bulb.
6     $P = I^2 \times R$

### Exam Questions
1 a)   electrical power = current × potential difference / $P = I \times V$ *[1 mark]*
  b)   $I = P \div V$
$\quad = (2.8 \times 1000) \div 230$
$\quad =$ **12.17...A**
$\quad =$ **12 A (to 2 s.f.)**
*[3 marks for correct answer, otherwise 1 mark for correct rearrangement and 1 mark for correct substitution]*
  c)   She should choose kettle B because it has the higher power rating *[1 mark]*. This means that it transfers more energy to heat the water per unit time, so it will boil the water faster *[1 mark]*.

2 a) $E = I \times V \times t$
$t = 0.5$ hours $= 30$ minutes
Convert minutes into seconds: $30 \times 60 = 1800$ s
$E = 0.5 \times 3.0 \times 1800$
$= \mathbf{2700\ J}$
*[3 marks for correct answer, otherwise 1 mark for correctly converting time into seconds and 1 mark for correct substitution]*

b) The power of the torch will be halved *[1 mark]*.
*The current has been halved, and as P = I × V, halving the current and keeping the potential difference the same means the power will also be halved.*

3 Calculate the lifetime of a single battery:
$E = I \times V \times t$
$t = \dfrac{E}{I \times V}$
$= \dfrac{13\,000}{(0.2 \times 10^{-3}) \times 1.5} = 4.333... \times 10^7$ s

Then calculate the number of batteries required for ten years:
$= \dfrac{\text{ten years (seconds)}}{\text{lifetime of one battery (seconds)}}$
$= \dfrac{10 \times 365 \times 24 \times 60 \times 60}{4.333... \times 10^7} = 7.2775...$ batteries

So **8 batteries** are needed to power the clock for ten years.
*[3 marks for correct answer, otherwise 1 mark for correctly calculating the lifetime of a single battery and 1 mark for dividing the number of seconds in ten years by the lifetime of a single battery]*

Alternative method:
Number of seconds in ten years $= 10 \times 365 \times 24 \times 60 \times 60$
$= 315\,360\,000$ s
Calculate the energy required by the clock in ten years:
$E = I \times V \times t$
$= (0.2 \times 10^{-3}) \times 1.5 \times 315\,360\,000$
$= 94\,608$ J

Then calculate the total number of batteries needed to supply this amount of energy:
Number of batteries $= 94\,608 \div 13\,000$
$= 7.2775...$
So **8 batteries** are needed to power the clock for ten years.
*[3 marks for correct answer, otherwise 1 mark for correctly calculating the total energy required for ten years and 1 mark for dividing this by the energy of a single battery]*

## Page 151
## Warm-Up Questions

1 direct current
2 The neutral wire completes the circuit, allowing current to flow out of the appliance.
3 230 V
4 the live wire
5 false
*Fuses should be rated as near as possible but just higher than the normal operating current.*

## Exam Questions

1 a) In alternating current the movement of charges constantly changes direction *[1 mark]*.
b) Your body is at 0 V, so there's a potential difference of around 230 V between the live wire and you *[1 mark]*. Touching the wire forms a link from the supply to the earth through your body *[1 mark]*, causing a large current to flow through you, which is an electric shock *[1 mark]*.
2 a) The earth wire is connected to the kettle's metal casing *[1 mark]*. When the casing becomes live, a large current is able to surge from the live wire, through the casing and out through the earth wire *[1 mark]*. The surge in current causes the fuse attached to the live wire to melt, isolating the kettle from the live supply *[1 mark]*.
b) a circuit breaker *[1 mark]*
c) Because plastic is a good electrical insulator, the casing cannot become live, so an earth wire is not needed *[1 mark]*.

## Section 8 — Electric and Magnetic Fields

## Page 156
## Electric Fields
Q1

*[1 mark for at least 8 straight lines at right angles to the surface, 1 mark for arrows on the lines pointing away from the sphere, 1 mark for lines equally spaced]*

## Page 157
## Warm-Up Questions

1 electrons
2 attract
3 The droplets all have the same charge so repel one another, which creates a very fine, even spray of paint. The parts pointing away from the spray will also be painted, because the paint droplets are oppositely charged to the bike, so they will be attracted to all parts of the bike.
4 Earthing provides an easy route for charges to travel to or from the ground. This prevents a spark from occurring, as static charge won't be able to build up enough to cause a spark.
5 The region around a charged object where, if a second charge was placed inside it, a force will be exerted on both of the charges.
6

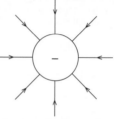

7 The greater the distance from a charged object, the weaker the electric field produced by the charged object. / The smaller the distance from a charged object, the stronger the electric field produced by the charged object.

## Exam Questions

1 a) Electrons are transferred from the cloth and onto the sphere *[1 mark]*.
b) B *[1 mark]*
*The field strength is bigger the closer you are to the charged sphere, so the electrostatic force is greatest when the point charge is closest to the sphere.*
c)

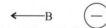

*[1 mark for arrow drawn at answer to part b), pointing away from sphere]*
*Like charges repel, so the direction of the force is directly away from the charged sphere.*
d) The electric field of the sphere ionised the particles in the air *[1 mark]*. This made the air more conductive and allowed charge to flow to the earthed conductor in the form of a spark *[1 mark]*.
2 A *[1 mark]*. The rod is negatively charged so would repel the negative charges in the balloon *[1 mark]*, making them move away from the rod and leaving a positive charge near to where the rod is being held *[1 mark]*.

## Page 161
## The Motor Effect
Q1 Into the page *[1 mark]*.

## Page 164
## Warm-Up Questions

1 a) attraction
*Opposite poles are facing each other and opposite poles attract.*
b)

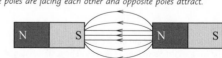

*The magnetic field is uniform between the two bar magnets, so you need to draw at least 3 parallel field lines that are equally spaced.*

2    Put the magnet on a piece of paper and put a compass next to it. Make a mark on the paper at each end of the compass needle. Then move the compass so that the tail of the compass needle is where the tip of the needle was previously, and mark again where the needle is pointing. Repeat this several times and then join up the markings for a complete sketch of a field line around the magnet. Do this several times for different points around the magnet to get several field lines. Add arrows to each field line, pointing from north to south.

3    north/towards the Earth's North Pole

4    false
*A permanent magnet will always attract an induced magnet/magnetic material.*

5    It swaps the electrical contacts every half rotation, allowing the motor to keep rotating in the same direction.

## Exam Questions

1  a)

*[1 mark]*

   b)  The interaction between the magnetic field generated by the wire and the magnetic field between the north and south poles of the bar magnets *[1 mark]*.

   c)  $l = 7.0$ cm $= 0.070$ m
   $F = B \times I \times l$
   $= 0.028 \times 5.5 \times 0.070$
   $= 0.01078$ N $= \mathbf{0.011}$ **N (to 2 s.f.)**
   *[2 marks for correct answer, otherwise 1 mark for correct substitution]*

   d)  The direction of the force would be reversed *[1 mark]*.

2  a)  The field lines inside each loop of the solenoid all point in the same direction, so they add together to create a strong uniform field *[1 mark]*.

   b)  e.g. iron / nickel / cobalt *[1 mark]*

   c)  E.g. increase the current flowing through the solenoid *[1 mark]*.

## Page 168
### Transformers

Q1   Power output $= V_s \times I_s = 320$ W
   $V_p \times I_p = V_s \times I_s$, so
   $I_p = (V_s \times I_s) \div V_p$
   $= 320 \div 1.6$ *[1 mark]*
   $= \mathbf{200}$ **A** *[1 mark]*

## Page 170
### Warm-Up Questions

1    A dynamo generates a direct current whereas an alternator generates an alternating current.

2    More turns on the secondary coil.

3    Because the high current would result in inefficient transmission of power/a large loss of energy to thermal energy stores.

### Exam Questions

1  a)  The coil experiences a change in magnetic field, so a potential difference is induced *[1 mark]*.

   b)  Any one from: e.g. move the magnet out of the coil / move the coil away from the magnet / insert the south pole of the magnet into the same end of the coil / insert the north pole of the magnet into the other end of the coil *[1 mark]*.

   c)  Any one from: e.g. push the magnet into the coil more quickly / use a stronger magnet / add more turns per unit length of wire *[1 mark]*.

   d)  Zero / no reading *[1 mark]*.
*A moving/changing magnetic field is needed to generate a potential difference.*

2  a)  A potential difference will not be induced in the secondary coil when using the d.c. supply because the magnetic field generated in the iron core is not changing *[1 mark]*. A p.d. is only induced if the secondary coil experiences a change in magnetic field *[1 mark]*.

   b)  $V_p \times I_p = V_s \times I_s$
   $I_s = \dfrac{V_p \times I_p}{V_s} = \dfrac{12 \times 2.5}{4}$
   $I_s = \mathbf{7.5}$ **A**
   *[2 marks for correct answer, otherwise 1 mark for correct substitution]*

   c)  $V_s \div V_p = N_s \div N_p$
   So, $N_s = (V_s \div V_p) \times N_p$
   $N_s = (4 \div 12) \times 15$
   $= \mathbf{5}$ **turns**
   *[2 marks for correct answer, otherwise 1 mark for correct substitution]*

3    When the a.c. current flows through the coil of wire in the magnetic field of the permanent magnet, the coil of wire experiences a force *[1 mark]*. The force causes the coil, and so the cone, to move *[1 mark]*. The alternating current is constantly changing direction and so the direction of the force on the coil is constantly changing and the cone vibrates back and forth *[1 mark]*. The vibrations cause pressure variations in the air that cause sound waves *[1 mark]*.

## Section 9 — Matter

## Page 172
### Density

Q1   First find the cube's volume:
   $0.015 \times 0.015 \times 0.015 = 3.375 \times 10^{-6}$ m³ *[1 mark]*
   The cube's density is 3500 kg/m³.
   $m = \rho \times V$
   $= 3500 \times (3.375 \times 10^{-6})$ *[1 mark]*
   $= 0.01181...$ kg
   $= \mathbf{12}$ **g (to 2 s.f.)** *[1 mark]*

## Page 175
### Warm-Up Questions

1    Density is a measure of the amount of mass in a given volume / compactness of a substance.

2    gas

3    sublimation

4    physical changes

5    Cooling a system decreases its internal energy.

6    $- 273$ °C

7    subtract 273

### Exam Questions

1  a)  Particles are held close together in a fixed, regular pattern *[1 mark]*. They vibrate about fixed positions *[1 mark]*.

   b)  density = mass ÷ volume = $850.5 \div 75.0 = \mathbf{11.34}$ **g/cm³**
   *[2 marks for correct answer, otherwise 1 mark for correct substitution]*

   c)  melting *[1 mark]*

2  a)  C *[1 mark]*

   b)  The volume of the toy soldier / the volume of water displaced by the toy soldier *[1 mark]*. The mass of the toy soldier *[1 mark]*.

   c)  How to grade your answer:
   Level 0:    There is no relevant information. *[No marks]*
   Level 1:    There is a brief description of an experiment to measure the density of the toy soldier, but the answer isn't very clear. The points made do not link together. *[1 to 2 marks]*
   Level 2:    There is a description of an experiment to measure the mass and volume of the toy soldier, with reference to the equipment needed. The answer has some structure. *[3 to 4 marks]*
   Level 3:    There is a clear and detailed description of an experiment to measure the density of the toy soldier. The method includes details of how to use the equipment and how to process the results to work out the density of the toy soldier. The answer is well structured. *[5 to 6 marks]*
   Here are some points your answer may include:
   Measure and record the mass of the toy soldier using the mass balance.
   Fill a eureka can with water.
   Place an empty measuring cylinder beneath the spout of the eureka can.
   Submerge the toy soldier in the eureka can.
   Measure the volume of water displaced from the eureka can using the measuring cylinder.
   The volume of water displaced is equal to the volume of the soldier.
   Use the equation density = mass ÷ volume / $\rho = m \div V$
   to calculate the density of the toy soldier.
*With questions where you have to describe a method, make sure your description is clear and detailed.*

## Page 176
### Specific Heat Capacity

Q1   $\Delta Q = mc\Delta\theta$ so
   $\Delta\theta = \Delta Q \div (m \times c)$ *[1 mark]*
   $= 50\,000 \div (5 \times 4200)$
   $= 2.380...$ °C *[1 mark]*
   So the new temperature $= 5 + 2.380... = 7.380...$
   $= \mathbf{7}$ **°C (to 1 s.f.)** *[1 mark]*

## Page 177
### Specific Latent Heat

Q1   $Q = m \times L = 0.25 \times 120\,000$ *[1 mark]*
   $= \mathbf{30\,000}$ **J** *[1 mark]*

## Page 179
### Warm-Up Questions

1    The change in energy in the substance's thermal energy store needed to raise the temperature of 1 kg of that substance by 1 °C.

2     The thermally insulating material reduces unwanted energy transfers to the surroundings. More of the energy supplied is transferred to the thermal energy stores of the water, so the $\Delta E$ value used to calculate the specific heat capacity is a more accurate value. This improves the accuracy of the value of specific heat capacity.

3     J/kg

4

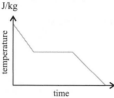

## Exam Questions

1     $Q = m \times L$
So, $L = Q \div m$
$m = 40.8 \text{ g} = (40.8 \div 1000) \text{ kg} = 0.0408 \text{ kg}$
$L = 47\,100 \div 0.0408 = 1.1544... \times 10^6 \text{ J/kg}$
    $= 1.15 \times 10^6 \text{ J/kg (to 3 s.f.)}$
*[2 marks for correct answer, otherwise 1 mark for correct substitution]*

2  a)   $\Delta Q = m \times c \times \Delta\theta$
So, $c = \Delta Q \div (m \times \Delta\theta)$
$\Delta\theta = 100 - 20 = 80 \text{ °C}$
$c = 36\,000 \div (0.5 \times 80) = \textbf{900 J/kg°C}$
*[2 marks for correct answer, otherwise 1 mark for correct substitution]*

   b)   Concrete has a higher specific heat capacity *[1 mark]* and so will be able to store a lot more energy in its thermal energy store for the same temperature change, and therefore emit a lot more energy during the day *[1 mark]*. This means it will be able to heat the room to a higher temperature / for longer *[1 mark]*.

3  a)   In the graph, $y = \Delta\theta$ and $x = \Delta Q$.
$\Delta Q = m \times c \times \Delta\theta$
Rearrange this equation to make it look like $y = mx + c$:

$\Delta\theta = \dfrac{1}{m \times c} \times \Delta Q$

Comparing this to $y = mx + c$,

the gradient of the graph must equal $\dfrac{1}{m \times c}$ *[1 mark]*

Coordinates of two points on the line of best fit are (0,0) and (3000, 0.70), where $x$ has been converted from kJ to J.
Gradient $= \Delta y \div \Delta x = (0.70 - 0) \div (3000 - 0)$
    $= 0.0002333...$ *[1 mark]*

$c = \dfrac{1}{m \times \text{gradient}}$

$m = 1.0 \text{ kg, so } c = \dfrac{1}{1 \times 0.0002333...} = 4285.71... \text{ J/kg °C}$
    $= \textbf{4300 J/kg °C (to 2 s.f.)}$ *[1 mark]*

   b)   Lower — in the investigation, some of the energy transferred by the heater would have been transferred to the thermal energy stores of the surroundings rather than the water *[1 mark]*. For the same temperature change to have occurred for a smaller amount of energy transferred, the specific heat capacity must be smaller *[1 mark]*.

## Page 181

### Gas Pressure

Q1     When gas particles collide with the walls of their container, they exert a force on it *[1 mark]*. Across many particles, this force acting on the container causes an outward pressure *[1 mark]*.

Q2     $P_1 V_1 = P_2 V_2$, so when $V_1 = 3.5 \text{ m}^3$,
$P_1 V_1 = 520 \times 3.5 = 1820$ *[1 mark]*
When $V_2 = 1 \text{ m}^3$,
$P_2 V_2 = P_2 \times 1 = 1820$ *[1 mark]*,
so $P_2 = \textbf{1820 Pa}$ *[1 mark]*

## Page 183

### Fluid Pressure

Q1     $P = h\rho g$ so $\rho = P \div gh$
$\rho = 450 \div (10 \times 0.05)$ *[1 mark]*
$\rho = \textbf{900 kg/m}^3$ *[1 mark]*

## Page 185

### Warm-Up Questions

1     The higher the temperature of the gas, the faster the gas particles move. This means the gas particles collide with the walls of the container more often and with a greater force. This causes the gas pressure to increase.

2     Atmospheric pressure decreases with height, so as the helium balloon floats upwards, the pressure outside the balloon decreases. This causes the balloon to expand until the pressure inside drops to the same as the atmospheric pressure.

3     Doing work against the air pressure transfers energy to the kinetic energy stores of the air particles, so the temperature of the air increases.

---

4     Pressure is the force (on a surface) per unit area.

5     A denser fluid has more particles in a set volume. This means there are more particles colliding in a given volume, so the fluid pressure is greater.

6     3.5 N

### Exam Questions

1  a)   It has a higher density than water *[1 mark]*.

   b)   depth of water = 50 cm = 0.50 m
diameter of ball = 8 cm = 0.08 m
$P = h \times \rho \times g$
$h = 0.50 - 0.08 = 0.42 \text{ m}$
$P = 0.42 \times 1000 \times 10 = \textbf{4200 Pa}$
*[3 marks for correct answer, otherwise 1 mark for correct calculation of h and 1 mark for correct substitution]*

2  a)   $P = F \div A$
$P = 175 \div 0.25 = \textbf{700 Pa}$
*[2 marks for correct answer, otherwise 1 mark for correct substitution]*

   b)   Since the pressure is the same at all points in the liquid, the pressure on piston 2 is equal to the pressure applied by piston 1.
$P = F \div A$
So, $F = P \times A = 700 \times 1.3 = \textbf{910 N}$
*[3 marks for correct answer, otherwise 1 mark for correct rearrangement and 1 mark for correct substitution]*

3     $P_1 \times V_1 = P_2 \times V_2$
Rearrange for $P_2$:
$P_2 = (P_1 \times V_1) \div V_2$
    $= (0.034 \times 98) \div 0.031$
    $= 107.4... \text{ kPa}$
    $= \textbf{110 kPa (to 2 s.f.)}$
*[4 marks for correct answer, otherwise 1 mark for correct rearrangement, 1 mark for correct substitution and 1 mark for correct unrounded answer]*
*You don't need to convert $P_1$ into Pa before substituting into the equation here — you just need to make sure both pressures use the same units.*

## Page 187

### Elasticity

Q1     $k = F \div x = 1 \div 0.02$ *[1 mark]*
    $= \textbf{50 N/m}$ *[1 mark]*

## Page 188

### Investigating Elasticity

Q1     $E = \frac{1}{2}kx^2$
    $= \frac{1}{2} \times 40 \times (0.025)^2$ *[1 mark]*
    $= \textbf{0.0125 J}$ *[1 mark]*

## Page 189

### Warm-Up Questions

1     false
*In order to distort a spring, at least two forces must be applied to the spring.*

2     An object undergoing elastic distortion will go back to its original shape and length after the distorting forces have been removed.

3     force = spring constant × extension / $F = k \times x$

### Exam Questions

1     extension = 4 cm = 0.04 m
work done = area under graph
    $= \frac{1}{2} \times 8 \times 0.04$
    $= \textbf{0.16 J}$
*[2 marks for correct answer, otherwise 1 mark for attempting to find the area under the graph]*

2  a)   The mass on the bottom of the spring / the force applied to the bottom of the spring *[1 mark]*.

   b)   Any one from: e.g. the spring used throughout the experiment / the temperature the experiment is carried out at *[1 mark]*.

   c)   extension = 2.5 cm = 0.025 m
$F = k \times x$
so $k = F \div x = 4 \div 0.025 = \textbf{160 N/m}$
*[3 marks for correct answer, otherwise 1 mark for correct rearrangement and 1 mark for correct substitution]*
*Remember to convert the measurement of extension from cm into m before you do your calculation.*

   d)   The spring has been inelastically distorted *[1 mark]*.

3     $E = \frac{1}{2} \times k \times x^2$
Rearrange for $x$:
$x = \sqrt{\dfrac{2 \times E}{k}} = \sqrt{\dfrac{2 \times 36}{400}} = 0.42426... \text{ m}$

So length of spring after compression = 1.20 − 0.42426...
    $= \textbf{0.77573... m}$
    $= \textbf{0.78 m (to 2 s.f.)}$
*[3 marks for correct answer, otherwise 1 mark for correct substitution and 1 mark for calculating compression = 0.42426... m]*

<u>Practice Paper 1</u>
<u>Pages 195-215</u>

1 a) i) E.g. total energy must be conserved / energy cannot be created or destroyed, only transferred. *[1 mark]*
   ii) C *[1 mark]*
   iii) C *[1 mark]*
   b) i) E.g. measure the temperature after a set number of bounces instead of after a set time *[1 mark]*.
   *This is a sensible idea as the number of bounces in a given time may vary.*
   ii) E.g. energy is transferred mechanically from the ball's kinetic energy store *[1 mark]* to its elastic potential energy store as it hits the wall and deforms *[1 mark]*. Some energy is transferred by heating to the thermal energy store of the ball *[1 mark]*. Energy is transferred mechanically from the elastic potential energy store of the ball to the kinetic energy store of the ball as the ball rebounds from the wall *[1 mark]*.
   c) change in GPE = 0.03 × 10 × 1.75
   = **0.525 J**
   *[2 marks for correct answer, otherwise 1 mark for correct substitution]*

2 a) i) E.g. biofuel / wind power / hydroelectricity / the tides *[1 mark]*
   ii) Efficiency = useful energy transferred by the device ÷ total energy transferred to the device. *[1 mark]*
   iii) Efficiency = useful energy transferred by the device ÷ total energy transferred to the device
   = 0.2 ÷ 1.2
   = 0.1666...
   = **0.17 (= 17%) (to 2 s.f.)**
   *[2 marks for correct answer, otherwise 1 mark for correct substitution]*
   b) i) The amount of energy used has decreased over time *[1 mark]*. E.g. this could be because electrical devices have become more efficient over time *[1 mark]*.
   ii) Any two from: e.g. building renewable power plants is expensive / using fossil fuels is fairly cheap / some people don't want to live near renewable power plants / renewable energy resources are not as reliable as fossil fuels / research into improving the reliability and reducing the cost of renewable resources is expensive and time consuming / making personal changes (such as installing solar panels) can be expensive for an individual *[2 marks — 1 mark for each correct point]*
   c) The home owner should use brick Y *[1 mark]*, because brick Y has the lowest thermal conductivity of all the options. This means the rate of energy transfer by heating will be slowest through this type of brick *[1 mark]*. Also brick Y is the thickest brick and the thicker the walls of a building, the lower the rate of cooling of the building will be *[1 mark]*.

3 a) The first skater travels at a constant speed for the first 15 s (travelling 33 m) *[1 mark]*. She then remains stationary (at 33 m) for 10 s *[1 mark]* before accelerating away for the next 10 s (and travelling another 12 m) *[1 mark]*.
   b) The gradient of the line between 0 and 15 s will give speed.
   speed = gradient = $\frac{\text{change in } y}{\text{change in } x}$
   = $\frac{33-0}{15-0}$
   = **2.2 m/s**
   *[2 marks for correct answer, otherwise 1 mark for correct method for calculating speed from the graph]*
   c) i) Speed = distance ÷ time *[1 mark]*
   ii) Time = distance ÷ speed
   = 14 ÷ 3.5
   = **4 s**
   *[3 marks for the correct answer, otherwise 1 mark for correct rearrangement and 1 mark for correct substitution]*
   d) i) A *[1 mark]*
   ii) The total frictional force must be larger than the total driving forces *[1 mark]*.

4 a) The outward pressure/thermal expansion due to nuclear fusion *[1 mark]* balances the inwards force due to gravitational attraction / gravity *[1 mark]*.
   b) Nuclear fusion occurs in the core of stars *[1 mark]*. During fusion, larger nuclei are created from smaller nuclei, resulting in a loss of mass and a release of energy *[1 mark]*.
   c) B *[1 mark]*
   d) B *[1 mark]*
   e) W = m × g
   = 1400 × 9
   = **12 600 N**
   *[2 marks for correct answer, otherwise 1 mark for correct substitution]*

5 a) E.g. place a block on a sheet of paper and draw around it. Shine a light beam through the block *[1 mark]*. Trace the path of the ray using a pencil and a ruler. Measure and record the angles of incidence and refraction *[1 mark]*. Repeat this for different materials, keeping the angle of incidence the same *[1 mark]*.
   b) i) e.g. ray box *[1 mark]*
   ii) E.g. it allows the centre of the beam to be traced more accurately, meaning better angle measurements *[1 mark]*.

c) i) Flint glass *[1 mark]*
   ii) Flint glass refracts the light beam by the greatest amount *[1 mark]* and refraction is caused by light being slowed down by a material *[1 mark]*.
   d) $v = f \times \lambda$
   = $(5.1 \times 10^{14}) \times (353 \times 10^{-9})$
   = **1.800... × 10⁸**
   = **1.8 × 10⁸ m/s (to 2 s.f.)**
   *[2 marks for correct answer, otherwise 1 mark for correct substitution]*

6 a) How to grade your answer:
   Level 0: There is no relevant information. *[No marks]*
   Level 1: There is a brief description of both models of the atom. The points made do not link together. *[1 to 2 marks]*
   Level 2: There is a description of both models of the atom, and some description of the scientific discoveries that led to the development of the nuclear model. The answer has some structure. *[3 to 4 marks]*
   Level 3: There is a clear and detailed description of both models of the atom, and of the scientific discoveries and experiments which led to the development of the nuclear model. The answer is well structured. *[5 to 6 marks]*
   Here are some points your answer may include:
   Model X is the plum pudding model of the atom.
   The plum pudding model describes the atom as a sphere of positive charge, with negatively charged electrons within it.
   Model Y is the nuclear/Bohr model of the atom.
   The nuclear/Bohr model of the atom describes the atom as a nucleus, made up of positively charged protons and uncharged neutrons, orbited by electrons.
   In the early 20th century (1909), Rutherford and Marsden performed the alpha scattering experiment.
   They fired a beam of positively charged alpha particles at a thin gold foil.
   Based on the plum pudding model, they expected all the alpha particles to pass through the foil, with some deflection.
   However, they found that most alpha particles passed through the foil without deflecting, while a small few were deflected back towards the emitter.
   This suggested that most of the atom is empty space, since so many of the alpha particles passed through without deflecting.
   It also suggested there was a small, positively charged 'nucleus' in the centre of the atom, which caused the backwards deflection of the alpha particles.
   Later, Bohr proposed that the electrons in an atom could only be found in fixed orbits named energy levels.
   b) i) E.g. a Geiger-Müller tube *[1 mark]*
   ii) The charge on a beta particle, B = –1
   83 = A – 1
   A = **84** *[1 mark]*
   iii) The initial count-rate was 80 cps.
   80 ÷ 2 = 40
   So after one half-life, the count-rate will be 40 cps.
   From the graph, 40 cps is reached after 60 minutes.
   So half-life = **60 minutes**.
   *[2 marks for correct answer, otherwise 1 mark for correct method of calculating half-life graphically]*
   c) A thicker lead lining blocks more gamma radiation *[1 mark]*, which improves the safety of people nearby since gamma radiation can damage or kill cells *[1 mark]*.

7 a) 10 dB *[1 mark]*
   b) wavelength = 2 × 0.625 = 1.25 m
   wave speed = frequency × wavelength
   = 5500 × 1.25
   = 6875 m/s
   = **6900 m/s (to 2 s.f.)**
   *[4 marks for correct answer, otherwise 1 mark for correctly calculating wavelength, 1 mark for correct substitution and 1 mark for correct unrounded answer]*
   c) A *[1 mark]*

8 a) i)
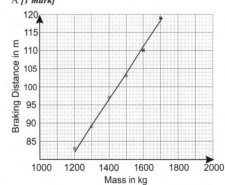
   ii) E.g. as mass increases, so does braking distance *[1 mark]*.

*[1 mark for plotting points correctly, 1 mark for line of best fit]*

b) i)  Work done = 7000 × 18
       = **126 000 J**
       *[2 marks for correct answer,*
       *otherwise 1 mark for correct substitution]*

   ii) ½ × m × v² = W
       $v = \sqrt{\dfrac{2 \times W}{m}}$
       $= \sqrt{\dfrac{2 \times 126\,000}{1100}}$
       = **15.135... m/s**
       = **15 m/s (to 2 s.f.)**
       *[3 marks for the correct answer, otherwise 1 mark for correct*
       *rearrangement and 1 mark for correct substitution]*

  iii) Force = mass × acceleration
       a = F ÷ m
       = 7000 ÷ 1100
       = **6.363... m/s²**
       = **6.4 m/s² (to 2 s.f.)**
       *[2 marks for the correct answer, otherwise 1 mark for*
       *correct rearrangement and correct substitution]*

*You could have used the equation v² − u² = 2 × a × x too.*

9 a)  E.g. this ensures the accelerating force (gravity)
       will be equal for all of the tests. *[1 mark]*

   b)  The student could look at the footage and see how long it takes for
       the can to stop completely after hitting the concrete block *[1 mark]*.
       The can's change in velocity will equal 4.4 m/s as it comes to a
       complete stop *[1 mark]*. These values for time and change in velocity
       can be substituted into the equation $a = (v - u) \div t$ *[1 mark]*.

   c) i)  (10 + 10 + 7) ÷ 3 = **9 m/s²**
          *[2 marks for correct answer, otherwise 1 mark for*
          *correct method for calculating the mean]*

     ii)  Material C *[1 mark]*. Since mass is kept constant, a smaller
          acceleration will lead to a smaller impact force ($F = m \times a$)
          which will reduce the risk of injury *[1 mark]*.

   d)  $F = \dfrac{(mv - mu)}{t}$
       $= \dfrac{(60 \times 0) - (60 \times 3)}{0.4}$
       = −450 N
       So, the size of the force is 450 N.
       *[2 marks for correct answer, otherwise 1 mark for correct substitution]*

10 a)  E.g. the atmosphere absorbs 100% of gamma radiation
       *[1 mark]* which could cause cell damage/cancer in
       humans if it reached the Earth's surface *[1 mark]*.

   b)  How to grade your answer:
       Level 0:    There is no relevant information. *[No marks]*
       Level 1:    There are some relevant points made about radio waves,
                   but there is little attempt to describe or evaluate their use
                   by satellites. The points made are not linked together.
                   *[1 to 2 marks]*
       Level 2:    There is an explanation of why radio waves are suited
                   to use by satellites. A brief description is given of how
                   they are produced and received. The answer has some
                   structure. *[3 to 4 marks]*
       Level 3:    There is a clear evaluation of why radio waves are suited
                   to use in satellite communications. A coherent and logical
                   description of how radio waves are produced and received
                   in communication technology is included. The answer is
                   well structured. *[5 to 6 marks]*
       Here are some points your answer may include:
       As shown in Figure 20, almost all types of radio wave can pass through
       the Earth's atmosphere.
       This means that radio waves can travel between the Earth's surface and a
       satellite in orbit (without being absorbed).
       Radio waves are electromagnetic waves and are made up of oscillating
       electric and magnetic fields.
       Oscillating electric and magnetic fields can be produced by an oscillating
       charged particle (e.g. an electron).
       Alternating currents are made up of oscillating electrons.
       So radio waves can be produced by passing an alternating current through
       a transmitter.
       The oscillating charges in the transmitter produce oscillating electric and
       magnetic fields (a radio wave) with the same frequency as the
       alternating current.
       When these radio waves reach a receiver, they are absorbed by the
       electrons in the receiver.
       This causes the electrons to oscillate at the same frequency as the
       radio wave.
       This induces an alternating current in the receiver.
       So the frequency of the alternating current in the transmitter
       is the same as the frequency in the receiver.

c)  The temperature of an object is affected by the amount of radiation it
    absorbs and emits — absorbing radiation increases temperature and
    emitting radiation decreases temperature *[1 mark]*. At night at a point on
    the Earth, no radiation is absorbed from the Sun but radiation is emitted
    from the surface, so the temperature decreases *[1 mark]*. On a cloudy
    night, this temperature decrease is less, because some radiation emitted
    will be reflected back towards the surface, where it is re-absorbed,
    reducing the rate of temperature decrease *[1 mark]*. Some radiation
    will also be absorbed by the clouds, and later re-emitted back towards
    the surface, again reducing the rate of temperature decrease *[1 mark]*.

# Practice Paper 2
## Pages 216-237

1 a) i)   A *[1 mark]*

   ii)  time = charge ÷ current = 1440 ÷ 12 = **120 s**
      *[3 marks for correct answer, otherwise 1 mark for correct rearrangement and 1 mark for correct substitution]*

 b)  E.g. the maximum safe power that an appliance can operate at / the maximum amount of energy an appliance can transfer between stores per second *[1 mark]*.

 c)  Energy is transferred from the thermal energy store of the heating element *[1 mark]* to the thermal energy store of the water *[1 mark]* by heating *[1 mark]*.

 d)  E.g.

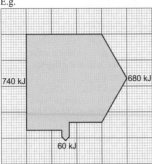

740 kJ    680 kJ

60 kJ

*[2 marks for a correctly drawn diagram, otherwise 1 mark for correct width of one arrow or correct calculation of waste energy]*

2 a)  Any one from: e.g. to improve the precision of the results / to improve the accuracy of the results / to check the repeatability of the results / to check the reliability of the results *[1 mark]*.

 b)  E.g. the scientist could wait for the temperature of the gas to reach room temperature before taking any pressure measurements *[1 mark]*.

 c)  The gas pressure would have increased *[1 mark]*. Decreasing the volume of the syringe would increase the number of collisions of gas particles on the syringe wall in a given time *[1 mark]*. This would increase the force on a unit area of the syringe wall, which is an increase in the gas pressure *[1 mark]*.

 d)  D *[1 mark]*

3 a) i)   B *[1 mark]*
The clamp must apply 1 N of force to balance the weight of the mass. Otherwise, there will be a resultant force on the spring causing it to move.

   ii)  If only one force was applied, this would simply cause the spring to move in the direction of the force *[1 mark]*.

 b)  D *[1 mark]*

 c)  How to grade your answer:

   Level 0:   There is no relevant information. *[No marks]*
   Level 1:   There is a brief description of an experiment using the equipment shown. The points made are not linked together. *[1 to 2 marks]*
   Level 2:   There is a description of an experiment that can be performed with the equipment shown, and a valid statement of how to calculate the spring constant. The answer has some structure. *[3 to 4 marks]*
   Level 3:   There is a clear and detailed description of an experiment that can be performed using the equipment shown, and of how to calculate the spring constant from the resulting force-extension graph. The answer is well structured. *[5 to 6 marks]*

Here are some points your answer may include:
Measure the mass of the masses that are to be hung from the spring using a mass balance.
Calculate the weight of each of the masses using $W = m \times g$.
Using the ruler, measure the length of the spring when it has no masses hanging from it (the unstretched length).
Hang a mass from the spring, and record the new length of the spring.
Calculate the extension of the spring by subtracting the unstretched length from the new length.
Increase the number of masses hanging from the spring in steps, recording the new weight and calculating the extension each time.
Once there are a suitable number of points, plot the results on a force-extension graph, with force on the $y$-axis, and extension on the $x$-axis.
Draw a line of best fit through the results.
Spring constant = force ÷ extension ($k = F \div e$).
So the spring constant can be calculated by finding the gradient of the linear part of the graph.

 d)  Work done is equal to area under the graph up to point A.
   Extension = 3.0 cm = 0.030 m
   Area = area of a triangle = ½ × base × height
      = ½ × 0.030 × 6.0
      = **0.09 J**
   *[3 marks for correct answer, otherwise 1 mark for correctly converting cm to m and 1 mark for a correct method of calculating the area under the graph]*
You could have used the counting the squares method here instead if you had wanted to. Either method used correctly will get you full marks.

 e)  The rubber band did behave elastically, as it returned to its original shape and size once the forces acting on it were removed *[1 mark]*. However, the force-extension graph for the rubber band was a curve, so the relationship between force and extension was not linear *[1 mark]*.

4 a)  E.g.

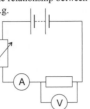

A

V

*[1 mark for variable resistor, fixed resistor and ammeter drawn in series with the battery, 1 mark for voltmeter drawn in parallel to the fixed resistor, 1 mark for all circuit symbols drawn correctly]*

 b)  mean = $\frac{2.53 + 2.52 + 2.51}{3}$ = **2.52 A** *[1 mark]*

 c)  E.g. when a current flows through the resistor, electrons collide with the ions in the lattice that make up the resistor *[1 mark]*. This gives energy to the ions, which makes them vibrate more (causing the resistor to heat up) *[1 mark]*.

 d)  $V = I \times R = 5 \times 2 = $ **10 V**
   *[2 marks for correct answer, otherwise 1 mark for correct substitution]*

 e)  D *[1 mark]*

5 a)  A *[1 mark]*

 b)  An alternating potential difference across the primary coil produces an alternating magnetic field *[1 mark]*. The iron core is magnetic, so the core is magnetised, and the magnetisation in the core also alternates *[1 mark]*. The changing magnetic field in the core induces an alternating potential difference across the secondary coil *[1 mark]*.

 c)  $\frac{V_p}{V_s} = \frac{N_p}{N_s}$ so $N_s = \frac{V_s \times N_p}{V_p} = \frac{400 \times 5000}{25} = $ **80 000**

   *[3 marks for correct answer, otherwise 1 mark for correct rearrangement and 1 mark for correct substitution]*
You could have also converted kV to volts to get the correct answer.

 d)  How to grade your answer:

   Level 0:   There is no relevant information. *[No marks]*
   Level 1:   There is a brief description of the transformers used in the national grid. The points made are not linked together. *[1 to 2 marks]*
   Level 2:   There is a description of the transformers used in the national grid, and some explanation of how they are used to efficiently transmit electricity. The answer has some structure. *[3 to 4 marks]*
   Level 3:   There is a clear and detailed description of how transformers are used in the national grid to transmit electricity efficiently. There is also a description of how the electricity is made suitable for home use after transmission. The answer is well structured. *[5 to 6 marks]*

Here are some points your answer may include:
The national grid needs to transmit high power electricity from power stations to consumers.
Because the power is high, and $P = V \times I$, the electricity must be transmitted with either a high potential difference ($V$) or a high current ($I$).
A high current causes lots of energy to be wasted to thermal stores. This is because the power lost due to resistive heating, $P$, is found from $P = I^2 \times R$.
In the national grid, step-up transformers are used to increase the potential difference of the electricity before transmission.
Transformers are almost 100% efficient, so the input power is roughly equal to the output power.
This means a step-up transformer decreases the current as the potential difference is increased.
As electricity is transmitted at a low current, less energy is dissipated to thermal energy stores.
So transmission at a low current is more efficient.
The transmission potential difference is too large to be used by consumers.
Before reaching the consumer, step-down transformers are used.
Step-down transformers decrease the potential difference back to a safe, usable level for consumer appliances.

6 a) Friction between the overalls and the worker's hair has caused electrons to move *[1 mark]* from the hair to the overalls *[1 mark]*.

b) There is a potential difference between the positively charged worker and the 0 V door *[1 mark]*. This potential difference creates an electric field between the worker's hand and the door handle that ionises the air between them *[1 mark]*. This makes the air more conductive, so electricity can easily flow between the door handle and the worker's hand (this is the spark) *[1 mark]*.

c) $E = Q \times V$
$12 \ \mu C = 12 \times 10^{-6}$ C
$10 \ kV = 10 \times 10^{3}$ V
$E = (12 \times 10^{-6}) \times (10 \times 10^{3}) = \textbf{0.12 J}$
*[3 marks for correct answer, otherwise 1 mark for correctly converting the charge into coulombs and the voltage into volts, 1 mark for correct substitution]*

d) i) Sparks could ignite the fuel/cause a fire/explosion *[1 mark]*.
   ii) E.g. the aircraft and the filler pipe can be earthed *[1 mark]*.

7 a) i) E.g. wear insulated gloves to move the container / don't move the container until it is cool / keep all electronics (apart from the immersion heater) away from the water *[1 mark]*
   ii) E.g. joulemeter *[1 mark]*

b) Comparing $y = mx + c$ and $Q = m \times L$, with $Q$ on the $y$-axis and $m$ on the $x$-axis, you can see that the gradient of the graph is equal to $L$.
Gradient = change in $y$ ÷ change in $x$
$= 0.34 \div 0.15 = 2.266... = \textbf{2.3 MJ/kg (to 2 s.f.)}$
**(accept between 2.2 and 2.3 MJ/kg)**
*[2 marks for correct answer, otherwise 1 mark for correct method for calculating the gradient of the graph]*

c) A *[1 mark]*
*Reading from the graph, 0.42 MJ of energy was required to boil off 0.185 kg of water.*
$E = IVt$, so $t = \dfrac{E}{IV} = \dfrac{0.42 \times 10^{6}}{8 \times 12} = 4375$ s.

d) E.g. particles of liquid water are closer together than particles of water vapour. / Particles of liquid water have less energy in their kinetic stores/move slower than particles of water vapour *[1 mark]*.

8 a) C *[1 mark]*
b) B *[1 mark]*
$Q = It = 3 \times (30 \times 60) = 5400$ C
c) clockwise/side A will move upwards *[1 mark]*
d) Force on one length of wire in the coil is given by $F = B \times I \times l$
$F = 0.75 \times 2.4 \times 0.050 = 0.09$ N
There are 4 loops on the wire, so multiply by 4 to find the total force.
$F = 4 \times 0.9 = \textbf{0.36 N}$
*[3 marks for correct answer, otherwise 1 mark for correct substitution and 1 mark for multiplying the force on one wire by 4.]*

e) Any one from: e.g. increase the current through the coil / increase the strength of the magnetic field / increase the number of turns on the coil / increase the length of side A inside the magnetic field *[1 mark]*.

9 a) i) electrical power = current × potential difference / $P = I \times V$ *[1 mark]*
   ii) Potential difference across the motor = $12.0 - 4.0 = 8.0$ V
   Current through the motor = $5.0 - 3.0 = 2.0$ A
   $P = I \times V = 2.0 \times 8.0 = \textbf{16 W}$
   *[3 marks for correct answer, otherwise 1 mark for correct calculation of potential difference across the motor or current through the motor and 1 mark for correct substitution into the power equation.]*

b) i) The motors transfer energy to the kinetic energy store of the fan blades *[1 mark]*. Power is the rate of energy transfer, so using a more powerful motor will cause the fan blades to increase their speed at a higher rate / reach a higher maximum speed *[1 mark]*. So motor A has the highest power *[1 mark]*.
   ii) E.g. lubricate the motors *[1 mark]*.

c) As the temperature increases, the resistance of the thermistor will decrease *[1 mark]*, so the potential difference across the thermistor will decrease *[1 mark]*. As the thermistor is in parallel with the heater, the potential difference across the heater will decrease *[1 mark]*.

d) Energy usefully transferred = $\Delta Q = m \times c \times \Delta\theta$
$\Delta\theta = 65 - 16 = 49$ °C
$\Delta Q = 2.1 \times 4200 \times 49 = 432 \ 180$ J
Total useful energy transferred by device = 432 180 J
efficiency = $\dfrac{\text{useful energy transferred by device}}{\text{total energy supplied to device}}$
total energy supplied to device
= useful energy transferred by device ÷ efficiency
= 432 180 ÷ 0.85
= **508 447.058... J = 510 000 J (to 2 s.f.)**
*[4 marks for correct answer, otherwise 1 mark for correct substitution to find energy usefully transferred, 1 mark for correct rearrangement of efficiency equation and 1 mark for correct substitution into rearranged efficiency equation]*

10 a) i) E.g. using a scale of 1 cm = 10 N

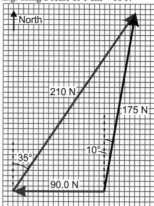

*[1 mark for correct conversion of forces using a suitable scale factor, 1 mark for forces drawn correctly in closed triangle]*

   ii) Line of resultant force is 17.5 cm, so:
   Magnitude of resultant force = 17.5 × 10
   = **175 N (accept between 173 N and 177 N)** *[1 mark]*
   Direction = **10° (accept between 9° and 11°)** *[1 mark]*

b) E.g. the pressure acting on the diver is due to the force applied by the water particles on her body *[1 mark]*. As depth increases, the number of water particles above the diver increases *[1 mark]*. The weight of water above the diver adds to the force acting on the diver, and so the pressure acting on the diver is larger *[1 mark]*.

c) $p = h \times \rho \times g$ so $h = p \div (\rho \times g)$
$= (255 \times 10^{3}) \div (1020 \times 10)$
= **25 m**
*[3 marks for correct answer, otherwise 1 mark for correct rearrangement and 1 mark for correct conversion and substitution]*

# Glossary

| | |
|---|---|
| **Absolute zero** | Theoretically the coldest temperature an object could reach. At absolute zero, particles have the minimum amount of energy in their kinetic energy stores. Absolute zero is at 0 K, or −273 °C. |
| **Absorption (of waves)** | When a wave transfers energy to the energy stores of a material. |
| **Acceleration** | A change in velocity in a certain amount of time. |
| **Accurate result** | A result that is very close to the true answer. |
| **Activity (radioactive)** | The number of nuclei of a sample that decay per second, measured in Bq. |
| **Air resistance** | The frictional force caused by air on a moving object. |
| **Alpha decay** | A type of radioactive decay in which an alpha particle is given out from a decaying nucleus. |
| **Alpha particle** | A positively-charged particle made up of two protons and two neutrons (a helium nucleus). |
| **Alpha particle scattering experiment** | An experiment in which alpha particles were fired at gold foil to see if they were deflected. It led to the plum pudding model being abandoned in favour of the nuclear model of the atom. |
| **Alternating current (a.c.)** | Current that is constantly changing direction. |
| **Alternator** | A device which generates an a.c. supply using electromagnetic induction. |
| **Ammeter** | A component used to measure the current through a component. It is always connected in series with the component. |
| **Amplitude** | The maximum displacement of a point on a wave from its rest position. |
| **Angle of incidence** | The angle the incoming ray makes with the normal at a boundary. |
| **Angle of reflection** | The angle a reflected ray makes with the normal at a boundary. |
| **Angle of refraction** | The angle a refracted ray makes with the normal when a wave refracts at a boundary. |
| **Anomalous result** | A result that doesn't seem to fit with the rest of the data. |
| **Aperture (of a telescope)** | The diameter of the objective lens. |
| **Artificial satellite** | A man-made satellite (normally orbiting the Earth in a fairly circular orbit). |
| **Asteroid** | A lump of rock and metal that orbits the Sun. |
| **Atmosphere** | A relatively thin layer of air that surrounds the Earth. |
| **Atmospheric pressure** | The pressure felt by any surface within the atmosphere, due to air molecules colliding with the surface. |
| **Atom** | A small particle that makes up matter. It is made up of a small, central, positively-charged nucleus, consisting of protons and neutrons, surrounded by negatively-charged electrons. |
| **Atomic (proton) number** | The number of protons in the nucleus of an atom. |
| **Axis (of a lens)** | A line passing through the middle of a lens, perpendicular to the lens. |
| **Background radiation** | The low-level radiation which surrounds us at all times, arising from both natural and man-made sources. |

# Glossary

| | |
|---|---|
| **Beta decay** | A type of radioactive decay in which either a beta-minus particle or a beta-plus particle is given out from a decaying nucleus. |
| **Beta-minus particle** | A high-speed electron emitted by the nucleus. |
| **Beta-plus particle** | A high-speed positron emitted by the nucleus. |
| **Bias** | Unfairness in the way data is presented, possibly because the presenter is trying to make a particular point (sometimes without knowing they're doing it). |
| **Big Bang theory** | The idea that the Universe began from a small, very hot and dense region of space, which exploded and has been expanding ever since. |
| **Bio-fuel** | A renewable energy resource made from plant products or animal dung. |
| **Black hole** | A super dense point in space that light cannot escape from, left behind when a red supergiant explodes in a supernova. |
| **Braking distance** | The braking distance is the distance a vehicle travels after the brakes are applied until it comes to a complete stop, as a result of the braking force. |
| **Calibrate** | Measure something with a known quantity to see if the instrument being used to measure that quantity gives the correct value. |
| **Categoric data** | Data that comes in distinct categories, e.g. metals (copper, zinc, etc.). |
| **Centripetal force** | The resultant force that acts on any object moving in a circle. It acts towards the centre of the circle. |
| **Chain reaction** | A reaction which keeps going (without any outside input) because the products of the reaction cause further reactions (e.g. nuclear fission). |
| **Circuit breaker** | A circuit component that 'trips' and breaks the circuit when the current through it goes above a certain point. They are used to protect circuits and to prevent electrical fires and electric shocks. |
| **Closed system** | A system where the net change in energy is zero. |
| **Comet** | A lump of ice and dust that orbits the Sun in a highly elliptical orbit. |
| **Conclusion** | A summary of the findings of a scientific investigation. |
| **Conduction** | A method of energy transfer by heating where vibrating particles transfer energy through a material by colliding with neighbouring particles and transferring energy between their kinetic energy stores. |
| **Conductor (electrical)** | A material through which electrical charges can easily move. |
| **Conservation of energy** | Energy can be stored, transferred between energy stores and dissipated — but it can never be created or destroyed. The total energy of a closed system has no net change. |
| **Conservation of momentum** | In a closed system, the total momentum before an event is the same as the total momentum after the event. |
| **Contact force** | A force that only acts between touching objects. |
| **Contamination (radioactive)** | The presence of unwanted radioactive atoms on or inside an object. |
| **Continuous data** | Numerical data that can have any value within a range (e.g. length, volume or temperature). |

# Glossary

| | |
|---|---|
| **Control experiment** | An experiment that's kept under the same conditions as the rest of the investigation, but where the independent variable isn't altered. |
| **Control rod** | A rod used to absorb excess neutrons to control the chain reaction in a nuclear reactor. |
| **Control variable** | A variable in an experiment that is kept the same. |
| **Converging lens** | A lens that bulges outwards and causes rays of light parallel to the axis to converge (come together) at the principal focus. |
| **Conversion factor** | A number which you must multiply or divide a unit by to convert it to a different unit. |
| **Correlation** | A relationship between two variables. |
| **Cosmic microwave background (CMB) radiation** | Radiation mainly in the microwave section of the electromagnetic spectrum that is present all over the Universe.  It is thought to be leftover energy from the initial Big Bang explosion. |
| **Cosmic ray** | Radiation from space. |
| **Critical angle** | The angle of incidence above which total internal reflection occurs. |
| **Current** | The flow of electric charge.  The size of the current is the rate of flow of charge.  Measured in amperes (A). |
| **Density** | A substance's mass per unit volume. |
| **Dependent variable** | The variable in an experiment that is measured. |
| **Diffuse reflection** | When parallel waves are reflected by a rough surface (e.g. a piece of paper) and the reflected rays are scattered in lots of different directions. |
| **Diode** | A circuit component that only allows current to flow through it in one direction.  It has a very high resistance in the other direction. |
| **Direct current (d.c.)** | A current where the charges only move in one direction. |
| **Discrete data** | Numerical data that can only take a certain value, with no in-between value (e.g. number of protons). |
| **Displacement** | The straight-line distance and direction from an object's starting position to its finishing position. |
| **Dissipation** | The transfer of energy to thermal energy stores of an object and its surroundings.  Also called wasted energy. |
| **Distance/time graph** | A graph showing how the distance travelled by an object changes over a period of time. |
| **Diverging lens** | A lens that curves inwards and causes rays of light parallel to the axis to diverge (spread out) so they appear to have come from the principal focus. |
| **Dwarf planet** | A planet-like object in space that orbits a star but which doesn't match all of the rules for being a planet. |
| **Dynamo** | A device which generates a d.c. supply using electromagnetic induction. |
| **Eardrum** | The part of the ear which vibrates when sound waves enter the ear. It passes on these vibrations to other parts of the ear, which convert them to electrical signals that cause the sensation of hearing. |
| **Earth wire** | The green and yellow wire in an electrical cable that only carries current when there's a fault. It stops exposed metal parts of an appliance from becoming live.  It is at 0 V. |

# Glossary

| | |
|---|---|
| **Earthing** | Connecting a charged object to the ground using a conductor. |
| **Efficiency** | The proportion of energy supplied to a device which is usefully transferred. |
| **Elastic distortion** | An object undergoing elastic distortion will return to its original shape and length once any forces being applied to it are removed. |
| **Elastic object** | An object which can be elastically distorted. |
| **Elastic potential energy store** | Anything that has been stretched or compressed, e.g. a spring, has energy in its elastic potential energy store. |
| **Electric field** | A region in which an electrically charged object experiences an electrostatic force. |
| **Electromagnet** | A magnet whose magnetic field can be turned on and off by an electric current. |
| **Electromagnetic induction** | The induction of a potential difference across a conductor which is experiencing a change in external magnetic field.  If the conductor is part of a complete circuit, this will cause a current to flow. |
| **Electromagnetic (EM) spectrum** | A continuous spectrum of all the possible wavelengths of electromagnetic waves. |
| **Electron** | A subatomic particle with a relative charge of $-1$ and a relative mass of 0.0005. |
| **Electrostatic force** | The non-contact force which acts to bring together opposite charges (attraction) / push apart like charges (repulsion). |
| **Electrostatic induction** | Electrostatic attraction between a charged and an uncharged object. Caused by the induction of a small charge on the surface of the uncharged object. |
| **Energy store** | A means by which an object stores energy.  Common energy stores are: thermal, kinetic, gravitational potential, elastic potential, chemical, magnetic, electrostatic and nuclear. |
| **Equilibrium** | A state in which all the forces acting on an object are balanced, so the resultant force is zero. |
| **Evaluation** | A critical analysis of a scientific investigation. |
| **Fair test** | A controlled experiment where the only thing being changed is the independent variable. |
| **Fleming's left-hand rule** | The rule used to work out the direction of the force produced by the motor effect. Your first finger points in the direction of the magnetic field, your second finger points in the direction of the current and your thumb points in the direction of the force (or motion). |
| **Fluid** | A substance that can flow — either a liquid or a gas. |
| **Focal length (of a lens)** | The distance from the centre of a lens to its principal focus. |
| **Force** | A push or a pull on an object caused by it interacting with something. |
| **Fossil fuel** | The fossil fuels are coal, oil and natural gas. They're non-renewable energy resources that we burn to generate electricity. |
| **Free body force diagram** | A diagram that shows all the forces acting on an isolated object, the direction in which the forces are acting and their (relative) magnitudes. |
| **Frequency** | The number of complete wave cycles passing a certain point per second.  Measured in hertz, Hz. |
| **Friction** | A force that opposes an object's motion.  It acts in the opposite direction to motion. |

# Glossary

| | |
|---|---|
| **Fuse** | A circuit component that contains a thin piece of wire which melts when the current through the fuse goes above a certain point. Fuses are used to protect circuits and to prevent electrical fires and electric shocks. |
| **Gamma decay** | A type of radioactive decay in which a gamma ray is given out from a decaying nucleus. |
| **Gamma ray** | A high-frequency, short-wavelength electromagnetic wave. |
| **Gear** | A circular disc with teeth round its edge. It can be used to transmit the rotational effect of a force. |
| **Geiger-Müller tube** | A radiation detector that is used with a counter to measure count-rate. |
| **Geocentric model** | A model of the Solar System, with the Earth at the centre being orbited by the Sun, Moon and the other planets. |
| **Gradient** | The slope of a line graph. It shows how quickly the variable on the y-axis changes with the variable on the x-axis. |
| **Gravitational potential energy (GPE) store** | Anything that has mass and is in a gravitational field has energy in its gravitational potential energy store. |
| **Gravity** | The force of attraction between all objects with mass. |
| **Half-life** | The average time taken for the number of radioactive nuclei in an isotope to halve. |
| **Hazard** | Something that has the potential to cause harm (e.g. fire, electricity, etc.). |
| **Heliocentric model** | A model of the Solar System, with the Sun at the centre being orbited by the planets. |
| **Hydroelectric dam** | A power station in which a dam is built across a valley or river. This holds back water, forming a reservoir. Water is allowed to flow out of the reservoir through turbines at a controlled rate. This turns the turbines, which are attached to generators and can generate electricity. |
| **Hypothesis** | A possible explanation for a scientific observation. |
| **Independent variable** | The variable in an experiment that is changed. |
| **Induced (temporary) magnet** | A magnetic material that only has its own magnetic field while it is inside another magnetic field. |
| **Inelastic distortion** | An object undergoing inelastic distortion will not return to its original shape and length once the forces being applied to it are removed. |
| **Inertia** | The tendency of an object to remain stationary or continue travelling at a constant velocity. |
| **Inertial mass** | The ratio of the force on an object over its acceleration. |
| **Infrasound** | Sound with a frequency less than 20 Hz. |
| **Insulator (electrical)** | A material in which electrical charges cannot easily move. |
| **Intensity** | The power per unit area, i.e. how much energy is transferred to a given area in a certain amount of time. |
| **Internal energy** | The total energy that a system's particles have in their kinetic and potential energy stores. |
| **Ion** | An atom in which the number of electrons is different to the number of protons, giving it an overall charge. |

# Glossary

| | |
|---|---|
| **Ionising radiation** | Radiation that has enough energy to knock electrons off atoms. |
| **Irradiation** | Exposure to radiation. |
| **Isotope** | A different form of the same element, which has atoms with the same number of protons (atomic number), but a different number of neutrons (and so different mass number). |
| **Kinetic energy store** | Anything that's moving has energy in its kinetic energy store. |
| **Kinetic theory of matter** | A theory explaining how particles in matter behave by modelling these particles as tiny balls. |
| **Law of reflection** | The angle of reflection of a reflected ray is always equal to the angle of incidence. |
| **Lever** | A device that makes it easier to do work by increasing the distance between an applied force and a pivot. |
| **Light-dependent resistor (LDR)** | A resistor whose resistance is dependent on light intensity. The resistance decreases as light intensity increases. |
| **Limit of proportionality** | The point beyond which the force applied to an object is no longer directly proportional to the extension of the object. |
| **Linear graph** | A straight line graph. |
| **Live wire** | The brown wire in an electrical cable that carries an alternating potential difference from the mains. It is at 230 V. |
| **Longitudinal wave** | A wave in which the vibrations are parallel to the direction the wave travels. |
| **Lubricant** | A substance (usually a liquid) that can flow easily between two objects. Used to reduce friction between surfaces. |
| **Magnetic field** | A region where magnets, magnetic materials (like iron and steel) and current-carrying wires experience a force. |
| **Magnetic flux density** | The number of magnetic field lines per unit area. Its symbol is B and it is measured in tesla, T. |
| **Magnetic material** | A material (such as iron, steel, cobalt or nickel) which can become an induced magnet while it's inside another magnetic field. |
| **Main sequence star** | A star in the main sequence of its life, which is stable because the nuclear fusion in the star provides an outward pressure that balances the inward pull of gravity. |
| **Mass (nucleon) number** | The number of neutrons and protons in the nucleus of an atom. |
| **Mean (average)** | A measure of average found by adding up all the data and dividing by the number of values there are. |
| **Median (average)** | A measure of average found by selecting the middle value from a data set arranged in ascending order. |
| **Mode (average)** | A measure of average found by selecting the most frequent value from a data set. |
| **Model** | Used to describe or display how an object or system behaves in reality. |
| **Moderator** | A substance such as graphite that slows down fast-moving neutrons in a nuclear reactor. |
| **Moment** | The turning effect of a force. |

# Glossary

| | |
|---|---|
| **Momentum** | A property of a moving object that is the product of its mass and velocity. |
| **Moon** | A natural satellite which orbits a planet. |
| **Motor effect** | When a current-carrying conductor is placed in a magnetic field, the conductor and the magnet producing the magnetic field exert a force on each other. |
| **National grid** | The network of transformers and cables that distributes electrical power from power stations to consumers. |
| **Natural satellite** | A natural object which orbits a second, more massive object, e.g. a moon orbiting a planet. |
| **Nebula** | A cloud of dust and gas in space. |
| **Neutral wire** | The blue wire in an electrical cable that current in an appliance normally flows through. It is around 0 V. |
| **Neutron** | A subatomic particle with a relative charge of 0 and a relative mass of 1. |
| **Neutron star** | The very dense core of a star that is left behind when a red supergiant explodes in a supernova. |
| **Newton's First Law** | An object will remain at rest or travelling at a constant velocity unless it is acted on by a resultant force. |
| **Newton's Second Law** | The acceleration of an object is directly proportional to the resultant force acting on it, and inversely proportional to its mass. Often given as $F = m \times a$. |
| **Newton's Third Law** | When two objects interact, they exert equal and opposite forces on each other. |
| **Non-contact force** | A force that can act between objects that are not touching, usually as a result of interacting fields. |
| **Non-renewable energy resource** | An energy resource that is non-renewable cannot be made at the same rate as it's being used, so it will run out one day. |
| **Normal (at a boundary)** | A line that's perpendicular (at 90°) to a boundary at the point of incidence (where a wave hits the boundary). |
| **Normal contact force** | A force that acts between all touching objects. |
| **Nuclear fission** | When an atomic nucleus splits up to form two smaller nuclei. |
| **Nuclear fuel** | Nuclear fuels (e.g. uranium and plutonium) release energy through nuclear fission reactions to heat water into steam, which drives turbines and generators to generate electricity. |
| **Nuclear fusion** | When two nuclei join to create a heavier nucleus. |
| **Nuclear model** | A model of the atom that says that the atom has a small, central positively-charged nucleus with negatively-charged electrons moving around the nucleus, and that most of the atom is empty space. |
| **Nucleus (atom)** | The centre of an atom, containing protons and neutrons. |
| **Orbit** | The path on which one object moves around another. |
| **Parallel circuit** | A circuit in which every component is connected separately to the positive and negative ends of the supply. |
| **Partial reflection** | When waves are incident on a boundary, some are reflected and some are transmitted. |
| **Peak wavelength** | The wavelength of the radiation with the highest intensity that is emitted by an object. |

# Glossary

| | |
|---|---|
| **Peer-review** | The process in which other scientists check the results and explanations of an investigation before they are published. |
| **Period (of a wave)** | The time taken for one full cycle of a wave to be completed. |
| **Permanent magnet** | A magnetic material that always has its own magnetic field around it. |
| **Physical change** | A change where you don't end up with a new substance — it's the same substance as before, just in a different form. (A change of state is a physical change.) |
| **Planet** | A natural object in space which orbits a star. |
| **Positron** | A subatomic particle with a relative charge of +1 and a relative mass of 0.0005. It is the antiparticle of an electron. |
| **Positron emission tomography (PET scanning)** | A medical imaging technique that detects the gamma rays produced during electron-positron annihilation. |
| **Potential difference** | The driving force that pushes electric charge around a circuit, measured in volts (V). Also known as p.d. or voltage. |
| **Power** | The rate of transferring energy (or doing work). Normally measured in watts (W). |
| **Power rating** | The maximum safe power an appliance can operate at. |
| **Precise result** | When all the data is close to the mean. |
| **Prediction** | A statement that can be tested and is based on a hypothesis. |
| **Pressure** | The force per unit area exerted on a surface. |
| **Principal focus of a converging lens** | The point where rays hitting the lens parallel to the axis all meet. |
| **Principal focus of a diverging lens** | The point where rays hitting the lens parallel to the axis appear to have come from. |
| **Principle of moments** | The statement that for a body in equilibrium, the total clockwise moments are equal to the total anticlockwise moments, and so the body will not turn. |
| **Proton** | A subatomic particle with a relative charge of +1 and a relative mass of 1. |
| **Protostar** | An early stage in the life cycle of a star. Protostars are formed when the force of gravity causes clouds of dust and gas to pull together. |
| **Radioactive decay** | The random process of a radioactive substance giving out radiation from the nuclei of its atoms. |
| **Radioactive substance** | A substance that spontaneously gives out radiation from the nuclei of its atoms. |
| **Radiotherapy** | A treatment of cancer that uses ionising radiation (such as gamma rays) to kill cancer cells. |
| **Random error** | A difference in the results of an experiment caused by unpredictable events, e.g. human error in measuring. |
| **Range** | The difference between the smallest and largest values in a set of data. |
| **Range of human hearing** | The range of frequencies of sound waves that humans can hear. It's 20 Hz to 20 kHz. |

# Glossary

| | |
|---|---|
| **Ray** | A straight line showing the path along which a wave moves. |
| **Reaction time** | The time taken for a person to react after an event (e.g. seeing a hazard). |
| **Real image** | An image formed when light rays from a point on an object come together at another point — the light rays actually pass through that point. |
| **Red giant** | A type of star that is formed when a star around the same mass as the Sun expands after it runs out of hydrogen in its core. |
| **Red-shift** | The shift in observed wavelength of light from a source moving away from a stationary observer. The wavelength is shifted towards the red end of the electromagnetic spectrum. |
| **Red supergiant** | A type of star that is formed when a large star (with a mass much greater than the Sun) expands after it runs out of hydrogen in its core. |
| **Reflection** | When a wave bounces back as it meets a boundary between two materials. |
| **Refraction** | When a wave changes direction as it passes across the boundary between two materials at an angle to the normal. |
| **Reliable result** | A result that is repeatable and reproducible. |
| **Renewable energy resource** | An energy resource that is renewable is one that is being, or can be, made at the same rate (or faster) than it's being used, and so will never run out. |
| **Repeatable result** | A result that will come out the same if the experiment is repeated by the same person using the same method and equipment. |
| **Reproducible result** | A result that will come out the same if someone different does the experiment, or a slightly different method or piece of equipment is used. |
| **Resistance** | Anything in a circuit that reduces the flow of current. Measured in ohms, $\Omega$. |
| **Resolution** | The smallest change a measuring instrument can detect. |
| **Resultant force** | A single force that can replace all the forces acting on an object to give the same effect as the original forces acting altogether. |
| **Right-hand thumb rule** | The rule to work out the direction of the magnetic field around a current-carrying wire. Your thumb on your right hand points in the direction of the current, and your fingers curl in the direction of the magnetic field. |
| **Risk** | The chance that a hazard will cause harm. |
| **Scalar** | A quantity that has magnitude but no direction. |
| **Scaling prefix** | A word or symbol which goes before a unit to indicate a multiplying factor (e.g. 1 km = 1000 m). |
| **Seismic wave** | A wave which travels through (or over the surface of) the Earth when an earthquake occurs. Two important types are P-waves and S-waves. |
| **Series circuit** | A circuit in which every component is connected in a line, end to end. |
| **S.I. unit** | A unit recognised as standard by scientists all over the world. |
| **Significant figure** | The first significant figure of a number is the first non-zero digit. The second, third and fourth significant figures follow on immediately after it. |

# Glossary

| | |
|---|---|
| **Solar cell** | A device that generates electricity directly from the Sun's radiation. |
| **Solar System** | The Sun and all of the objects that orbit it. |
| **Solenoid** | A coil of wire often used in the construction of electromagnets. |
| **Sound wave** | A longitudinal wave of vibrating particles caused by vibrating objects. |
| **Spark** | The passage of electrons across a (usually) small gap between a charged object and an earthed conductor (or the earth). |
| **Specific heat capacity (SHC)** | The amount of energy (in joules) needed to raise the temperature of 1 kg of a material by 1°C. |
| **Specific latent heat (SLH)** | The amount of energy needed to change 1 kg of a substance from one state to another without changing its temperature. (For cooling, it is the energy released by a change in state.) |
| **Specific latent heat of fusion** | The specific latent heat for changing between a solid and a liquid (melting or freezing). |
| **Specific latent heat of vaporisation** | The specific latent heat for changing between a liquid and a gas (evaporating, boiling or condensing). |
| **Specular reflection** | When parallel waves are reflected in a single direction by a smooth surface. |
| **Split-ring commutator** | A ring with gaps in it that swaps the electrical contacts of a device every half-turn. |
| **Standard form** | A number written in the form $A \times 10^n$, where A is a number between 1 and 10. |
| **State of matter** | The form which a substance can take — e.g. solid, liquid or gas. |
| **Static charge** | An electric charge that cannot move. It often forms on electrical insulators, where charge cannot flow freely. |
| **Steady State theory** | The idea that the Universe has no beginning or end. It has always looked as it does and always will do. |
| **Stopping distance** | The distance covered by a vehicle in the time between the driver spotting a hazard and the vehicle coming to a complete stop. It's the sum of the thinking distance and the braking distance. |
| **Supernova** | The explosion of a red supergiant. |
| **System** | The object, or group of objects, that you're considering. |
| **Systematic error** | An error that is consistently made throughout an experiment. |
| **Tangent** | A straight line that touches a curve at a point but doesn't cross it. |
| **Theory** | A hypothesis which has been accepted by the scientific community because there is good evidence to back it up. |
| **Thermal conductivity** | A measure of how quickly an object transfers energy by heating through conduction. |
| **Thermal insulator** | A material with a low thermal conductivity. |
| **Thermistor** | A resistor whose resistance is dependent on the temperature. The resistance decreases as temperature increases. |
| **Thinking distance** | The distance a vehicle travels during the driver's reaction time (the time between seeing a hazard and applying the brakes). |

# Glossary

| | |
|---|---|
| **Three-core cable** | An electrical cable containing a live wire, a neutral wire and an earth wire. |
| **Tidal barrage** | A dam built across a river estuary, containing turbines connected to generators. When there's a difference in water height on either side, water flows through the dam, turning the turbines and generating electricity. |
| **Total internal reflection (TIR)** | When a wave is reflected back into a material instead of being transmitted into the new material. Occurs when a wave travels into a less dense material at an angle of incidence larger than the critical angle of the boundary. |
| **Tracers** | A radioactive isotope whose path through a system can be followed. Medical tracers can be used to diagnose illness and medical conditions. |
| **Transformer** | A device which can change the size of an alternating potential difference. |
| **Transmission (of waves)** | When a wave passes across a boundary from one material into another and continues travelling. |
| **Transverse wave** | A wave in which the vibrations are perpendicular (at 90°) to the direction the wave travels. |
| **Ultrasound** | Sound with a frequency greater than 20 000 Hz. |
| **Uncertainty** | The amount by which a given result may differ from the true value. |
| **Uniform field** | A field that has the same strength everywhere. |
| **Upthrust** | The resultant force acting upwards on an object submerged in a liquid, due to the pressure of the liquid being greater at the bottom of the object than at the top. |
| **Valid result** | A result that is repeatable, reproducible and answers the original question. |
| **Vector** | A quantity which has both magnitude (size) and a direction. |
| **Velocity** | The speed and direction of an object. |
| **Velocity/time graph** | A graph showing how the velocity of an object changes over a period of time. |
| **Virtual image** | An image that is formed when light rays appear to have come from one point, but have actually come from another — the light rays don't actually pass through that point. |
| **Voltmeter** | A component used to measure the potential difference across a component. It is always connected in parallel with the component. |
| **Wave** | An oscillation that transfers energy and information without transferring any matter. |
| **Wavefront diagram** | A representation of a wave made up of a series of 'wavefronts'. These are lines drawn through identical points on a wave, e.g. through each crest, perpendicular to the wave's direction of travel. |
| **Wavelength** | The length of a full cycle of a wave, e.g. from a crest to the next crest. |
| **Weight** | The force acting on an object due to gravity. |
| **White dwarf** | The hot, dense core left behind when a red giant becomes unstable and ejects its outer layer of dust and gas. |
| **Work done** | Energy transferred, e.g. when a force moves an object through a distance, or by an appliance. |
| **Zero error** | A type of systematic error caused by using a piece of equipment that isn't zeroed properly. |

# Index

# Index

# Physics Equations Sheet

## You'll Be Given Certain **Equations** in the **Exams**

In each paper you have to sit for your Physics GCSE, you'll be given an equations sheet listing some of the equations you might need to use. That means you don't have to learn them (hurrah), but you still need to be able to pick out the correct equations to use and be really confident using them. The equations sheet won't give you any units for the equation quantities — so make sure you know them inside out.

The equations you'll be given in the exam are all on this page. You can use this page as a reference when you're doing the exam questions in each section, and the Practice Papers at the end of the book.

(final velocity)$^2$ – (initial velocity)$^2$ = 2 × acceleration × distance

$$v^2 - u^2 = 2 \times a \times x$$

force = change in momentum ÷ time

$$F = \frac{(mv - mu)}{t}$$

energy transferred = current × potential difference × time

$$E = I \times V \times t$$

force on a conductor at right angles to a magnetic field carrying a current = magnetic flux density × current × length

$$F = B \times I \times l$$

$$\frac{\text{potential difference across primary coil}}{\text{potential difference across secondary coil}} = \frac{\text{number of turns in primary coil}}{\text{number of turns in secondary coil}}$$

$$\frac{V_p}{V_s} = \frac{N_p}{N_s}$$

For transformers with 100% efficiency:

potential difference across primary coil × current in primary coil = potential difference across secondary coil × current in secondary coil

$$V_p \times I_p = V_s \times I_s$$

change in thermal energy = mass × specific heat capacity × change in temperature

$$\Delta Q = m \times c \times \Delta\theta$$

thermal energy for a change of state = mass × specific latent heat

$$Q = m \times L$$

For a fixed mass of gas at a constant temperature:
pressure at volume 1 × volume 1 = pressure at volume 2 × volume 2

$$P_1 \times V_1 = P_2 \times V_2$$

energy transferred in stretching = 0.5 × spring constant × (extension)$^2$

$$E = \tfrac{1}{2} \times k \times x^2$$

pressure due to a column of liquid = height of column × density of liquid × gravitational field strength

$$P = h \times \rho \times g$$